CASE CLOSED

VOLUME

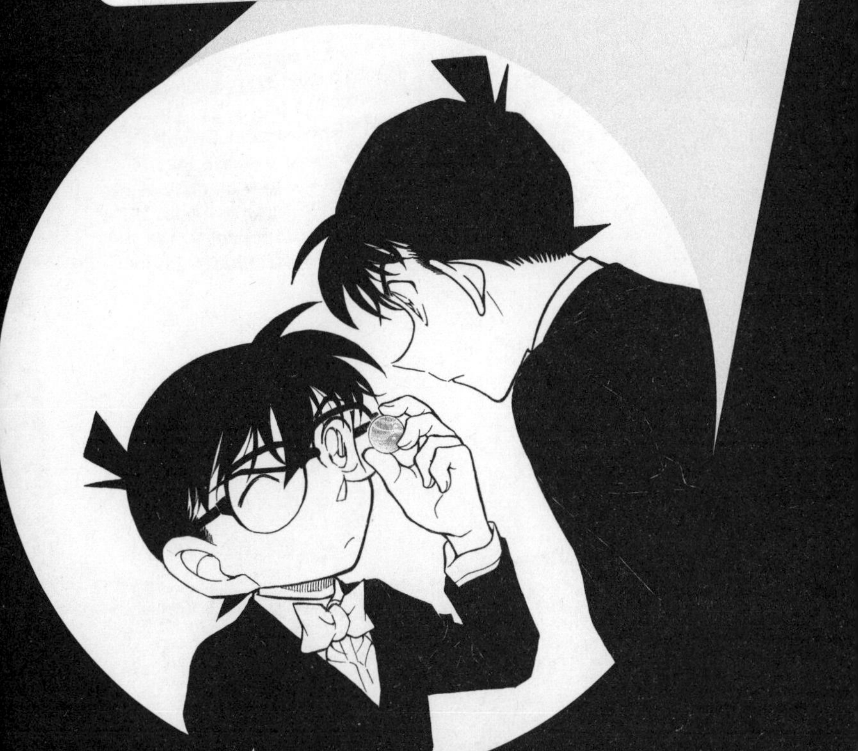

Gosho Aoyama

Case Briefing:

Subject:
Occupation:
Special Skills:
Equipment:

Jimmy Kudo, a.k.a. Conan Edogawa
High School Student/Detective
Analytical thinking and deductive reasoning, Soccer
Bow Tie Voice Transmitter, Super Sneakers,
Homing Glasses, Stretchy Suspenders

The subject is hot on the trail of a pair of suspicious men in black when he is attacked from behind and administered a strange substance which physically transforms him into a first grader. When the subject confides in the eccentric inventor Dr. Agasa, they decide to keep the subject's true identity a secret for the safety of everyone around him. Assuming the new identity of first-grader Conan Edogawa, the subject continues to assist the police force on their most baffling cases. The only problem is that most crime-solving professionals won't take a little kid's advice!

Table of Contents

CONFIDEN

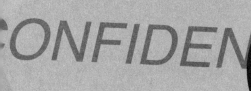

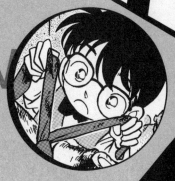

CASE CLOSED

Volume 70
Shonen Sunday Edition

Story and Art by GOSHO AOYAMA

MEITANTEI CONAN Vol. 70
by Gosho AOYAMA
© 1994 Gosho AOYAMA
All rights reserved.
Original Japanese edition published by SHOGAKUKAN.
English translation rights in the United States of America, Canada,
the United Kingdom and Ireland arranged with SHOGAKUKAN.

Translation
Tetsuichiro Miyaki

Touch-up & Lettering
Freeman Wong

Cover & Graphic Design
Andrea Rice

Editor
Shaenon K. Garrity

Printed in the U.S.A.

Published by VIZ Media, LLC
P.O. Box 77010
San Francisco, CA 94107

10 9 8 7 6 5 4 3 2 1
First printing, April 2019

VIZ MEDIA
viz.com

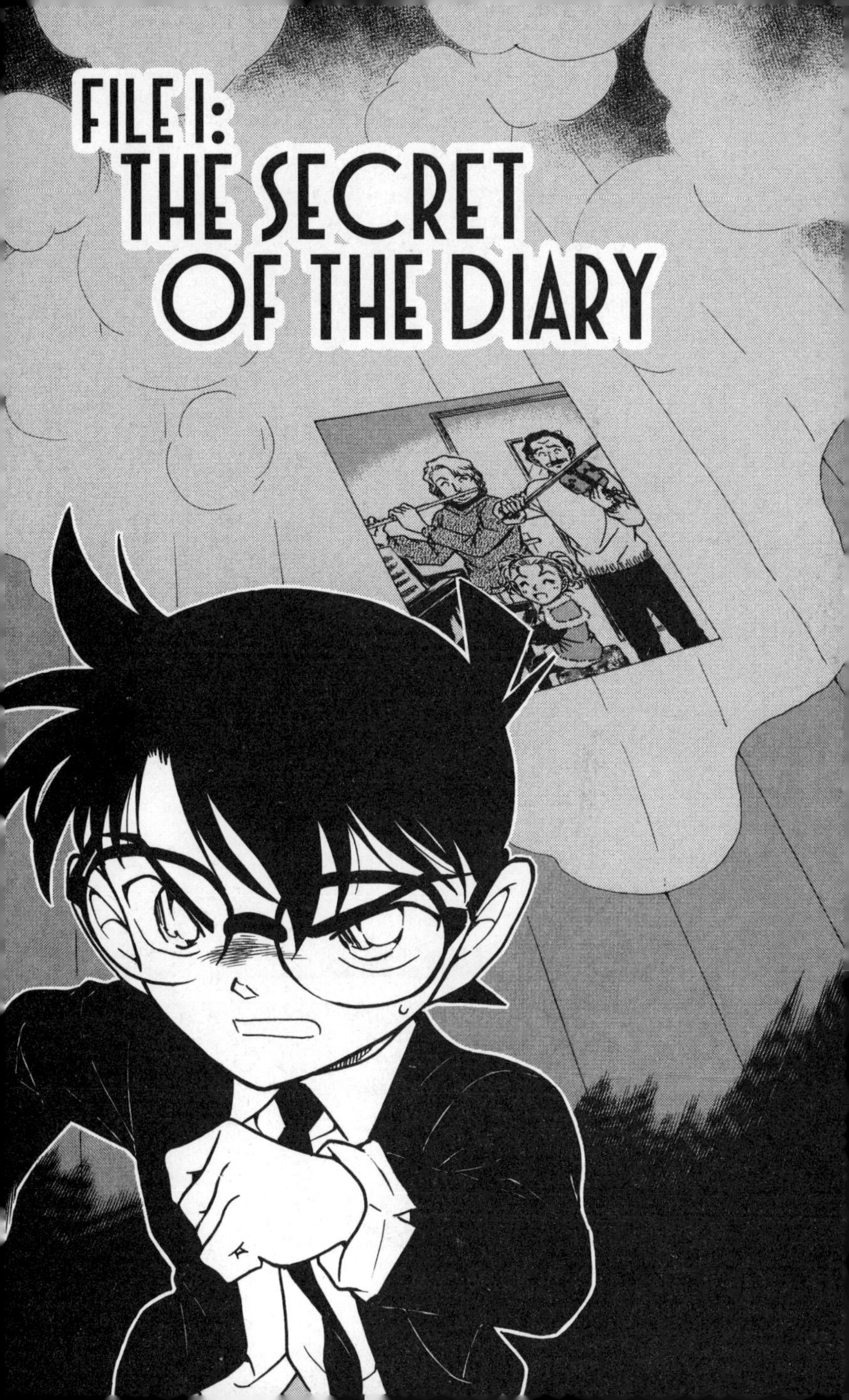
FILE 1:
THE SECRET OF THE DIARY

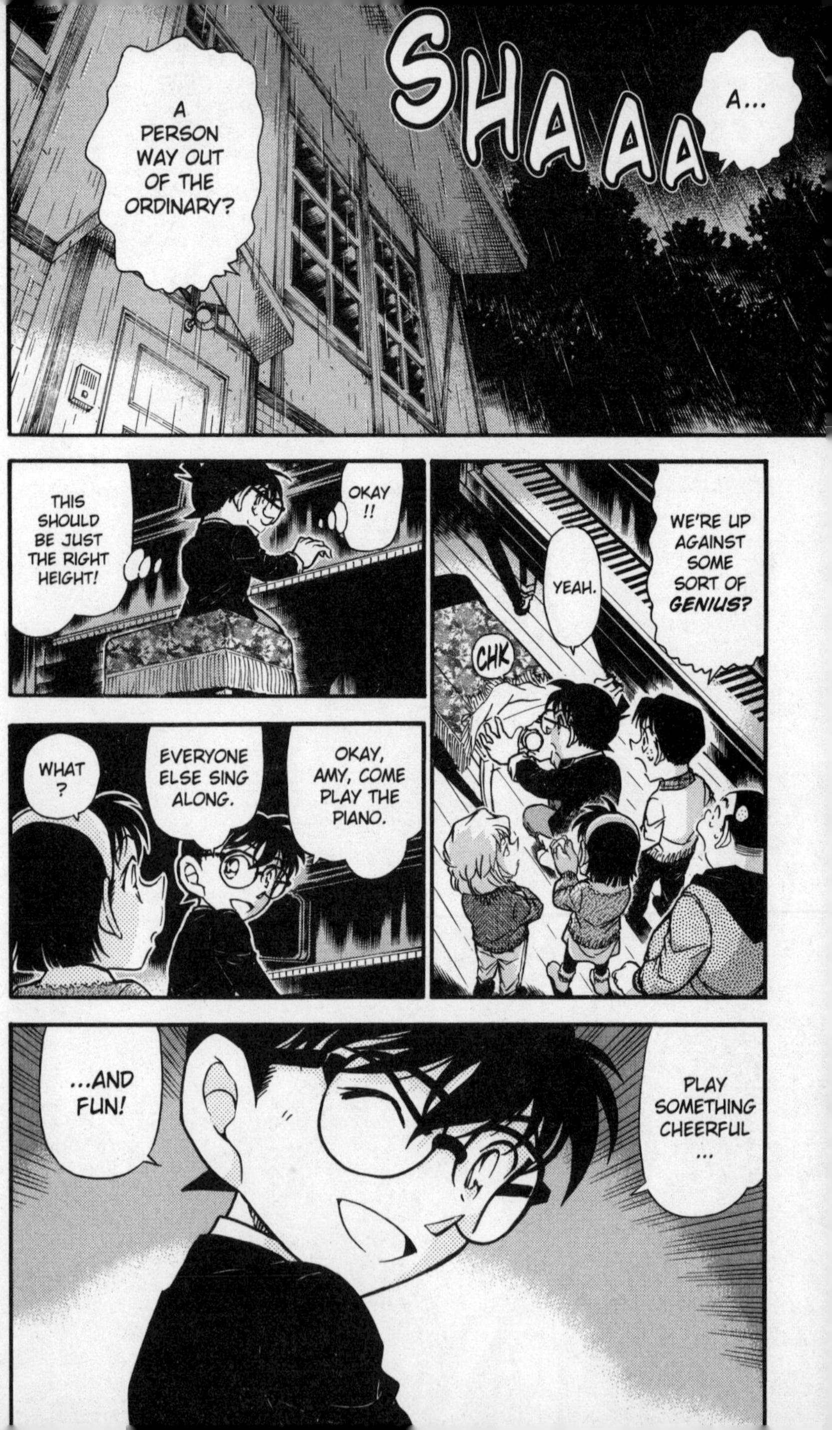
SHAAAA
A...
A PERSON WAY OUT OF THE ORDINARY?
WE'RE UP AGAINST SOME SORT OF **GENIUS?**
YEAH.
CHK
OKAY!!
THIS SHOULD BE JUST THE RIGHT HEIGHT!
OKAY, AMY, COME PLAY THE PIANO.
EVERYONE ELSE SING ALONG.
WHAT?
PLAY SOMETHING CHEERFUL...
...AND FUN!

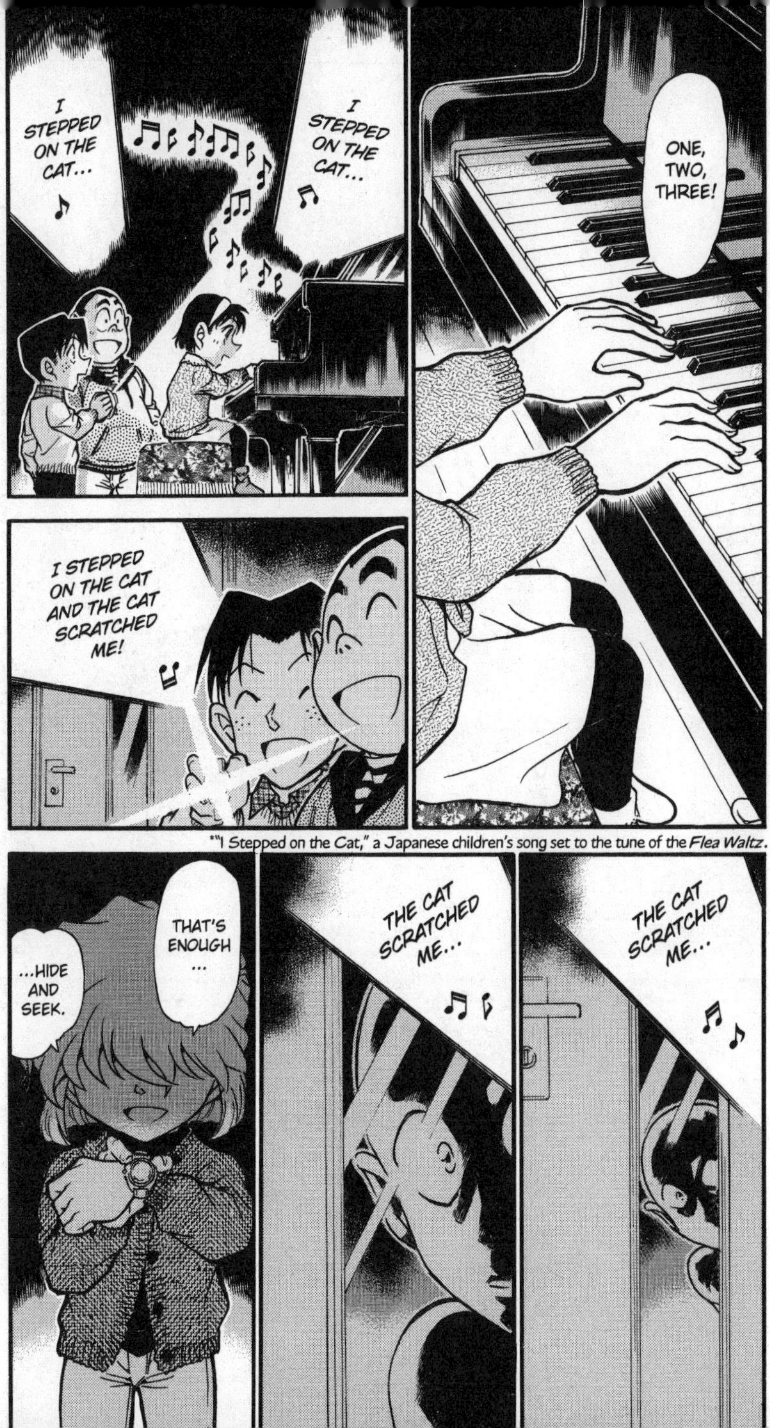
ONE, TWO, THREE!
I STEPPED ON THE CAT...
I STEPPED ON THE CAT...
I STEPPED ON THE CAT AND THE CAT SCRATCHED ME!
THE CAT SCRATCHED ME...
THE CAT SCRATCHED ME...
THAT'S ENOUGH ...
...HIDE AND SEEK.
*"I Stepped on the Cat," a Japanese children's song set to the tune of the *Flea Waltz*.

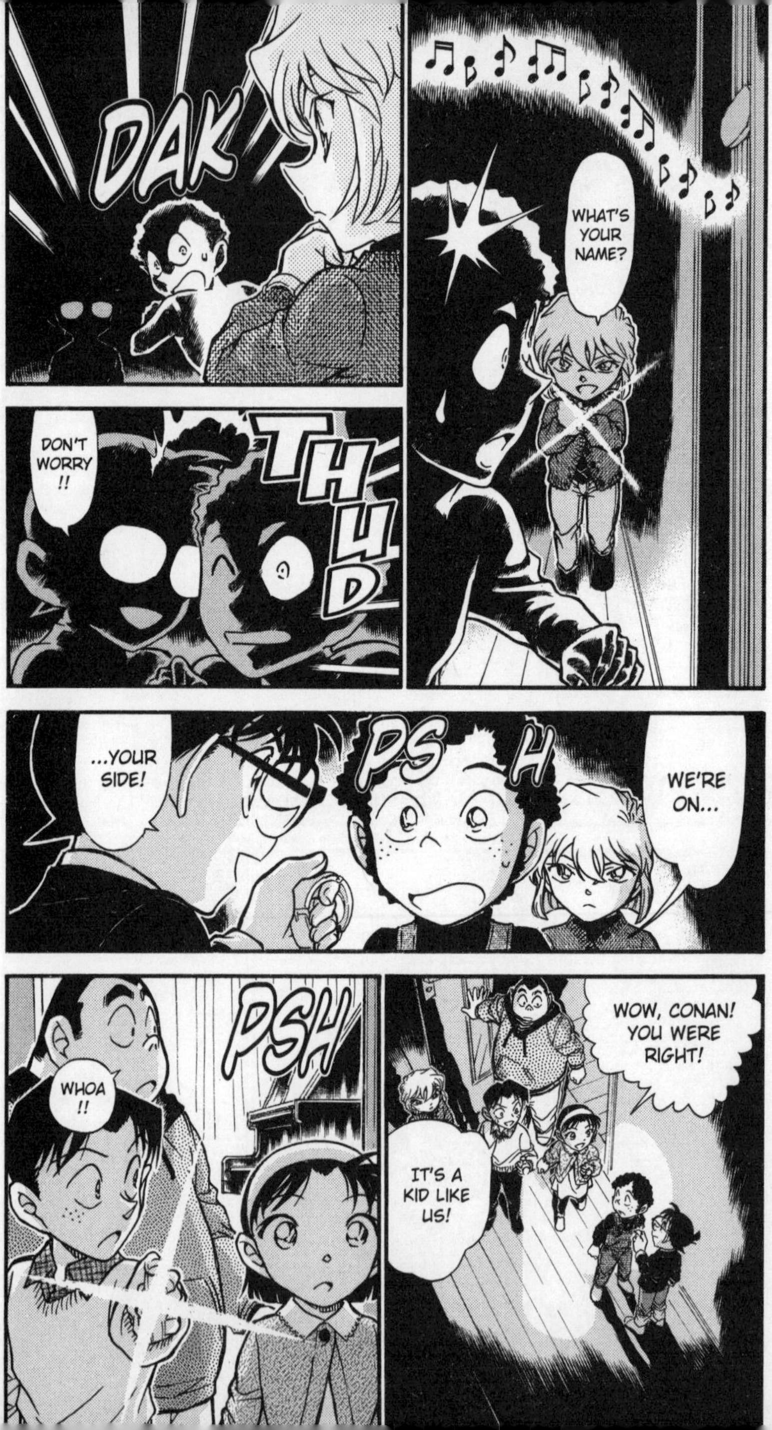
WHAT'S YOUR NAME?
DAK
DON'T WORRY !!
THUD
WE'RE ON...
PSH
...YOUR SIDE!
WOW, CONAN! YOU WERE RIGHT!
IT'S A KID LIKE US!
PSH
WHOA !!

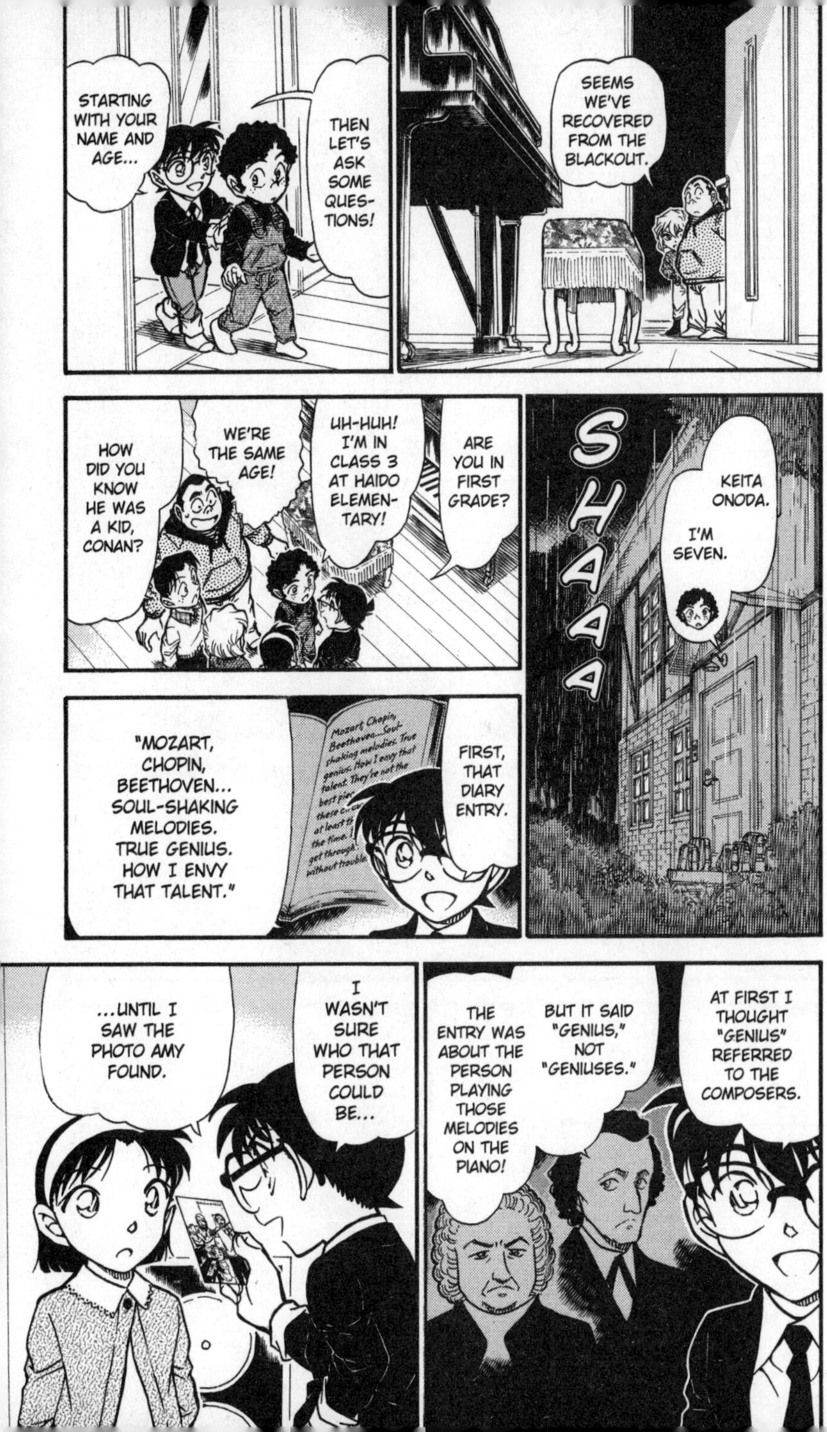
SEEMS WE'VE RECOVERED FROM THE BLACKOUT.
THEN LET'S ASK SOME QUES-TIONS!
STARTING WITH YOUR NAME AND AGE...
SHAAAA
KEITA ONODA.
I'M SEVEN.
ARE YOU IN FIRST GRADE?
UH-HUH! I'M IN CLASS 3 AT HAIDO ELEMEN-TARY!
WE'RE THE SAME AGE!
HOW DID YOU KNOW HE WAS A KID, CONAN?
FIRST, THAT DIARY ENTRY.
"MOZART, CHOPIN, BEETHOVEN... SOUL-SHAKING MELODIES. TRUE GENIUS. HOW I ENVY THAT TALENT."
AT FIRST I THOUGHT "GENIUS" REFERRED TO THE COMPOSERS.
BUT IT SAID "GENIUS," NOT "GENIUSES."
THE ENTRY WAS ABOUT THE PERSON PLAYING THOSE MELODIES ON THE PIANO!
I WASN'T SURE WHO THAT PERSON COULD BE...
...UNTIL I SAW THE PHOTO AMY FOUND.

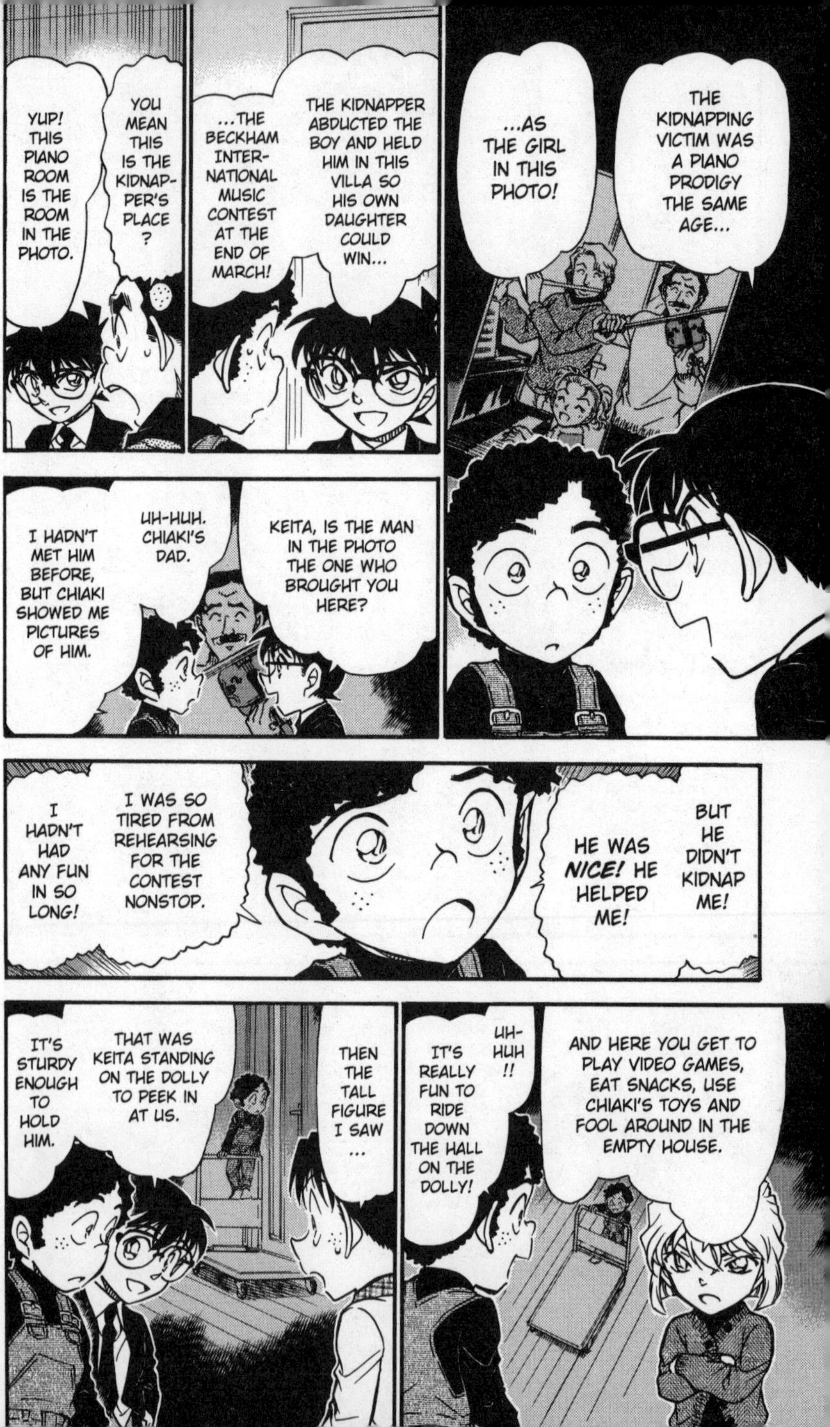
THE KIDNAPPING VICTIM WAS A PIANO PRODIGY THE SAME AGE...
...AS THE GIRL IN THIS PHOTO!
THE KIDNAPPER ABDUCTED THE BOY AND HELD HIM IN THIS VILLA SO HIS OWN DAUGHTER COULD WIN...
...THE BECKHAM INTERNATIONAL MUSIC CONTEST AT THE END OF MARCH!
YOU MEAN THIS IS THE KIDNAPPER'S PLACE?
YUP! THIS PIANO ROOM IS THE ROOM IN THE PHOTO.
KEITA, IS THE MAN IN THE PHOTO THE ONE WHO BROUGHT YOU HERE?
UH-HUH. CHIAKI'S DAD.
I HADN'T MET HIM BEFORE, BUT CHIAKI SHOWED ME PICTURES OF HIM.
BUT HE DIDN'T KIDNAP ME!
HE WAS *NICE!* HE HELPED ME!
I WAS SO TIRED FROM REHEARSING FOR THE CONTEST NONSTOP.
I HADN'T HAD ANY FUN IN SO LONG!
AND HERE YOU GET TO PLAY VIDEO GAMES, EAT SNACKS, USE CHIAKI'S TOYS AND FOOL AROUND IN THE EMPTY HOUSE.
UH-HUH!!
IT'S REALLY FUN TO RIDE DOWN THE HALL ON THE DOLLY!
THEN THE TALL FIGURE I SAW...
THAT WAS KEITA STANDING ON THE DOLLY TO PEEK IN AT US.
IT'S STURDY ENOUGH TO HOLD HIM.

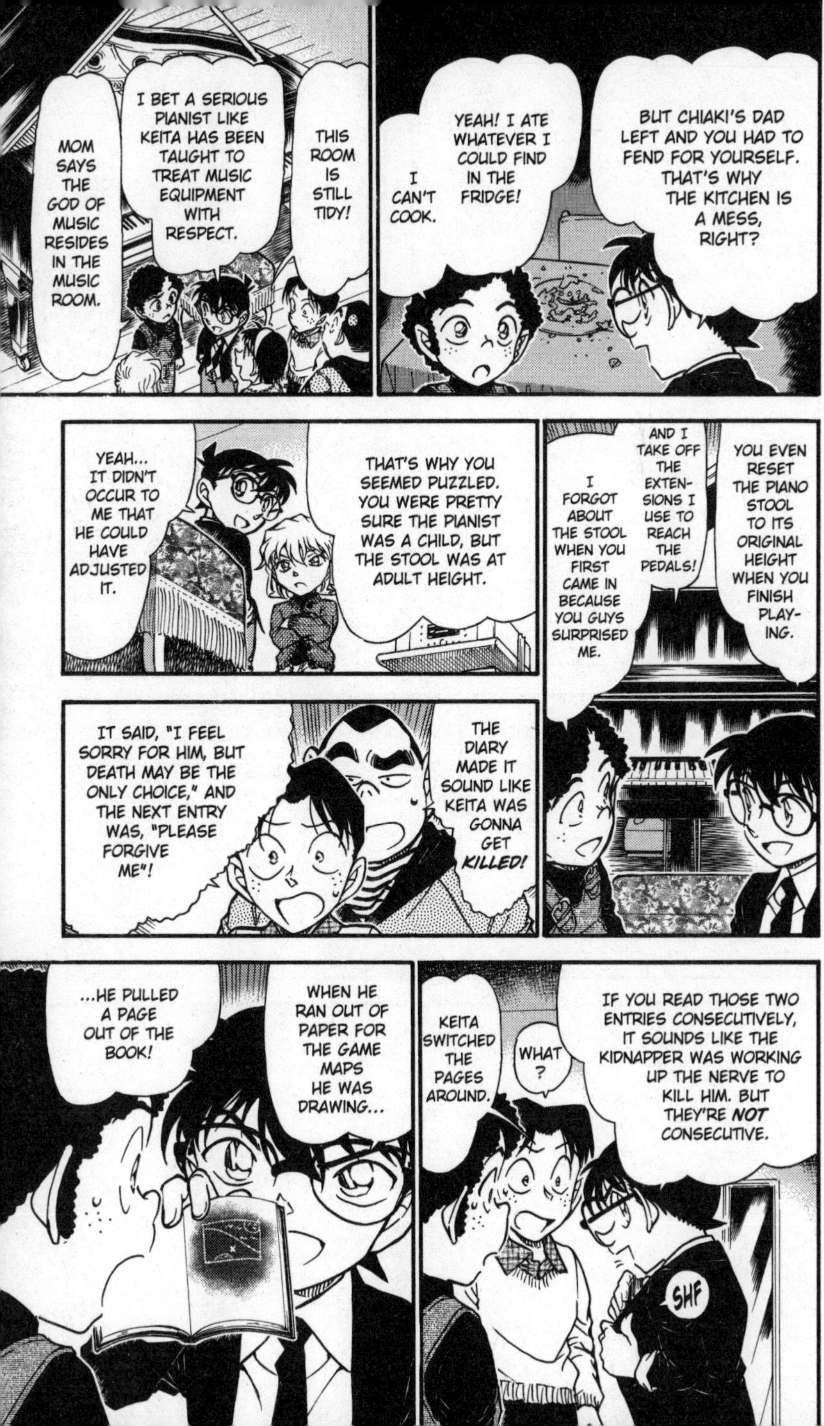
BUT CHIAKI'S DAD LEFT AND YOU HAD TO FEND FOR YOURSELF. THAT'S WHY THE KITCHEN IS A MESS, RIGHT?
YEAH! I ATE WHATEVER I COULD FIND IN THE FRIDGE!
I CAN'T COOK.
THIS ROOM IS STILL TIDY!
I BET A SERIOUS PIANIST LIKE KEITA HAS BEEN TAUGHT TO TREAT MUSIC EQUIPMENT WITH RESPECT.
MOM SAYS THE GOD OF MUSIC RESIDES IN THE MUSIC ROOM.
YOU EVEN RESET THE PIANO STOOL TO ITS ORIGINAL HEIGHT WHEN YOU FINISH PLAYING.
AND I TAKE OFF THE EXTENSIONS I USE TO REACH THE PEDALS!
I FORGOT ABOUT THE STOOL WHEN YOU FIRST CAME IN BECAUSE YOU GUYS SURPRISED ME.
THAT'S WHY YOU SEEMED PUZZLED. YOU WERE PRETTY SURE THE PIANIST WAS A CHILD, BUT THE STOOL WAS AT ADULT HEIGHT.
YEAH... IT DIDN'T OCCUR TO ME THAT HE COULD HAVE ADJUSTED IT.
THE DIARY MADE IT SOUND LIKE KEITA WAS GONNA GET *KILLED!*
IT SAID, "I FEEL SORRY FOR HIM, BUT DEATH MAY BE THE ONLY CHOICE," AND THE NEXT ENTRY WAS, "PLEASE FORGIVE ME"!
IF YOU READ THOSE TWO ENTRIES CONSECUTIVELY, IT SOUNDS LIKE THE KIDNAPPER WAS WORKING UP THE NERVE TO KILL HIM. BUT THEY'RE *NOT* CONSECUTIVE.
WHAT?
KEITA SWITCHED THE PAGES AROUND.
SHF
WHEN HE RAN OUT OF PAPER FOR THE GAME MAPS HE WAS DRAWING...
...HE PULLED A PAGE OUT OF THE BOOK!

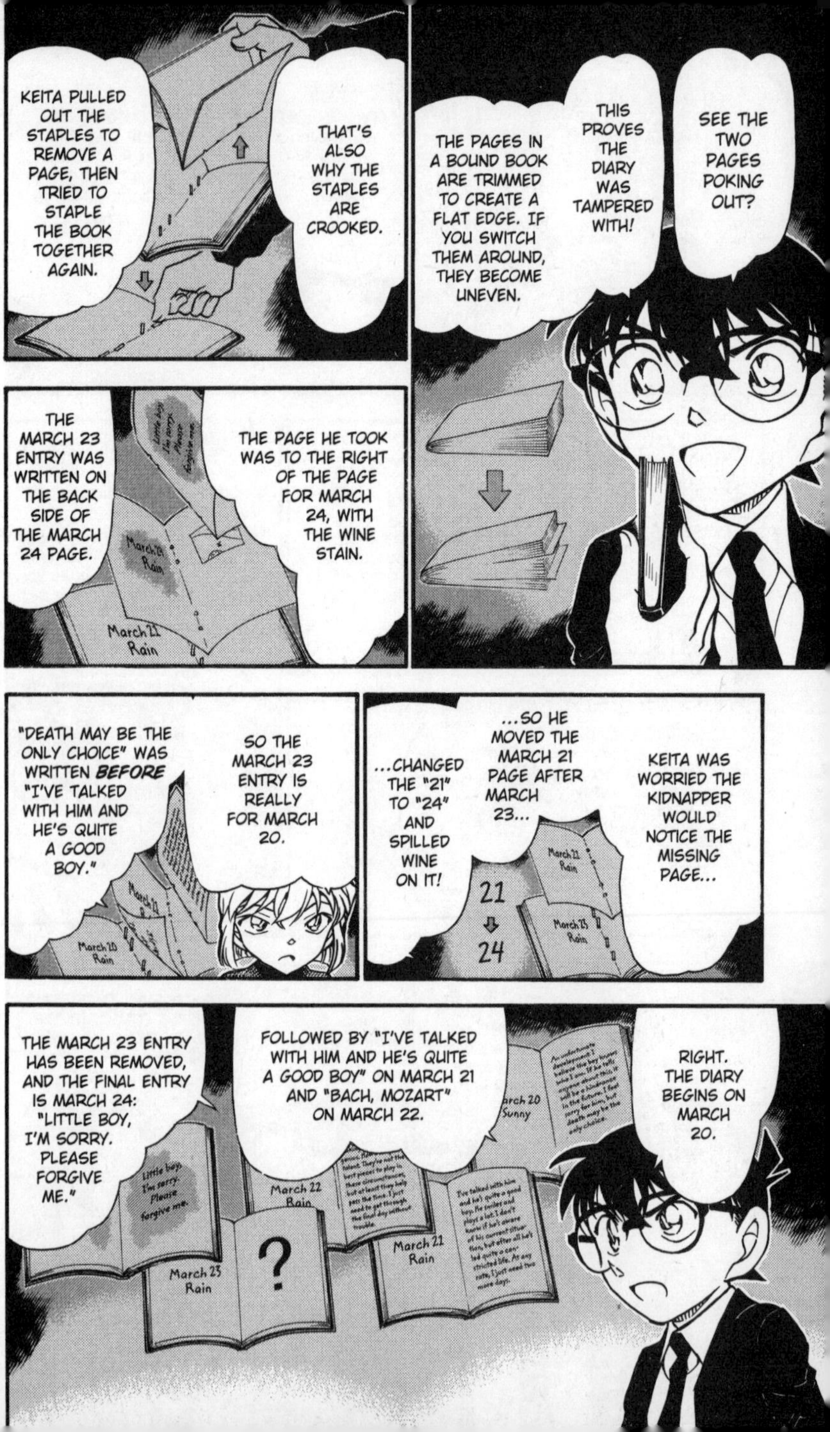
SEE THE TWO PAGES POKING OUT?
THIS PROVES THE DIARY WAS TAMPERED WITH!
THE PAGES IN A BOUND BOOK ARE TRIMMED TO CREATE A FLAT EDGE. IF YOU SWITCH THEM AROUND, THEY BECOME UNEVEN.
THAT'S ALSO WHY THE STAPLES ARE CROOKED.
KEITA PULLED OUT THE STAPLES TO REMOVE A PAGE, THEN TRIED TO STAPLE THE BOOK TOGETHER AGAIN.
THE PAGE HE TOOK WAS TO THE RIGHT OF THE PAGE FOR MARCH 24, WITH THE WINE STAIN.
THE MARCH 23 ENTRY WAS WRITTEN ON THE BACK SIDE OF THE MARCH 24 PAGE.
March 21 Rain
KEITA WAS WORRIED THE KIDNAPPER WOULD NOTICE THE MISSING PAGE...
...SO HE MOVED THE MARCH 21 PAGE AFTER MARCH 23...
...CHANGED THE "21" TO "24" AND SPILLED WINE ON IT!
21
24
March 21 Rain
March 23 Rain
SO THE MARCH 23 ENTRY IS REALLY FOR MARCH 20.
"DEATH MAY BE THE ONLY CHOICE" WAS WRITTEN BEFORE "I'VE TALKED WITH HIM AND HE'S QUITE A GOOD BOY."
March 20 Rain
RIGHT. THE DIARY BEGINS ON MARCH 20.
FOLLOWED BY "I'VE TALKED WITH HIM AND HE'S QUITE A GOOD BOY" ON MARCH 21 AND "BACH, MOZART" ON MARCH 22.
THE MARCH 23 ENTRY HAS BEEN REMOVED, AND THE FINAL ENTRY IS MARCH 24: "LITTLE BOY, I'M SORRY. PLEASE FORGIVE ME."
March 20 Sunny
March 22 Rain
March 21 Rain
March 23 Rain
?
Little boy, I'm sorry. Please forgive me.

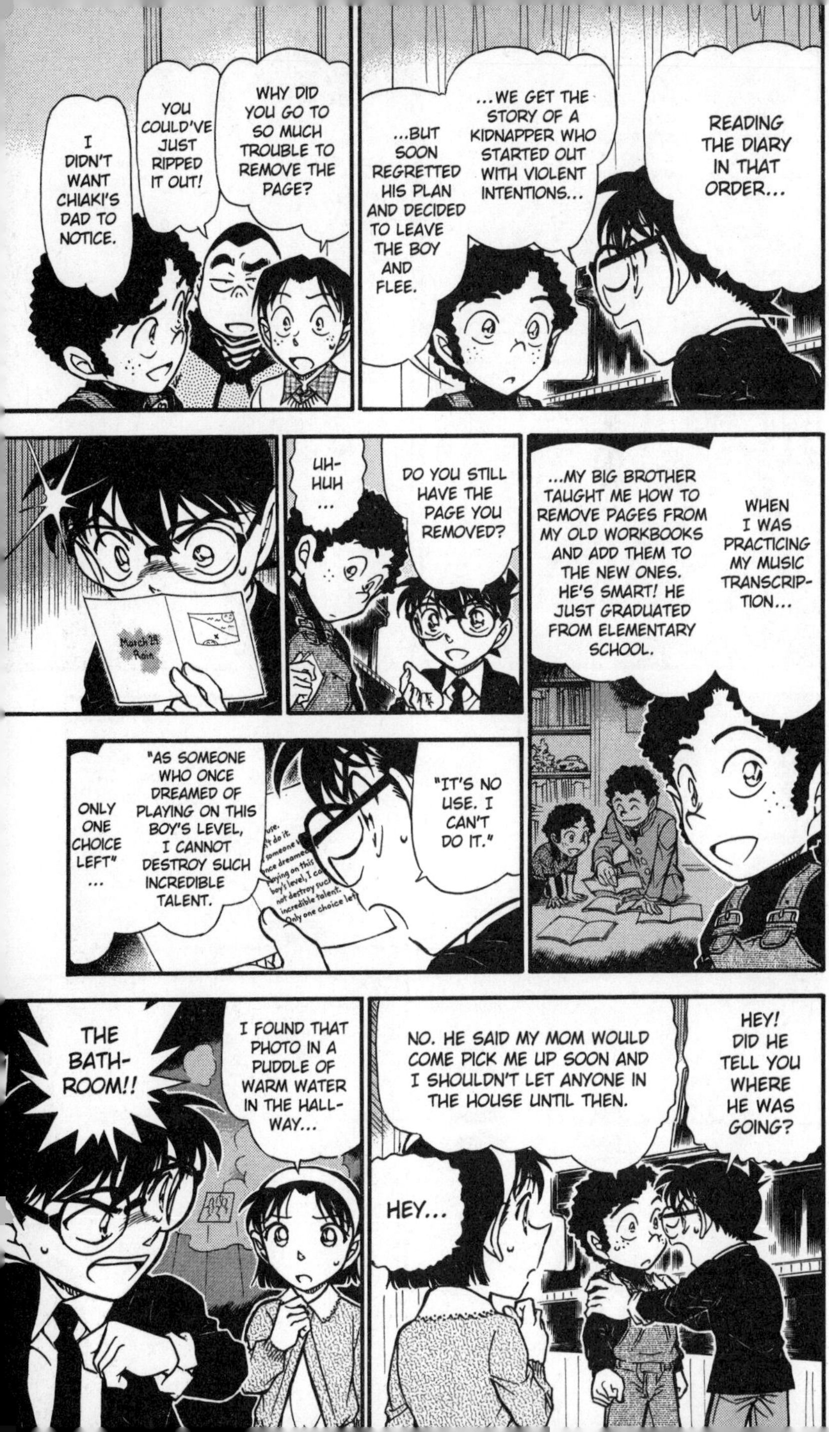
READING THE DIARY IN THAT ORDER...
...WE GET THE STORY OF A KIDNAPPER WHO STARTED OUT WITH VIOLENT INTENTIONS...
...BUT SOON REGRETTED HIS PLAN AND DECIDED TO LEAVE THE BOY AND FLEE.
WHY DID YOU GO TO SO MUCH TROUBLE TO REMOVE THE PAGE?
YOU COULD'VE JUST RIPPED IT OUT!
I DIDN'T WANT CHIAKI'S DAD TO NOTICE.
WHEN I WAS PRACTICING MY MUSIC TRANSCRIPTION...
...MY BIG BROTHER TAUGHT ME HOW TO REMOVE PAGES FROM MY OLD WORKBOOKS AND ADD THEM TO THE NEW ONES. HE'S SMART! HE JUST GRADUATED FROM ELEMENTARY SCHOOL.
DO YOU STILL HAVE THE PAGE YOU REMOVED?
UH-HUH...
March 29 Rain
"IT'S NO USE. I CAN'T DO IT."
"AS SOMEONE WHO ONCE DREAMED OF PLAYING ON THIS BOY'S LEVEL, I CANNOT DESTROY SUCH INCREDIBLE TALENT.
ONLY ONE CHOICE LEFT" ...
HEY! DID HE TELL YOU WHERE HE WAS GOING?
NO. HE SAID MY MOM WOULD COME PICK ME UP SOON AND I SHOULDN'T LET ANYONE IN THE HOUSE UNTIL THEN.
HEY...
I FOUND THAT PHOTO IN A PUDDLE OF WARM WATER IN THE HALL-WAY...
THE BATH-ROOM!!

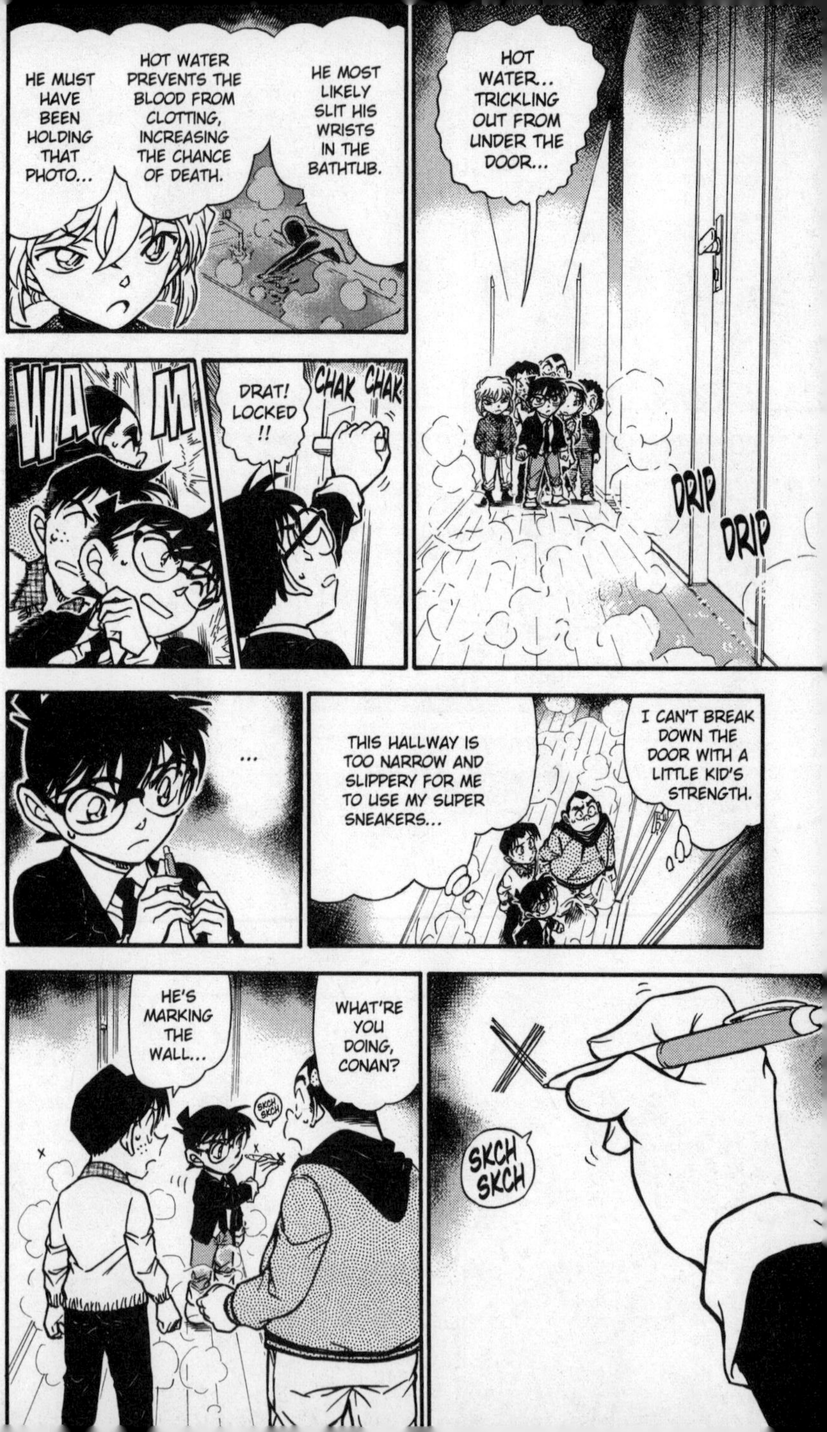
HOT WATER... TRICKLING OUT FROM UNDER THE DOOR...
DRIP
DRIP
HE MOST LIKELY SLIT HIS WRISTS IN THE BATHTUB.
HOT WATER PREVENTS THE BLOOD FROM CLOTTING, INCREASING THE CHANCE OF DEATH.
HE MUST HAVE BEEN HOLDING THAT PHOTO...
CHAK CHAK
DRAT! LOCKED !!
WAM
I CAN'T BREAK DOWN THE DOOR WITH A LITTLE KID'S STRENGTH.
THIS HALLWAY IS TOO NARROW AND SLIPPERY FOR ME TO USE MY SUPER SNEAKERS...
...
SKCH SKCH
WHAT'RE YOU DOING, CONAN?
HE'S MARKING THE WALL...
SKCH SKCH

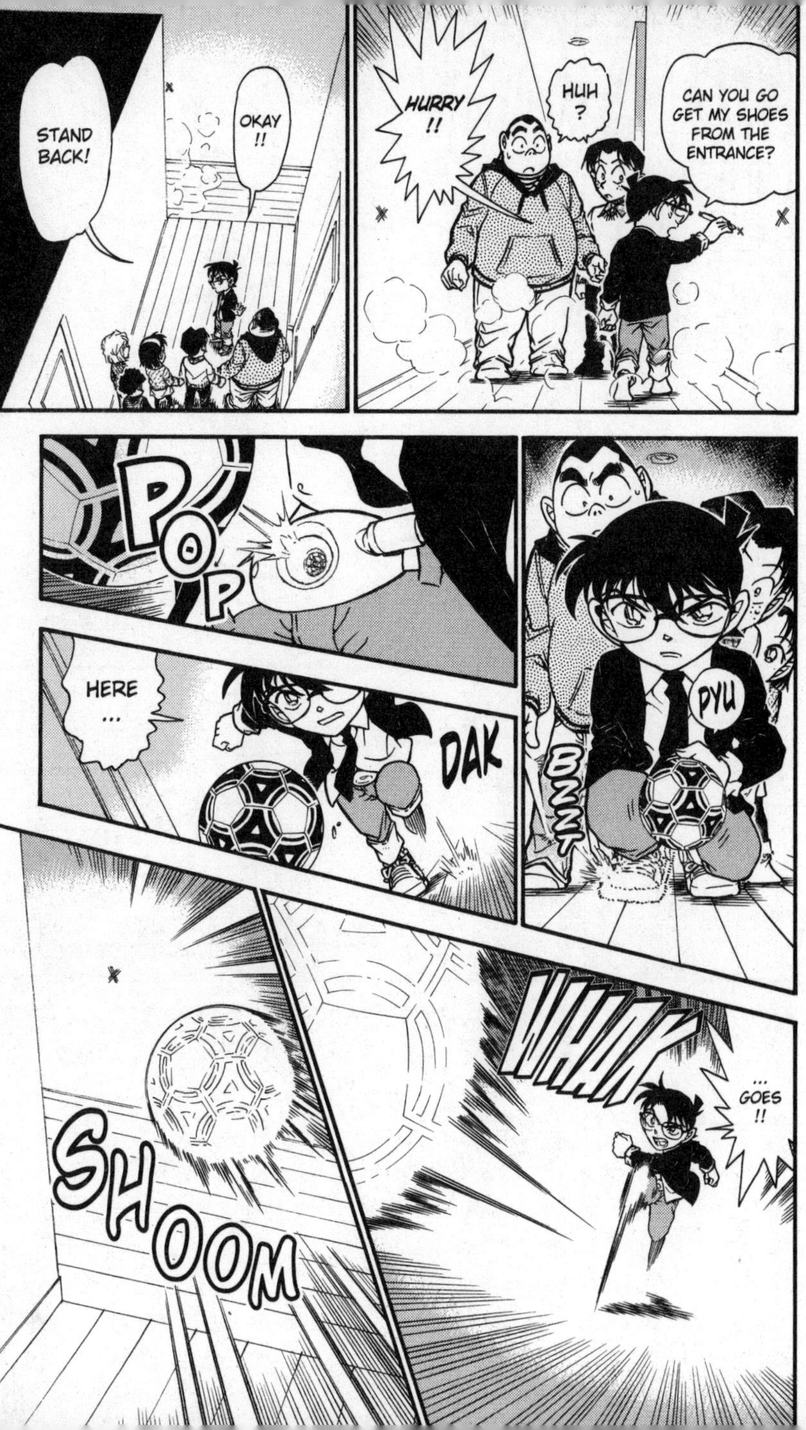
CAN YOU GO GET MY SHOES FROM THE ENTRANCE?
HUH ?
HURRY !!
OKAY !!
STAND BACK!
PYU
BZZT
POP
HERE ...
DAK
WHAK
... GOES !!
SHOOM

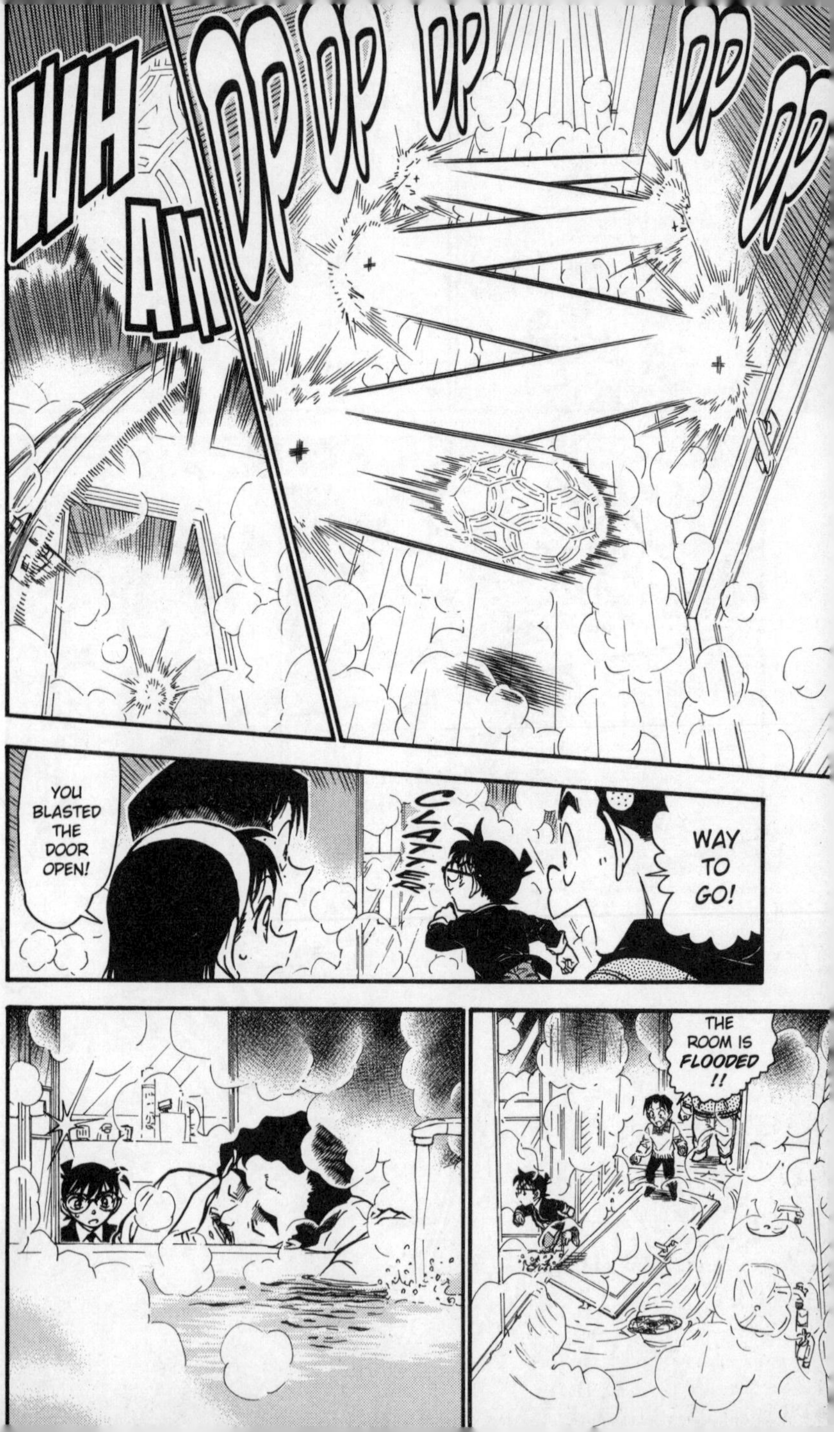
WHAM
DOOOOOOOOOOOOOOOOOOP
WAY TO GO!
CLATTER
YOU BLASTED THE DOOR OPEN!
THE ROOM IS FLOODED!!

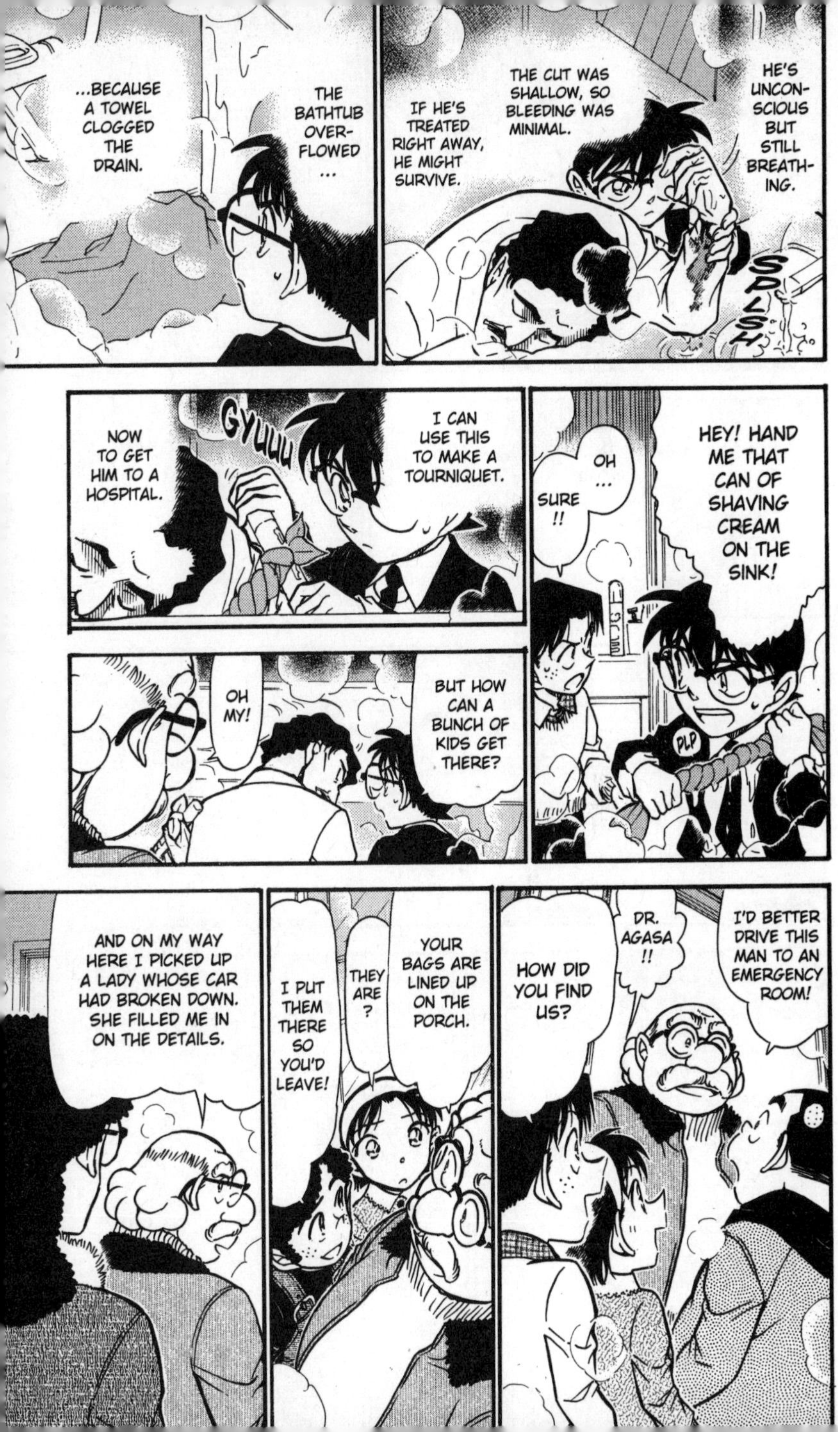
HE'S UNCONSCIOUS BUT STILL BREATHING.
THE CUT WAS SHALLOW, SO BLEEDING WAS MINIMAL.
IF HE'S TREATED RIGHT AWAY, HE MIGHT SURVIVE.
SPLISH
THE BATHTUB OVERFLOWED...
...BECAUSE A TOWEL CLOGGED THE DRAIN.
HEY! HAND ME THAT CAN OF SHAVING CREAM ON THE SINK!
OH... SURE!!
PLP
I CAN USE THIS TO MAKE A TOURNIQUET.
GYUUU
NOW TO GET HIM TO A HOSPITAL.
BUT HOW CAN A BUNCH OF KIDS GET THERE?
OH MY!
I'D BETTER DRIVE THIS MAN TO AN EMERGENCY ROOM!
DR. AGASA!!
HOW DID YOU FIND US?
YOUR BAGS ARE LINED UP ON THE PORCH.
THEY ARE?
I PUT THEM THERE SO YOU'D LEAVE!
AND ON MY WAY HERE I PICKED UP A LADY WHOSE CAR HAD BROKEN DOWN. SHE FILLED ME IN ON THE DETAILS.

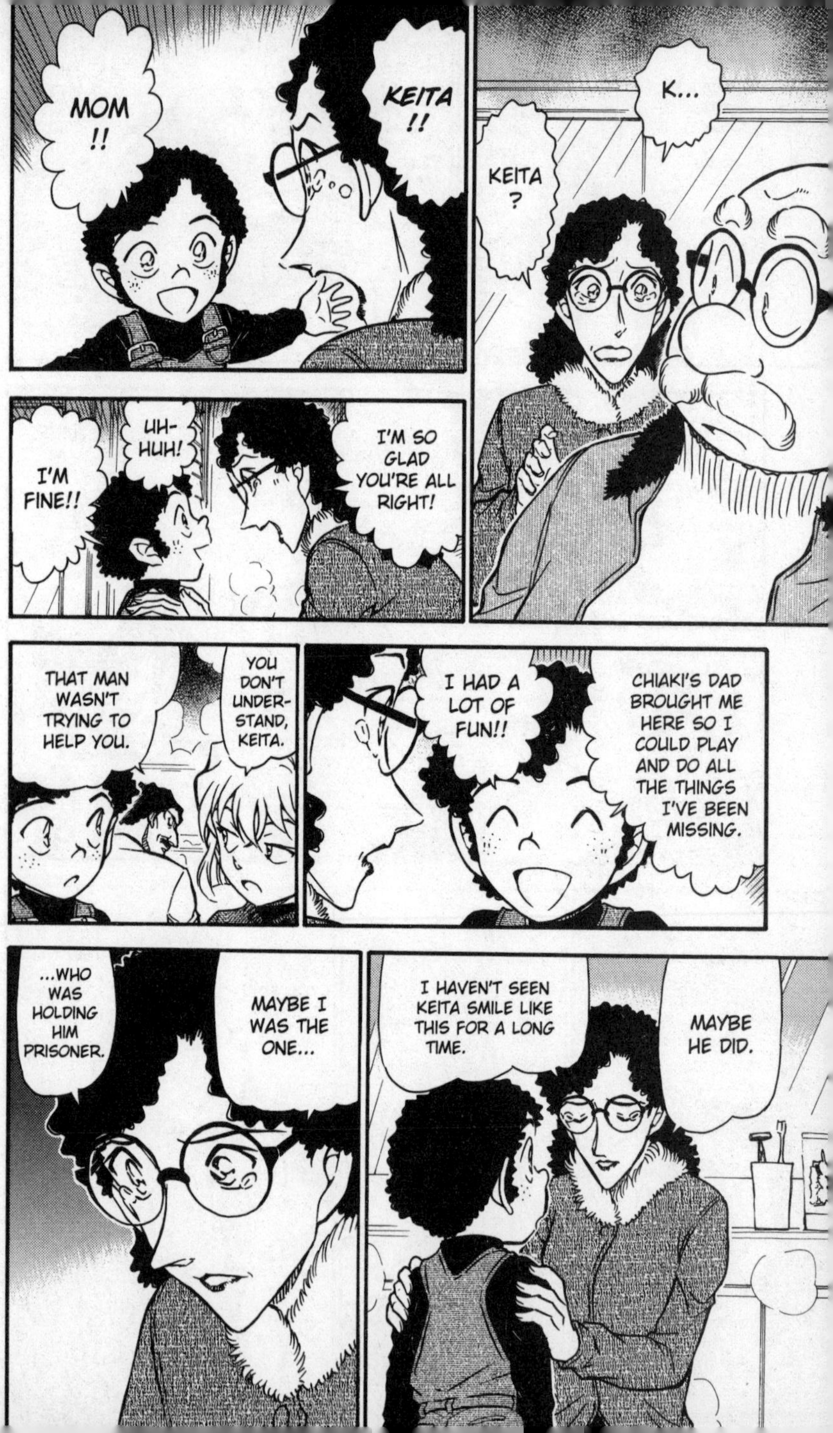
K...
KEITA ?
KEITA !!
MOM !!
I'M SO GLAD YOU'RE ALL RIGHT!
UH-HUH!
I'M FINE!!
CHIAKI'S DAD BROUGHT ME HERE SO I COULD PLAY AND DO ALL THE THINGS I'VE BEEN MISSING.
I HAD A LOT OF FUN!!
YOU DON'T UNDER-STAND, KEITA.
THAT MAN WASN'T TRYING TO HELP YOU.
MAYBE HE DID.
I HAVEN'T SEEN KEITA SMILE LIKE THIS FOR A LONG TIME.
MAYBE I WAS THE ONE...
...WHO WAS HOLDING HIM PRISONER.

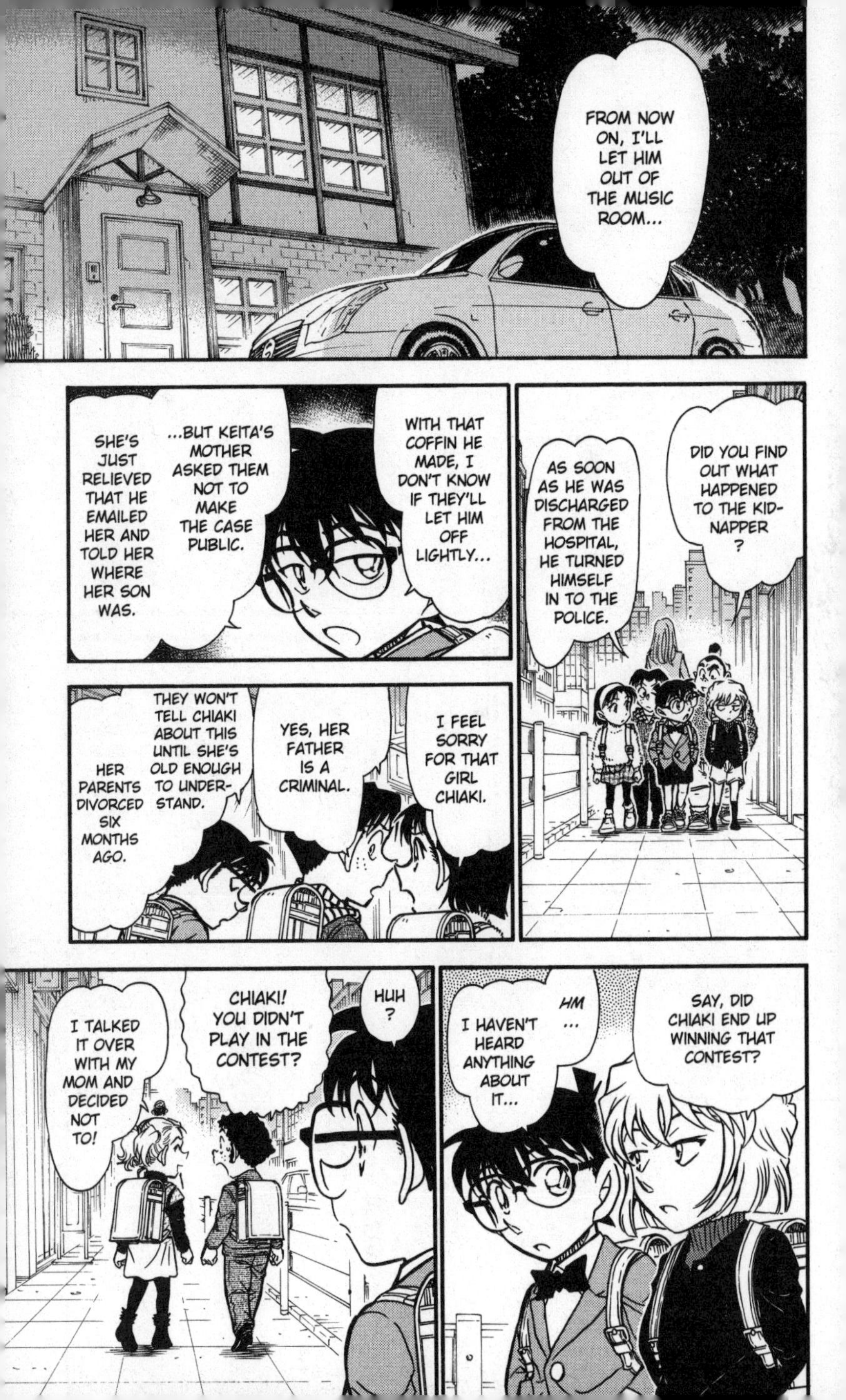
FROM NOW ON, I'LL LET HIM OUT OF THE MUSIC ROOM...
DID YOU FIND OUT WHAT HAPPENED TO THE KID-NAPPER?
AS SOON AS HE WAS DISCHARGED FROM THE HOSPITAL, HE TURNED HIMSELF IN TO THE POLICE.
WITH THAT COFFIN HE MADE, I DON'T KNOW IF THEY'LL LET HIM OFF LIGHTLY...
...BUT KEITA'S MOTHER ASKED THEM NOT TO MAKE THE CASE PUBLIC.
SHE'S JUST RELIEVED THAT HE EMAILED HER AND TOLD HER WHERE HER SON WAS.
I FEEL SORRY FOR THAT GIRL CHIAKI.
YES, HER FATHER IS A CRIMINAL.
THEY WON'T TELL CHIAKI ABOUT THIS UNTIL SHE'S OLD ENOUGH TO UNDER-STAND.
HER PARENTS DIVORCED SIX MONTHS AGO.
SAY, DID CHIAKI END UP WINNING THAT CONTEST?
HM...
I HAVEN'T HEARD ANYTHING ABOUT IT...
HUH?
CHIAKI! YOU DIDN'T PLAY IN THE CONTEST?
I TALKED IT OVER WITH MY MOM AND DECIDED NOT TO!

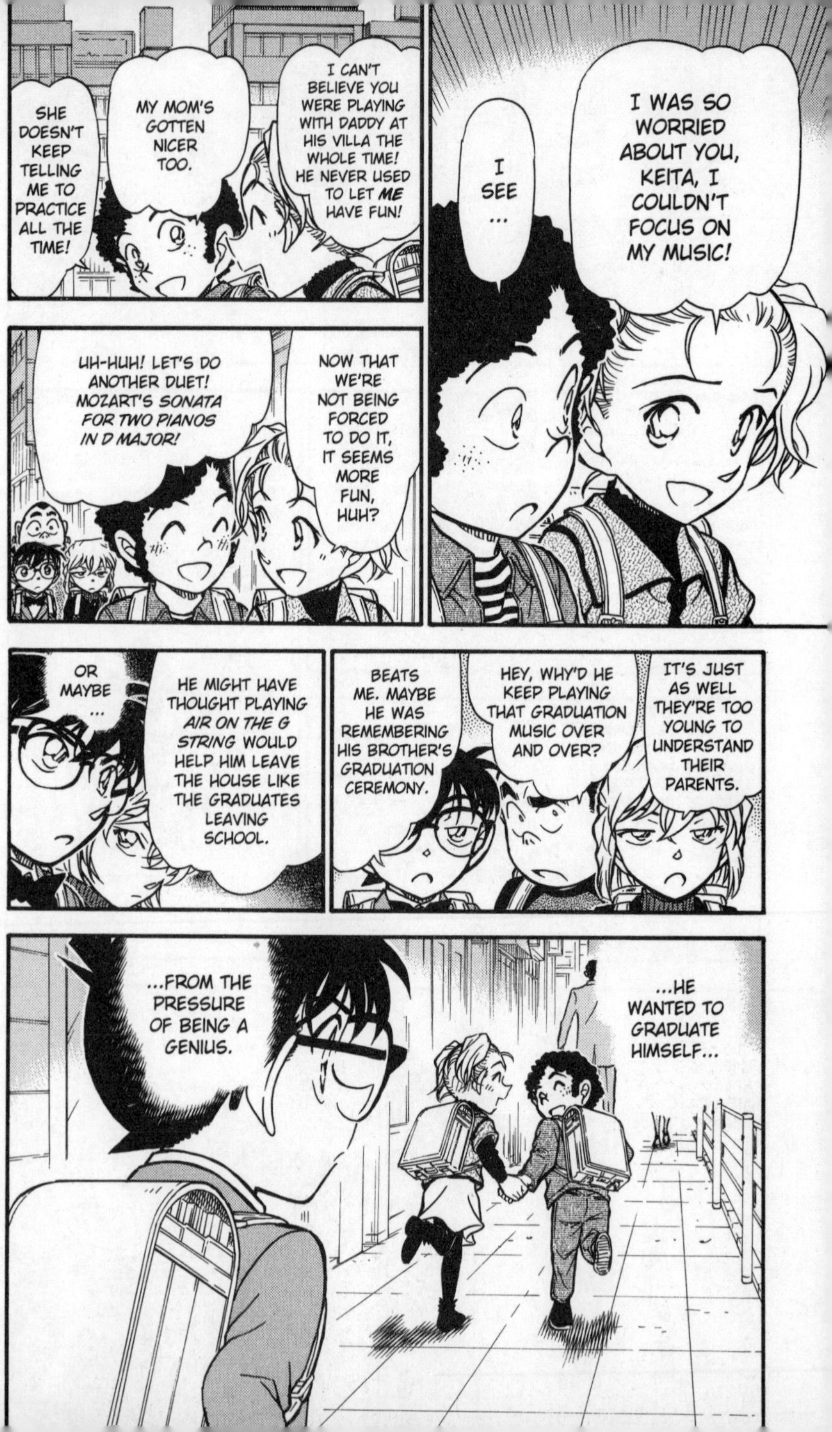
I WAS SO WORRIED ABOUT YOU, KEITA, I COULDN'T FOCUS ON MY MUSIC!
I SEE...
I CAN'T BELIEVE YOU WERE PLAYING WITH DADDY AT HIS VILLA THE WHOLE TIME! HE NEVER USED TO LET *ME* HAVE FUN!
MY MOM'S GOTTEN NICER TOO.
SHE DOESN'T KEEP TELLING ME TO PRACTICE ALL THE TIME!
NOW THAT WE'RE NOT BEING FORCED TO DO IT, IT SEEMS MORE FUN, HUH?
UH-HUH! LET'S DO ANOTHER DUET! MOZART'S *SONATA FOR TWO PIANOS IN D MAJOR!*
IT'S JUST AS WELL THEY'RE TOO YOUNG TO UNDERSTAND THEIR PARENTS.
HEY, WHY'D HE KEEP PLAYING THAT GRADUATION MUSIC OVER AND OVER?
BEATS ME. MAYBE HE WAS REMEMBERING HIS BROTHER'S GRADUATION CEREMONY.
HE MIGHT HAVE THOUGHT PLAYING *AIR ON THE G STRING* WOULD HELP HIM LEAVE THE HOUSE LIKE THE GRADUATES LEAVING SCHOOL.
OR MAYBE...
...HE WANTED TO GRADUATE HIMSELF...
...FROM THE PRESSURE OF BEING A GENIUS.

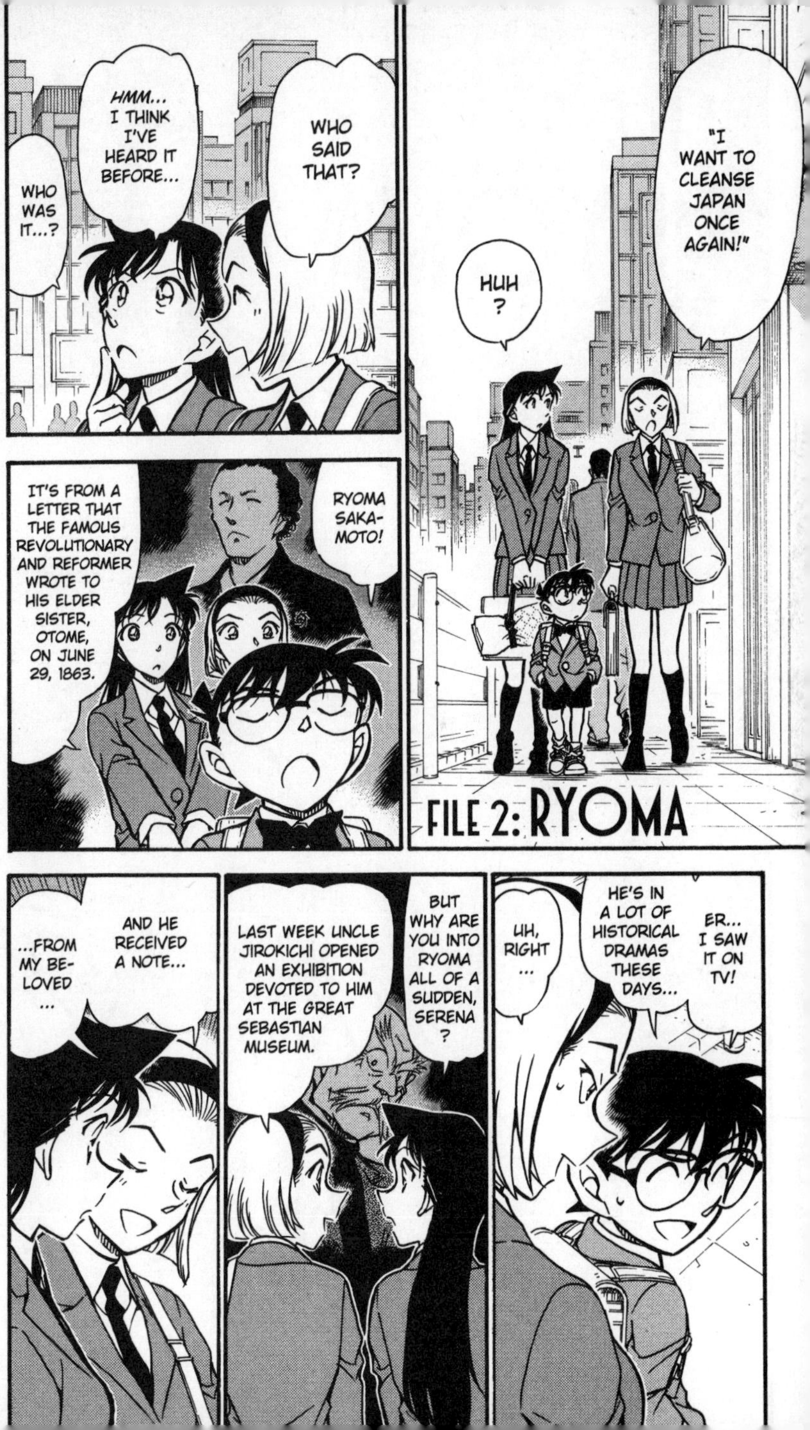
"I WANT TO CLEANSE JAPAN ONCE AGAIN!"
HUH?
FILE 2: RYOMA
WHO SAID THAT?
HMM... I THINK I'VE HEARD IT BEFORE...
WHO WAS IT...?
RYOMA SAKA-MOTO!
IT'S FROM A LETTER THAT THE FAMOUS REVOLUTIONARY AND REFORMER WROTE TO HIS ELDER SISTER, OTOME, ON JUNE 29, 1863.
ER... I SAW IT ON TV!
HE'S IN A LOT OF HISTORICAL DRAMAS THESE DAYS...
UH, RIGHT ...
BUT WHY ARE YOU INTO RYOMA ALL OF A SUDDEN, SERENA?
LAST WEEK UNCLE JIROKICHI OPENED AN EXHIBITION DEVOTED TO HIM AT THE GREAT SEBASTIAN MUSEUM.
AND HE RECEIVED A NOTE...
...FROM MY BE-LOVED ...

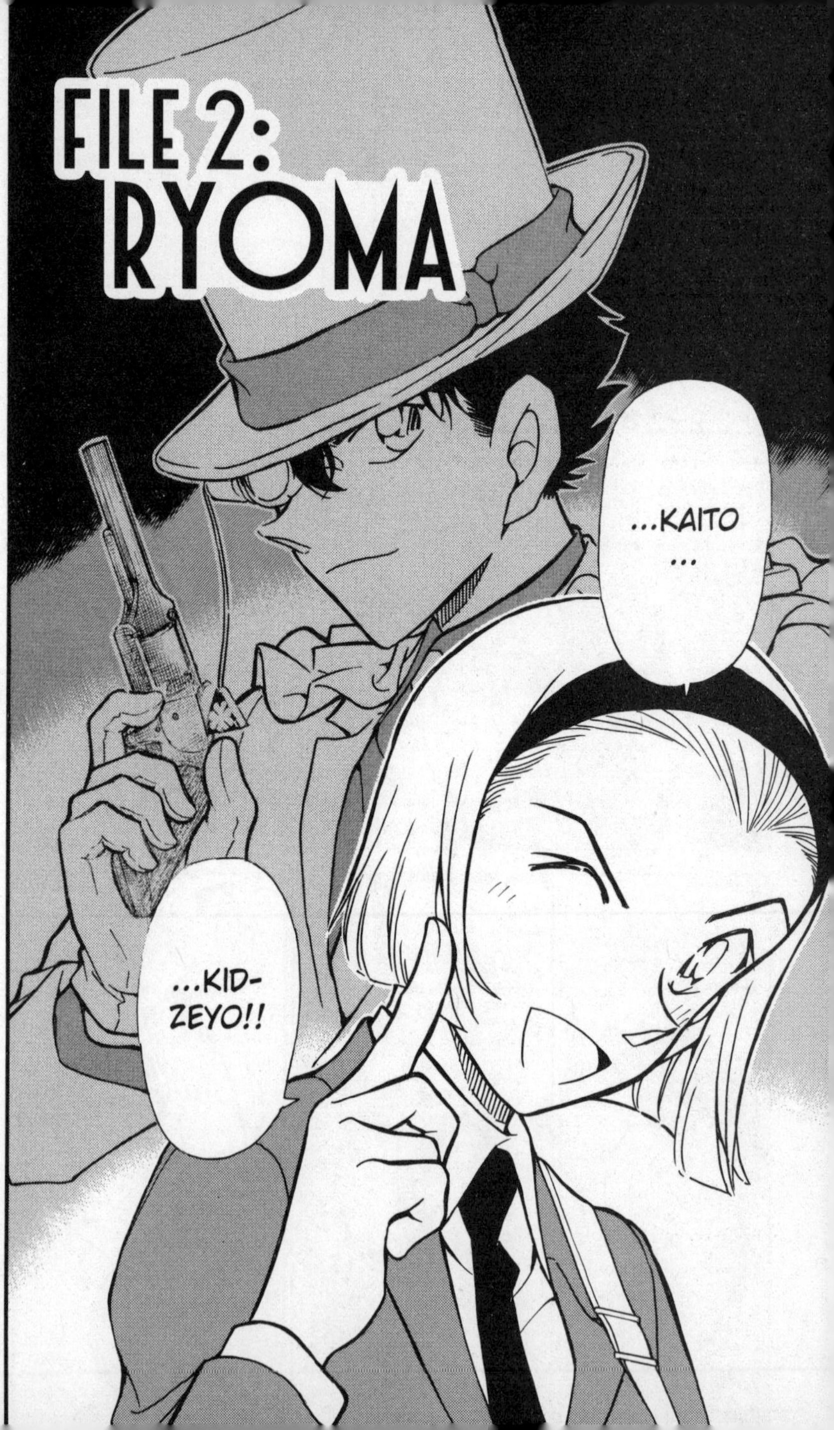
FILE 2: RYOMA
...KAITO ...
...KID-ZEYO!!

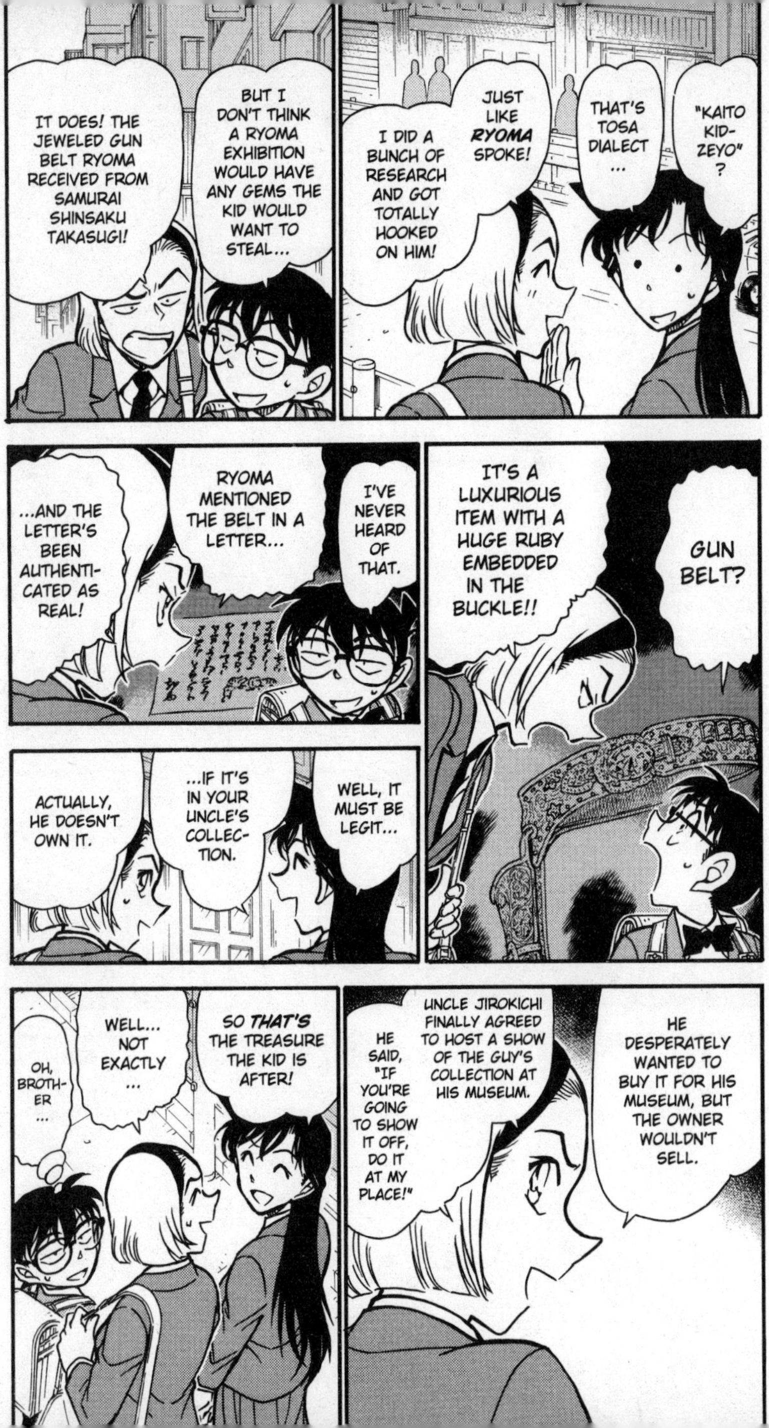
"KAITO KID-ZEYO"?
THAT'S TOSA DIALECT...
JUST LIKE *RYOMA* SPOKE!
I DID A BUNCH OF RESEARCH AND GOT TOTALLY HOOKED ON HIM!
BUT I DON'T THINK A RYOMA EXHIBITION WOULD HAVE ANY GEMS THE KID WOULD WANT TO STEAL...
IT DOES! THE JEWELED GUN BELT RYOMA RECEIVED FROM SAMURAI SHINSAKU TAKASUGI!
GUN BELT?
IT'S A LUXURIOUS ITEM WITH A HUGE RUBY EMBEDDED IN THE BUCKLE!!
I'VE NEVER HEARD OF THAT.
RYOMA MENTIONED THE BELT IN A LETTER...
...AND THE LETTER'S BEEN AUTHENTICATED AS REAL!
WELL, IT MUST BE LEGIT...
...IF IT'S IN YOUR UNCLE'S COLLECTION.
ACTUALLY, HE DOESN'T OWN IT.
HE DESPERATELY WANTED TO BUY IT FOR HIS MUSEUM, BUT THE OWNER WOULDN'T SELL.
UNCLE JIROKICHI FINALLY AGREED TO HOST A SHOW OF THE GUY'S COLLECTION AT HIS MUSEUM.
HE SAID, "IF YOU'RE GOING TO SHOW IT OFF, DO IT AT MY PLACE!"
SO *THAT'S* THE TREASURE THE KID IS AFTER!
WELL... NOT EXACTLY ...
OH, BROTHER ...

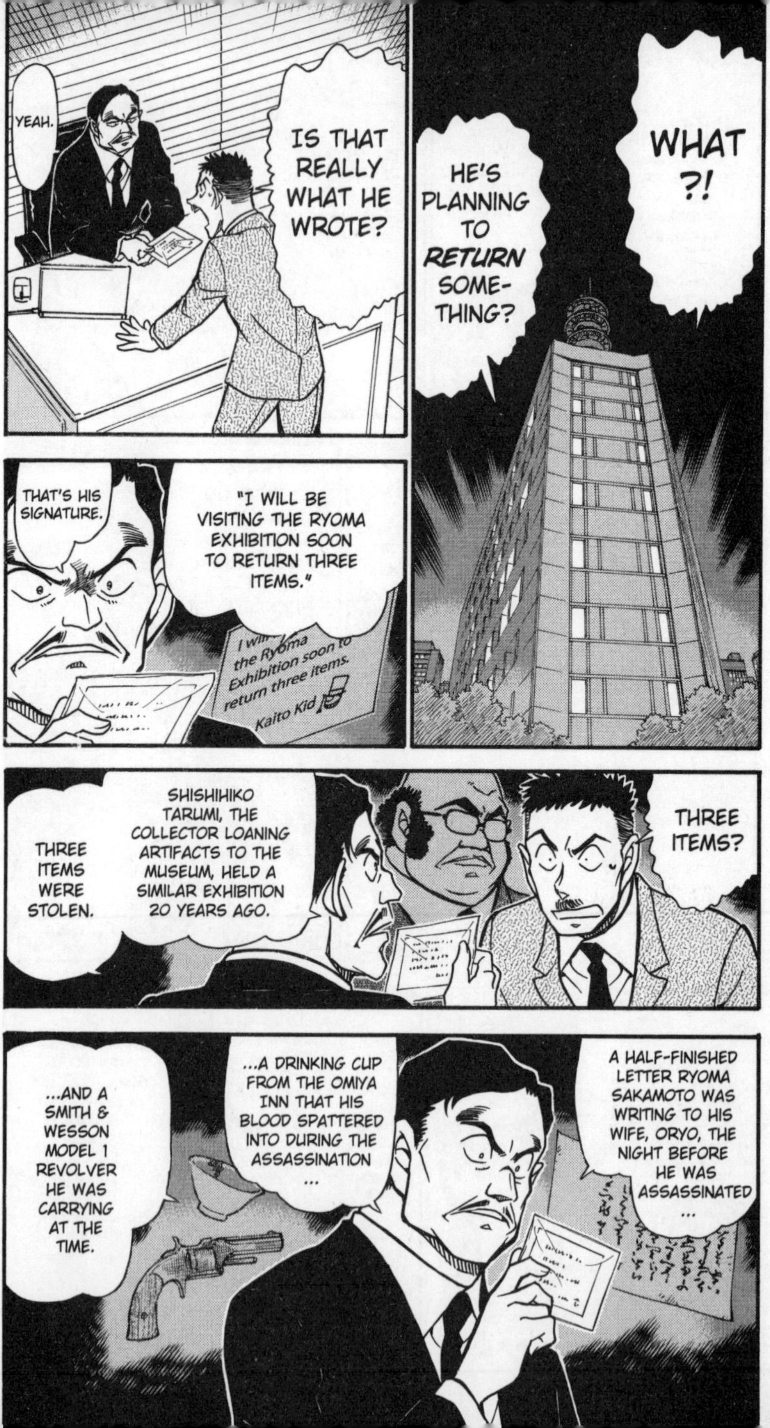
WHAT ?!
HE'S PLANNING TO *RETURN* SOME-THING?
IS THAT REALLY WHAT HE WROTE?
YEAH.
"I WILL BE VISITING THE RYOMA EXHIBITION SOON TO RETURN THREE ITEMS."
THAT'S HIS SIGNATURE.
the Ryoma Exhibition soon to return three items.
Kaito Kid
THREE ITEMS?
SHISHIHIKO TARUMI, THE COLLECTOR LOANING ARTIFACTS TO THE MUSEUM, HELD A SIMILAR EXHIBITION 20 YEARS AGO.
THREE ITEMS WERE STOLEN.
A HALF-FINISHED LETTER RYOMA SAKAMOTO WAS WRITING TO HIS WIFE, ORYO, THE NIGHT BEFORE HE WAS ASSASSINATED ...
...A DRINKING CUP FROM THE OMIYA INN THAT HIS BLOOD SPATTERED INTO DURING THE ASSASSINATION ...
...AND A SMITH & WESSON MODEL 1 REVOLVER HE WAS CARRYING AT THE TIME.

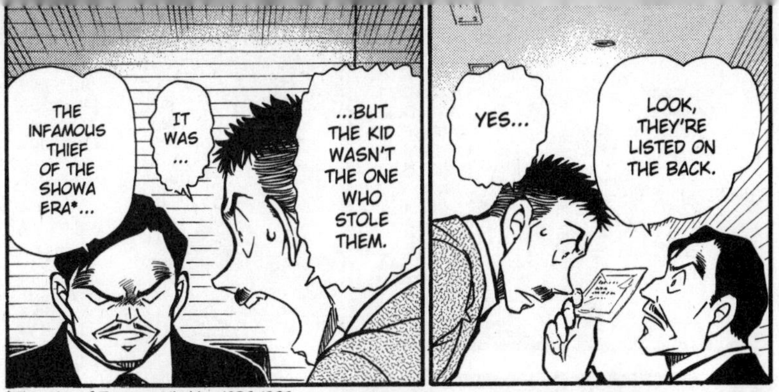
LOOK, THEY'RE LISTED ON THE BACK.
YES...
...BUT THE KID WASN'T THE ONE WHO STOLE THEM.
IT WAS...
THE INFAMOUS THIEF OF THE SHOWA ERA*...

*The reign of Emperor Hirohito, 1926-1989.

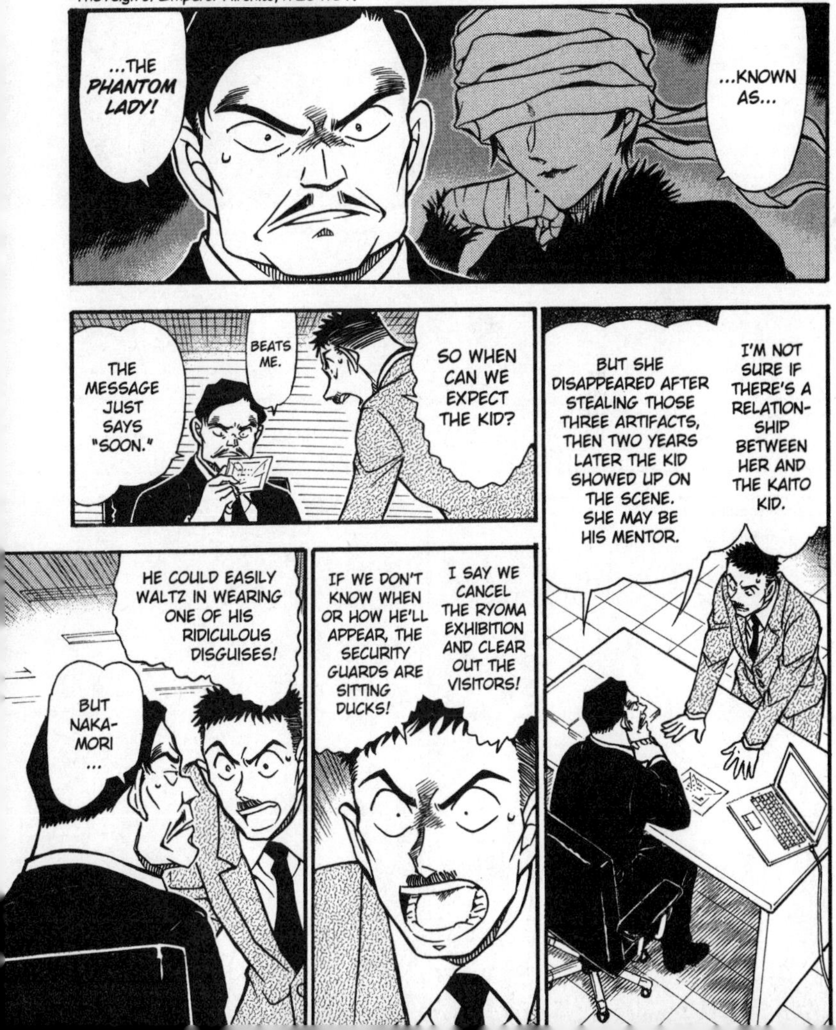
...KNOWN AS...
...THE *PHANTOM LADY!*
I'M NOT SURE IF THERE'S A RELATIONSHIP BETWEEN HER AND THE KAITO KID.
BUT SHE DISAPPEARED AFTER STEALING THOSE THREE ARTIFACTS, THEN TWO YEARS LATER THE KID SHOWED UP ON THE SCENE. SHE MAY BE HIS MENTOR.
SO WHEN CAN WE EXPECT THE KID?
BEATS ME.
THE MESSAGE JUST SAYS "SOON."
I SAY WE CANCEL THE RYOMA EXHIBITION AND CLEAR OUT THE VISITORS!
IF WE DON'T KNOW WHEN OR HOW HE'LL APPEAR, THE SECURITY GUARDS ARE SITTING DUCKS!
HE COULD EASILY WALTZ IN WEARING ONE OF HIS RIDICULOUS DISGUISES!
BUT NAKAMORI...

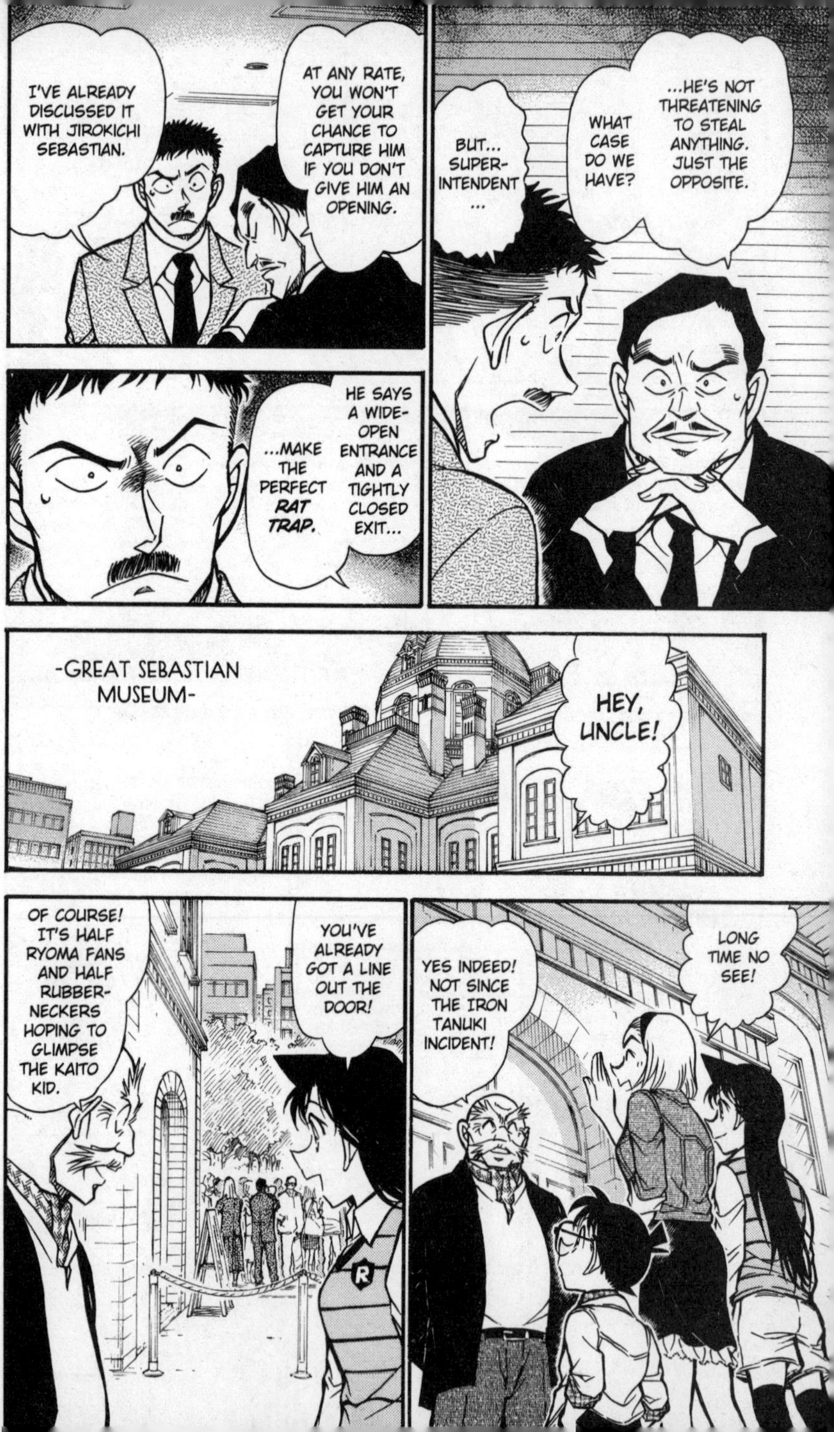
...HE'S NOT THREATENING TO STEAL ANYTHING. JUST THE OPPOSITE.
WHAT CASE DO WE HAVE?
BUT... SUPER-INTENDENT ...
AT ANY RATE, YOU WON'T GET YOUR CHANCE TO CAPTURE HIM IF YOU DON'T GIVE HIM AN OPENING.
I'VE ALREADY DISCUSSED IT WITH JIROKICHI SEBASTIAN.
HE SAYS A WIDE-OPEN ENTRANCE AND A TIGHTLY CLOSED EXIT...
...MAKE THE PERFECT *RAT TRAP.*
HEY, UNCLE!
-GREAT SEBASTIAN MUSEUM-
LONG TIME NO SEE!
YES INDEED! NOT SINCE THE IRON TANUKI INCIDENT!
YOU'VE ALREADY GOT A LINE OUT THE DOOR!
OF COURSE! IT'S HALF RYOMA FANS AND HALF RUBBER-NECKERS HOPING TO GLIMPSE THE KAITO KID.

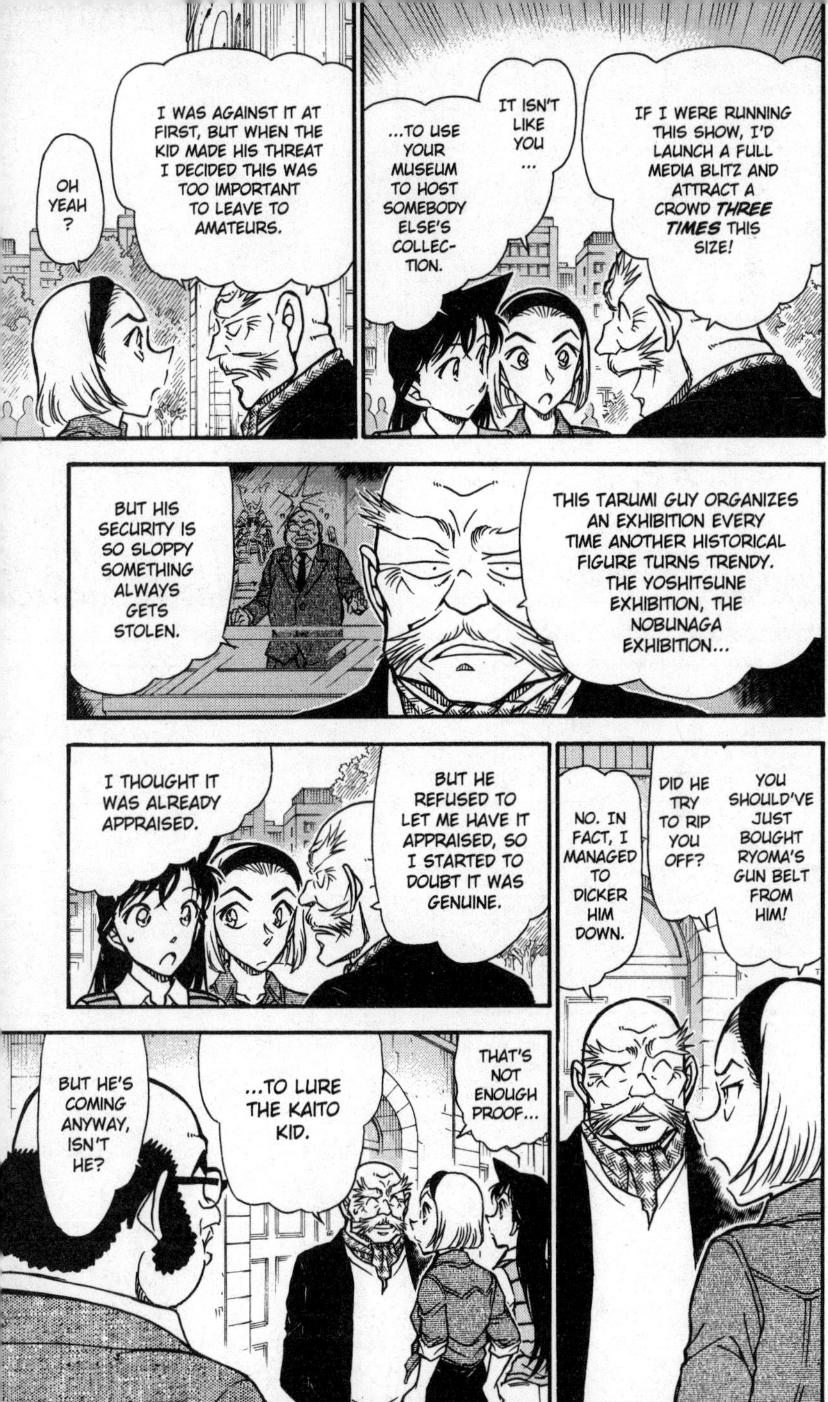
IF I WERE RUNNING THIS SHOW, I'D LAUNCH A FULL MEDIA BLITZ AND ATTRACT A CROWD ***THREE TIMES*** THIS SIZE!
IT ISN'T LIKE YOU ...
...TO USE YOUR MUSEUM TO HOST SOMEBODY ELSE'S COLLEC-TION.
I WAS AGAINST IT AT FIRST, BUT WHEN THE KID MADE HIS THREAT I DECIDED THIS WAS TOO IMPORTANT TO LEAVE TO AMATEURS.
OH YEAH ?
THIS TARUMI GUY ORGANIZES AN EXHIBITION EVERY TIME ANOTHER HISTORICAL FIGURE TURNS TRENDY. THE YOSHITSUNE EXHIBITION, THE NOBUNAGA EXHIBITION...
BUT HIS SECURITY IS SO SLOPPY SOMETHING ALWAYS GETS STOLEN.
YOU SHOULD'VE JUST BOUGHT RYOMA'S GUN BELT FROM HIM!
DID HE TRY TO RIP YOU OFF?
NO. IN FACT, I MANAGED TO DICKER HIM DOWN.
BUT HE REFUSED TO LET ME HAVE IT APPRAISED, SO I STARTED TO DOUBT IT WAS GENUINE.
I THOUGHT IT WAS ALREADY APPRAISED.
THAT'S NOT ENOUGH PROOF...
...TO LURE THE KAITO KID.
BUT HE'S COMING ANYWAY, ISN'T HE?

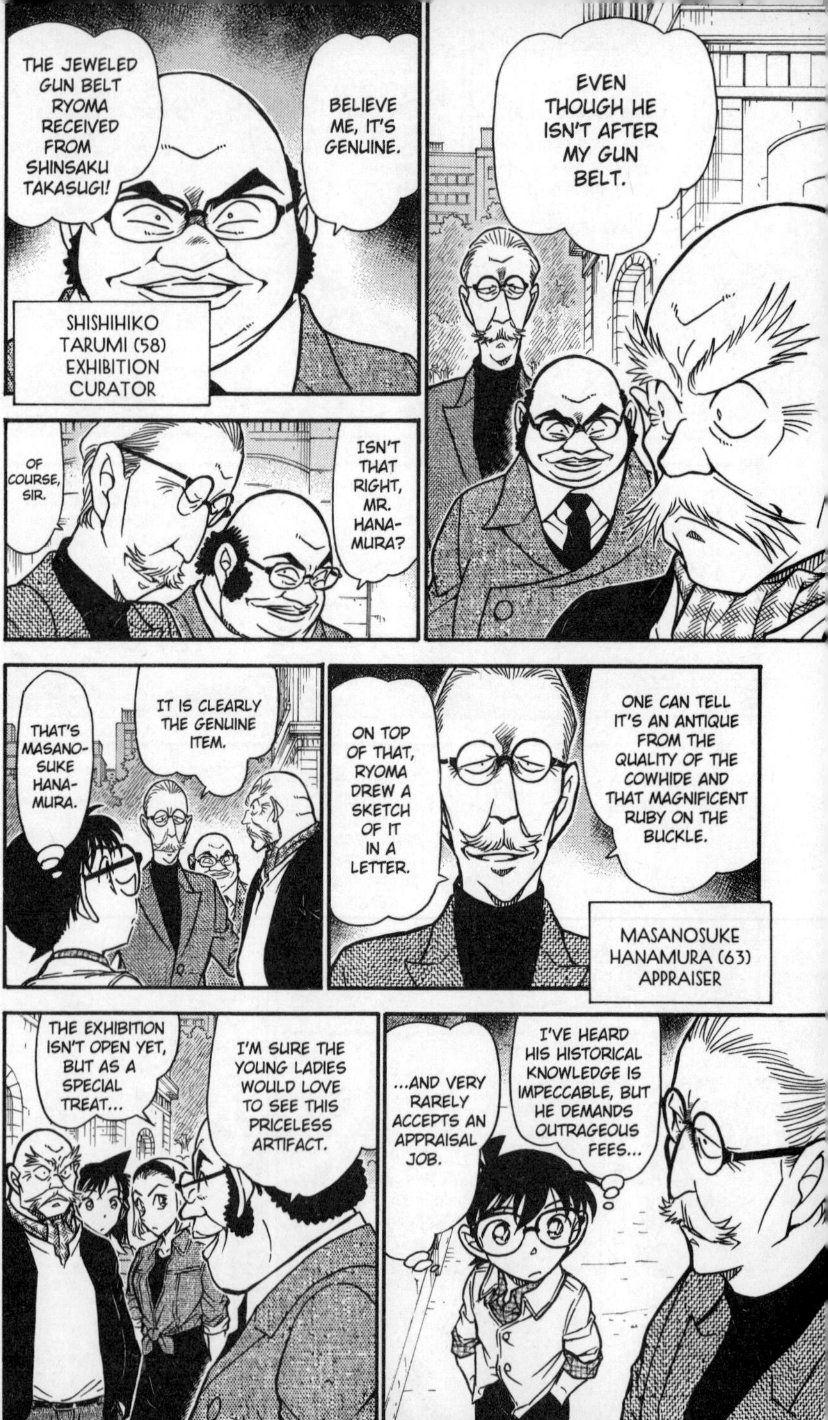
EVEN THOUGH HE ISN'T AFTER MY GUN BELT.
BELIEVE ME, IT'S GENUINE.
THE JEWELED GUN BELT RYOMA RECEIVED FROM SHINSAKU TAKASUGI!
SHISHIHIKO TARUMI (58) EXHIBITION CURATOR
ISN'T THAT RIGHT, MR. HANAMURA?
OF COURSE, SIR.
ONE CAN TELL IT'S AN ANTIQUE FROM THE QUALITY OF THE COWHIDE AND THAT MAGNIFICENT RUBY ON THE BUCKLE.
ON TOP OF THAT, RYOMA DREW A SKETCH OF IT IN A LETTER.
MASANOSUKE HANAMURA (63) APPRAISER
IT IS CLEARLY THE GENUINE ITEM.
THAT'S MASANOSUKE HANAMURA.
I'VE HEARD HIS HISTORICAL KNOWLEDGE IS IMPECCABLE, BUT HE DEMANDS OUTRAGEOUS FEES...
...AND VERY RARELY ACCEPTS AN APPRAISAL JOB.
I'M SURE THE YOUNG LADIES WOULD LOVE TO SEE THIS PRICELESS ARTIFACT.
THE EXHIBITION ISN'T OPEN YET, BUT AS A SPECIAL TREAT...

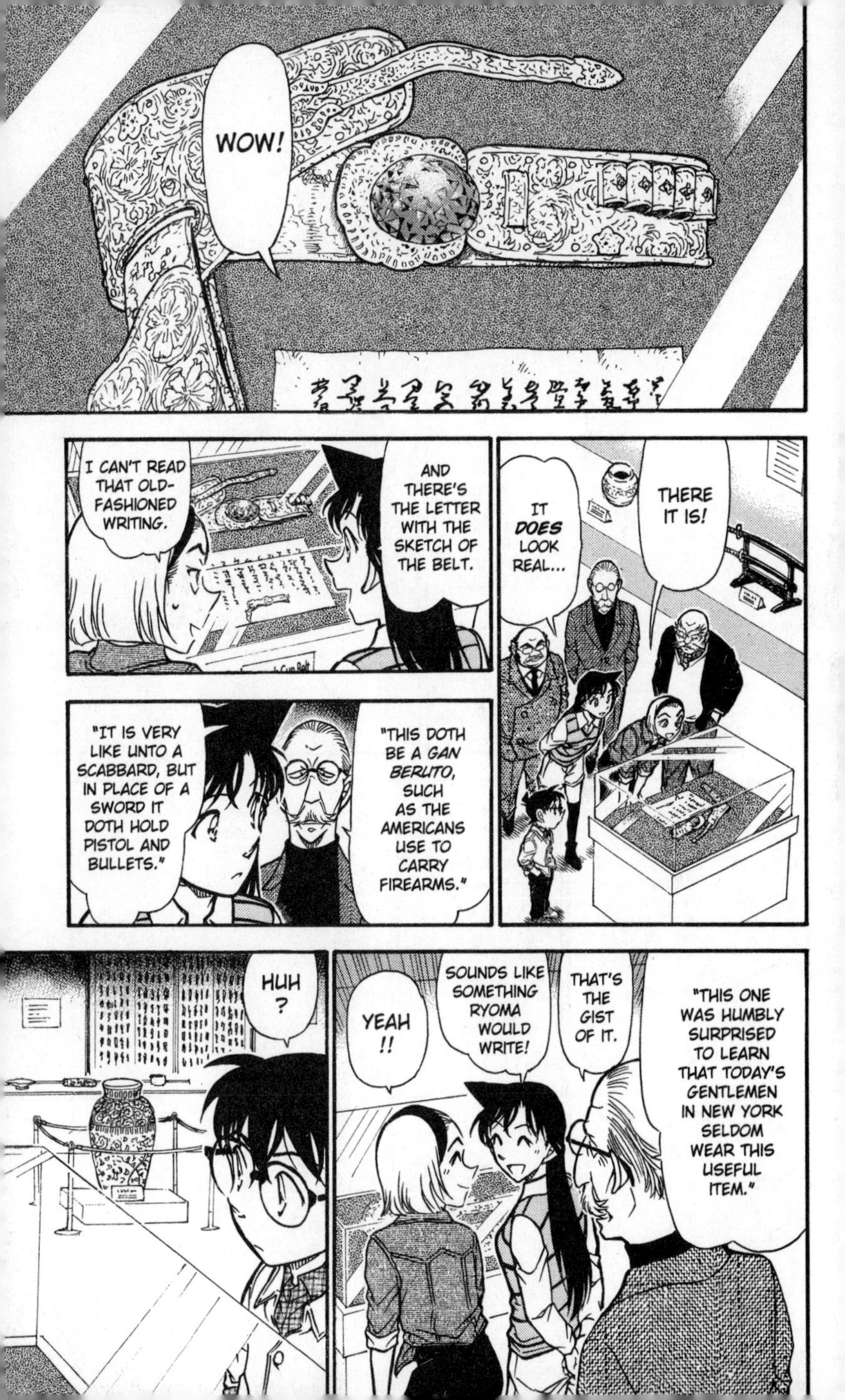
WOW!
THERE IT IS!
IT *DOES* LOOK REAL...
AND THERE'S THE LETTER WITH THE SKETCH OF THE BELT.
I CAN'T READ THAT OLD-FASHIONED WRITING.
"THIS DOTH BE A *GAN BERUTO*, SUCH AS THE AMERICANS USE TO CARRY FIREARMS."
"IT IS VERY LIKE UNTO A SCABBARD, BUT IN PLACE OF A SWORD IT DOTH HOLD PISTOL AND BULLETS."
"THIS ONE WAS HUMBLY SURPRISED TO LEARN THAT TODAY'S GENTLEMEN IN NEW YORK SELDOM WEAR THIS USEFUL ITEM."
THAT'S THE GIST OF IT.
SOUNDS LIKE SOMETHING RYOMA WOULD WRITE!
YEAH!!
HUH?

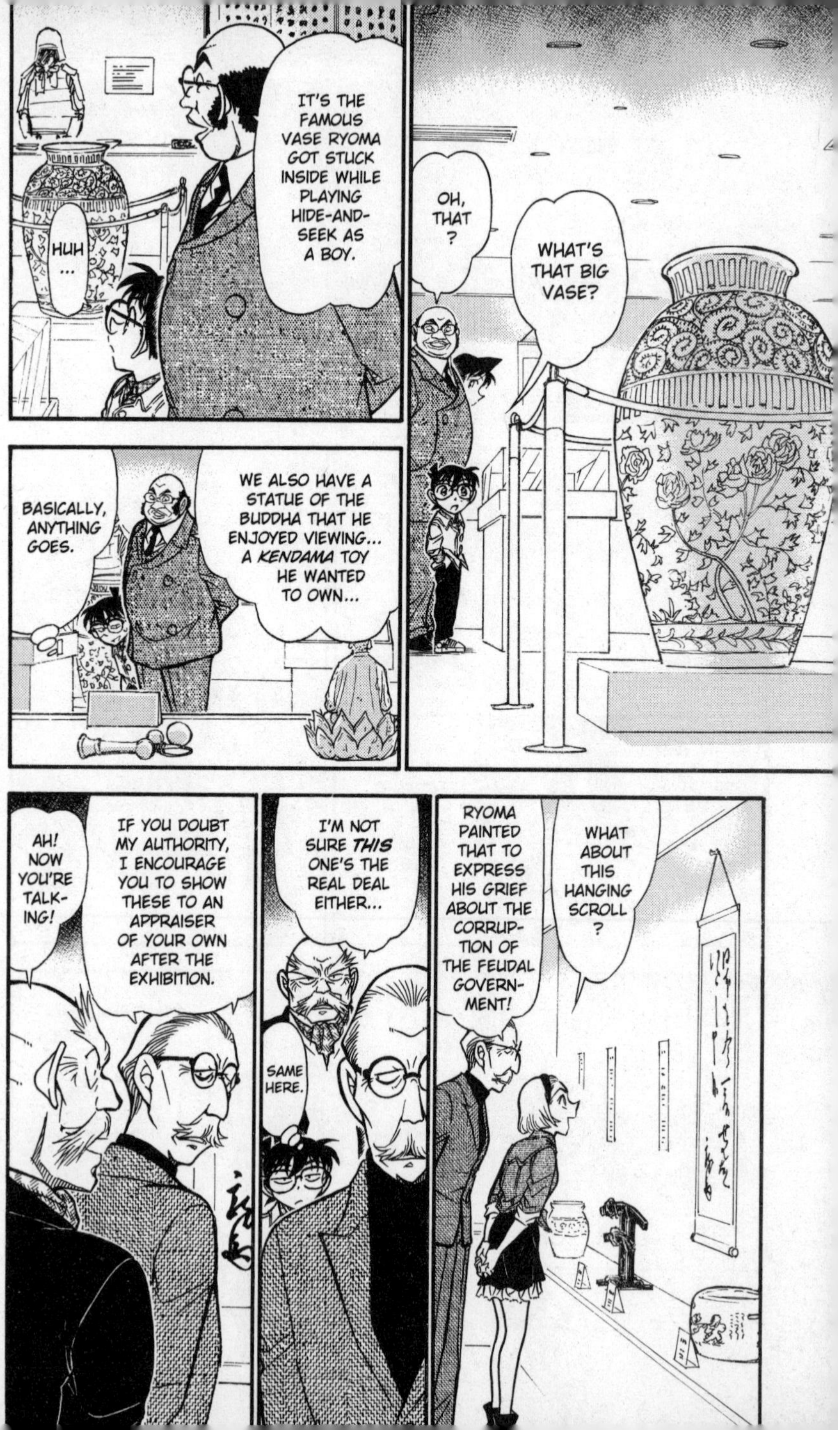
WHAT'S THAT BIG VASE?
OH, THAT?
IT'S THE FAMOUS VASE RYOMA GOT STUCK INSIDE WHILE PLAYING HIDE-AND-SEEK AS A BOY.
HUH...
WE ALSO HAVE A STATUE OF THE BUDDHA THAT HE ENJOYED VIEWING... A *KENDAMA* TOY HE WANTED TO OWN...
BASICALLY, ANYTHING GOES.
WHAT ABOUT THIS HANGING SCROLL?
RYOMA PAINTED THAT TO EXPRESS HIS GRIEF ABOUT THE CORRUPTION OF THE FEUDAL GOVERNMENT!
I'M NOT SURE ***THIS*** ONE'S THE REAL DEAL EITHER...
SAME HERE.
IF YOU DOUBT MY AUTHORITY, I ENCOURAGE YOU TO SHOW THESE TO AN APPRAISER OF YOUR OWN AFTER THE EXHIBITION.
AH! NOW YOU'RE TALKING!

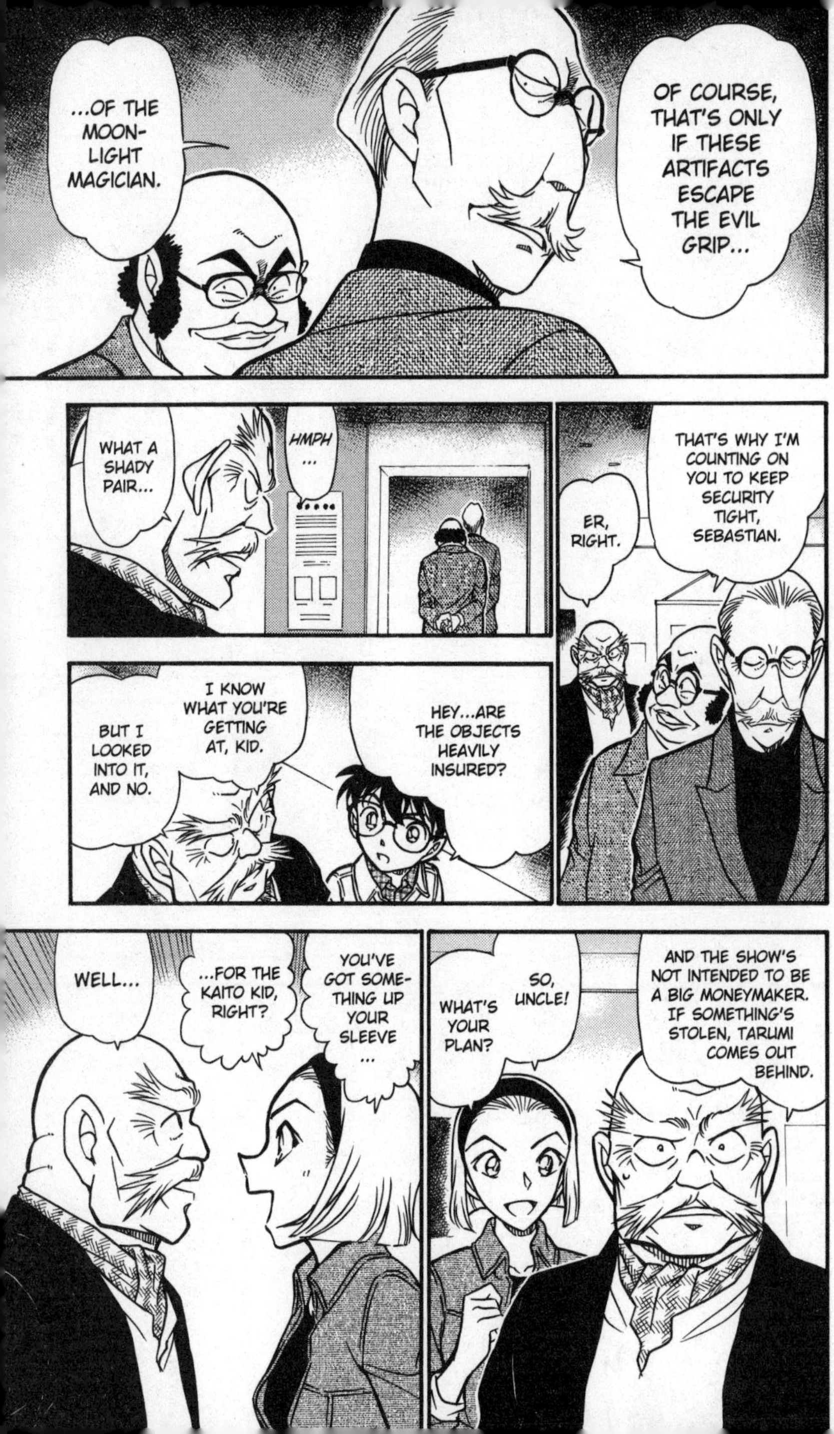
OF COURSE, THAT'S ONLY IF THESE ARTIFACTS ESCAPE THE EVIL GRIP...
...OF THE MOON-LIGHT MAGICIAN.
THAT'S WHY I'M COUNTING ON YOU TO KEEP SECURITY TIGHT, SEBASTIAN.
ER, RIGHT.
HMPH...
WHAT A SHADY PAIR...
HEY...ARE THE OBJECTS HEAVILY INSURED?
I KNOW WHAT YOU'RE GETTING AT, KID.
BUT I LOOKED INTO IT, AND NO.
AND THE SHOW'S NOT INTENDED TO BE A BIG MONEYMAKER. IF SOMETHING'S STOLEN, TARUMI COMES OUT BEHIND.
SO, UNCLE!
WHAT'S YOUR PLAN?
YOU'VE GOT SOME-THING UP YOUR SLEEVE...
...FOR THE KAITO KID, RIGHT?
WELL...

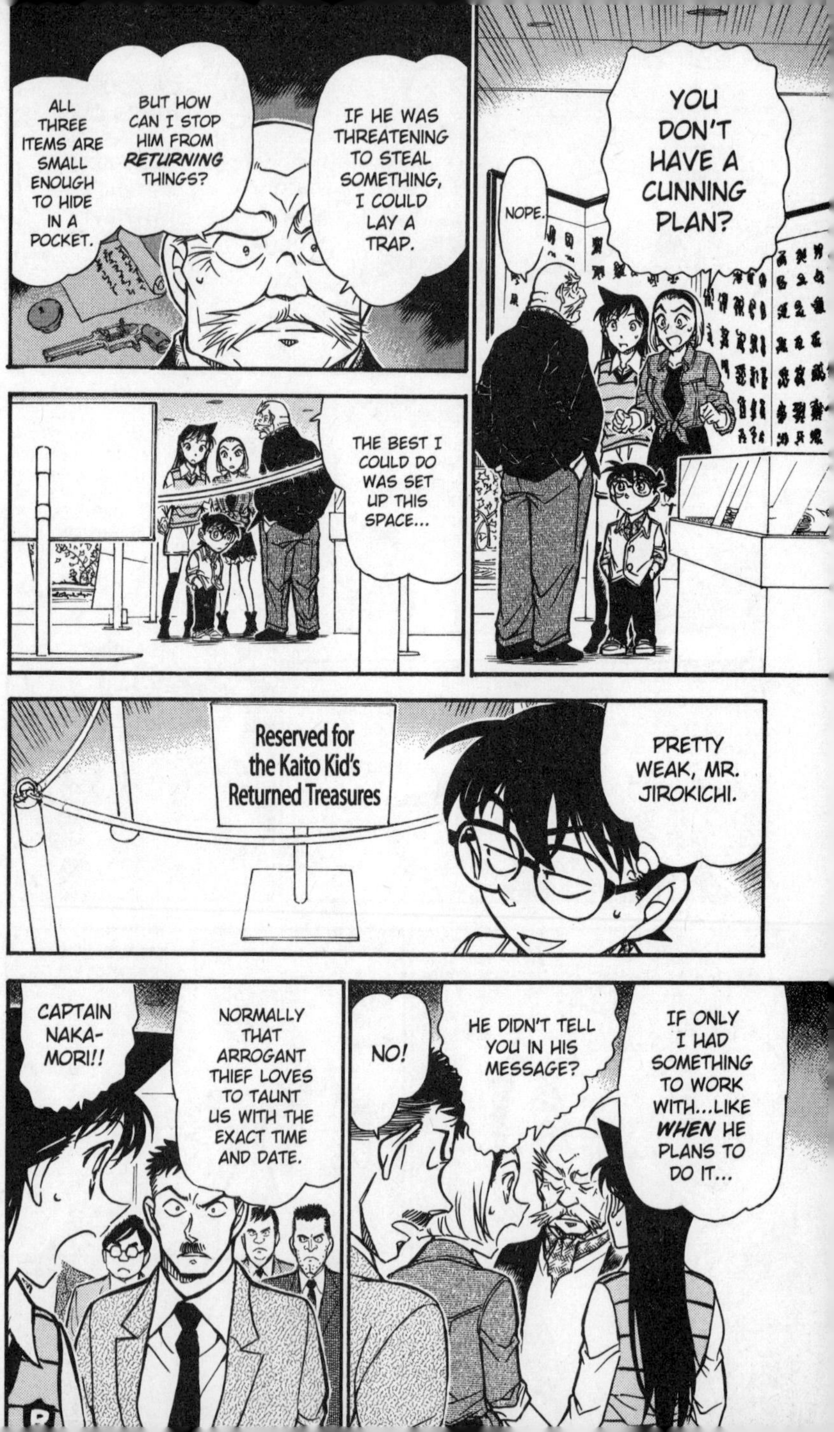
YOU DON'T HAVE A CUNNING PLAN?
NOPE.
IF HE WAS THREATENING TO STEAL SOMETHING, I COULD LAY A TRAP.
BUT HOW CAN I STOP HIM FROM *RETURNING* THINGS?
ALL THREE ITEMS ARE SMALL ENOUGH TO HIDE IN A POCKET.
THE BEST I COULD DO WAS SET UP THIS SPACE...
PRETTY WEAK, MR. JIROKICHI.
Reserved for the Kaito Kid's Returned Treasures
IF ONLY I HAD SOMETHING TO WORK WITH...LIKE *WHEN* HE PLANS TO DO IT...
HE DIDN'T TELL YOU IN HIS MESSAGE?
NO!
NORMALLY THAT ARROGANT THIEF LOVES TO TAUNT US WITH THE EXACT TIME AND DATE.
CAPTAIN NAKA-MORI!!

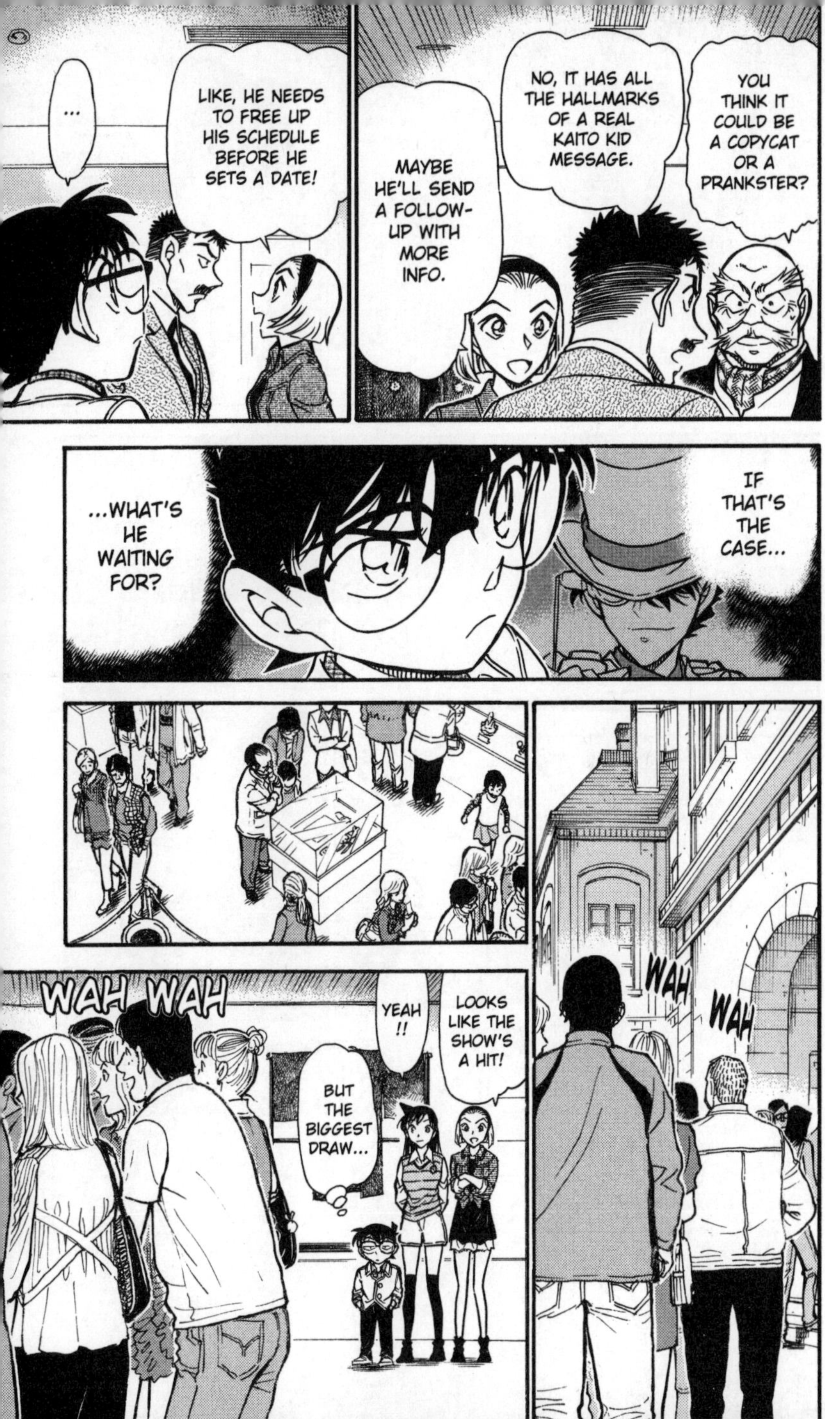
YOU THINK IT COULD BE A COPYCAT OR A PRANKSTER?
NO, IT HAS ALL THE HALLMARKS OF A REAL KAITO KID MESSAGE.
MAYBE HE'LL SEND A FOLLOW-UP WITH MORE INFO.
LIKE, HE NEEDS TO FREE UP HIS SCHEDULE BEFORE HE SETS A DATE!
...
IF THAT'S THE CASE...
...WHAT'S HE WAITING FOR?
WAH WAH
LOOKS LIKE THE SHOW'S A HIT!
YEAH!!
BUT THE BIGGEST DRAW...
WAH WAH

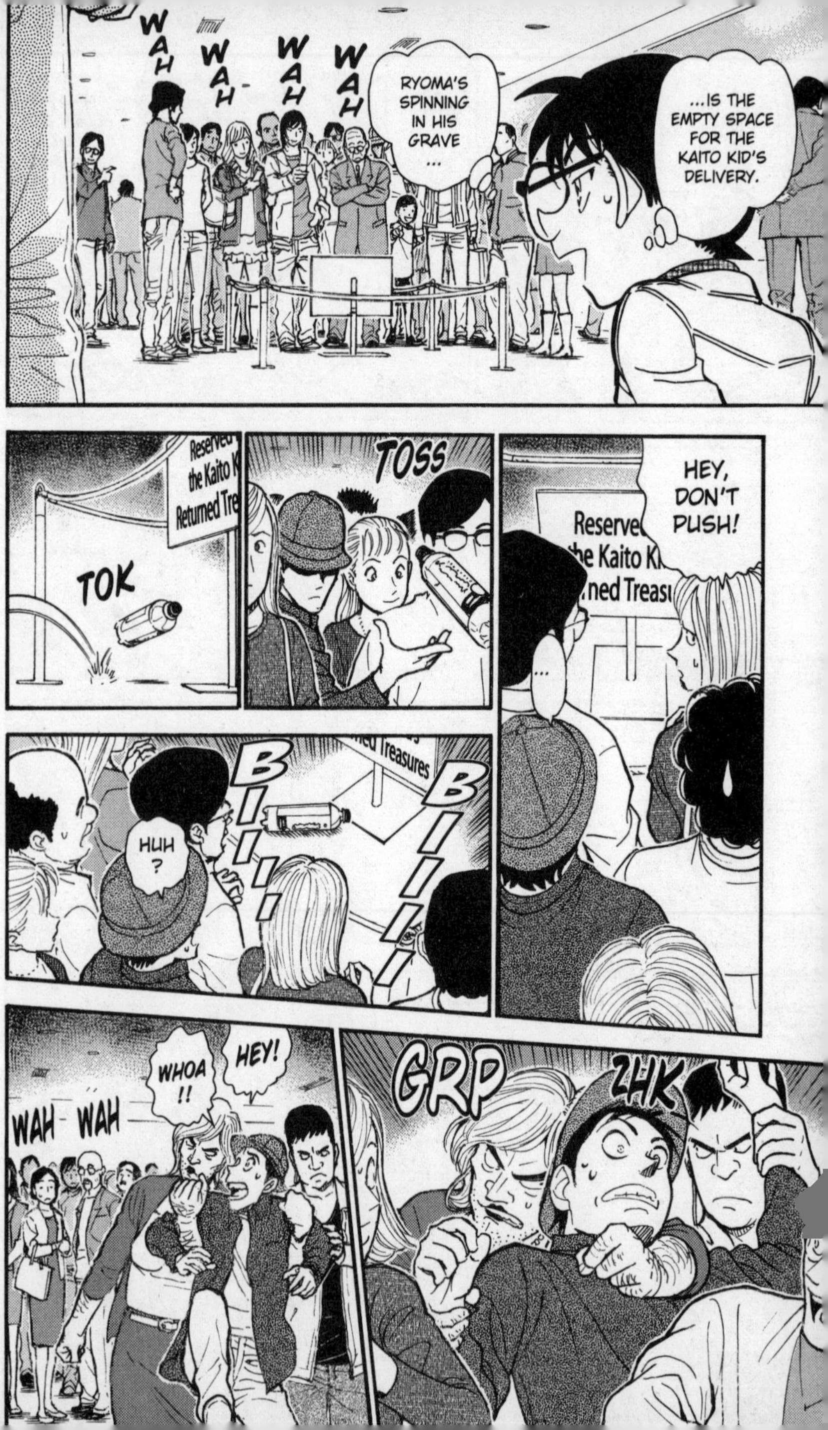
...IS THE EMPTY SPACE FOR THE KAITO KID'S DELIVERY.
RYOMA'S SPINNING IN HIS GRAVE ...
WAH
WAH
WAH
WAH
HEY, DON'T PUSH!
...
TOSS
TOK
BIIIII
BIIIII
HUH?
GRP
ZHK
HEY!
WHOA!!
WAH WAH

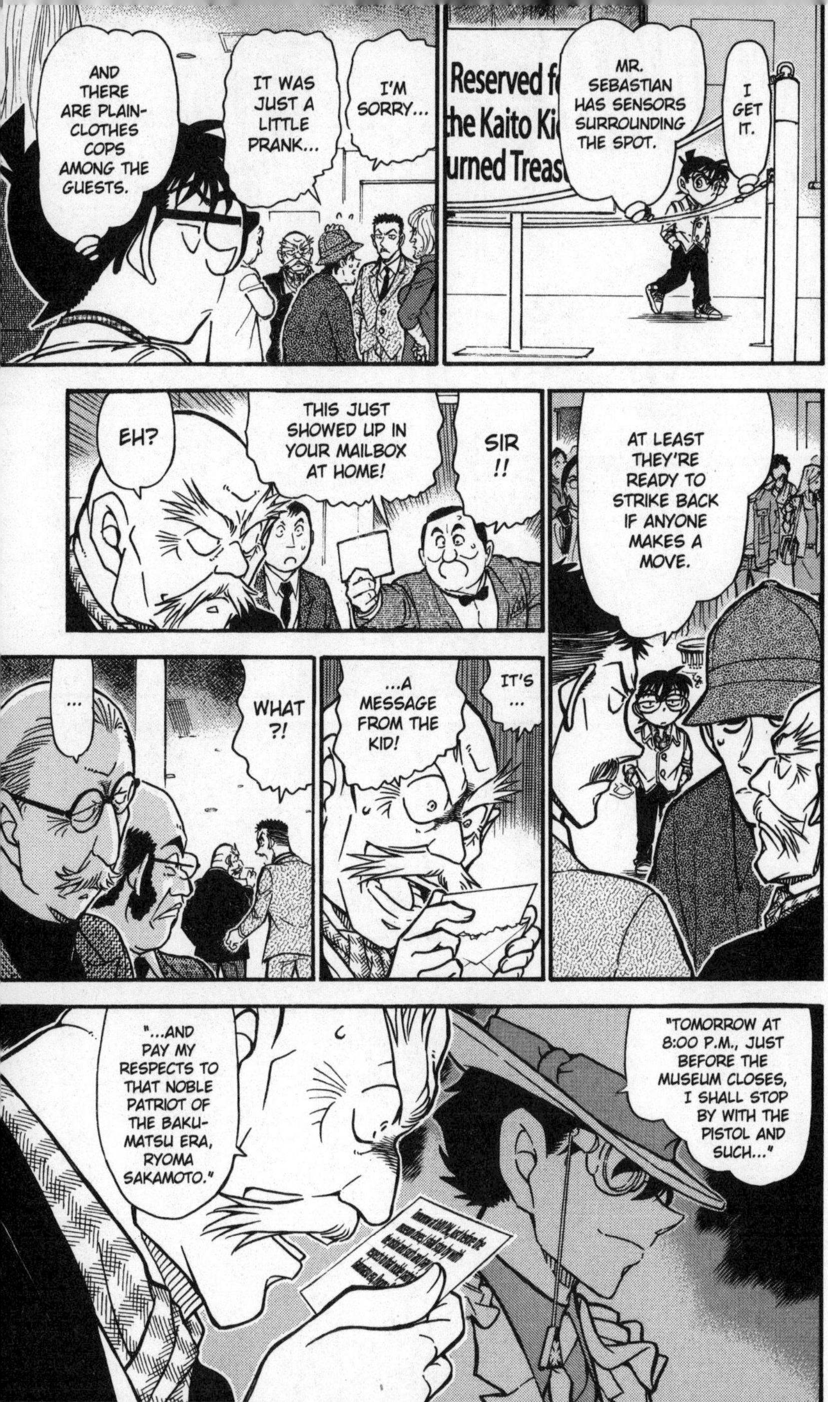
I GET IT.
MR. SEBASTIAN HAS SENSORS SURROUNDING THE SPOT.
I'M SORRY...
IT WAS JUST A LITTLE PRANK...
AND THERE ARE PLAIN-CLOTHES COPS AMONG THE GUESTS.
AT LEAST THEY'RE READY TO STRIKE BACK IF ANYONE MAKES A MOVE.
SIR !!
THIS JUST SHOWED UP IN YOUR MAILBOX AT HOME!
EH?
IT'S ...
...A MESSAGE FROM THE KID!
WHAT ?!
...
"TOMORROW AT 8:00 P.M., JUST BEFORE THE MUSEUM CLOSES, I SHALL STOP BY WITH THE PISTOL AND SUCH..."
"...AND PAY MY RESPECTS TO THAT NOBLE PATRIOT OF THE BAKU-MATSU ERA, RYOMA SAKAMOTO."

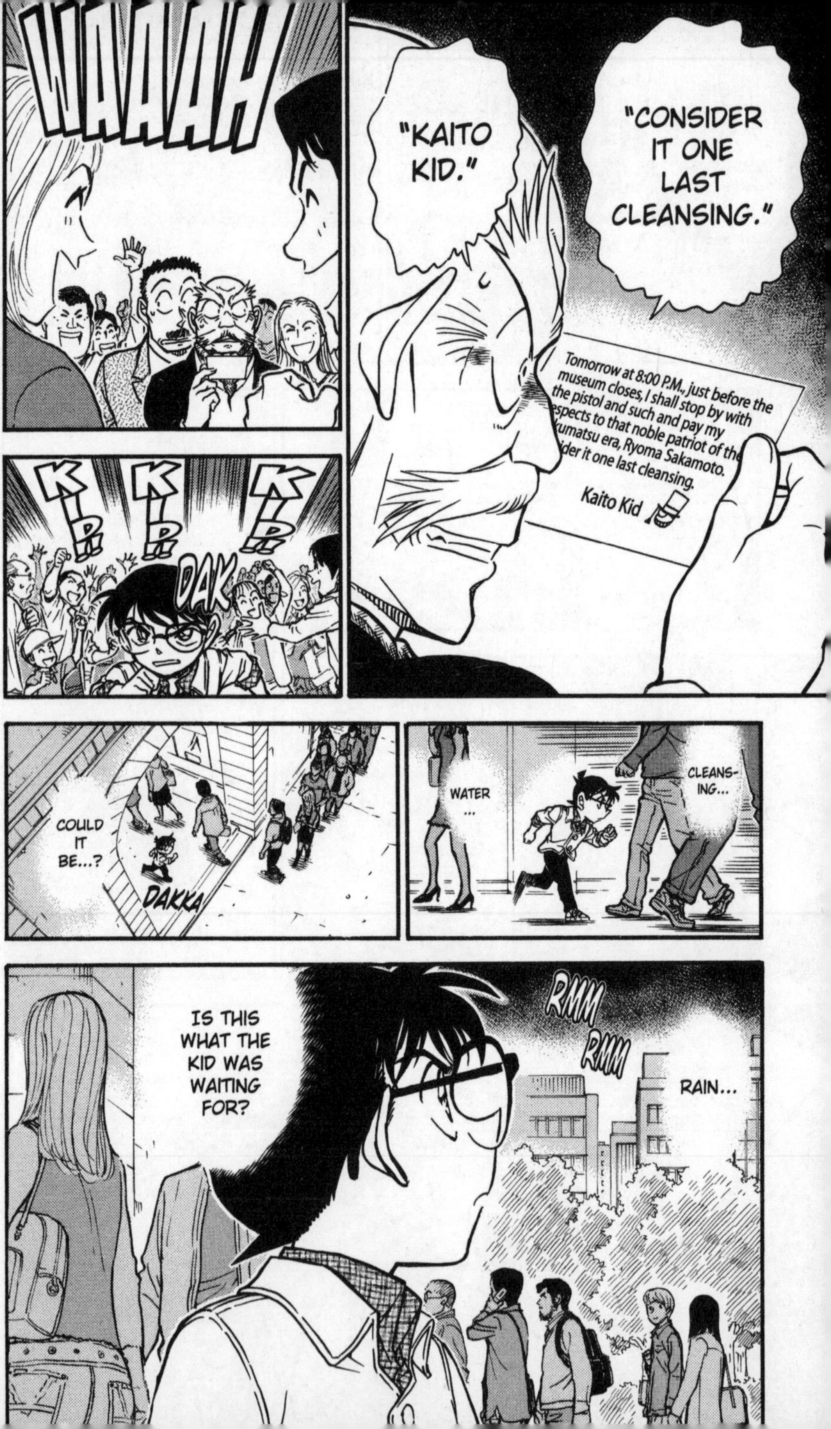
"CONSIDER IT ONE LAST CLEANSING."
"KAITO KID."
Tomorrow at 8:00 P.M., just before the museum closes, I shall stop by with the pistol and such and pay my espects to that noble patriot of the kumatsu era, Ryoma Sakamoto. ider it one last cleansing.
Kaito Kid
WAAAH
KID KID KID
DAK
CLEANS-ING...
WATER...
COULD IT BE...?
DAKKA
RMM RMM
RAIN...
IS THIS WHAT THE KID WAS WAITING FOR?

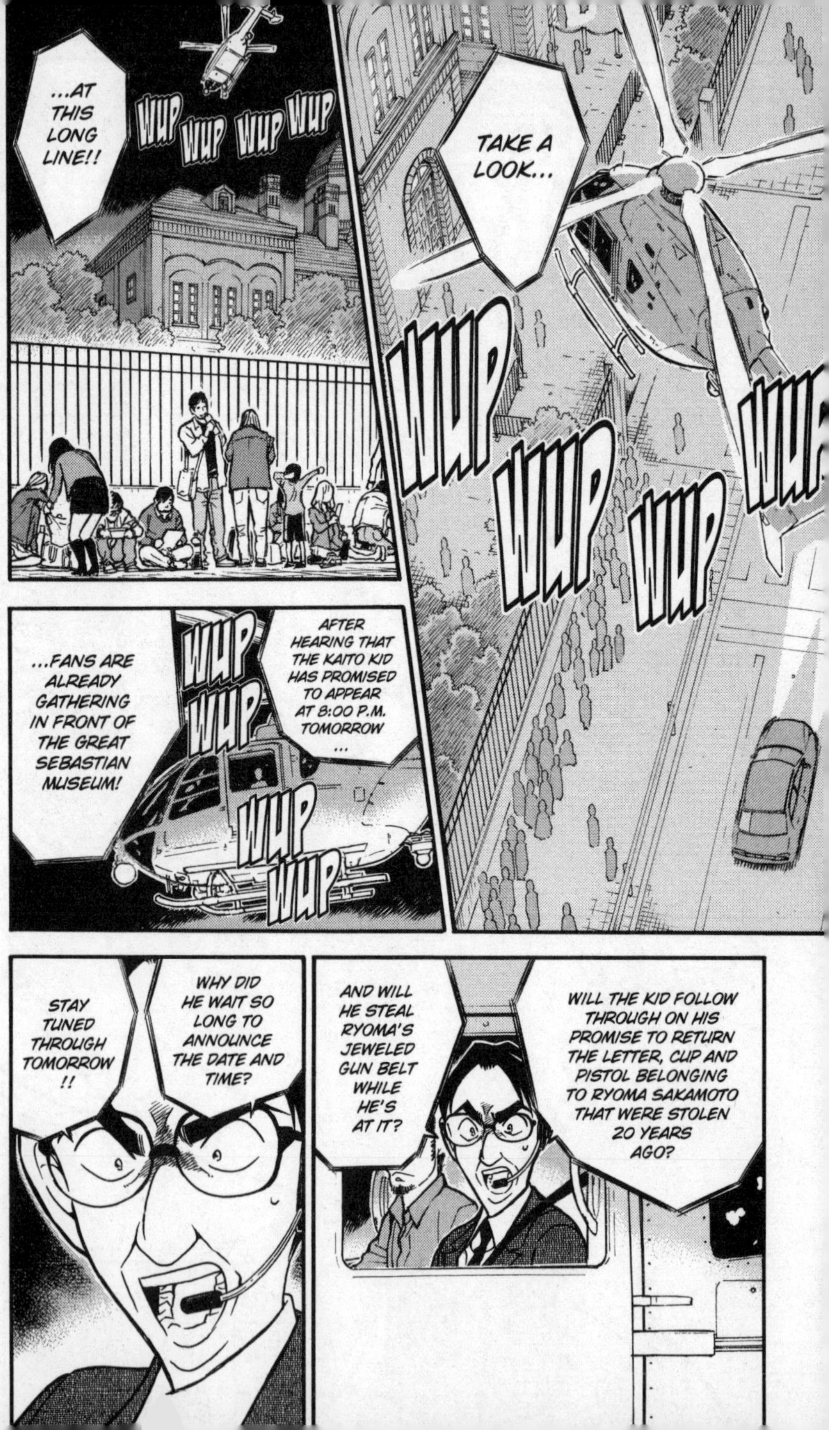
TAKE A LOOK...
WUP WUP WUP WUP
...AT THIS LONG LINE!!
WUP WUP WUP WUP
AFTER HEARING THAT THE KAITO KID HAS PROMISED TO APPEAR AT 8:00 P.M. TOMORROW...
...FANS ARE ALREADY GATHERING IN FRONT OF THE GREAT SEBASTIAN MUSEUM!
WUP WUP WUP WUP
WILL THE KID FOLLOW THROUGH ON HIS PROMISE TO RETURN THE LETTER, CUP AND PISTOL BELONGING TO RYOMA SAKAMOTO THAT WERE STOLEN 20 YEARS AGO?
AND WILL HE STEAL RYOMA'S JEWELED GUN BELT WHILE HE'S AT IT?
WHY DID HE WAIT SO LONG TO ANNOUNCE THE DATE AND TIME?
STAY TUNED THROUGH TOMORROW!!

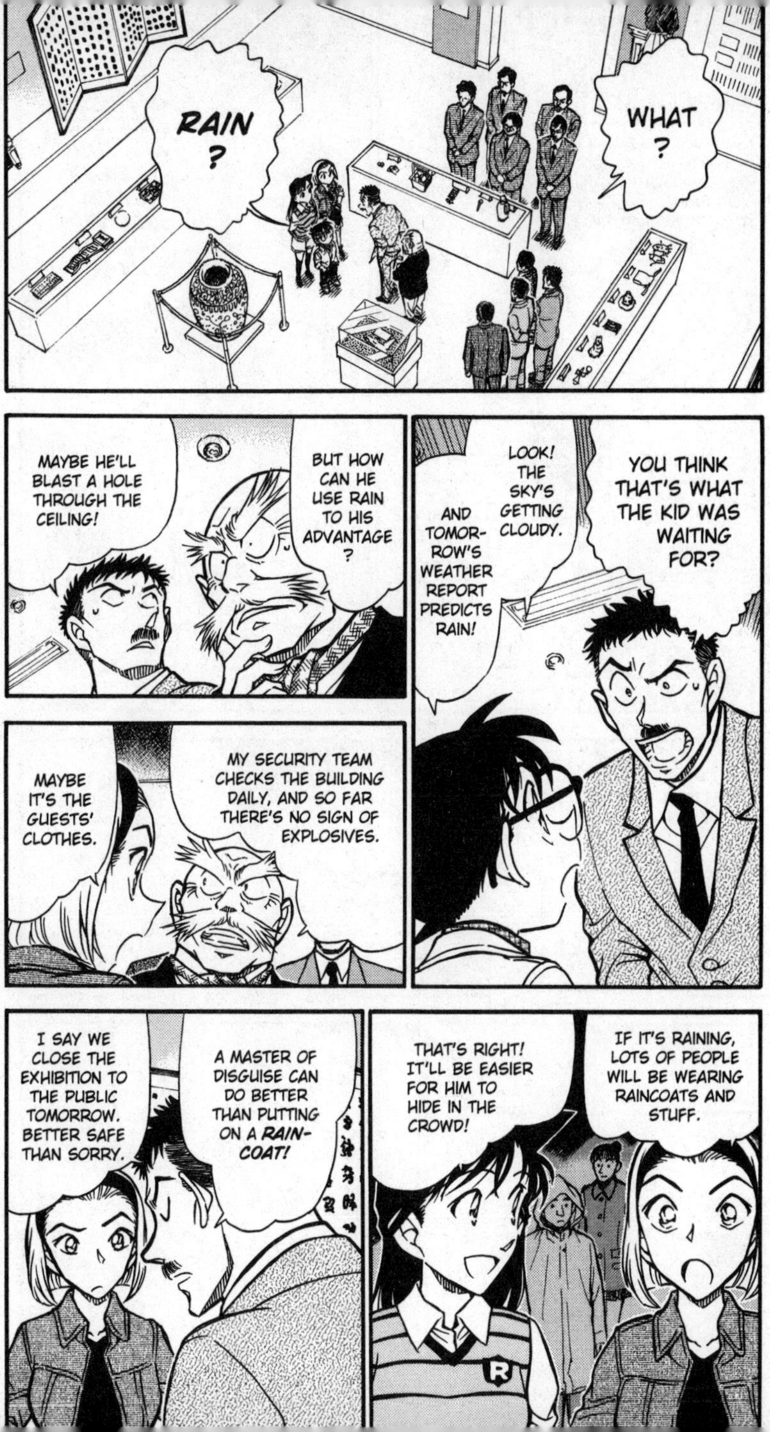
WHAT ?
RAIN ?
YOU THINK THAT'S WHAT THE KID WAS WAITING FOR?
LOOK! THE SKY'S GETTING CLOUDY.
AND TOMORROW'S WEATHER REPORT PREDICTS RAIN!
BUT HOW CAN HE USE RAIN TO HIS ADVANTAGE ?
MAYBE HE'LL BLAST A HOLE THROUGH THE CEILING!
MY SECURITY TEAM CHECKS THE BUILDING DAILY, AND SO FAR THERE'S NO SIGN OF EXPLOSIVES.
MAYBE IT'S THE GUESTS' CLOTHES.
IF IT'S RAINING, LOTS OF PEOPLE WILL BE WEARING RAINCOATS AND STUFF.
THAT'S RIGHT! IT'LL BE EASIER FOR HIM TO HIDE IN THE CROWD!
A MASTER OF DISGUISE CAN DO BETTER THAN PUTTING ON A RAINCOAT!
I SAY WE CLOSE THE EXHIBITION TO THE PUBLIC TOMORROW. BETTER SAFE THAN SORRY.

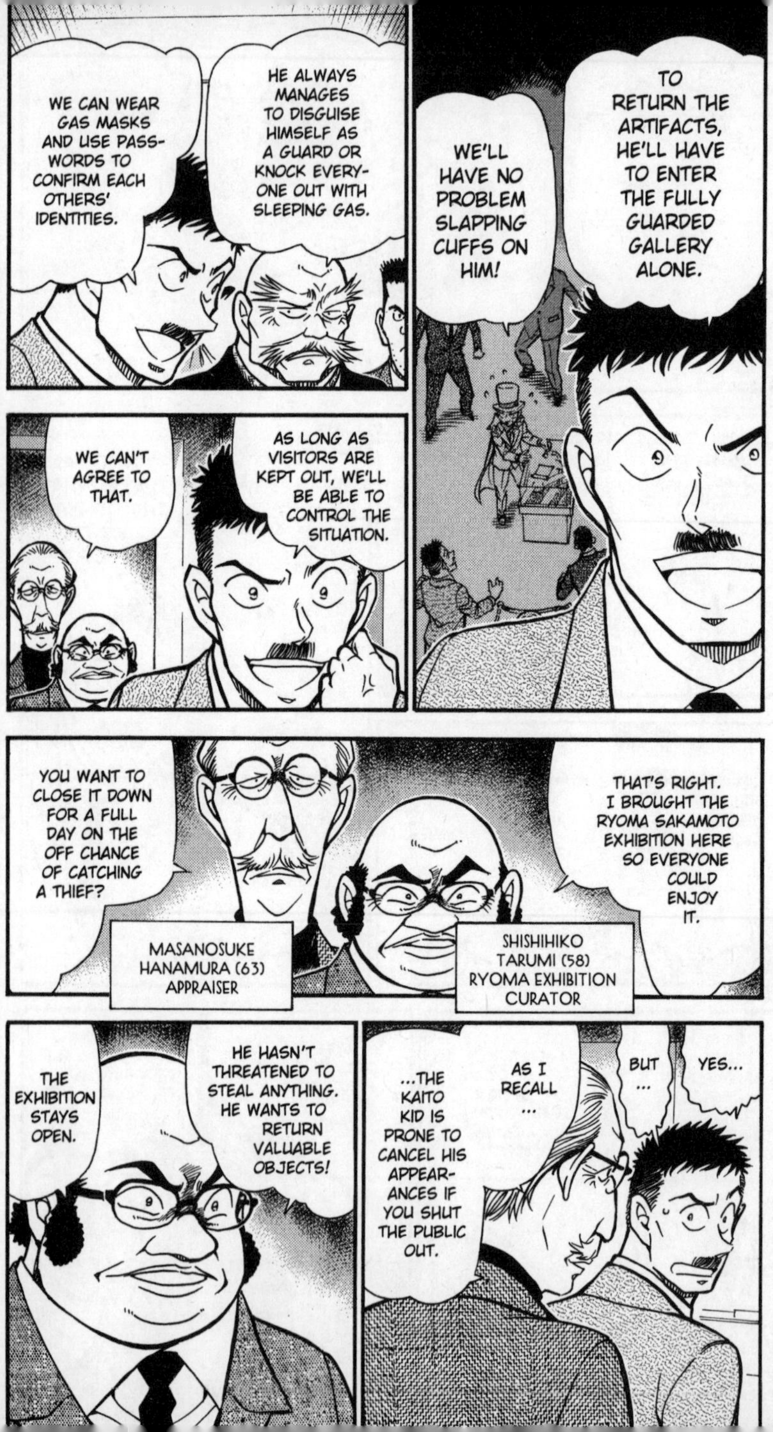
TO RETURN THE ARTIFACTS, HE'LL HAVE TO ENTER THE FULLY GUARDED GALLERY ALONE.
WE'LL HAVE NO PROBLEM SLAPPING CUFFS ON HIM!
HE ALWAYS MANAGES TO DISGUISE HIMSELF AS A GUARD OR KNOCK EVERY-ONE OUT WITH SLEEPING GAS.
WE CAN WEAR GAS MASKS AND USE PASS-WORDS TO CONFIRM EACH OTHERS' IDENTITIES.
AS LONG AS VISITORS ARE KEPT OUT, WE'LL BE ABLE TO CONTROL THE SITUATION.
WE CAN'T AGREE TO THAT.
THAT'S RIGHT. I BROUGHT THE RYOMA SAKAMOTO EXHIBITION HERE SO EVERYONE COULD ENJOY IT.
YOU WANT TO CLOSE IT DOWN FOR A FULL DAY ON THE OFF CHANCE OF CATCHING A THIEF?
SHISHIHIKO TARUMI (58) RYOMA EXHIBITION CURATOR
MASANOSUKE HANAMURA (63) APPRAISER
YES...
BUT...
AS I RECALL...
...THE KAITO KID IS PRONE TO CANCEL HIS APPEAR-ANCES IF YOU SHUT THE PUBLIC OUT.
HE HASN'T THREATENED TO STEAL ANYTHING. HE WANTS TO RETURN VALUABLE OBJECTS!
THE EXHIBITION STAYS OPEN.

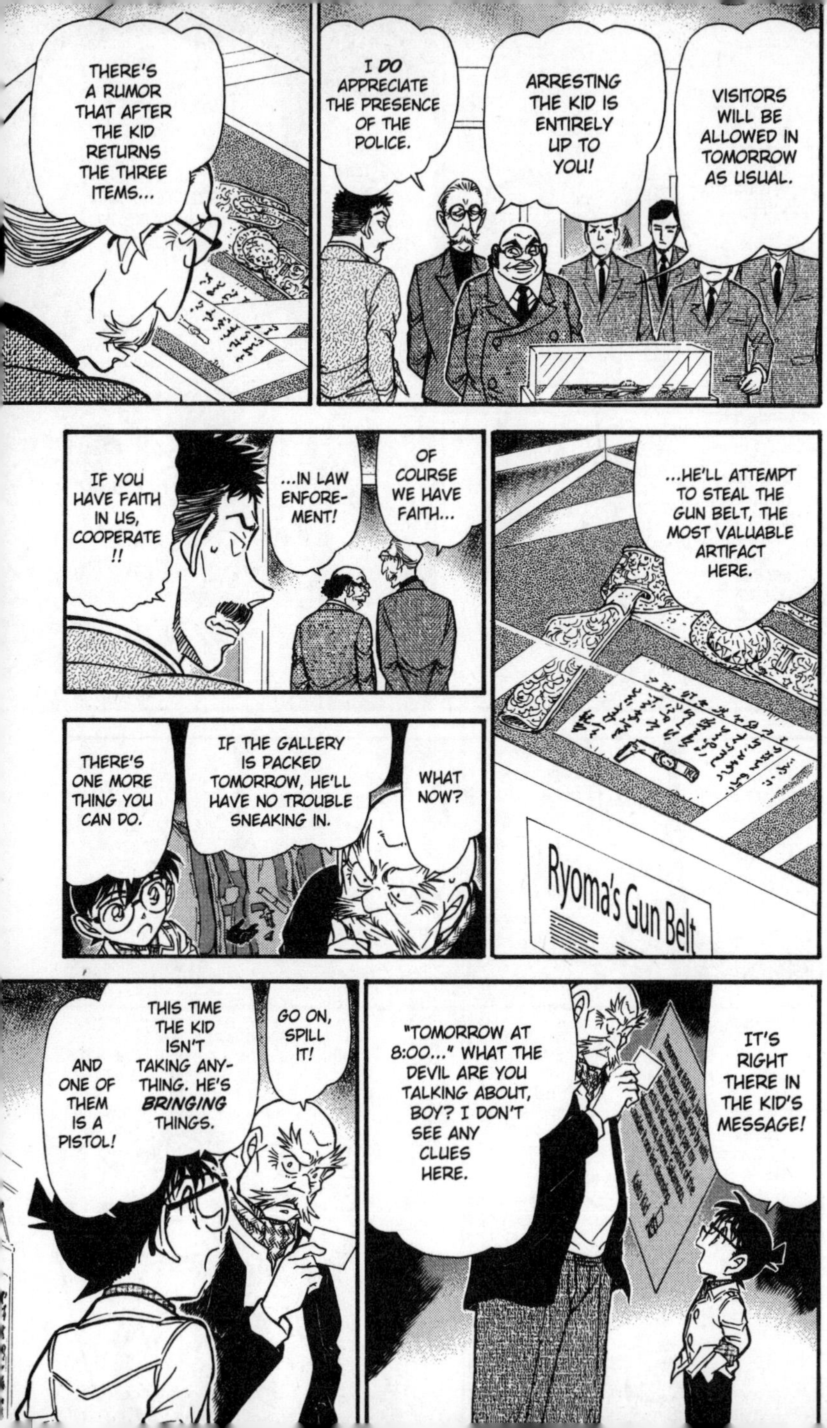
VISITORS WILL BE ALLOWED IN TOMORROW AS USUAL.
ARRESTING THE KID IS ENTIRELY UP TO YOU!
I ***DO*** APPRECIATE THE PRESENCE OF THE POLICE.
THERE'S A RUMOR THAT AFTER THE KID RETURNS THE THREE ITEMS...
...HE'LL ATTEMPT TO STEAL THE GUN BELT, THE MOST VALUABLE ARTIFACT HERE.
Ryoma's Gun Belt
OF COURSE WE HAVE FAITH...
...IN LAW ENFOREMENT!
IF YOU HAVE FAITH IN US, COOPERATE!!
WHAT NOW?
IF THE GALLERY IS PACKED TOMORROW, HE'LL HAVE NO TROUBLE SNEAKING IN.
THERE'S ONE MORE THING YOU CAN DO.
IT'S RIGHT THERE IN THE KID'S MESSAGE!
"TOMORROW AT 8:00..." WHAT THE DEVIL ARE YOU TALKING ABOUT, BOY? I DON'T SEE ANY CLUES HERE.
GO ON, SPILL IT!
THIS TIME THE KID ISN'T TAKING ANYTHING. HE'S ***BRINGING*** THINGS.
AND ONE OF THEM IS A PISTOL!

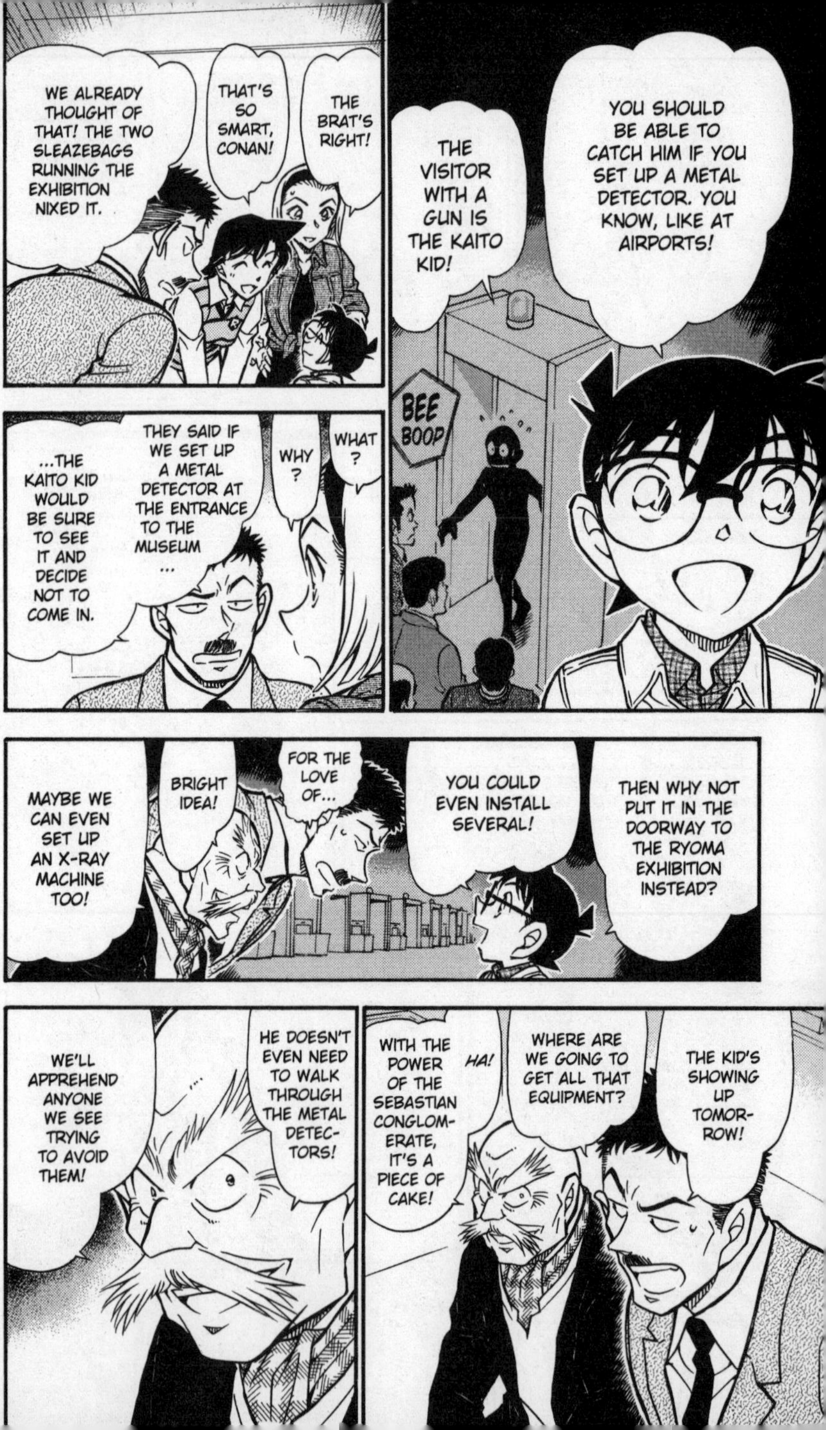
YOU SHOULD BE ABLE TO CATCH HIM IF YOU SET UP A METAL DETECTOR. YOU KNOW, LIKE AT AIRPORTS!
THE VISITOR WITH A GUN IS THE KAITO KID!
BEE BOOP
THE BRAT'S RIGHT!
THAT'S SO SMART, CONAN!
WE ALREADY THOUGHT OF THAT! THE TWO SLEAZEBAGS RUNNING THE EXHIBITION NIXED IT.
WHAT?
WHY?
THEY SAID IF WE SET UP A METAL DETECTOR AT THE ENTRANCE TO THE MUSEUM...
...THE KAITO KID WOULD BE SURE TO SEE IT AND DECIDE NOT TO COME IN.
THEN WHY NOT PUT IT IN THE DOORWAY TO THE RYOMA EXHIBITION INSTEAD?
YOU COULD EVEN INSTALL SEVERAL!
FOR THE LOVE OF...
BRIGHT IDEA!
MAYBE WE CAN EVEN SET UP AN X-RAY MACHINE TOO!
THE KID'S SHOWING UP TOMORROW!
WHERE ARE WE GOING TO GET ALL THAT EQUIPMENT?
HA!
WITH THE POWER OF THE SEBASTIAN CONGLOMERATE, IT'S A PIECE OF CAKE!
HE DOESN'T EVEN NEED TO WALK THROUGH THE METAL DETECTORS!
...
WE'LL APPREHEND ANYONE WE SEE TRYING TO AVOID THEM!

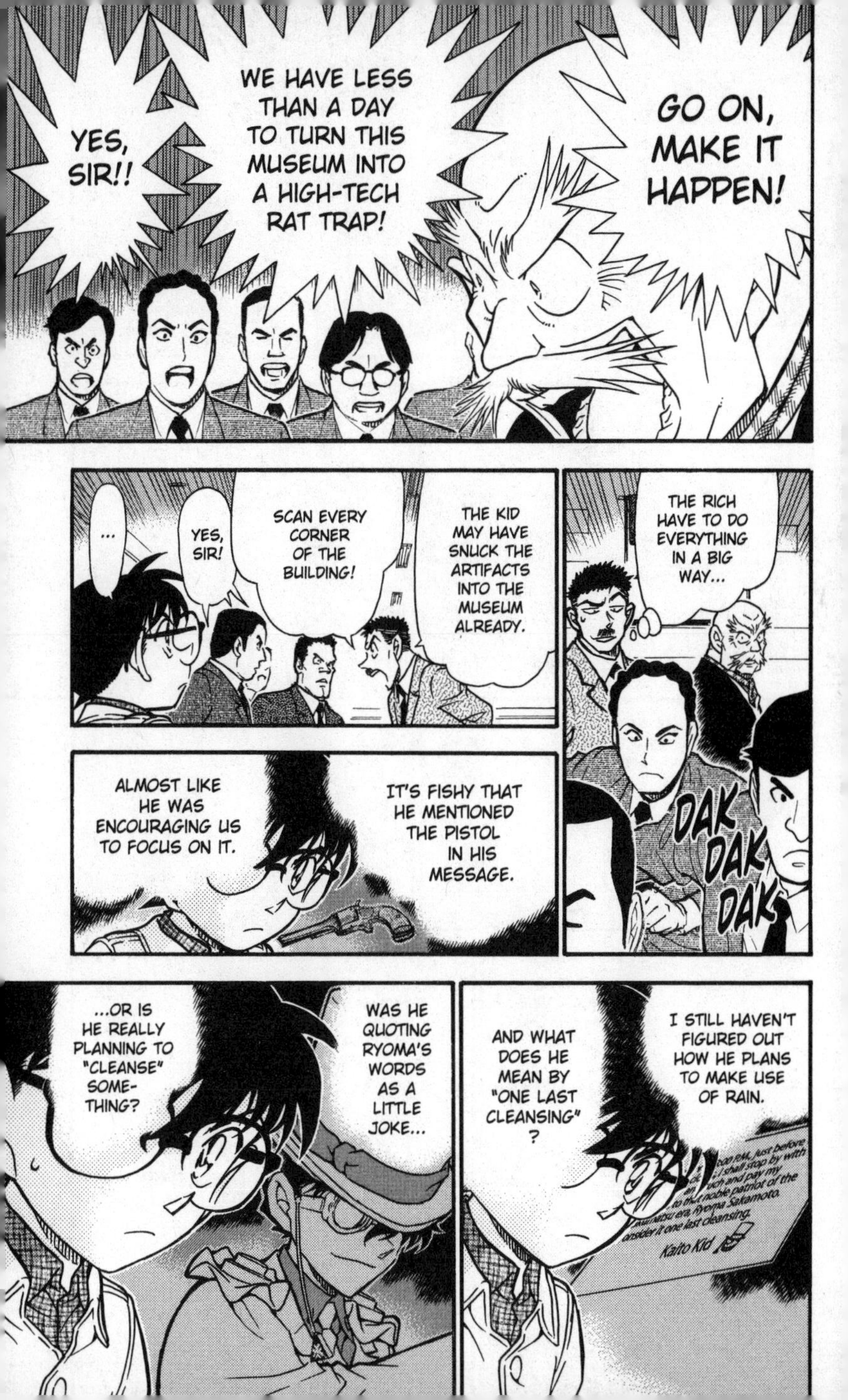
GO ON, MAKE IT HAPPEN!
WE HAVE LESS THAN A DAY TO TURN THIS MUSEUM INTO A HIGH-TECH RAT TRAP!
YES, SIR!!
THE RICH HAVE TO DO EVERYTHING IN A BIG WAY...
DAK DAK DAK
THE KID MAY HAVE SNUCK THE ARTIFACTS INTO THE MUSEUM ALREADY.
SCAN EVERY CORNER OF THE BUILDING!
YES, SIR!
...
IT'S FISHY THAT HE MENTIONED THE PISTOL IN HIS MESSAGE.
ALMOST LIKE HE WAS ENCOURAGING US TO FOCUS ON IT.
I STILL HAVEN'T FIGURED OUT HOW HE PLANS TO MAKE USE OF RAIN.
AND WHAT DOES HE MEAN BY "ONE LAST CLEANSING"?
Kaito Kid
WAS HE QUOTING RYOMA'S WORDS AS A LITTLE JOKE...
...OR IS HE REALLY PLANNING TO "CLEANSE" SOMETHING?

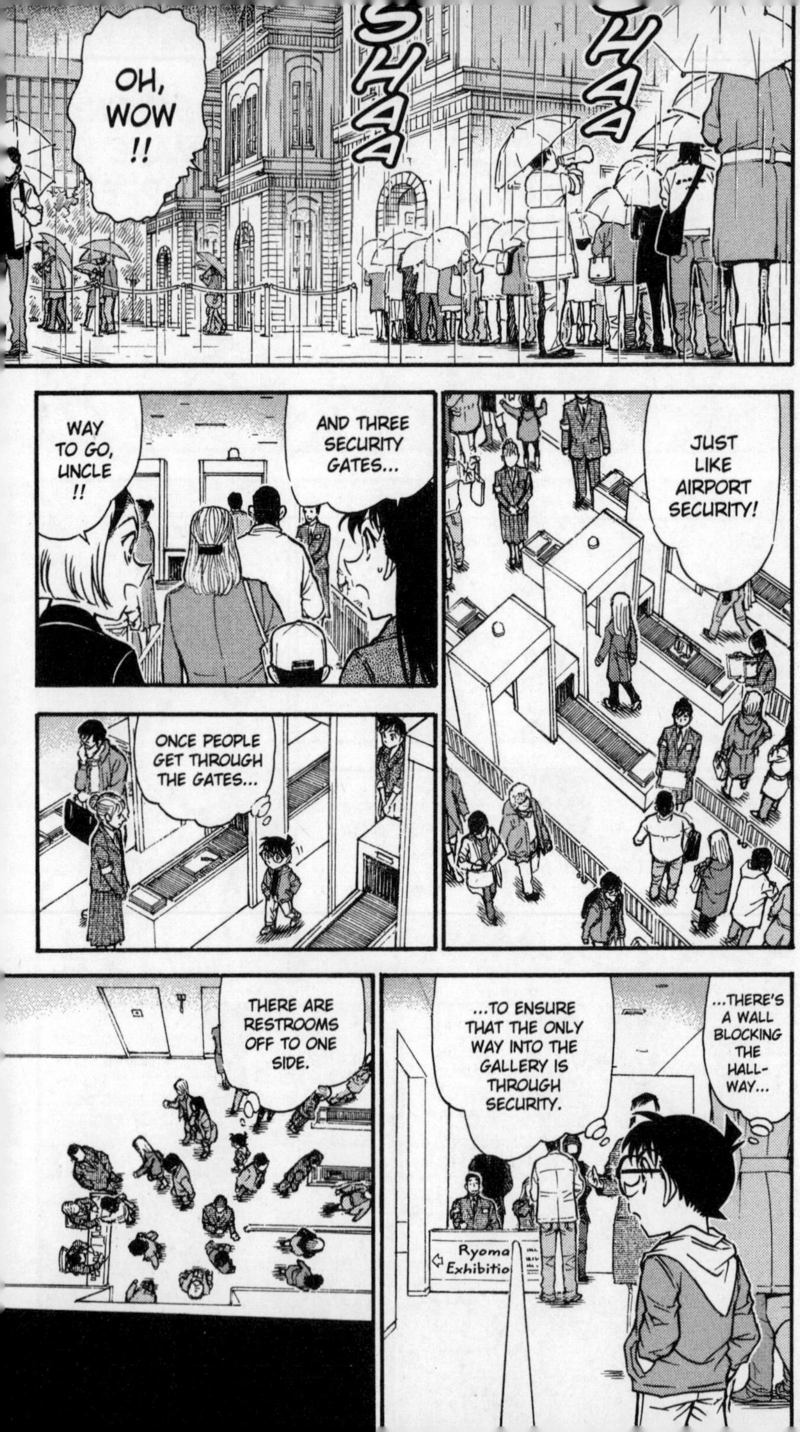
SHAAA
SHAAA
OH, WOW !!
JUST LIKE AIRPORT SECURITY!
AND THREE SECURITY GATES...
WAY TO GO, UNCLE !!
ONCE PEOPLE GET THROUGH THE GATES...
...THERE'S A WALL BLOCKING THE HALL-WAY...
...TO ENSURE THAT THE ONLY WAY INTO THE GALLERY IS THROUGH SECURITY.
Ryoma Exhibitio
THERE ARE RESTROOMS OFF TO ONE SIDE.

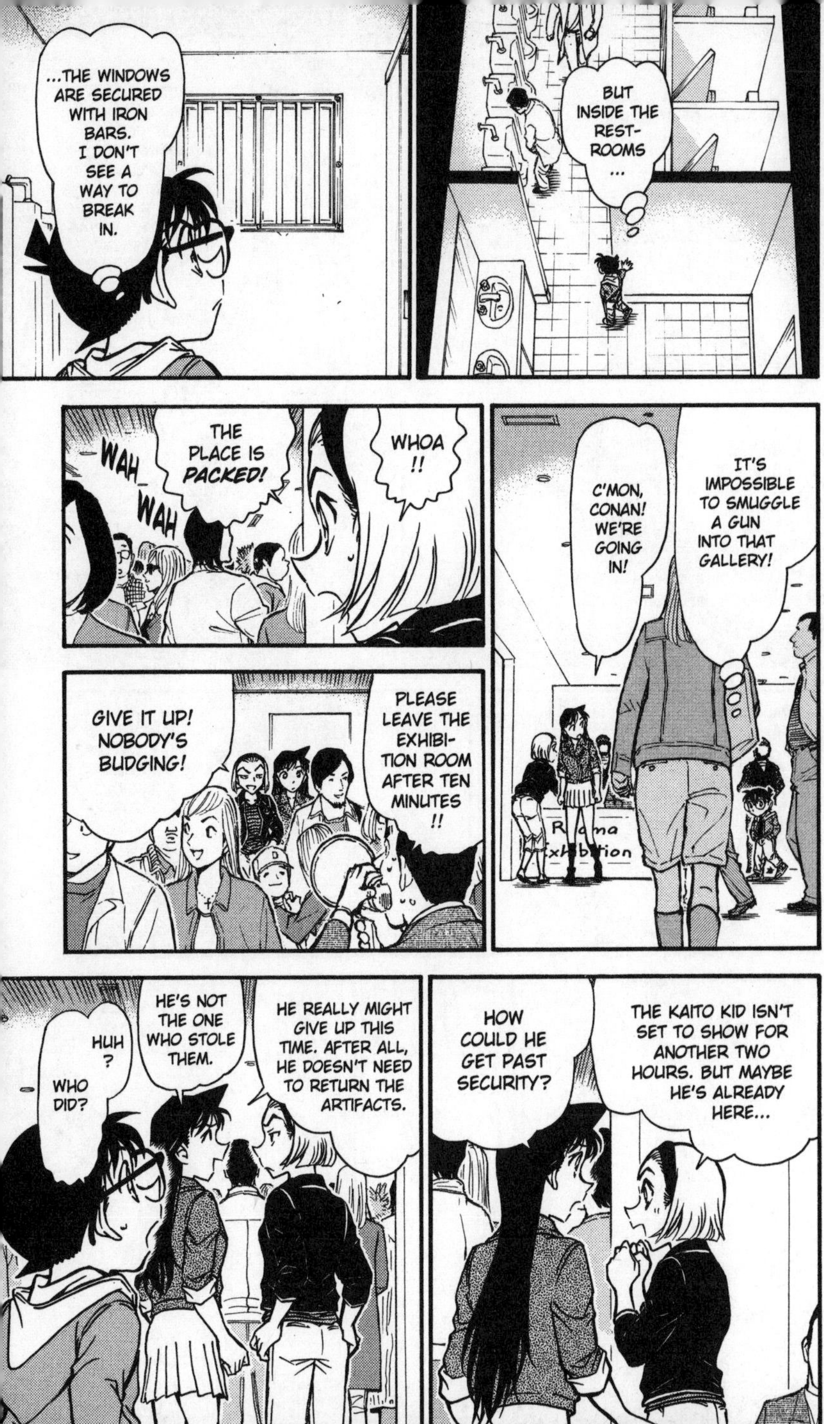
BUT INSIDE THE REST-ROOMS...
...THE WINDOWS ARE SECURED WITH IRON BARS. I DON'T SEE A WAY TO BREAK IN.
IT'S IMPOSSIBLE TO SMUGGLE A GUN INTO THAT GALLERY!
C'MON, CONAN! WE'RE GOING IN!
WHOA!!
THE PLACE IS PACKED!
WAH_ WAH
PLEASE LEAVE THE EXHIBITION ROOM AFTER TEN MINUTES!!
GIVE IT UP! NOBODY'S BUDGING!
THE KAITO KID ISN'T SET TO SHOW FOR ANOTHER TWO HOURS. BUT MAYBE HE'S ALREADY HERE...
HOW COULD HE GET PAST SECURITY?
HE REALLY MIGHT GIVE UP THIS TIME. AFTER ALL, HE DOESN'T NEED TO RETURN THE ARTIFACTS.
HE'S NOT THE ONE WHO STOLE THEM.
HUH?
WHO DID?

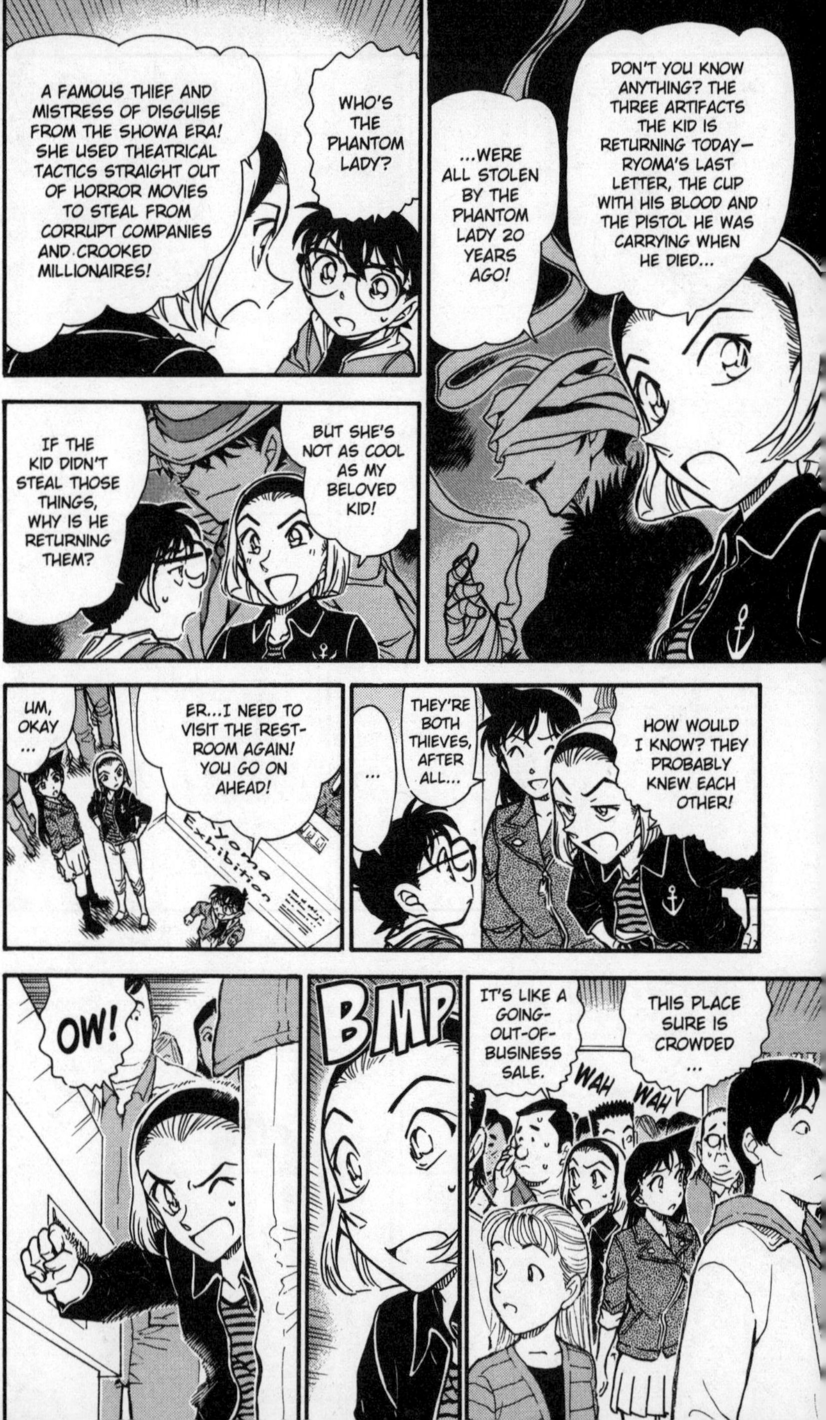
DON'T YOU KNOW ANYTHING? THE THREE ARTIFACTS THE KID IS RETURNING TODAY—RYOMA'S LAST LETTER, THE CUP WITH HIS BLOOD AND THE PISTOL HE WAS CARRYING WHEN HE DIED...
...WERE ALL STOLEN BY THE PHANTOM LADY 20 YEARS AGO!
WHO'S THE PHANTOM LADY?
A FAMOUS THIEF AND MISTRESS OF DISGUISE FROM THE SHOWA ERA! SHE USED THEATRICAL TACTICS STRAIGHT OUT OF HORROR MOVIES TO STEAL FROM CORRUPT COMPANIES AND CROOKED MILLIONAIRES!
BUT SHE'S NOT AS COOL AS MY BELOVED KID!
IF THE KID DIDN'T STEAL THOSE THINGS, WHY IS HE RETURNING THEM?
HOW WOULD I KNOW? THEY PROBABLY KNEW EACH OTHER!
THEY'RE BOTH THIEVES, AFTER ALL...
...
ER...I NEED TO VISIT THE REST-ROOM AGAIN! YOU GO ON AHEAD!
UM, OKAY...
Ryoma Exhibition
THIS PLACE SURE IS CROWDED...
IT'S LIKE A GOING-OUT-OF-BUSINESS SALE.
WAH
WAH
BMP
OW!

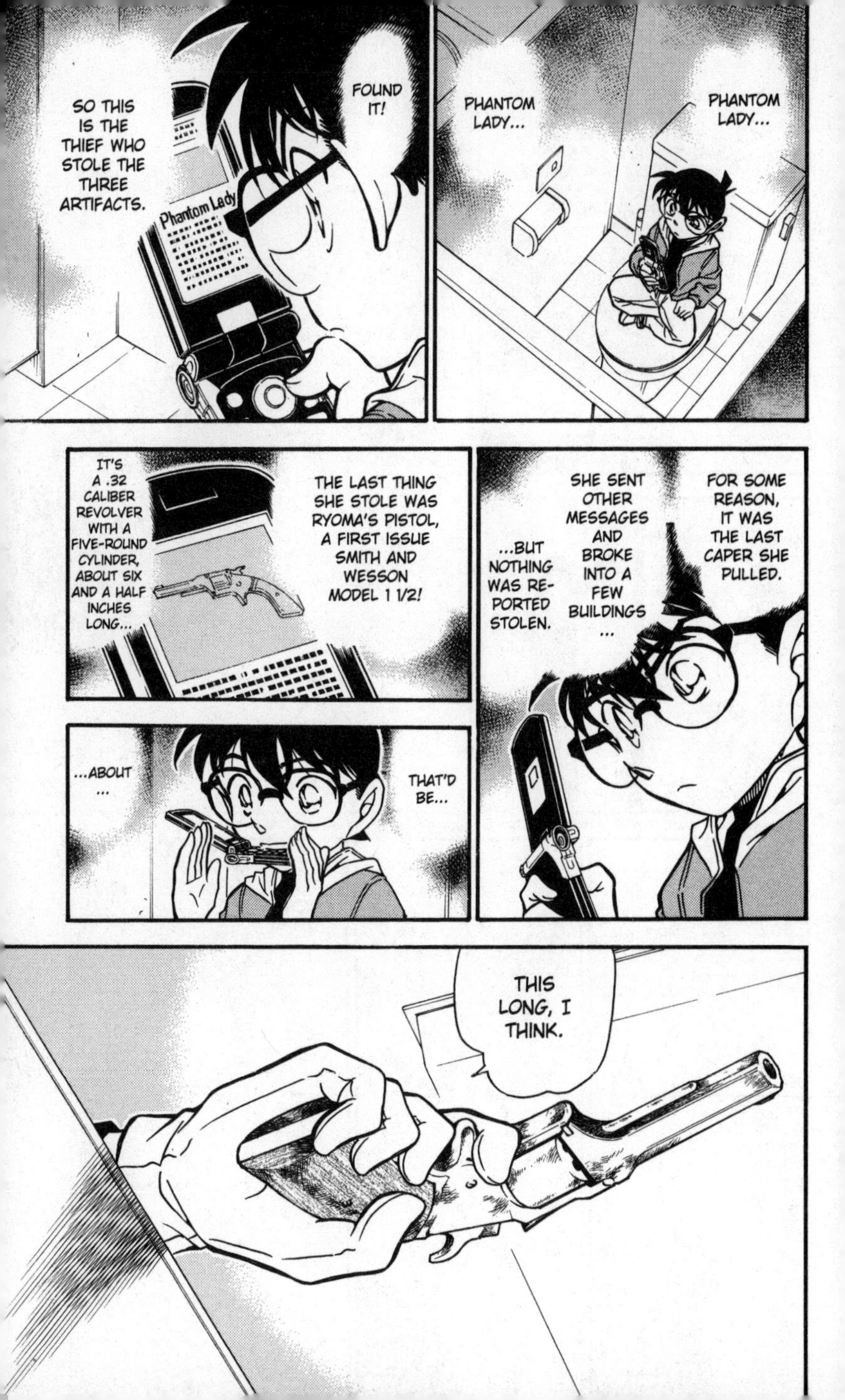
PHANTOM LADY...
PHANTOM LADY...
FOUND IT!
SO THIS IS THE THIEF WHO STOLE THE THREE ARTIFACTS.
Phantom Lady
FOR SOME REASON, IT WAS THE LAST CAPER SHE PULLED.
SHE SENT OTHER MESSAGES AND BROKE INTO A FEW BUILDINGS ...
...BUT NOTHING WAS RE-PORTED STOLEN.
THE LAST THING SHE STOLE WAS RYOMA'S PISTOL, A FIRST ISSUE SMITH AND WESSON MODEL 1 1/2!
IT'S A .32 CALIBER REVOLVER WITH A FIVE-ROUND CYLINDER, ABOUT SIX AND A HALF INCHES LONG...
THAT'D BE...
...ABOUT ...
THIS LONG, I THINK.

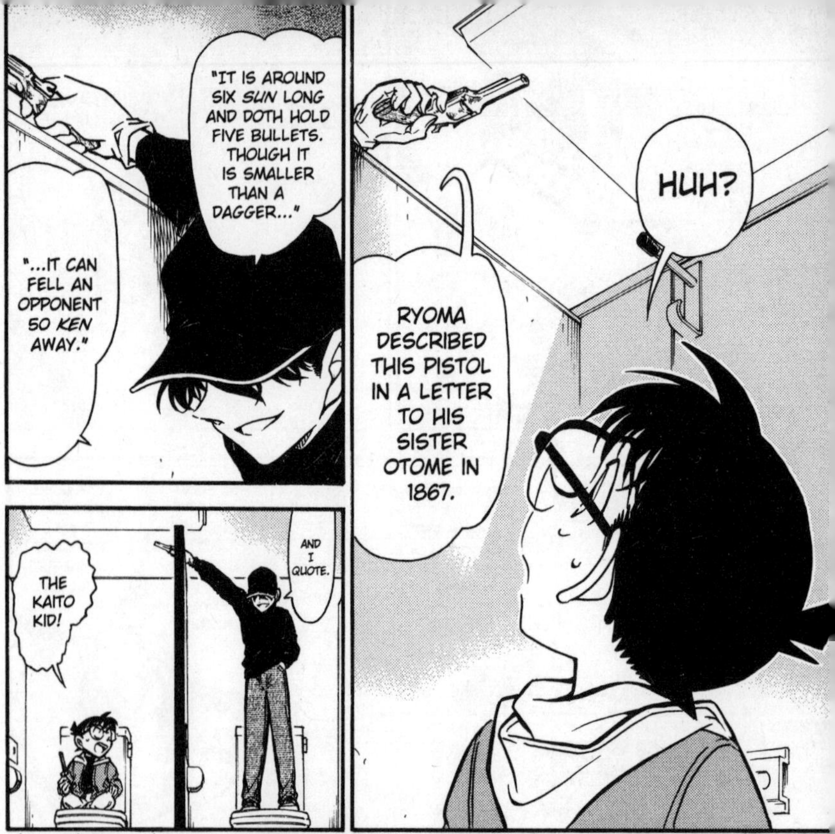
HUH?
RYOMA DESCRIBED THIS PISTOL IN A LETTER TO HIS SISTER OTOME IN 1867.
"IT IS AROUND SIX *SUN* LONG AND DOTH HOLD FIVE BULLETS. THOUGH IT IS SMALLER THAN A DAGGER..."
"...IT CAN FELL AN OPPONENT 50 *KEN* AWAY."
AND I QUOTE.
THE KAITO KID!

**Sun* and *ken* are old Japanese measurements. One *sun* is roughly one inch and one *ken* is roughly six feet.

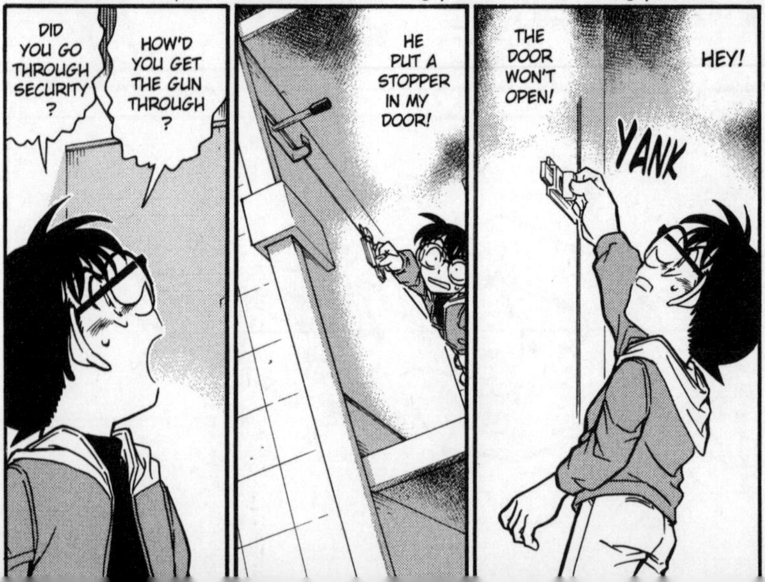
HEY!
YANK
THE DOOR WON'T OPEN!
HE PUT A STOPPER IN MY DOOR!
HOW'D YOU GET THE GUN THROUGH?
DID YOU GO THROUGH SECURITY?

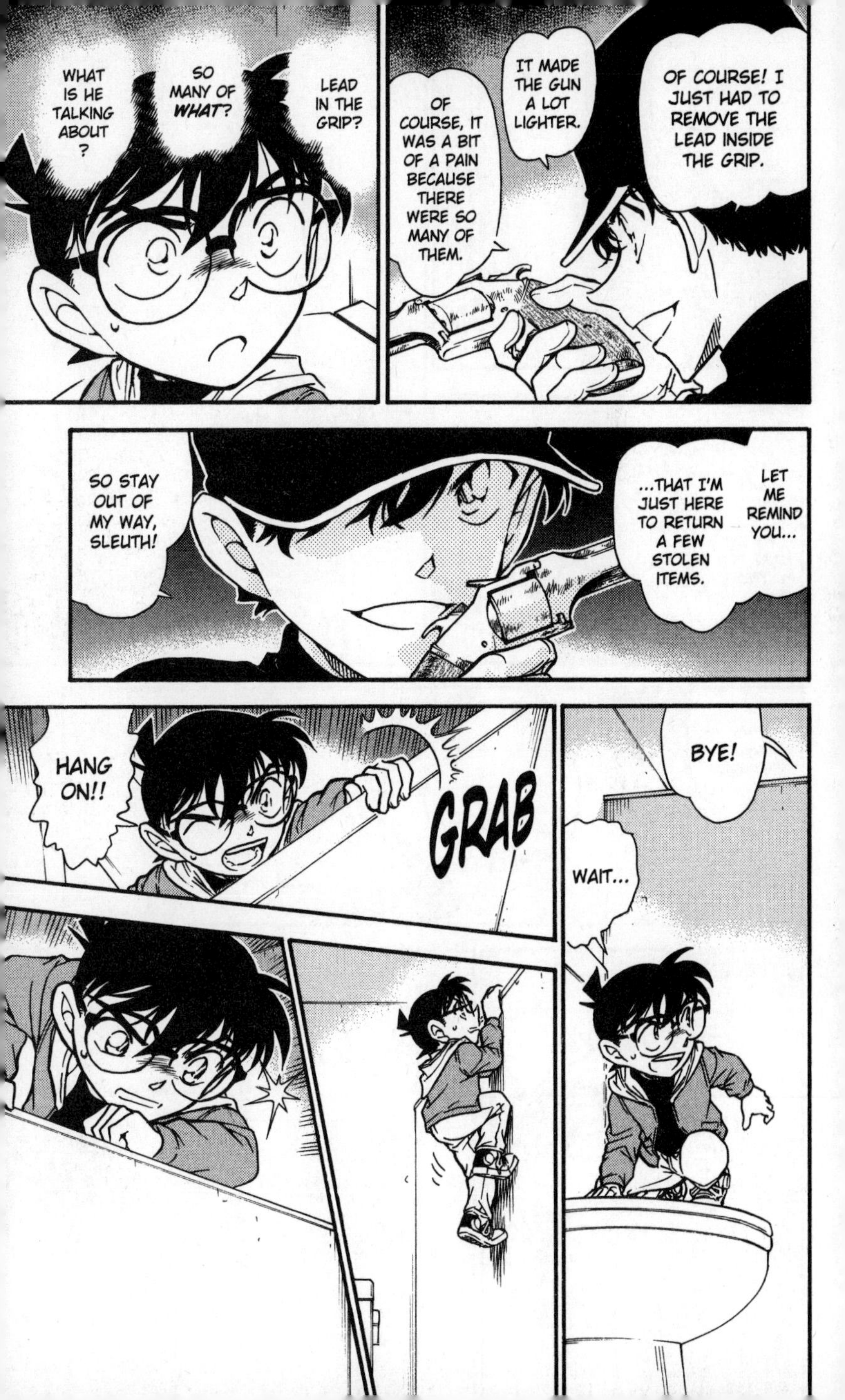
OF COURSE! I JUST HAD TO REMOVE THE LEAD INSIDE THE GRIP.
IT MADE THE GUN A LOT LIGHTER.
OF COURSE, IT WAS A BIT OF A PAIN BECAUSE THERE WERE SO MANY OF THEM.
LEAD IN THE GRIP?
SO MANY OF *WHAT*?
WHAT IS HE TALKING ABOUT?
LET ME REMIND YOU...
...THAT I'M JUST HERE TO RETURN A FEW STOLEN ITEMS.
SO STAY OUT OF MY WAY, SLEUTH!
BYE!
WAIT...
HANG ON!!
GRAB

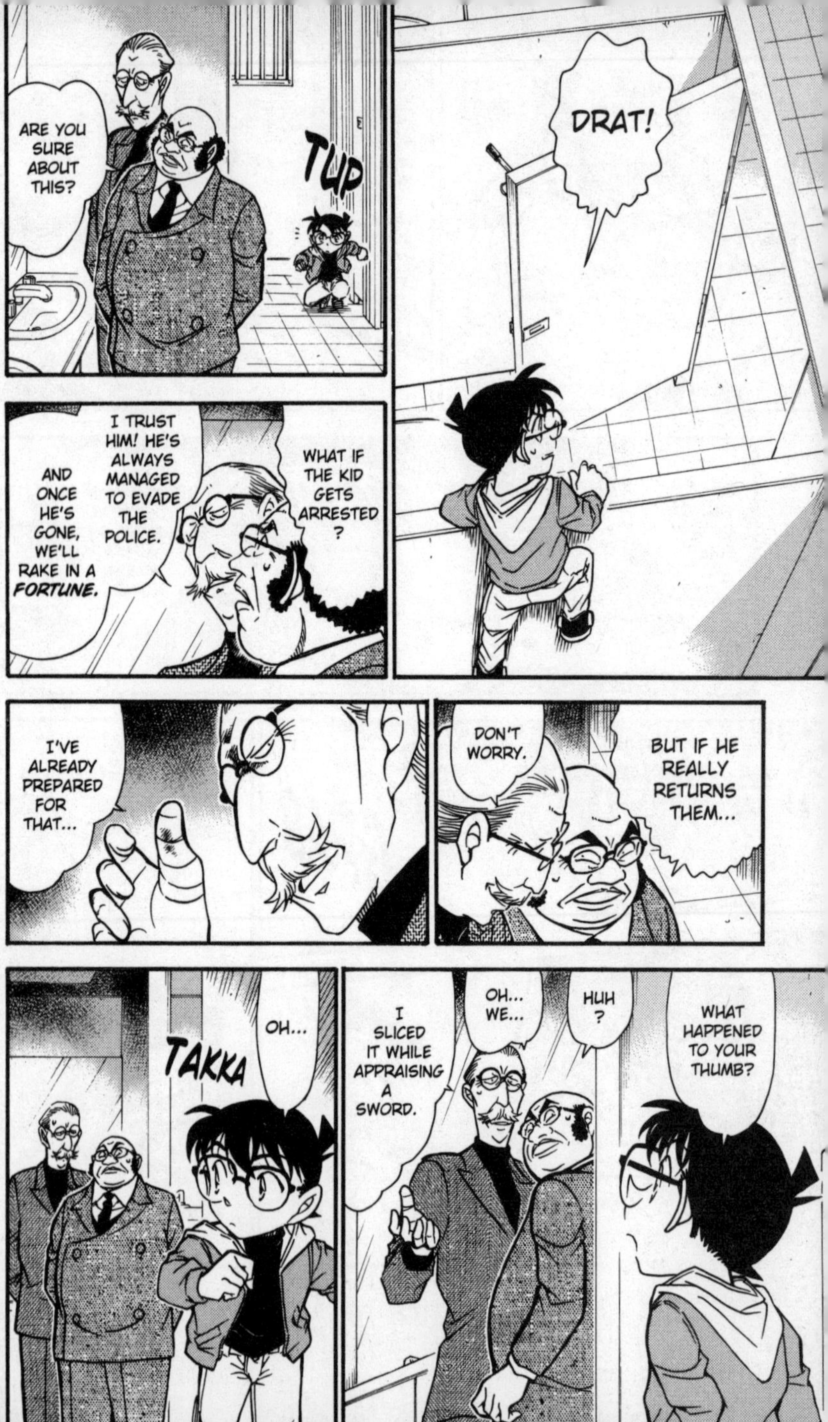
DRAT!
ARE YOU SURE ABOUT THIS?
TUP
WHAT IF THE KID GETS ARRESTED?
I TRUST HIM! HE'S ALWAYS MANAGED TO EVADE THE POLICE.
AND ONCE HE'S GONE, WE'LL RAKE IN A *FORTUNE.*
BUT IF HE REALLY RETURNS THEM...
DON'T WORRY.
I'VE ALREADY PREPARED FOR THAT...
WHAT HAPPENED TO YOUR THUMB?
HUH?
OH... WE...
I SLICED IT WHILE APPRAISING A SWORD.
OH...
TAKKA

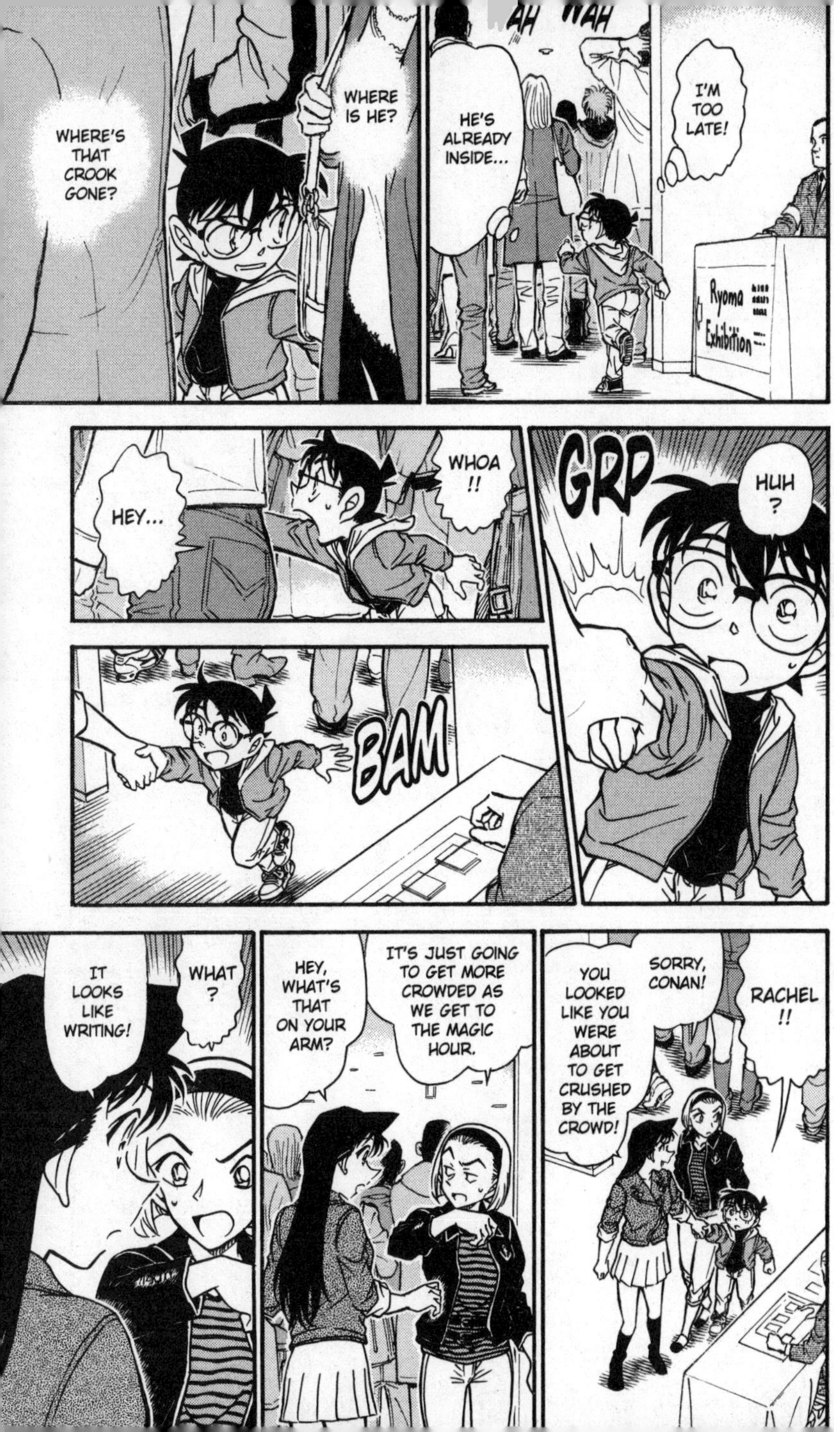

AH
WAH
I'M TOO LATE!
HE'S ALREADY INSIDE...
Ryoma Exhibition
WHERE IS HE?
WHERE'S THAT CROOK GONE?
HUH ?
GRP
WHOA !!
HEY...
BAM
RACHEL !!
SORRY, CONAN!
YOU LOOKED LIKE YOU WERE ABOUT TO GET CRUSHED BY THE CROWD!
IT'S JUST GOING TO GET MORE CROWDED AS WE GET TO THE MAGIC HOUR.
HEY, WHAT'S THAT ON YOUR ARM?
WHAT ?
IT LOOKS LIKE WRITING!

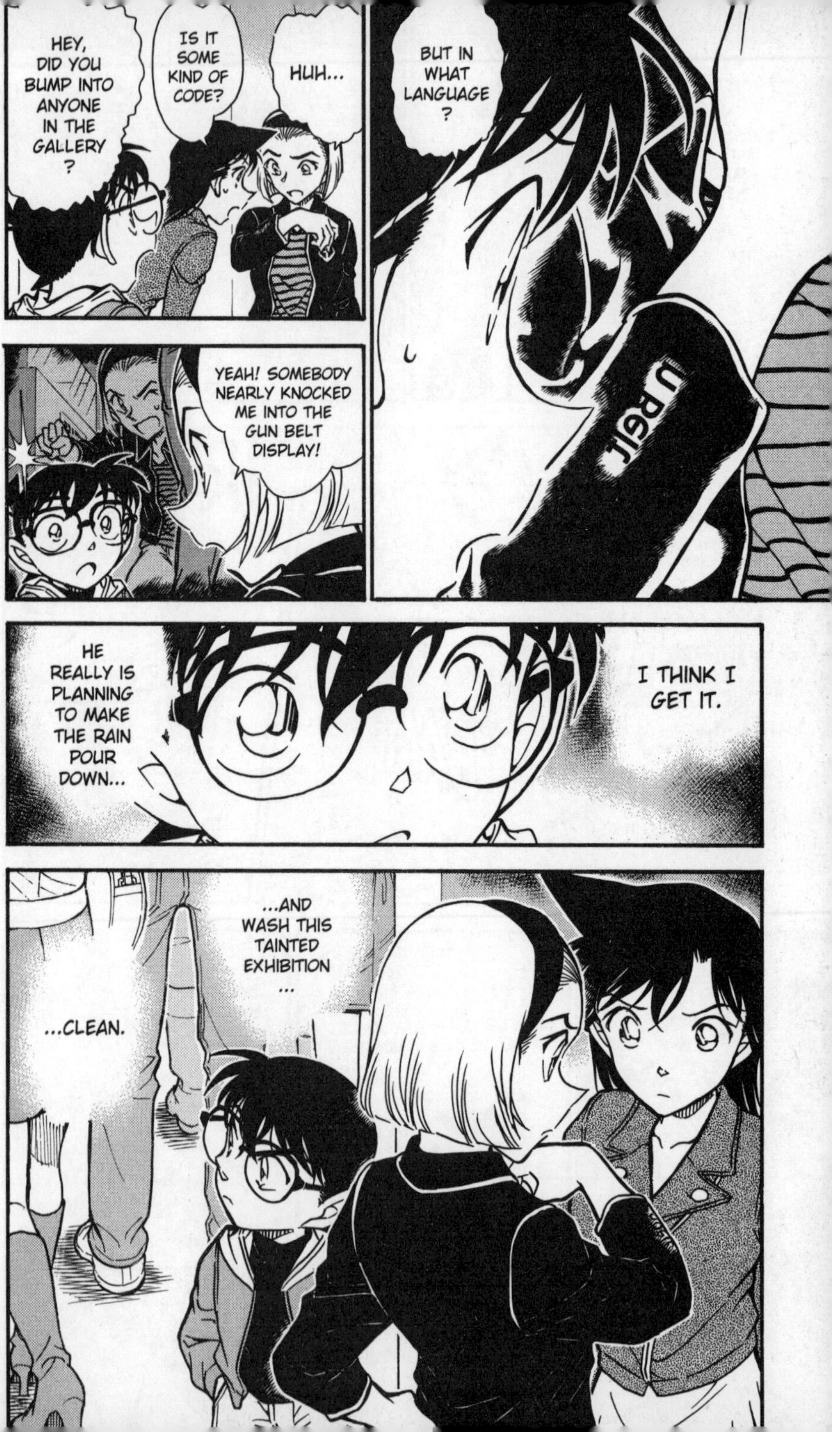
BUT IN WHAT LANGUAGE ?
HUH...
IS IT SOME KIND OF CODE?
HEY, DID YOU BUMP INTO ANYONE IN THE GALLERY ?
YEAH! SOMEBODY NEARLY KNOCKED ME INTO THE GUN BELT DISPLAY!
I THINK I GET IT.
HE REALLY IS PLANNING TO MAKE THE RAIN POUR DOWN...
...AND WASH THIS TAINTED EXHIBITION ...
...CLEAN.

FILE 4: CLEANSING

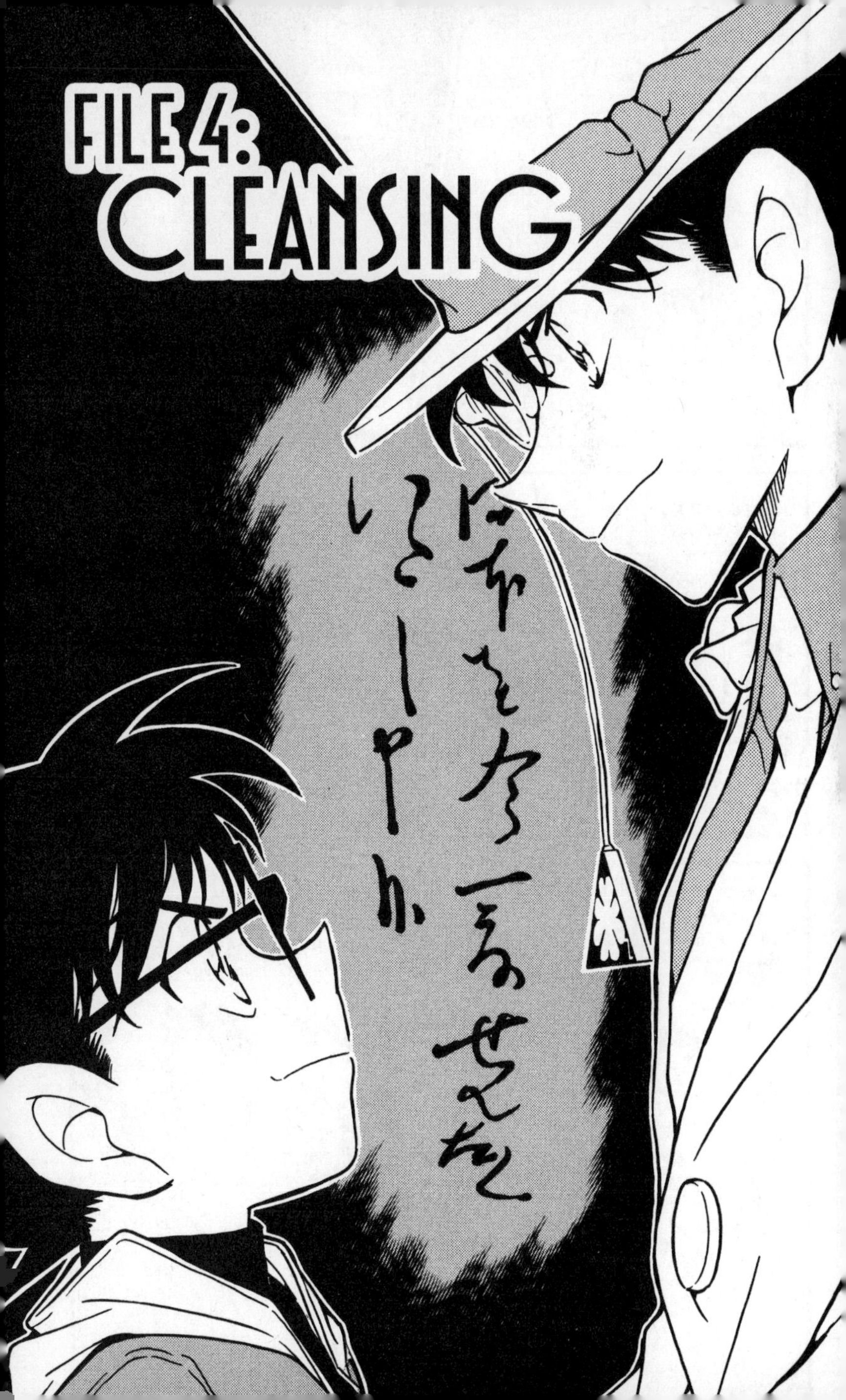

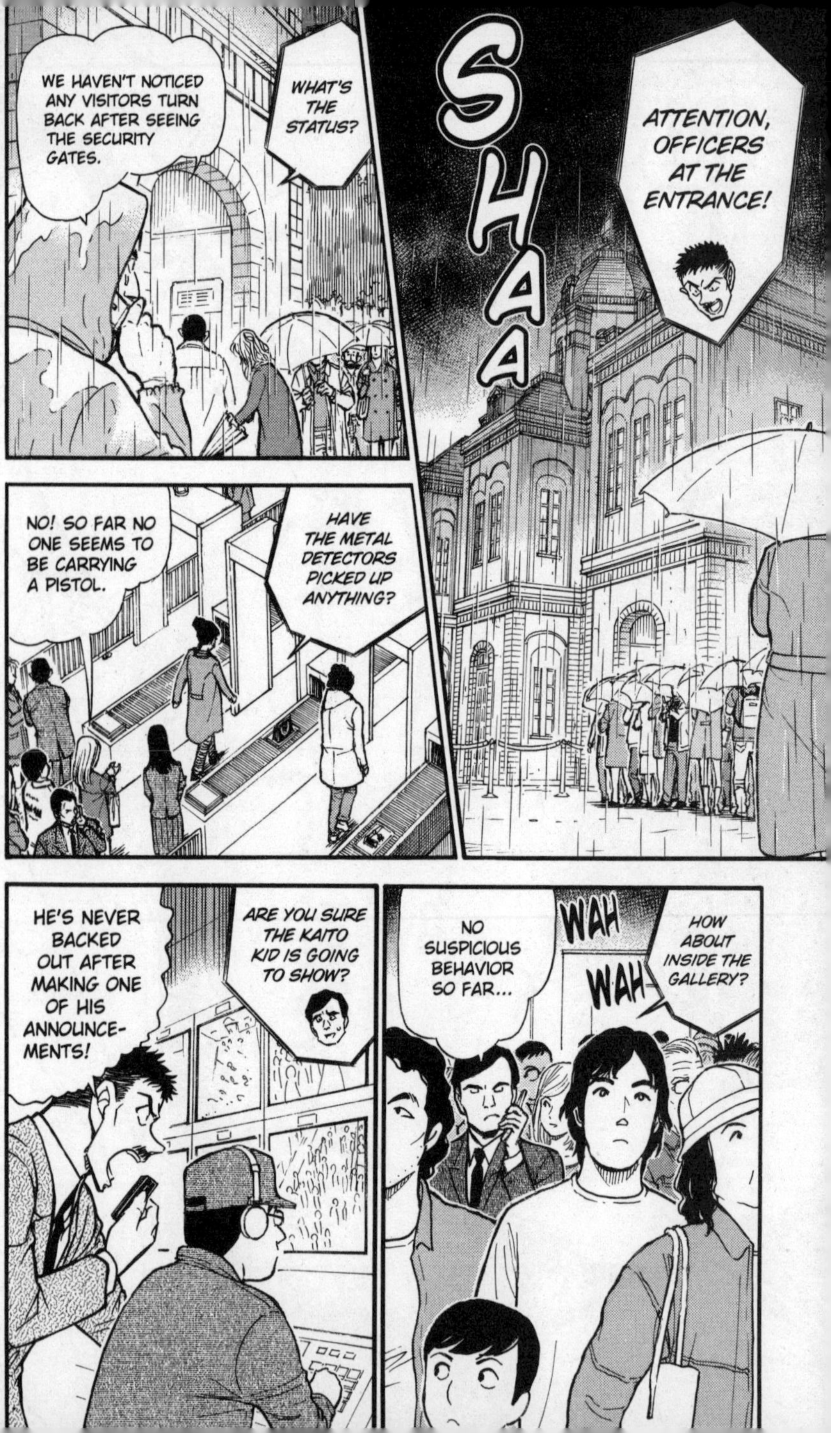
SHAA
ATTENTION, OFFICERS AT THE ENTRANCE!
WHAT'S THE STATUS?
WE HAVEN'T NOTICED ANY VISITORS TURN BACK AFTER SEEING THE SECURITY GATES.
HAVE THE METAL DETECTORS PICKED UP ANYTHING?
NO! SO FAR NO ONE SEEMS TO BE CARRYING A PISTOL.
HOW ABOUT INSIDE THE GALLERY?
WAH
WAH
NO SUSPICIOUS BEHAVIOR SO FAR...
ARE YOU SURE THE KAITO KID IS GOING TO SHOW?
HE'S NEVER BACKED OUT AFTER MAKING ONE OF HIS ANNOUNCE-MENTS!

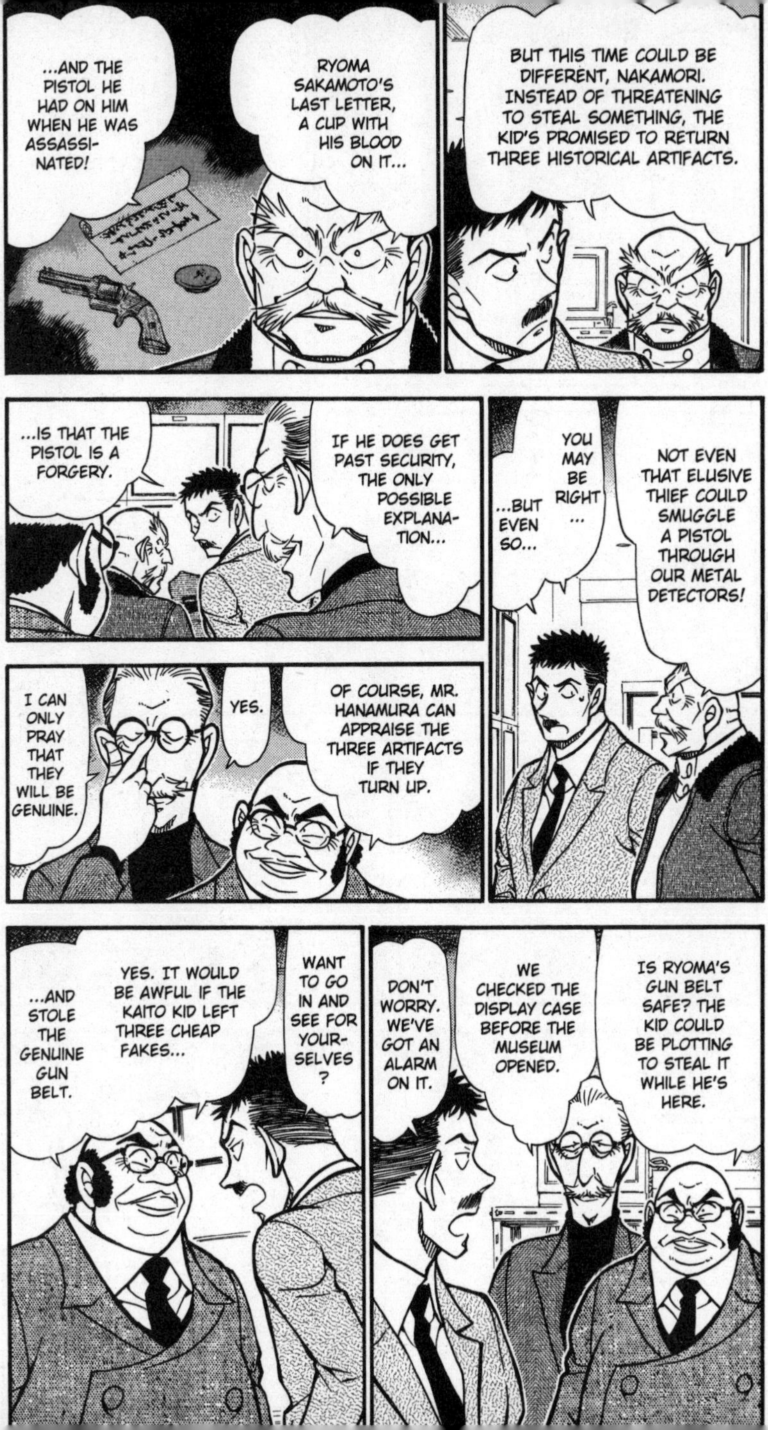
BUT THIS TIME COULD BE DIFFERENT, NAKAMORI. INSTEAD OF THREATENING TO STEAL SOMETHING, THE KID'S PROMISED TO RETURN THREE HISTORICAL ARTIFACTS.
RYOMA SAKAMOTO'S LAST LETTER, A CUP WITH HIS BLOOD ON IT...
...AND THE PISTOL HE HAD ON HIM WHEN HE WAS ASSASSI-NATED!
NOT EVEN THAT ELUSIVE THIEF COULD SMUGGLE A PISTOL THROUGH OUR METAL DETECTORS!
YOU MAY BE RIGHT...
...BUT EVEN SO...
IF HE DOES GET PAST SECURITY, THE ONLY POSSIBLE EXPLANA-TION...
...IS THAT THE PISTOL IS A FORGERY.
OF COURSE, MR. HANAMURA CAN APPRAISE THE THREE ARTIFACTS IF THEY TURN UP.
YES.
I CAN ONLY PRAY THAT THEY WILL BE GENUINE.
IS RYOMA'S GUN BELT SAFE? THE KID COULD BE PLOTTING TO STEAL IT WHILE HE'S HERE.
WE CHECKED THE DISPLAY CASE BEFORE THE MUSEUM OPENED.
DON'T WORRY. WE'VE GOT AN ALARM ON IT.
WANT TO GO IN AND SEE FOR YOUR-SELVES?
YES. IT WOULD BE AWFUL IF THE KAITO KID LEFT THREE CHEAP FAKES...
...AND STOLE THE GENUINE GUN BELT.

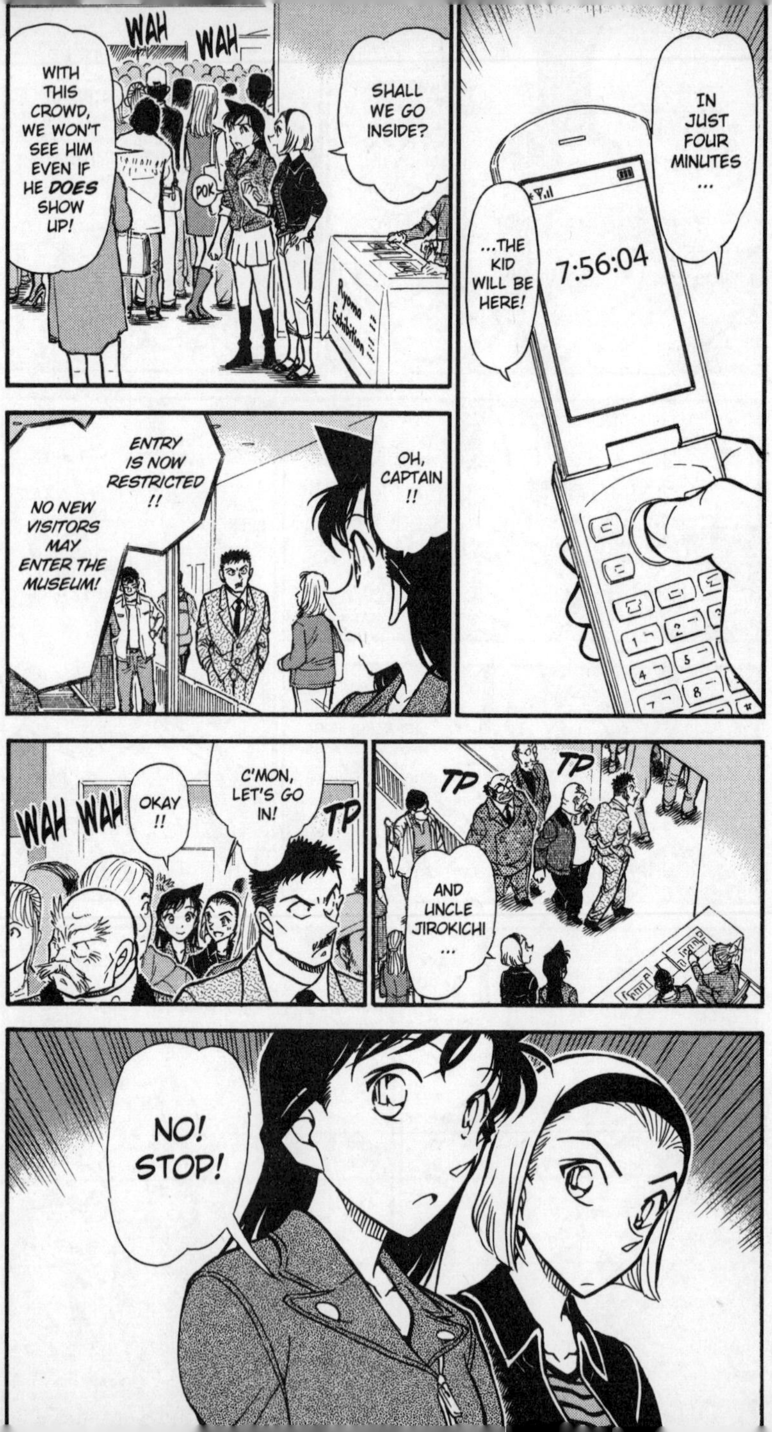
IN JUST FOUR MINUTES ...
7:56:04
...THE KID WILL BE HERE!
SHALL WE GO INSIDE?
WAH
WAH
POK
WITH THIS CROWD, WE WON'T SEE HIM EVEN IF HE **DOES** SHOW UP!
Ryoma Exhibition
OH, CAPTAIN !!
ENTRY IS NOW RESTRICTED !!
NO NEW VISITORS MAY ENTER THE MUSEUM!
TP
TP
AND UNCLE JIROKICHI ...
TP
C'MON, LET'S GO IN!
OKAY !!
WAH WAH
NO! STOP!

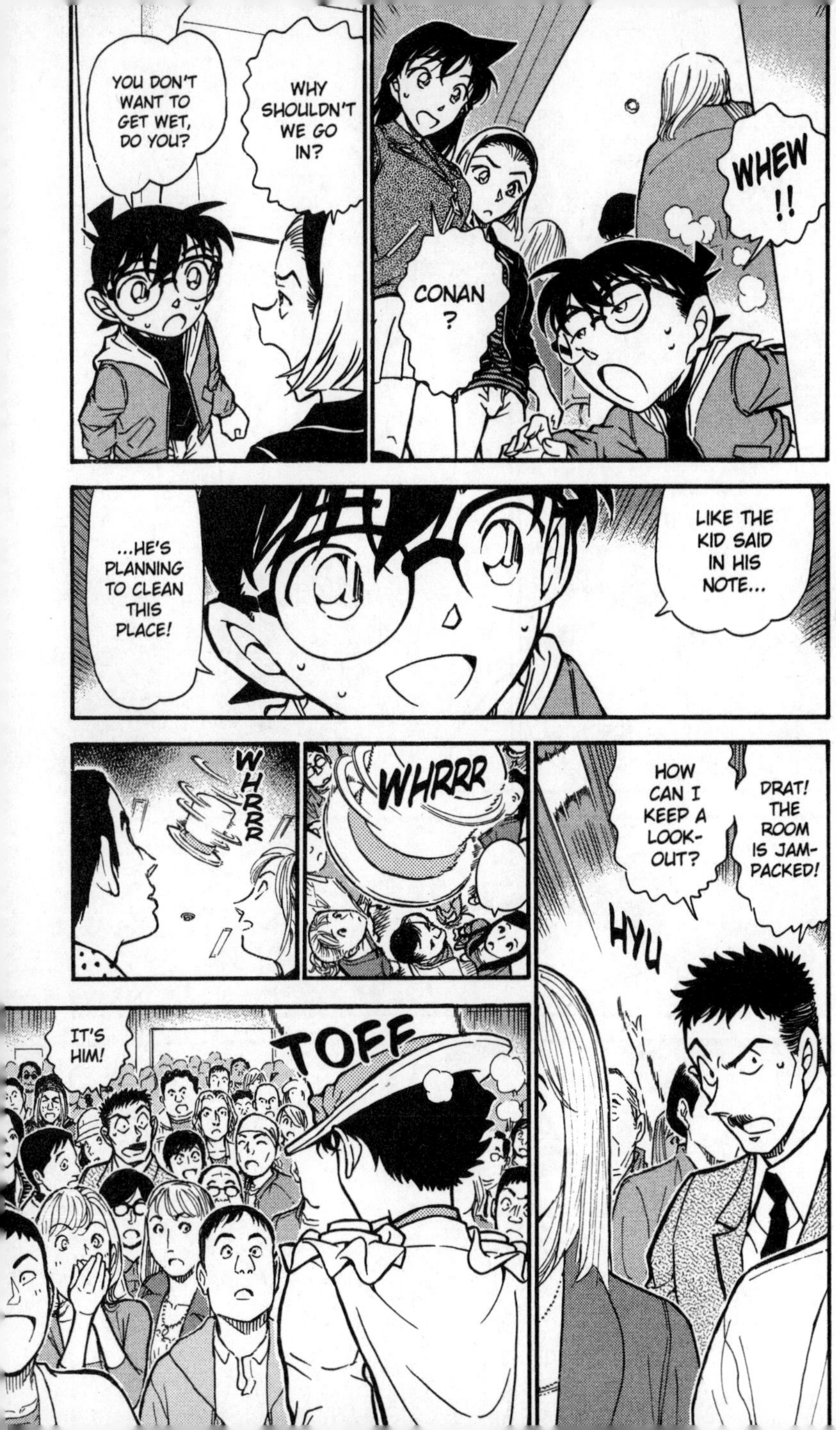
WHEW !!
CONAN ?
WHY SHOULDN'T WE GO IN?
YOU DON'T WANT TO GET WET, DO YOU?
LIKE THE KID SAID IN HIS NOTE...
...HE'S PLANNING TO CLEAN THIS PLACE!
DRAT! THE ROOM IS JAM-PACKED!
HOW CAN I KEEP A LOOK-OUT?
HYU
WHRRR
WHRRR
TOFF
IT'S HIM!

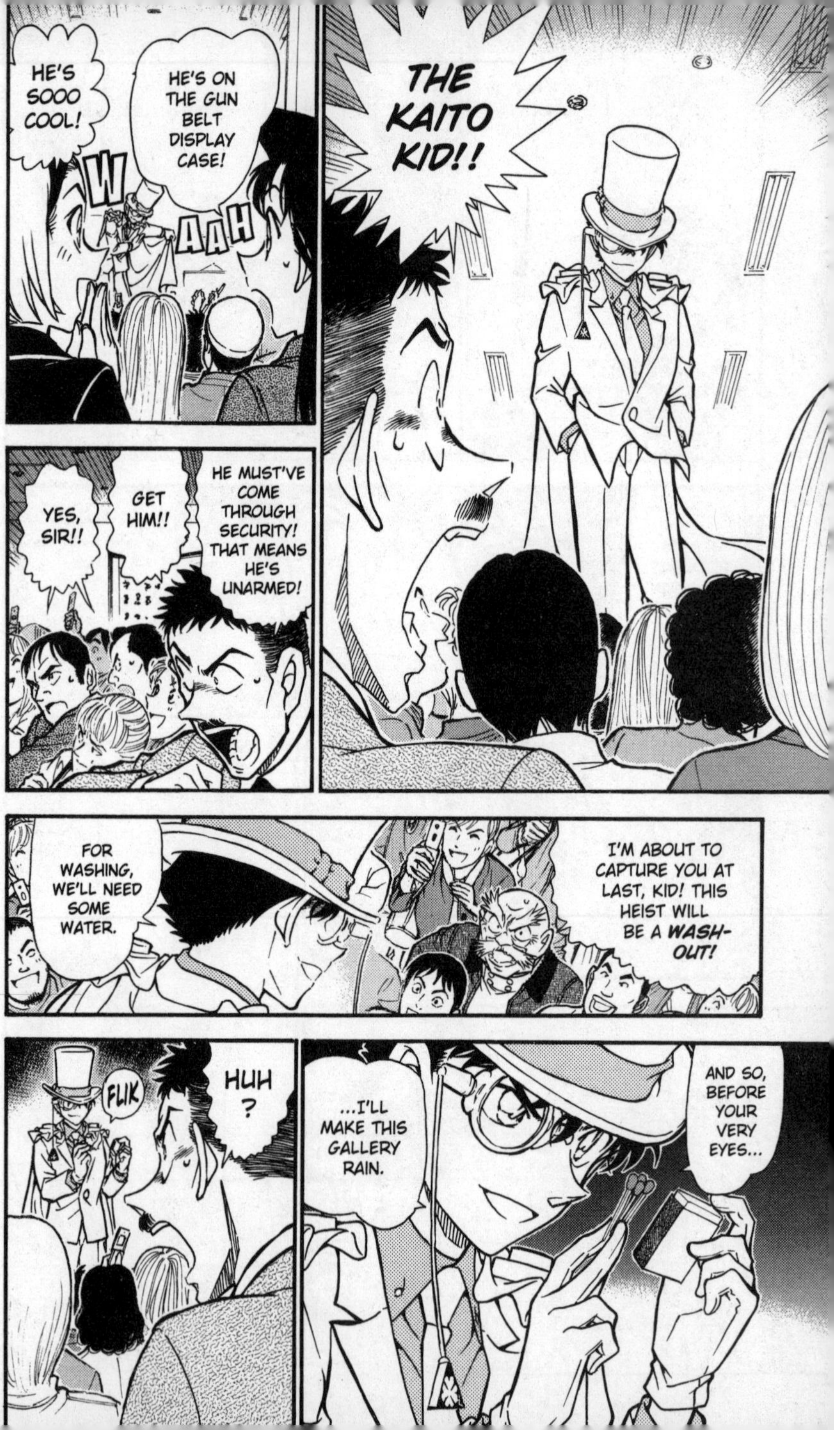
THE KAITO KID!!
HE'S ON THE GUN BELT DISPLAY CASE!
HE'S SOOO COOL!
WAAH
HE MUST'VE COME THROUGH SECURITY! THAT MEANS HE'S UNARMED!
GET HIM!!
YES, SIR!!
I'M ABOUT TO CAPTURE YOU AT LAST, KID! THIS HEIST WILL BE A ***WASH-OUT!***
FOR WASHING, WE'LL NEED SOME WATER.
AND SO, BEFORE YOUR VERY EYES...
...I'LL MAKE THIS GALLERY RAIN.
HUH?
FLIK

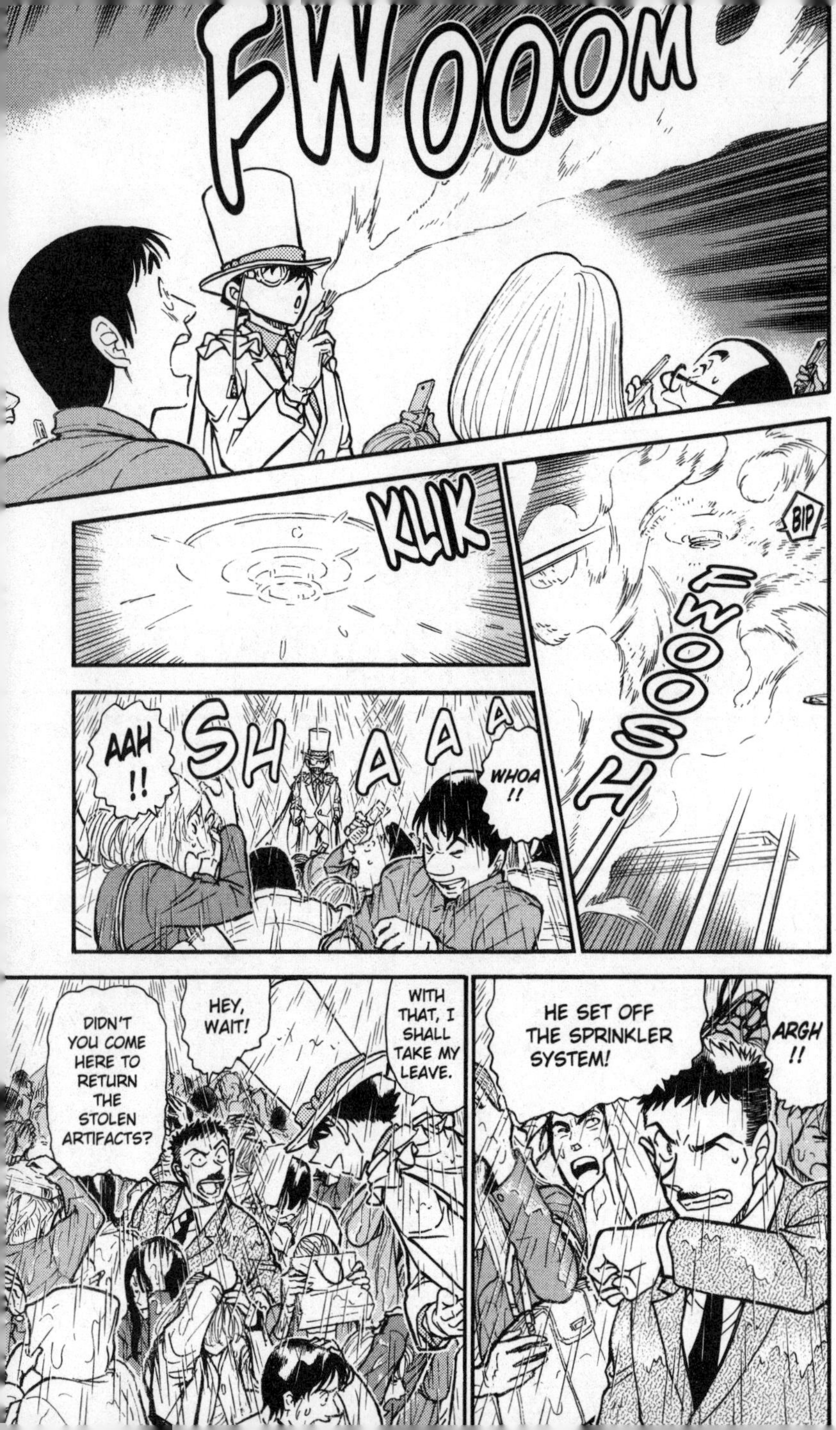
FWOOOM
BIP
FWOOSH
KLIK
SHAAA
WHOA !!
AAH !!
ARGH !!
HE SET OFF THE SPRINKLER SYSTEM!
WITH THAT, I SHALL TAKE MY LEAVE.
HEY, WAIT!
DIDN'T YOU COME HERE TO RETURN THE STOLEN ARTIFACTS?

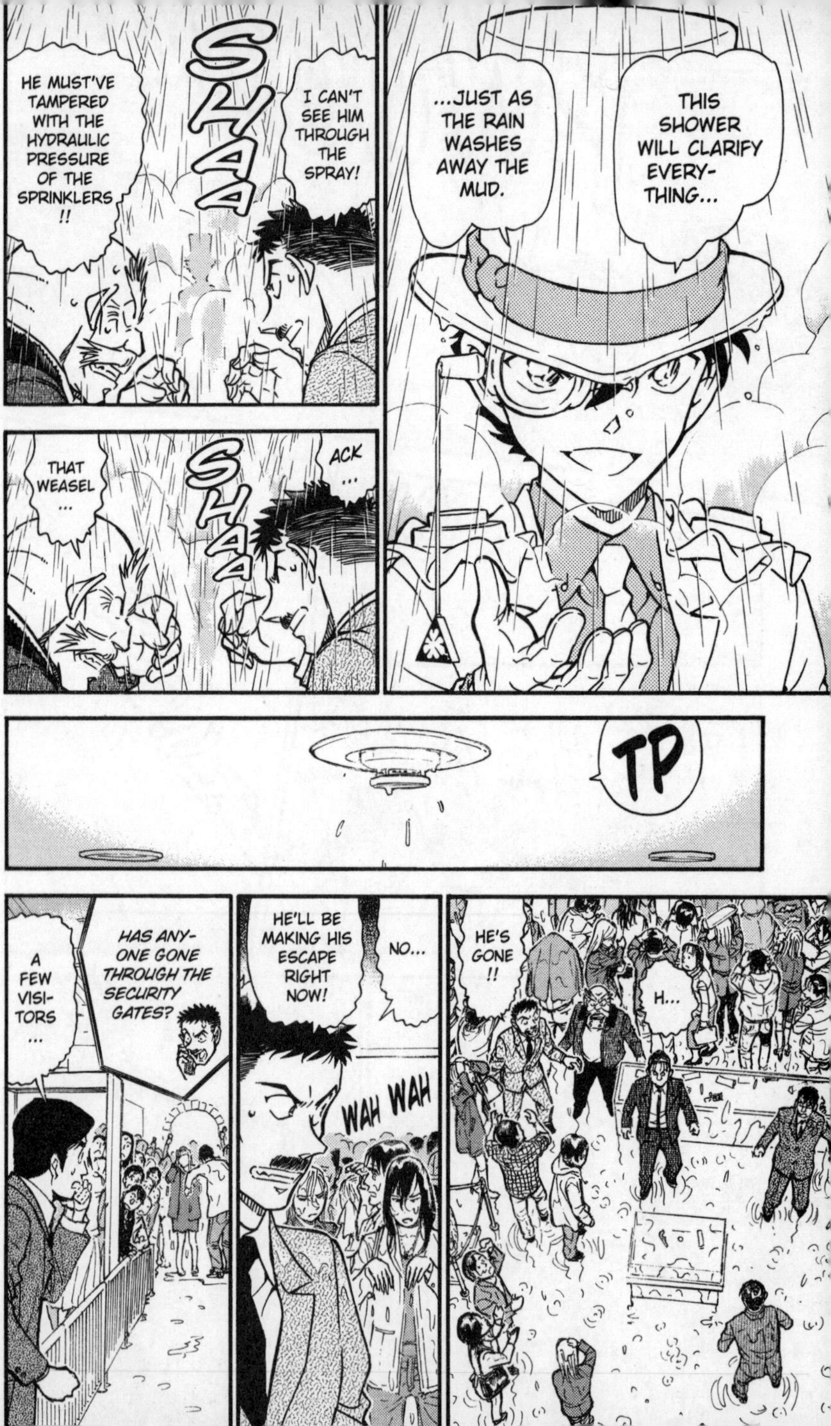
THIS SHOWER WILL CLARIFY EVERY-THING...
...JUST AS THE RAIN WASHES AWAY THE MUD.
SHAA
I CAN'T SEE HIM THROUGH THE SPRAY!
HE MUST'VE TAMPERED WITH THE HYDRAULIC PRESSURE OF THE SPRINKLERS !!
ACK ...
SHAA
THAT WEASEL ...
TP
HE'S GONE !!
H...
NO...
HE'LL BE MAKING HIS ESCAPE RIGHT NOW!
WAH WAH
HAS ANY-ONE GONE THROUGH THE SECURITY GATES?
A FEW VISI-TORS ...

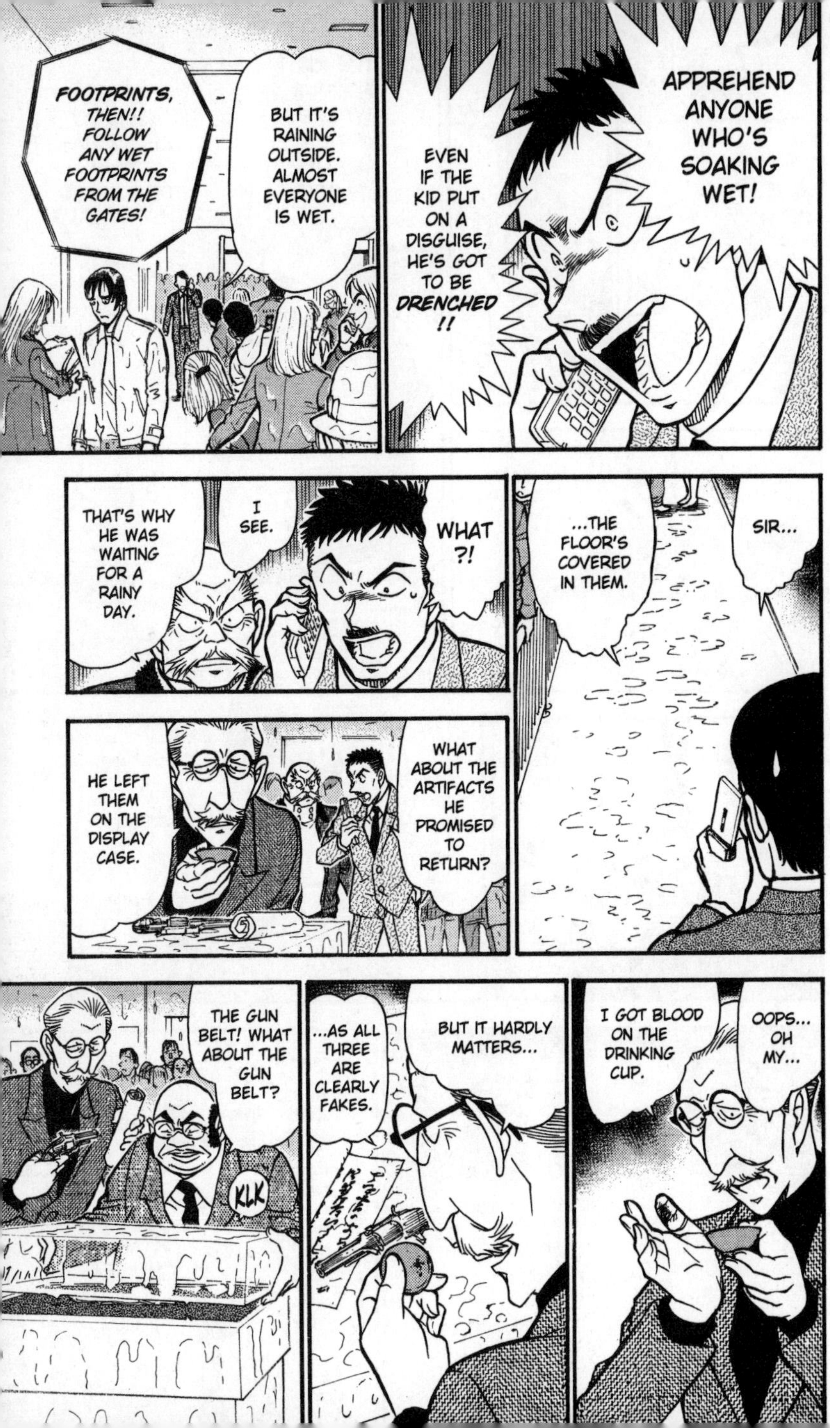
APPREHEND ANYONE WHO'S SOAKING WET!
EVEN IF THE KID PUT ON A DISGUISE, HE'S GOT TO BE DRENCHED!!
BUT IT'S RAINING OUTSIDE. ALMOST EVERYONE IS WET.
FOOTPRINTS, THEN!! FOLLOW ANY WET FOOTPRINTS FROM THE GATES!
SIR...
...THE FLOOR'S COVERED IN THEM.
WHAT?!
I SEE.
THAT'S WHY HE WAS WAITING FOR A RAINY DAY.
WHAT ABOUT THE ARTIFACTS HE PROMISED TO RETURN?
HE LEFT THEM ON THE DISPLAY CASE.
OOPS... OH MY...
I GOT BLOOD ON THE DRINKING CUP.
BUT IT HARDLY MATTERS...
...AS ALL THREE ARE CLEARLY FAKES.
THE GUN BELT! WHAT ABOUT THE GUN BELT?
KLK

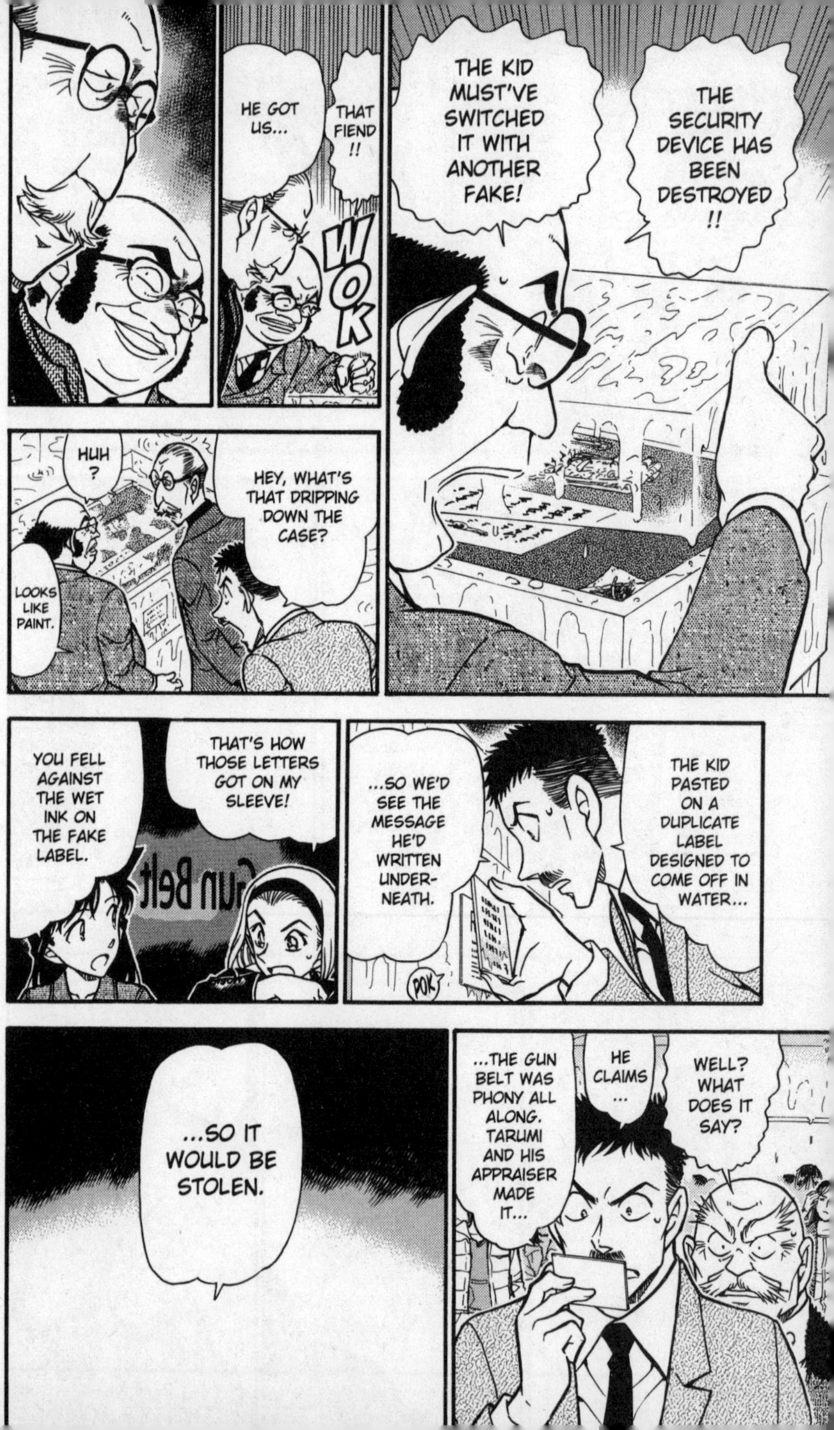
THE SECURITY DEVICE HAS BEEN DESTROYED!!
THE KID MUST'VE SWITCHED IT WITH ANOTHER FAKE!
THAT FIEND!!
WOK
HE GOT US...
HEY, WHAT'S THAT DRIPPING DOWN THE CASE?
HUH?
LOOKS LIKE PAINT.
THE KID PASTED ON A DUPLICATE LABEL DESIGNED TO COME OFF IN WATER...
...SO WE'D SEE THE MESSAGE HE'D WRITTEN UNDERNEATH.
POK
THAT'S HOW THOSE LETTERS GOT ON MY SLEEVE!
YOU FELL AGAINST THE WET INK ON THE FAKE LABEL.
Gun Belt
WELL? WHAT DOES IT SAY?
HE CLAIMS...
...THE GUN BELT WAS PHONY ALL ALONG. TARUMI AND HIS APPRAISER MADE IT...
...SO IT WOULD BE STOLEN.

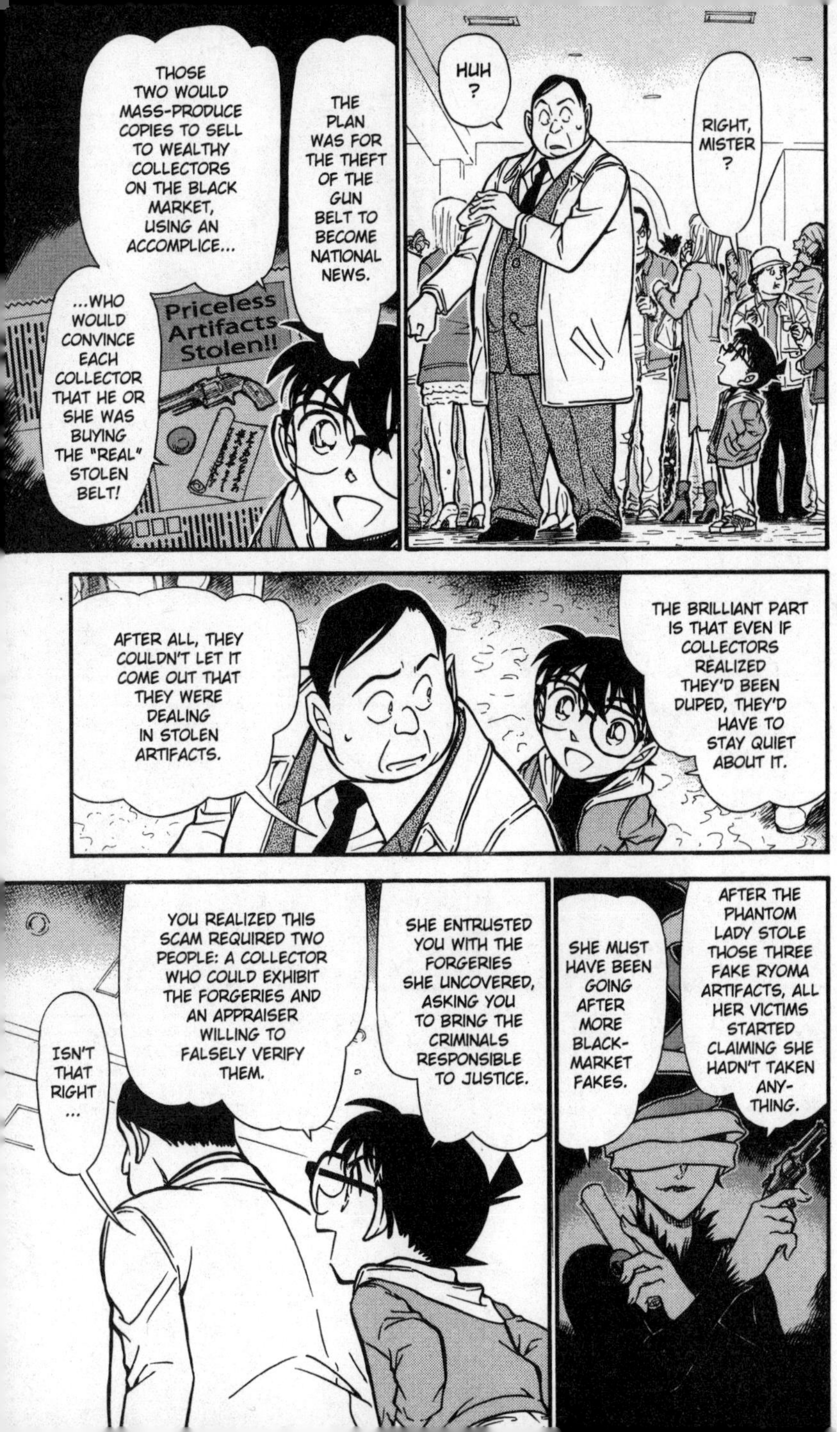
RIGHT, MISTER ?
HUH ?
THE PLAN WAS FOR THE THEFT OF THE GUN BELT TO BECOME NATIONAL NEWS.
THOSE TWO WOULD MASS-PRODUCE COPIES TO SELL TO WEALTHY COLLECTORS ON THE BLACK MARKET, USING AN ACCOMPLICE...
Priceless Artifacts Stolen!!
...WHO WOULD CONVINCE EACH COLLECTOR THAT HE OR SHE WAS BUYING THE "REAL" STOLEN BELT!
THE BRILLIANT PART IS THAT EVEN IF COLLECTORS REALIZED THEY'D BEEN DUPED, THEY'D HAVE TO STAY QUIET ABOUT IT.
AFTER ALL, THEY COULDN'T LET IT COME OUT THAT THEY WERE DEALING IN STOLEN ARTIFACTS.
AFTER THE PHANTOM LADY STOLE THOSE THREE FAKE RYOMA ARTIFACTS, ALL HER VICTIMS STARTED CLAIMING SHE HADN'T TAKEN ANY-THING.
SHE MUST HAVE BEEN GOING AFTER MORE BLACK-MARKET FAKES.
SHE ENTRUSTED YOU WITH THE FORGERIES SHE UNCOVERED, ASKING YOU TO BRING THE CRIMINALS RESPONSIBLE TO JUSTICE.
YOU REALIZED THIS SCAM REQUIRED TWO PEOPLE: A COLLECTOR WHO COULD EXHIBIT THE FORGERIES AND AN APPRAISER WILLING TO FALSELY VERIFY THEM.
ISN'T THAT RIGHT ...

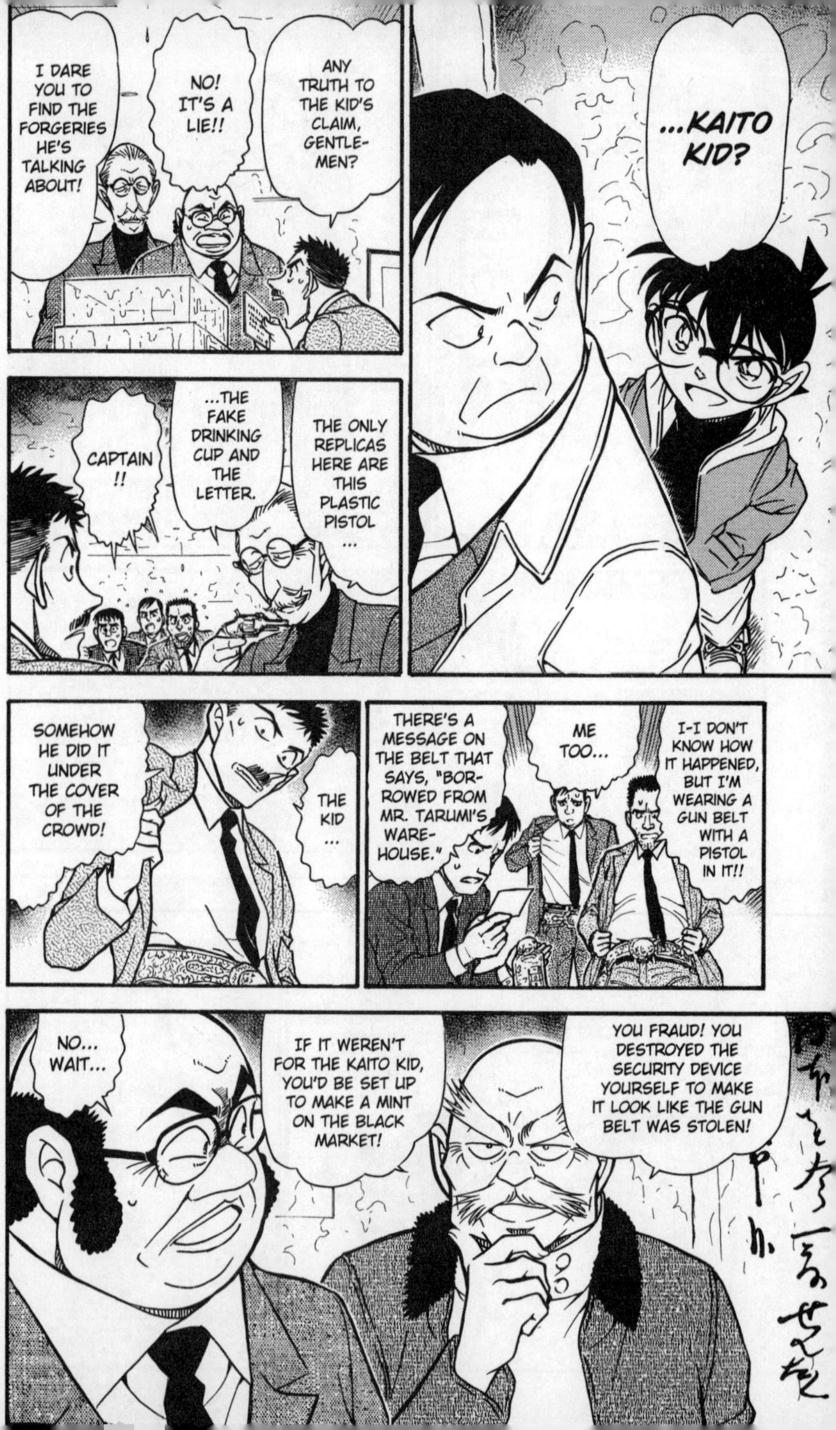
...KAITO KID?
ANY TRUTH TO THE KID'S CLAIM, GENTLEMEN?
NO! IT'S A LIE!!
I DARE YOU TO FIND THE FORGERIES HE'S TALKING ABOUT!
THE ONLY REPLICAS HERE ARE THIS PLASTIC PISTOL ...
...THE FAKE DRINKING CUP AND THE LETTER.
CAPTAIN !!
I-I DON'T KNOW HOW IT HAPPENED, BUT I'M WEARING A GUN BELT WITH A PISTOL IN IT!!
ME TOO...
THERE'S A MESSAGE ON THE BELT THAT SAYS, "BORROWED FROM MR. TARUMI'S WAREHOUSE."
THE KID ...
SOMEHOW HE DID IT UNDER THE COVER OF THE CROWD!
YOU FRAUD! YOU DESTROYED THE SECURITY DEVICE YOURSELF TO MAKE IT LOOK LIKE THE GUN BELT WAS STOLEN!
IF IT WEREN'T FOR THE KAITO KID, YOU'D BE SET UP TO MAKE A MINT ON THE BLACK MARKET!
NO... WAIT...

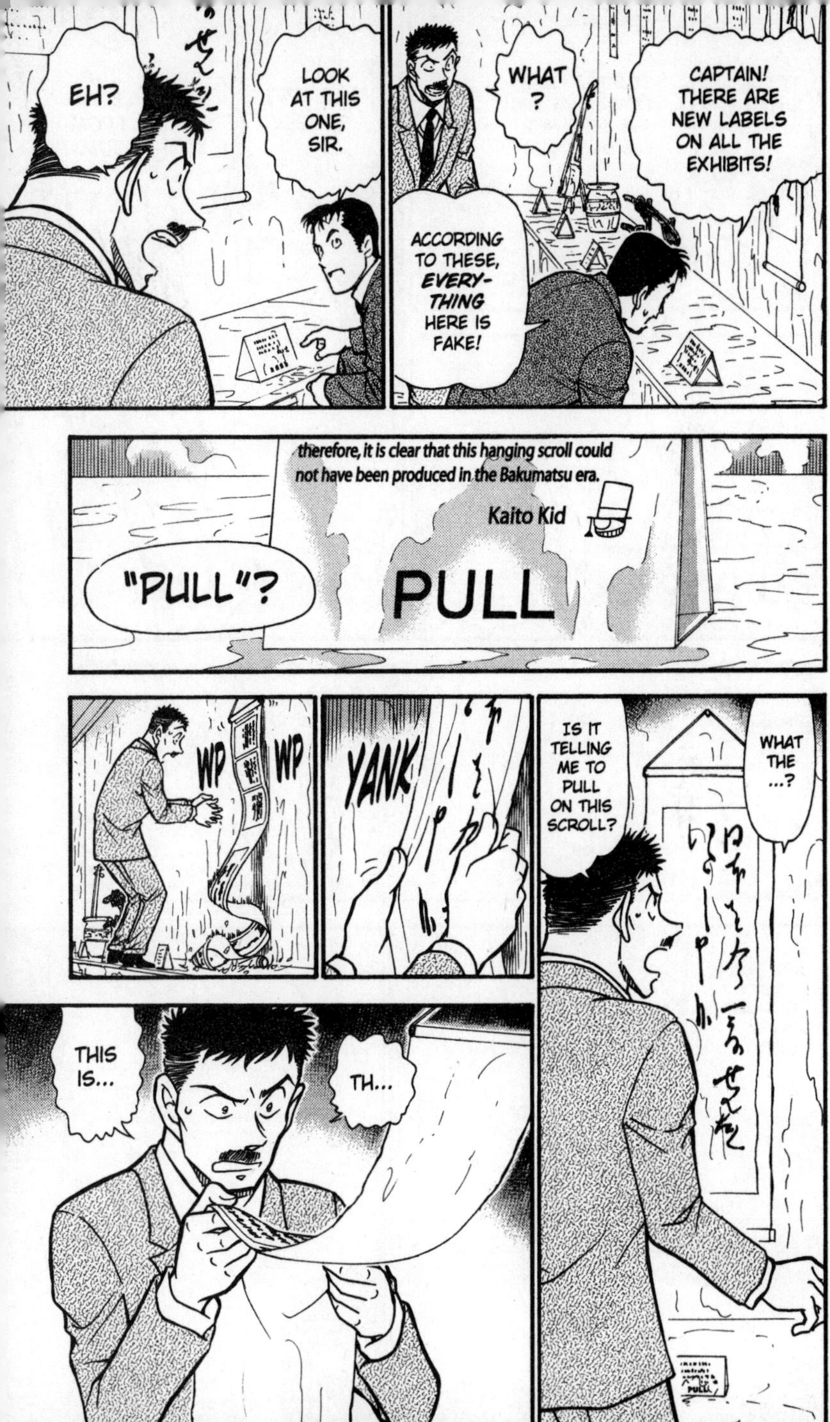
CAPTAIN! THERE ARE NEW LABELS ON ALL THE EXHIBITS!
WHAT?
ACCORDING TO THESE, *EVERYTHING* HERE IS FAKE!
LOOK AT THIS ONE, SIR.
EH?
therefore, it is clear that this hanging scroll could not have been produced in the Bakumatsu era.
Kaito Kid
PULL
"PULL"?
WHAT THE ...?
IS IT TELLING ME TO PULL ON THIS SCROLL?
PULL
YANK
WP
WP
TH...
THIS IS...

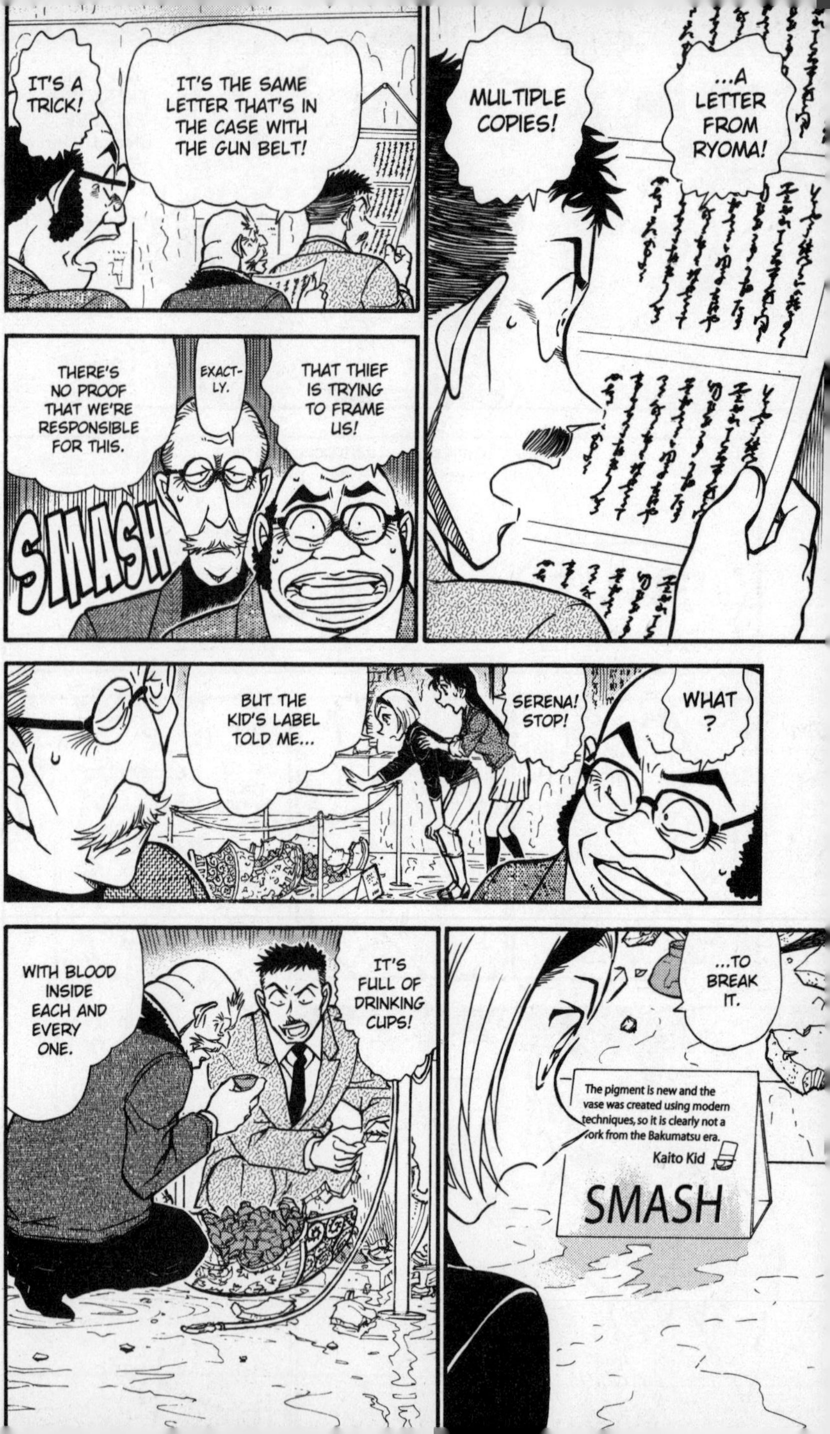
...A LETTER FROM RYOMA!
MULTIPLE COPIES!
IT'S THE SAME LETTER THAT'S IN THE CASE WITH THE GUN BELT!
IT'S A TRICK!
THAT THIEF IS TRYING TO FRAME US!
EXACT-LY.
THERE'S NO PROOF THAT WE'RE RESPONSIBLE FOR THIS.
SMASH
WHAT ?
SERENA! STOP!
BUT THE KID'S LABEL TOLD ME...
...TO BREAK IT.
The pigment is new and the vase was created using modern techniques, so it is clearly not a work from the Bakumatsu era.
Kaito Kid
SMASH
IT'S FULL OF DRINKING CUPS!
WITH BLOOD INSIDE EACH AND EVERY ONE.

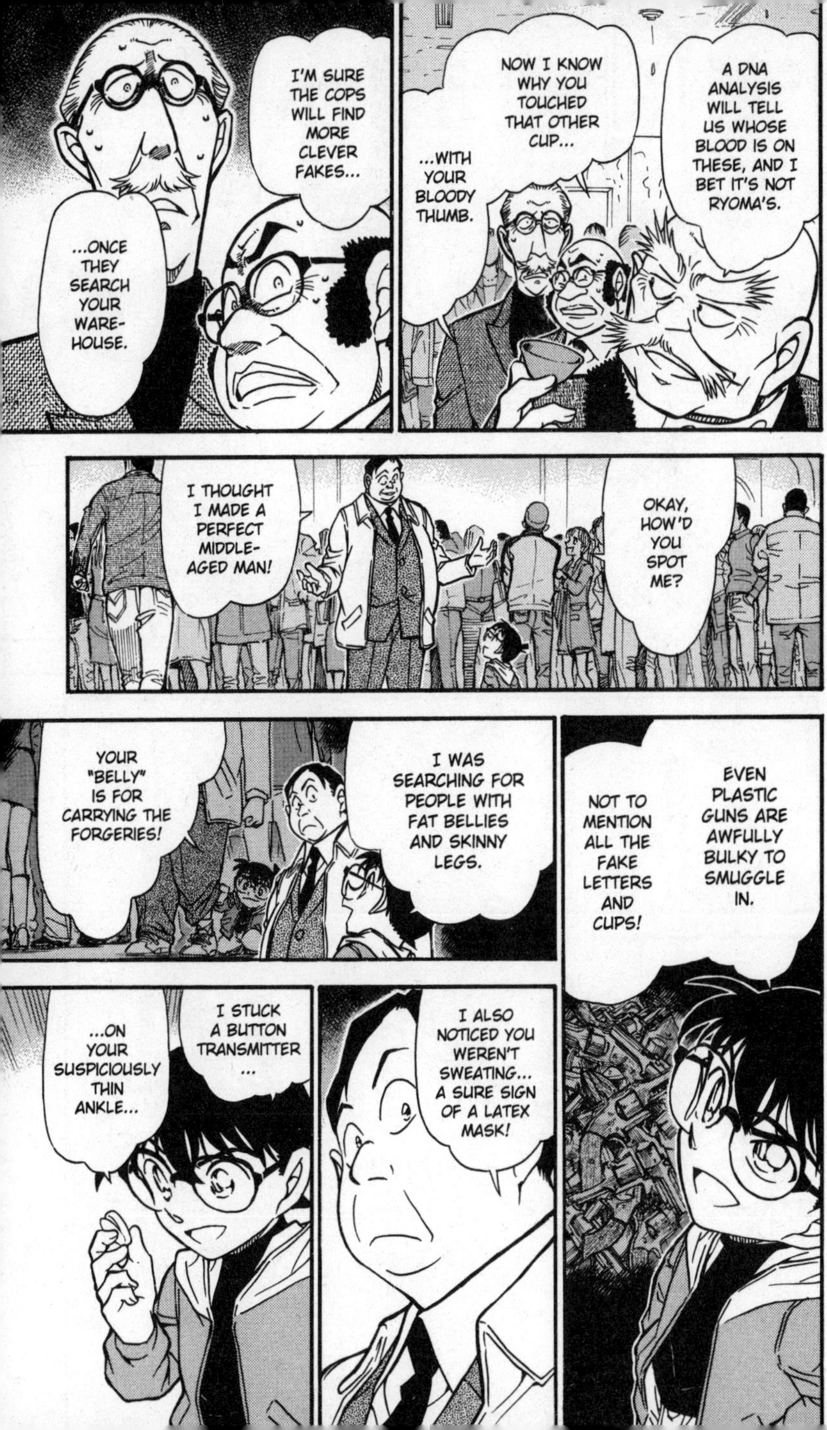
A DNA ANALYSIS WILL TELL US WHOSE BLOOD IS ON THESE, AND I BET IT'S NOT RYOMA'S.
NOW I KNOW WHY YOU TOUCHED THAT OTHER CUP...
...WITH YOUR BLOODY THUMB.
I'M SURE THE COPS WILL FIND MORE CLEVER FAKES...
...ONCE THEY SEARCH YOUR WARE-HOUSE.
OKAY, HOW'D YOU SPOT ME?
I THOUGHT I MADE A PERFECT MIDDLE-AGED MAN!
EVEN PLASTIC GUNS ARE AWFULLY BULKY TO SMUGGLE IN.
NOT TO MENTION ALL THE FAKE LETTERS AND CUPS!
I WAS SEARCHING FOR PEOPLE WITH FAT BELLIES AND SKINNY LEGS.
YOUR "BELLY" IS FOR CARRYING THE FORGERIES!
I ALSO NOTICED YOU WEREN'T SWEATING... A SURE SIGN OF A LATEX MASK!
I STUCK A BUTTON TRANSMITTER ...
...ON YOUR SUSPICIOUSLY THIN ANKLE...

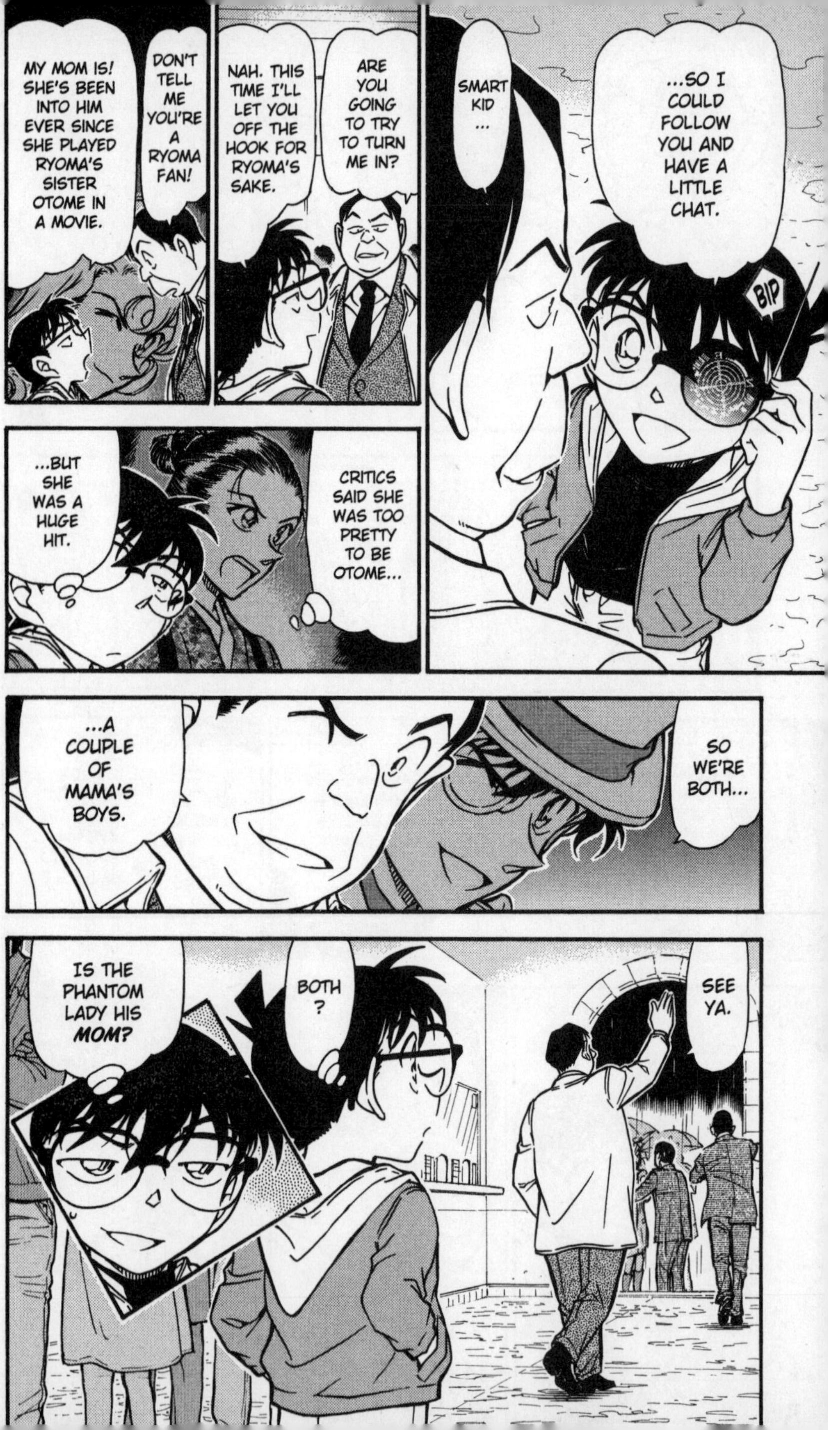
...SO I COULD FOLLOW YOU AND HAVE A LITTLE CHAT.
BIP
SMART KID ...
ARE YOU GOING TO TRY TO TURN ME IN?
NAH. THIS TIME I'LL LET YOU OFF THE HOOK FOR RYOMA'S SAKE.
DON'T TELL ME YOU'RE A RYOMA FAN!
MY MOM IS! SHE'S BEEN INTO HIM EVER SINCE SHE PLAYED RYOMA'S SISTER OTOME IN A MOVIE.
CRITICS SAID SHE WAS TOO PRETTY TO BE OTOME...
...BUT SHE WAS A HUGE HIT.
SO WE'RE BOTH...
...A COUPLE OF MAMA'S BOYS.
SEE YA.
BOTH?
IS THE PHANTOM LADY HIS *MOM?*

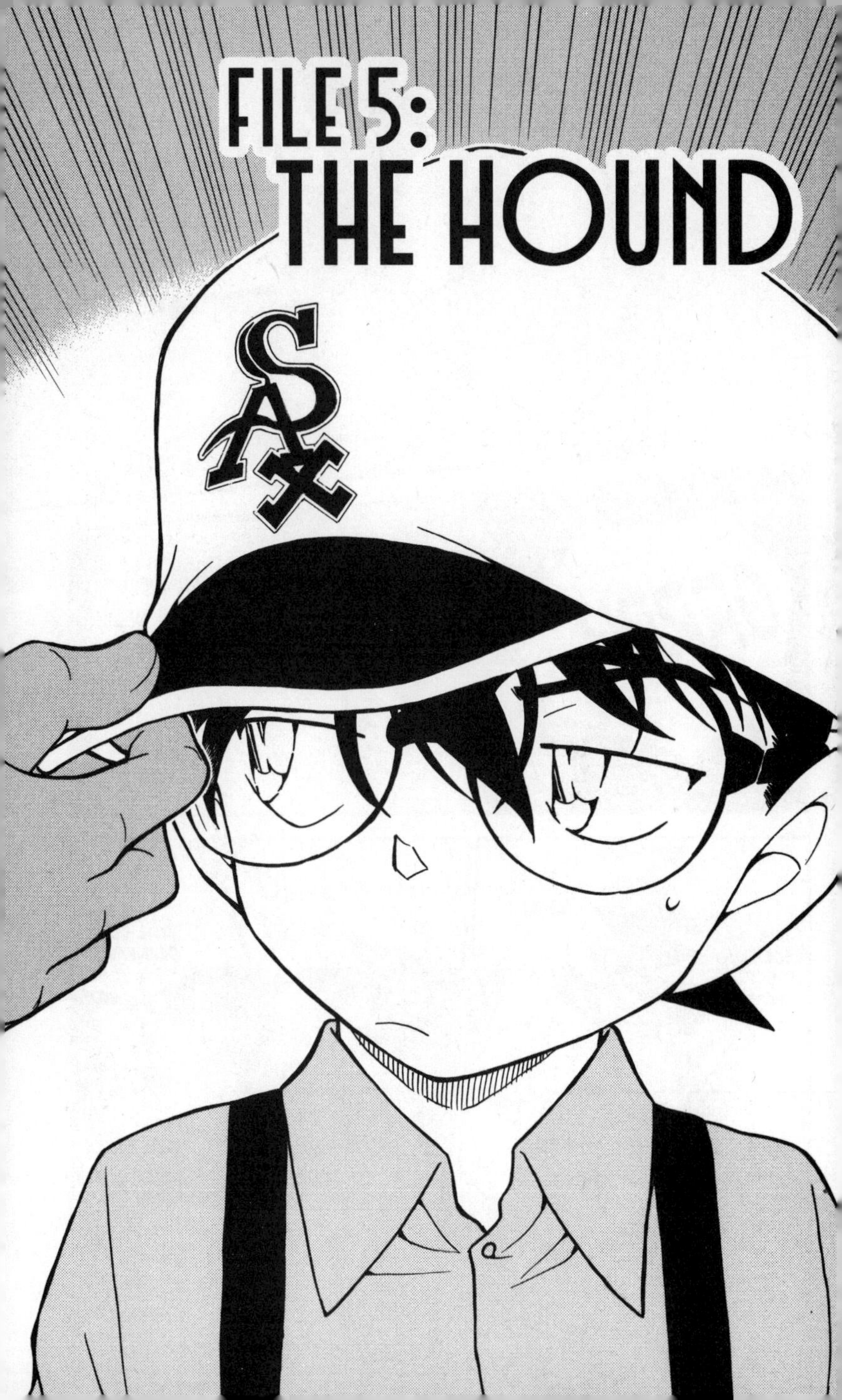
FILE 5:
THE HOUND

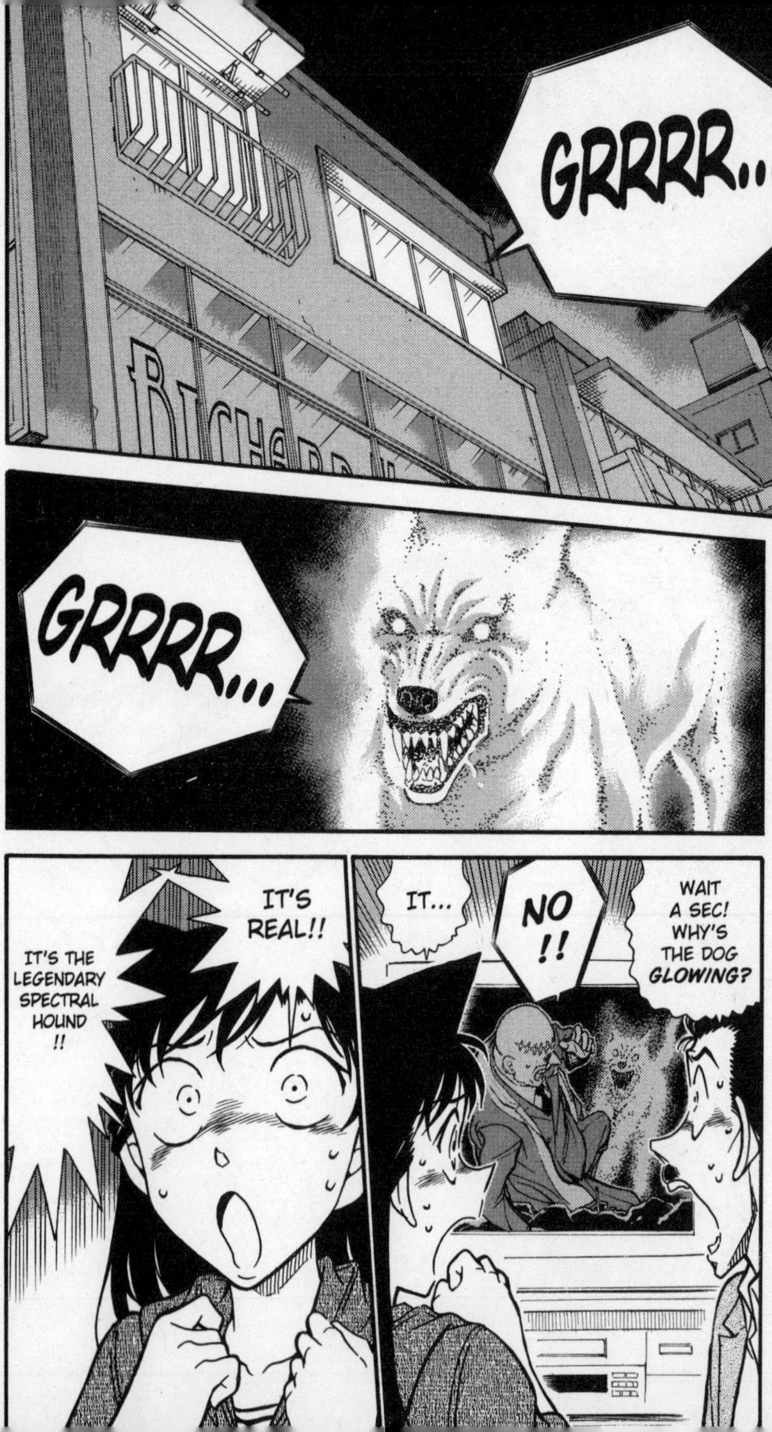
GRRRR...
GRRRR...
WAIT A SEC! WHY'S THE DOG GLOWING?
NO !!
IT...
IT'S REAL!!
IT'S THE LEGENDARY SPECTRAL HOUND !!

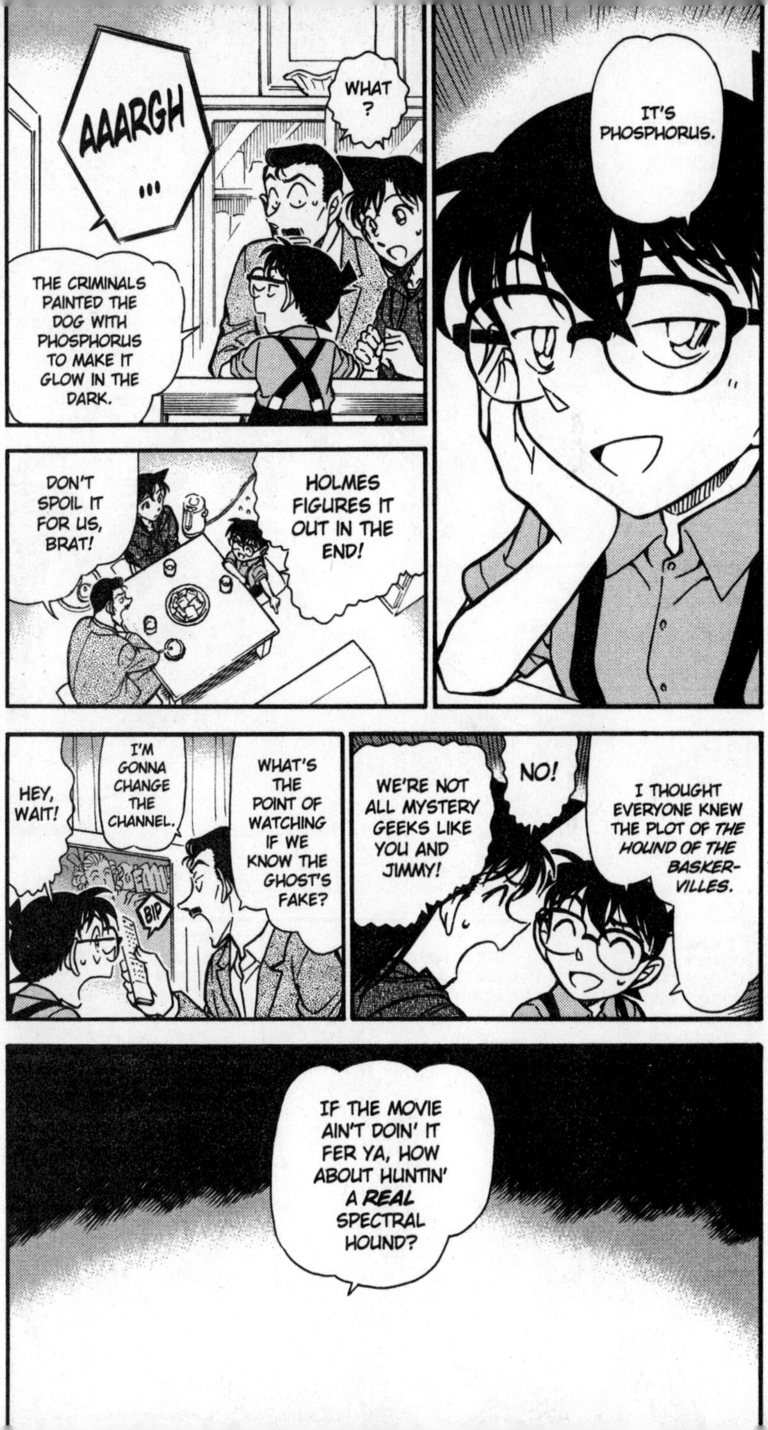
IT'S PHOSPHORUS.
WHAT ?
AAARGH ...
THE CRIMINALS PAINTED THE DOG WITH PHOSPHORUS TO MAKE IT GLOW IN THE DARK.
HOLMES FIGURES IT OUT IN THE END!
DON'T SPOIL IT FOR US, BRAT!
I THOUGHT EVERYONE KNEW THE PLOT OF *THE HOUND OF THE BASKERVILLES*.
NO!
WE'RE NOT ALL MYSTERY GEEKS LIKE YOU AND JIMMY!
WHAT'S THE POINT OF WATCHING IF WE KNOW THE GHOST'S FAKE?
I'M GONNA CHANGE THE CHANNEL.
HEY, WAIT!
BIP
IF THE MOVIE AIN'T DOIN' IT FER YA, HOW ABOUT HUNTIN' A ***REAL*** SPECTRAL HOUND?

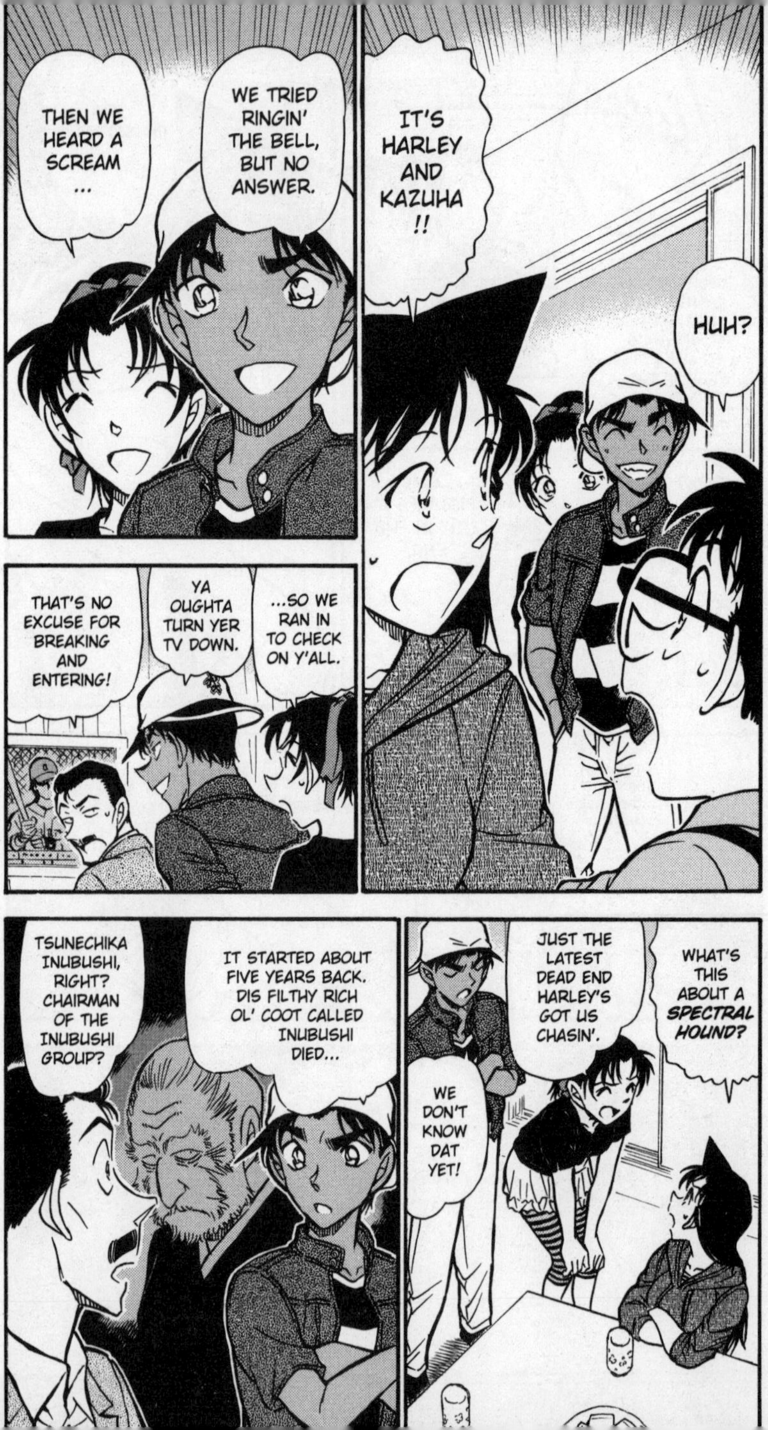
IT'S HARLEY AND KAZUHA !!
HUH?
WE TRIED RINGIN' THE BELL, BUT NO ANSWER.
THEN WE HEARD A SCREAM ...
...SO WE RAN IN TO CHECK ON Y'ALL.
YA OUGHTA TURN YER TV DOWN.
THAT'S NO EXCUSE FOR BREAKING AND ENTERING!
WHAT'S THIS ABOUT A SPECTRAL HOUND?
JUST THE LATEST DEAD END HARLEY'S GOT US CHASIN'.
WE DON'T KNOW DAT YET!
IT STARTED ABOUT FIVE YEARS BACK. DIS FILTHY RICH OL' COOT CALLED INUBUSHI DIED...
TSUNECHIKA INUBUSHI, RIGHT? CHAIRMAN OF THE INUBUSHI GROUP?

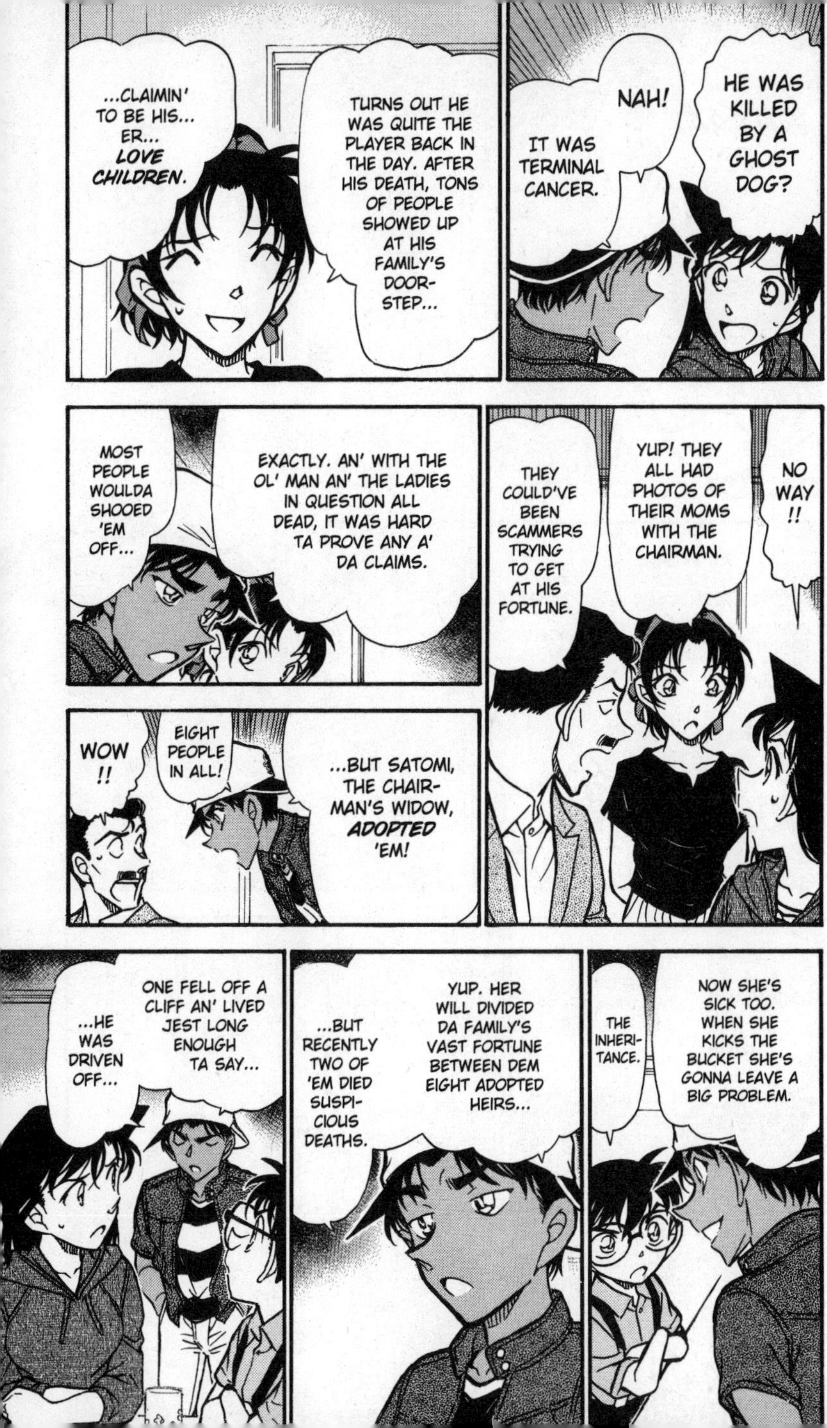
HE WAS KILLED BY A GHOST DOG?
NAH!
IT WAS TERMINAL CANCER.
TURNS OUT HE WAS QUITE THE PLAYER BACK IN THE DAY. AFTER HIS DEATH, TONS OF PEOPLE SHOWED UP AT HIS FAMILY'S DOOR-STEP...
...CLAIMIN' TO BE HIS... ER... *LOVE CHILDREN*.
NO WAY!!
YUP! THEY ALL HAD PHOTOS OF THEIR MOMS WITH THE CHAIRMAN.
THEY COULD'VE BEEN SCAMMERS TRYING TO GET AT HIS FORTUNE.
EXACTLY. AN' WITH THE OL' MAN AN' THE LADIES IN QUESTION ALL DEAD, IT WAS HARD TA PROVE ANY A' DA CLAIMS.
MOST PEOPLE WOULDA SHOOED 'EM OFF...
...BUT SATOMI, THE CHAIR-MAN'S WIDOW, *ADOPTED* 'EM!
EIGHT PEOPLE IN ALL!
WOW!!
NOW SHE'S SICK TOO. WHEN SHE KICKS THE BUCKET SHE'S GONNA LEAVE A BIG PROBLEM.
THE INHERI-TANCE.
YUP. HER WILL DIVIDED DA FAMILY'S VAST FORTUNE BETWEEN DEM EIGHT ADOPTED HEIRS...
...BUT RECENTLY TWO OF 'EM DIED SUSPI-CIOUS DEATHS.
ONE FELL OFF A CLIFF AN' LIVED JEST LONG ENOUGH TA SAY...
...HE WAS DRIVEN OFF...

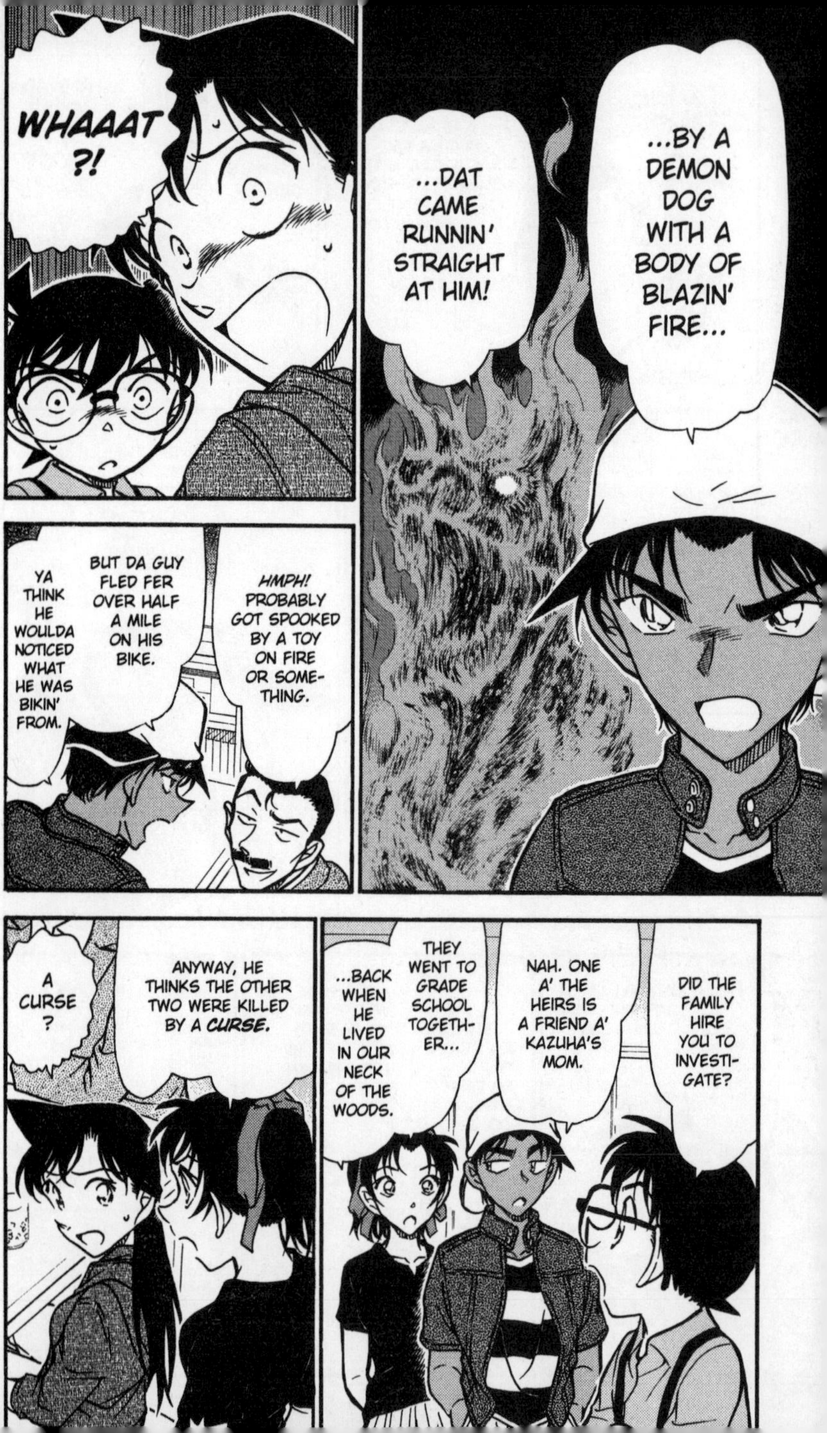
...BY A DEMON DOG WITH A BODY OF BLAZIN' FIRE...
...DAT CAME RUNNIN' STRAIGHT AT HIM!
WHAAAT ?!
HMPH! PROBABLY GOT SPOOKED BY A TOY ON FIRE OR SOME-THING.
BUT DA GUY FLED FER OVER HALF A MILE ON HIS BIKE.
YA THINK HE WOULDA NOTICED WHAT HE WAS BIKIN' FROM.
DID THE FAMILY HIRE YOU TO INVESTI-GATE?
NAH. ONE A' THE HEIRS IS A FRIEND A' KAZUHA'S MOM.
THEY WENT TO GRADE SCHOOL TOGETH-ER...
...BACK WHEN HE LIVED IN OUR NECK OF THE WOODS.
ANYWAY, HE THINKS THE OTHER TWO WERE KILLED BY A ***CURSE.***
A CURSE ?

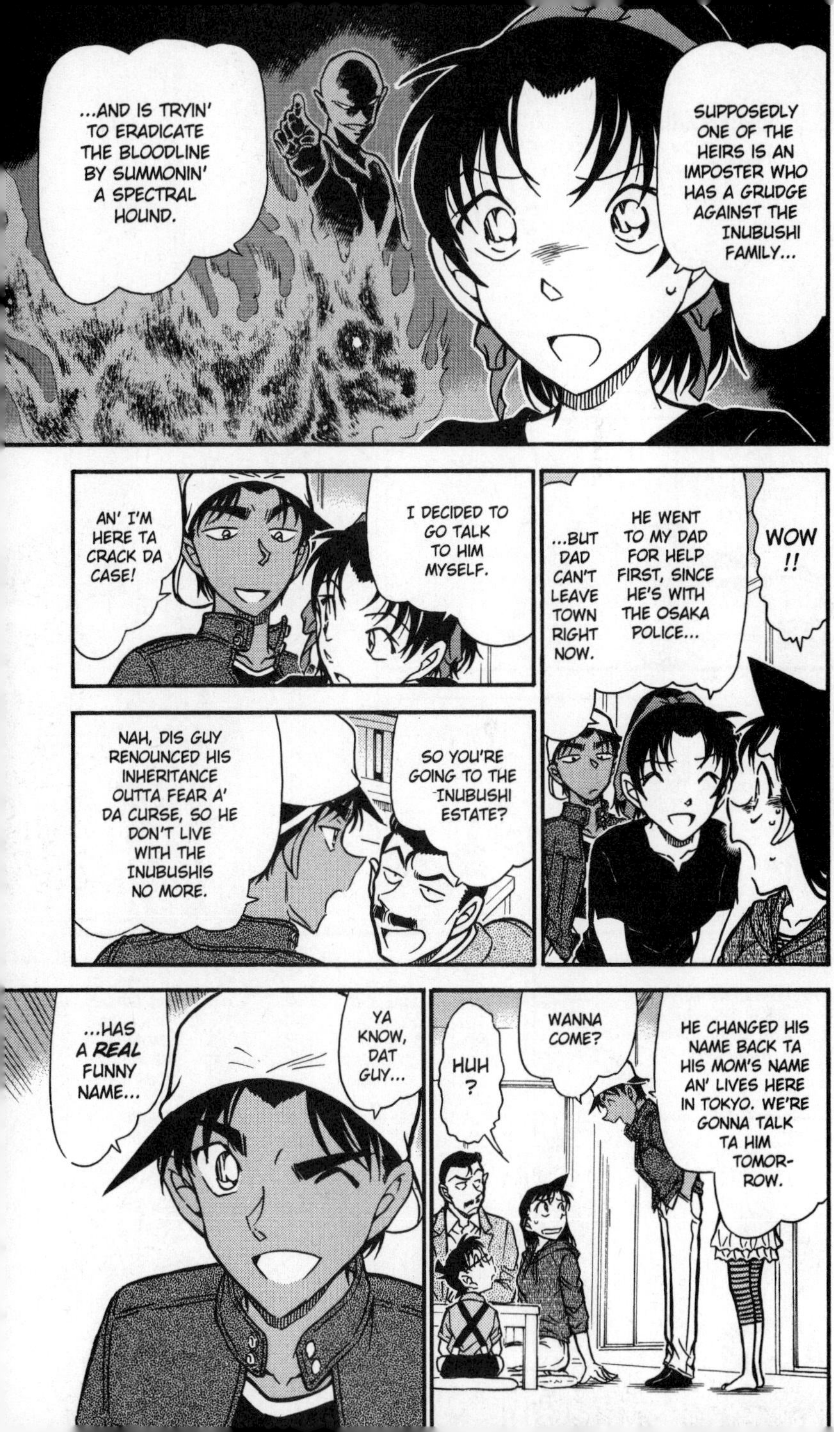
SUPPOSEDLY ONE OF THE HEIRS IS AN IMPOSTER WHO HAS A GRUDGE AGAINST THE INUBUSHI FAMILY...
...AND IS TRYIN' TO ERADICATE THE BLOODLINE BY SUMMONIN' A SPECTRAL HOUND.
WOW!!
HE WENT TO MY DAD FOR HELP FIRST, SINCE HE'S WITH THE OSAKA POLICE...
...BUT DAD CAN'T LEAVE TOWN RIGHT NOW.
I DECIDED TO GO TALK TO HIM MYSELF.
AN' I'M HERE TA CRACK DA CASE!
SO YOU'RE GOING TO THE INUBUSHI ESTATE?
NAH, DIS GUY RENOUNCED HIS INHERITANCE OUTTA FEAR A' DA CURSE, SO HE DON'T LIVE WITH THE INUBUSHIS NO MORE.
HE CHANGED HIS NAME BACK TA HIS MOM'S NAME AN' LIVES HERE IN TOKYO. WE'RE GONNA TALK TA HIM TOMORROW.
WANNA COME?
HUH?
YA KNOW, DAT GUY...
...HAS A ***REAL*** FUNNY NAME...

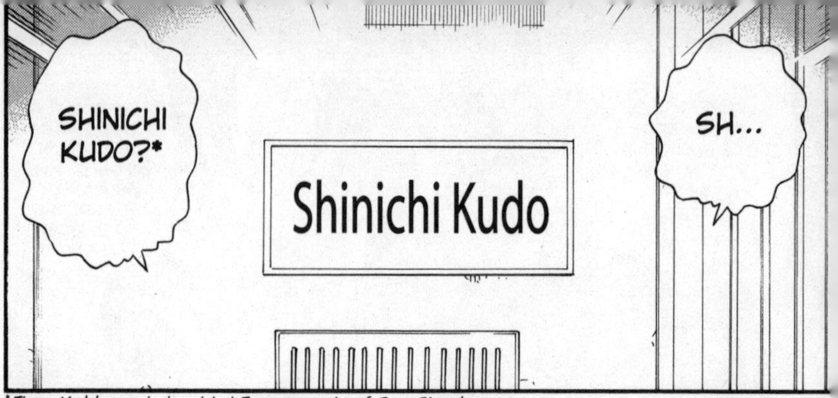
SH...
Shinichi Kudo
SHINICHI KUDO?*

*Jimmy Kudo's name in the original Japanese version of *Case Closed*.

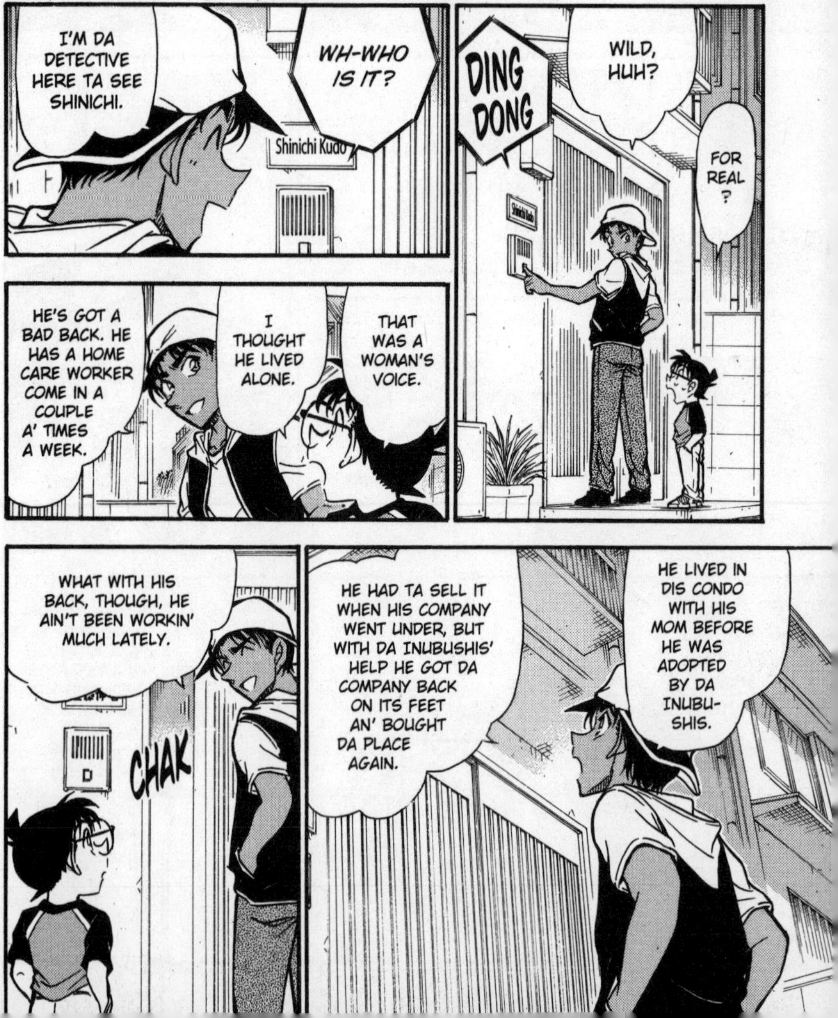
WILD, HUH?
FOR REAL?
DING DONG
Shinichi Kudo
WH-WHO IS IT?
I'M DA DETECTIVE HERE TA SEE SHINICHI.
Shinichi Kudo
THAT WAS A WOMAN'S VOICE.
I THOUGHT HE LIVED ALONE.
HE'S GOT A BAD BACK. HE HAS A HOME CARE WORKER COME IN A COUPLE A' TIMES A WEEK.
HE LIVED IN DIS CONDO WITH HIS MOM BEFORE HE WAS ADOPTED BY DA INUBUSHIS.
HE HAD TA SELL IT WHEN HIS COMPANY WENT UNDER, BUT WITH DA INUBUSHIS' HELP HE GOT DA COMPANY BACK ON ITS FEET AN' BOUGHT DA PLACE AGAIN.
WHAT WITH HIS BACK, THOUGH, HE AIN'T BEEN WORKIN' MUCH LATELY.
CHAK

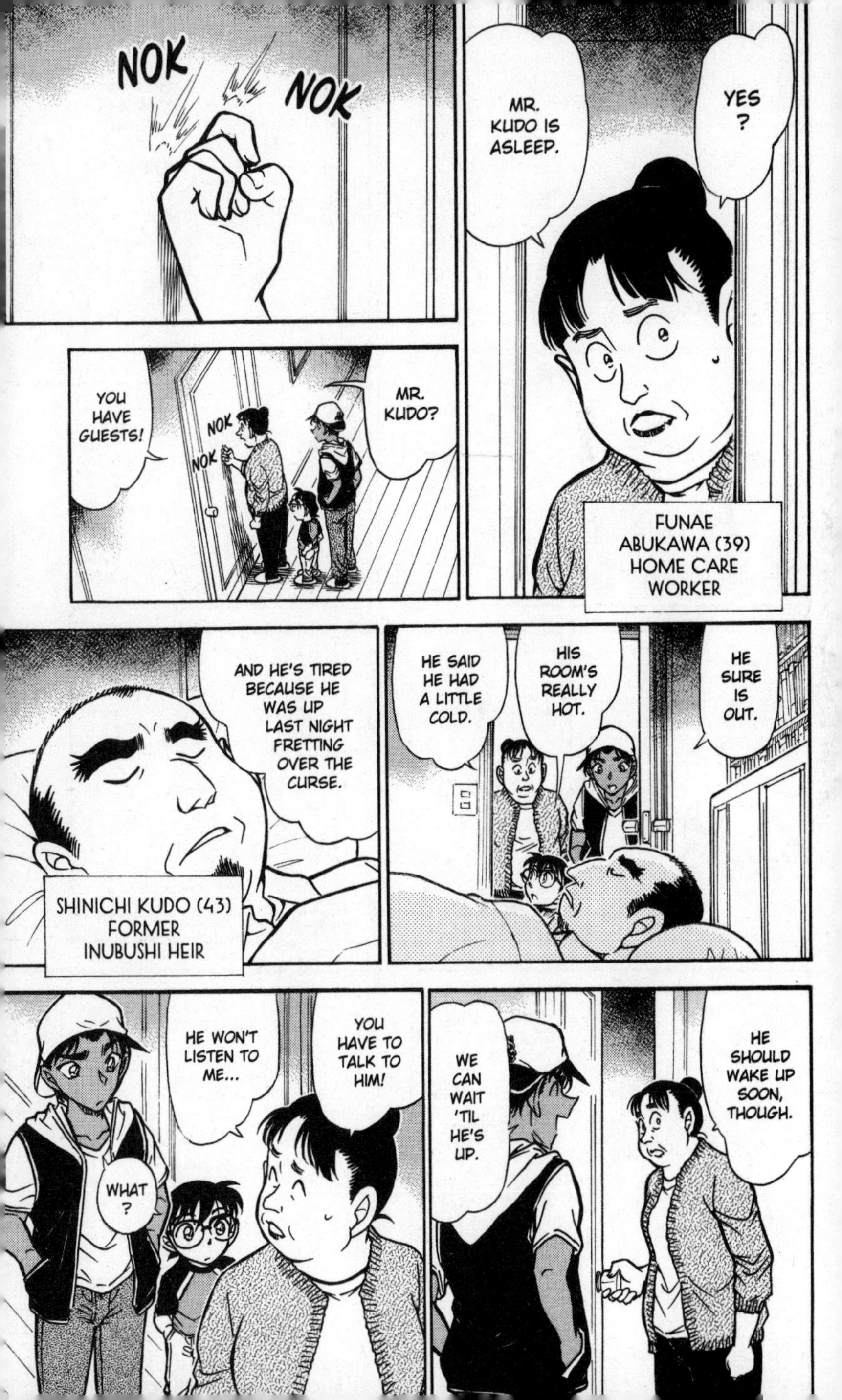
YES?
MR. KUDO IS ASLEEP.
FUNAE ABUKAWA (39) HOME CARE WORKER
NOK
NOK
MR. KUDO?
NOK
NOK
YOU HAVE GUESTS!
HE SURE IS OUT.
HIS ROOM'S REALLY HOT.
HE SAID HE HAD A LITTLE COLD.
AND HE'S TIRED BECAUSE HE WAS UP LAST NIGHT FRETTING OVER THE CURSE.
SHINICHI KUDO (43) FORMER INUBUSHI HEIR
HE SHOULD WAKE UP SOON, THOUGH.
WE CAN WAIT 'TIL HE'S UP.
YOU HAVE TO TALK TO HIM!
HE WON'T LISTEN TO ME...
WHAT?

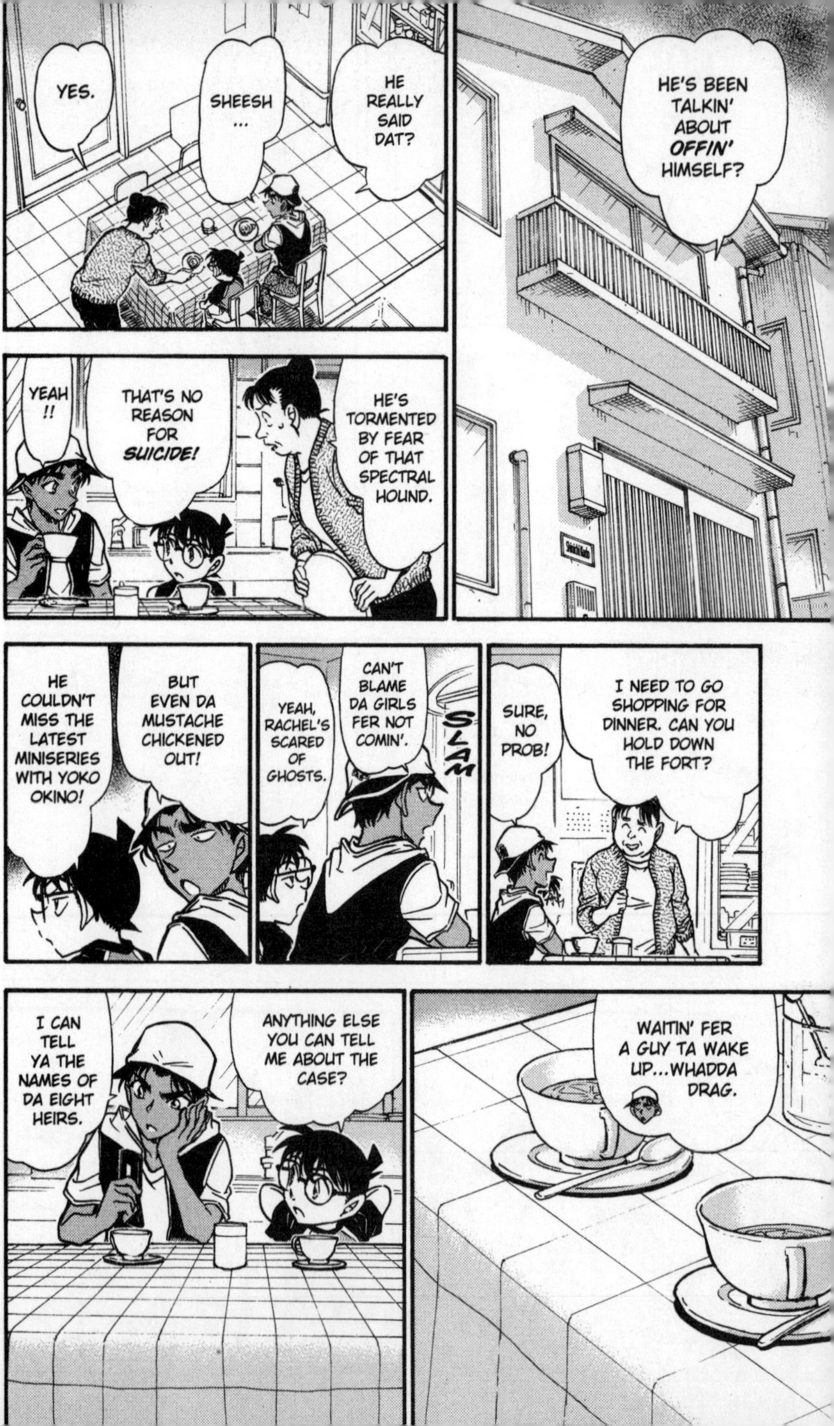
HE'S BEEN TALKIN' ABOUT *OFFIN'* HIMSELF?
HE REALLY SAID DAT?
SHEESH...
YES.
HE'S TORMENTED BY FEAR OF THAT SPECTRAL HOUND.
THAT'S NO REASON FOR *SUICIDE!*
YEAH!!
I NEED TO GO SHOPPING FOR DINNER. CAN YOU HOLD DOWN THE FORT?
SURE, NO PROB!
SLAM
CAN'T BLAME DA GIRLS FER NOT COMIN'.
YEAH, RACHEL'S SCARED OF GHOSTS.
BUT EVEN DA MUSTACHE CHICKENED OUT!
HE COULDN'T MISS THE LATEST MINISERIES WITH YOKO OKINO!
WAITIN' FER A GUY TA WAKE UP...WHADDA DRAG.
ANYTHING ELSE YOU CAN TELL ME ABOUT THE CASE?
I CAN TELL YA THE NAMES OF DA EIGHT HEIRS.

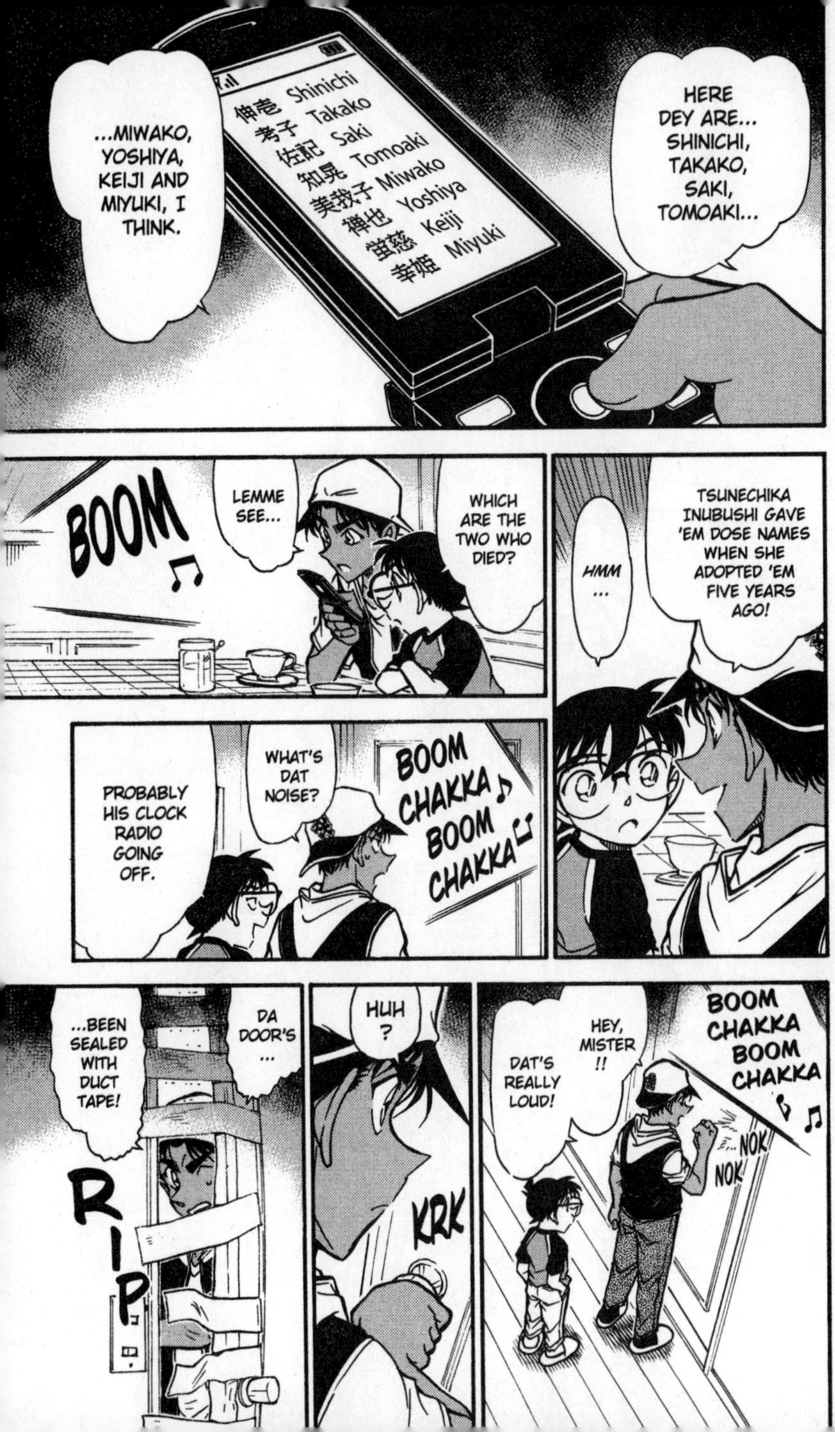
HERE DEY ARE... SHINICHI, TAKAKO, SAKI, TOMOAKI...
伸壱 Shinichi
孝子 Takako
佐記 Saki
知晃 Tomoaki
美我子 Miwako
禅也 Yoshiya
笛慈 Keiji
幸姫 Miyuki
...MIWAKO, YOSHIYA, KEIJI AND MIYUKI, I THINK.
TSUNECHIKA INUBUSHI GAVE 'EM DOSE NAMES WHEN SHE ADOPTED 'EM FIVE YEARS AGO!
HMM ...
WHICH ARE THE TWO WHO DIED?
LEMME SEE...
BOOM
BOOM CHAKKA BOOM CHAKKA
WHAT'S DAT NOISE?
PROBABLY HIS CLOCK RADIO GOING OFF.
BOOM CHAKKA BOOM CHAKKA
NOK NOK
HEY, MISTER !!
DAT'S REALLY LOUD!
HUH ?
KRK
DA DOOR'S ...
...BEEN SEALED WITH DUCT TAPE!
RIP

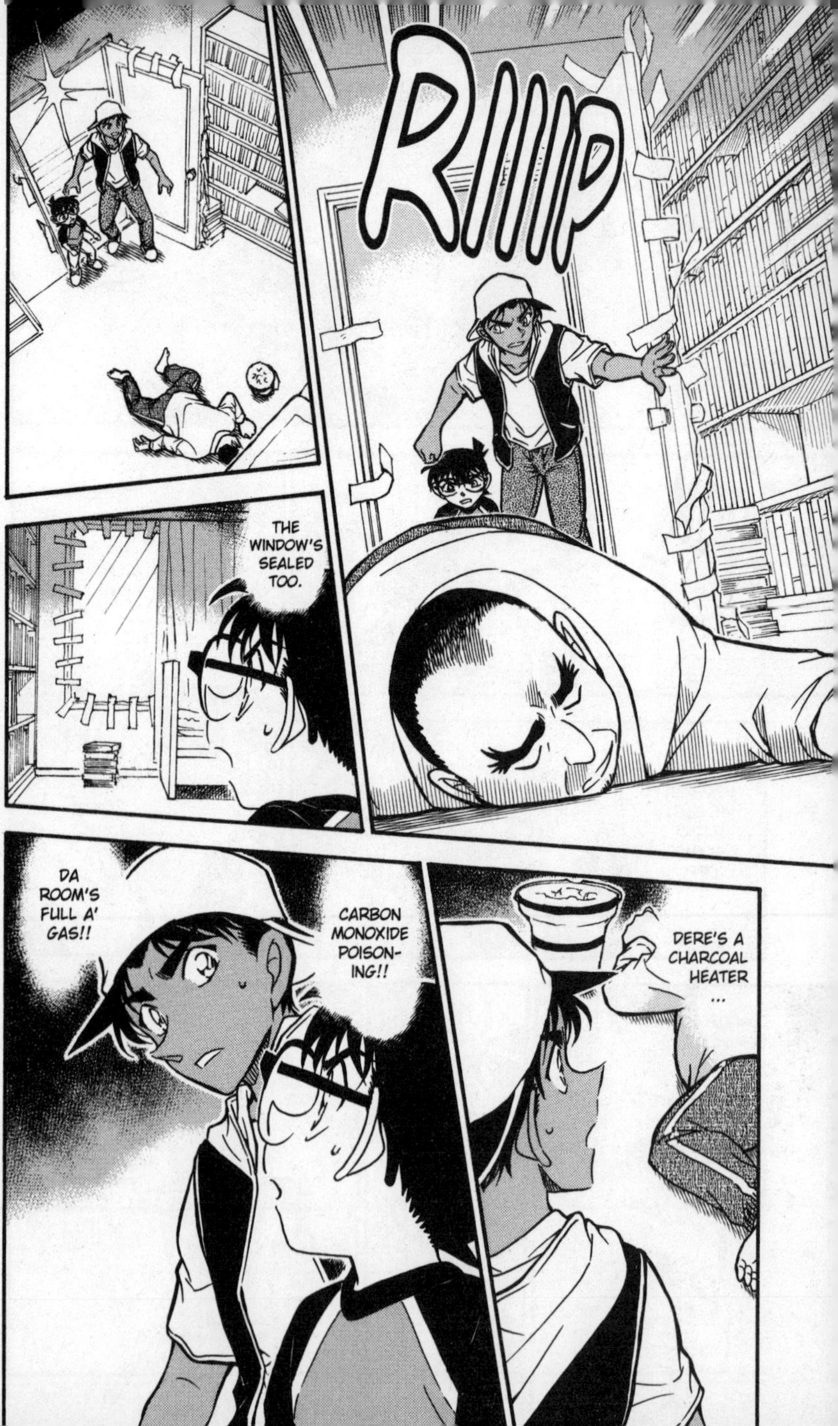
RIIIP
THE WINDOW'S SEALED TOO.
DERE'S A CHARCOAL HEATER ...
CARBON MONOXIDE POISON-ING!!
DA ROOM'S FULL A' GAS!!

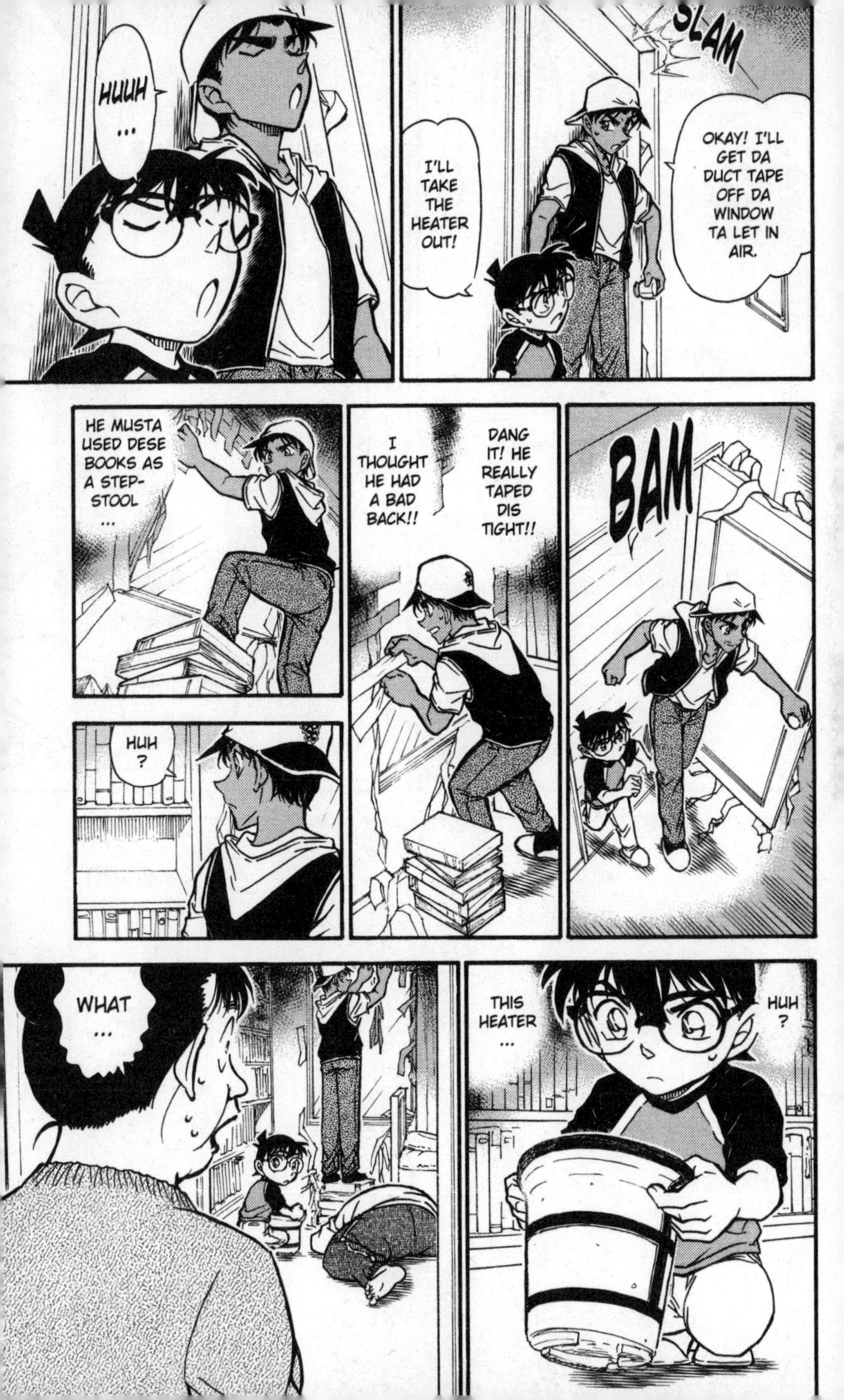
SLAM
OKAY! I'LL GET DA DUCT TAPE OFF DA WINDOW TA LET IN AIR.
I'LL TAKE THE HEATER OUT!
HUUH ...
BAM
DANG IT! HE REALLY TAPED DIS TIGHT!!
I THOUGHT HE HAD A BAD BACK!!
HE MUSTA USED DESE BOOKS AS A STEP-STOOL ...
HUH ?
HUH ?
THIS HEATER ...
WHAT ...

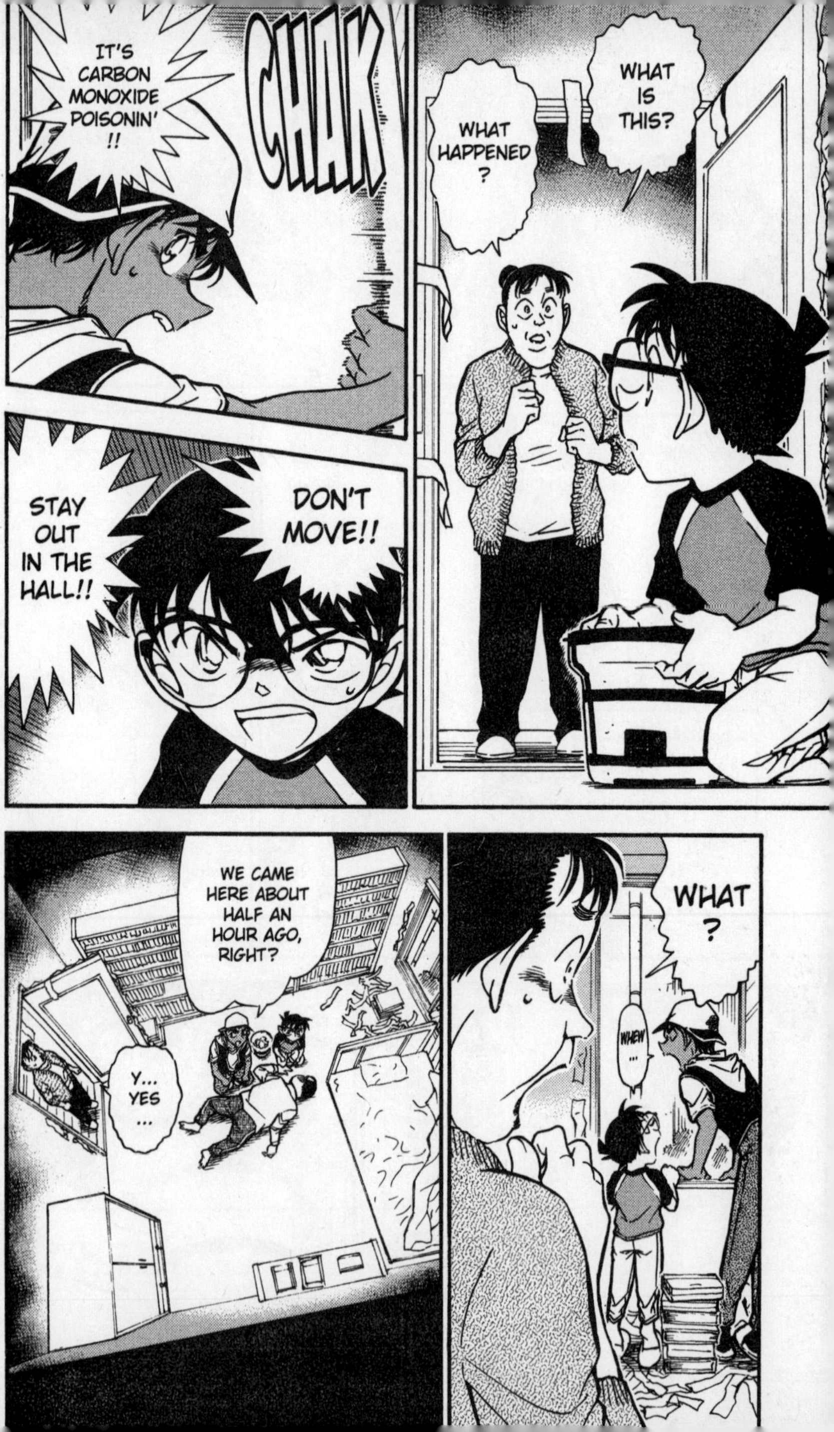
WHAT IS THIS?
WHAT HAPPENED?
CHAK
IT'S CARBON MONOXIDE POISONIN'!!
DON'T MOVE!!
STAY OUT IN THE HALL!!
WHAT?
WHEW...
WE CAME HERE ABOUT HALF AN HOUR AGO, RIGHT?
Y... YES...

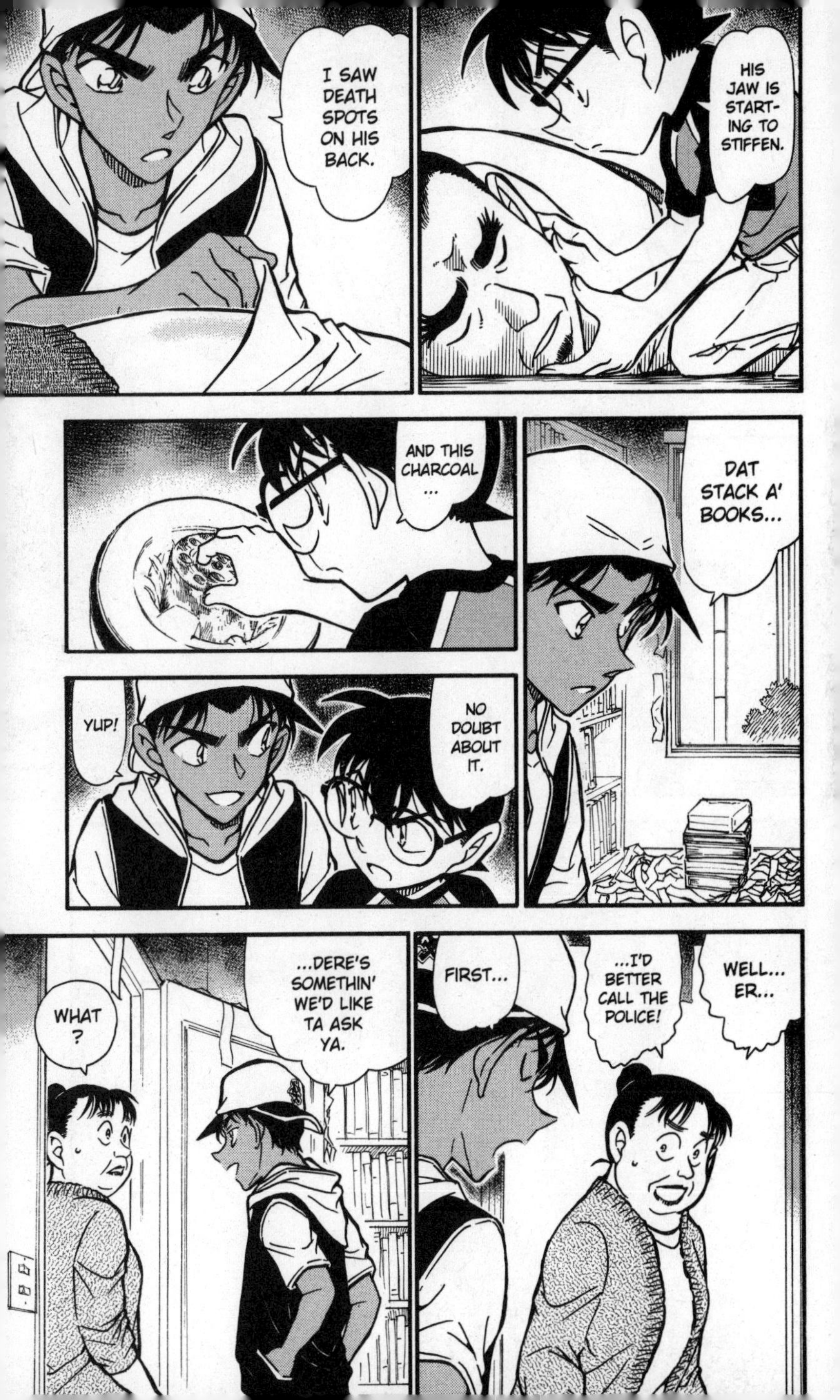
HIS JAW IS STARTING TO STIFFEN.
I SAW DEATH SPOTS ON HIS BACK.
DAT STACK A' BOOKS...
AND THIS CHARCOAL...
NO DOUBT ABOUT IT.
YUP!
WELL... ER...
...I'D BETTER CALL THE POLICE!
FIRST...
...DERE'S SOMETHIN' WE'D LIKE TA ASK YA.
WHAT?

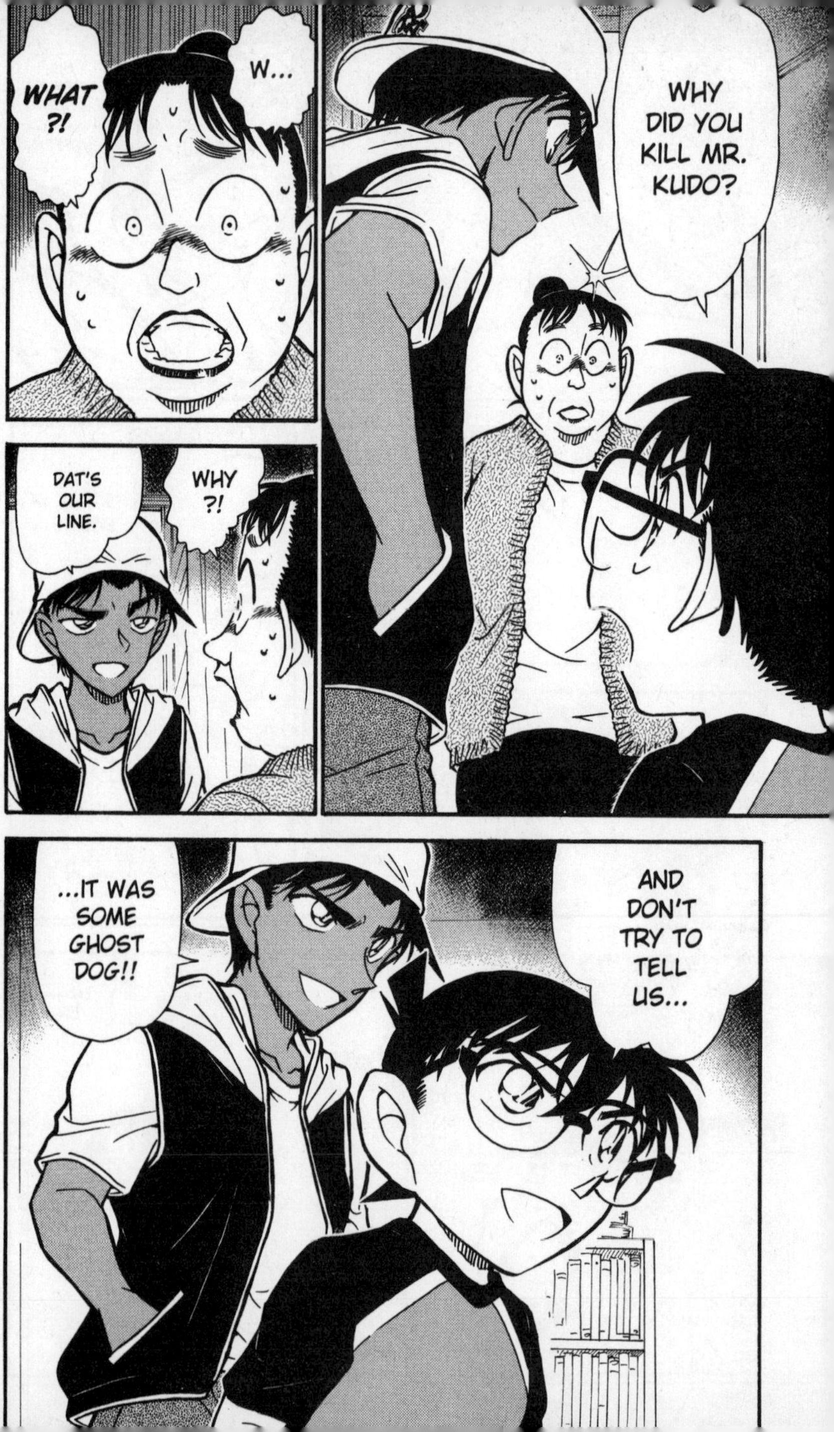
WHY DID YOU KILL MR. KUDO?
W...
WHAT?!
WHY?!
DAT'S OUR LINE.
AND DON'T TRY TO TELL US...
...IT WAS SOME GHOST DOG!!

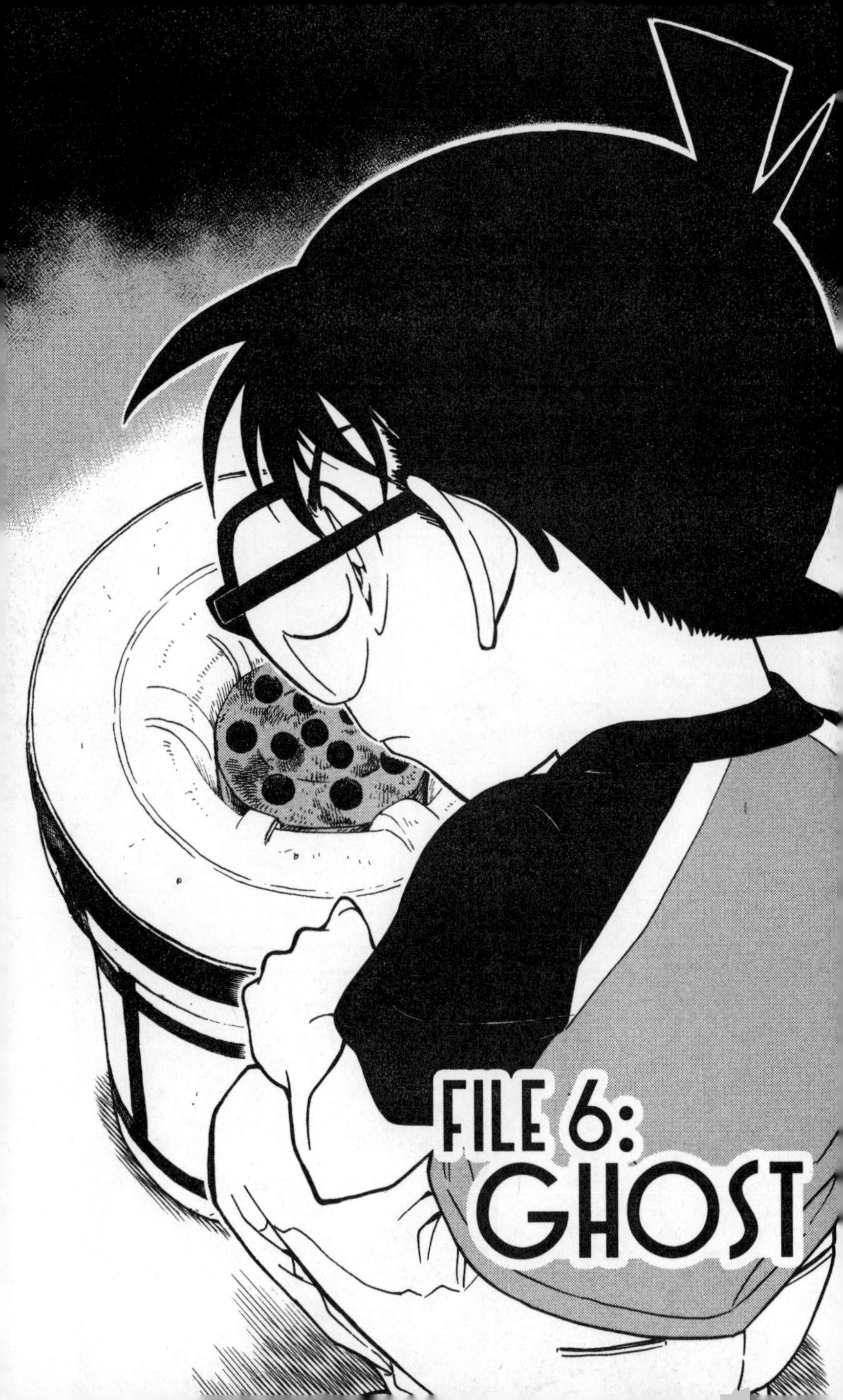
FILE 6:
GHOST

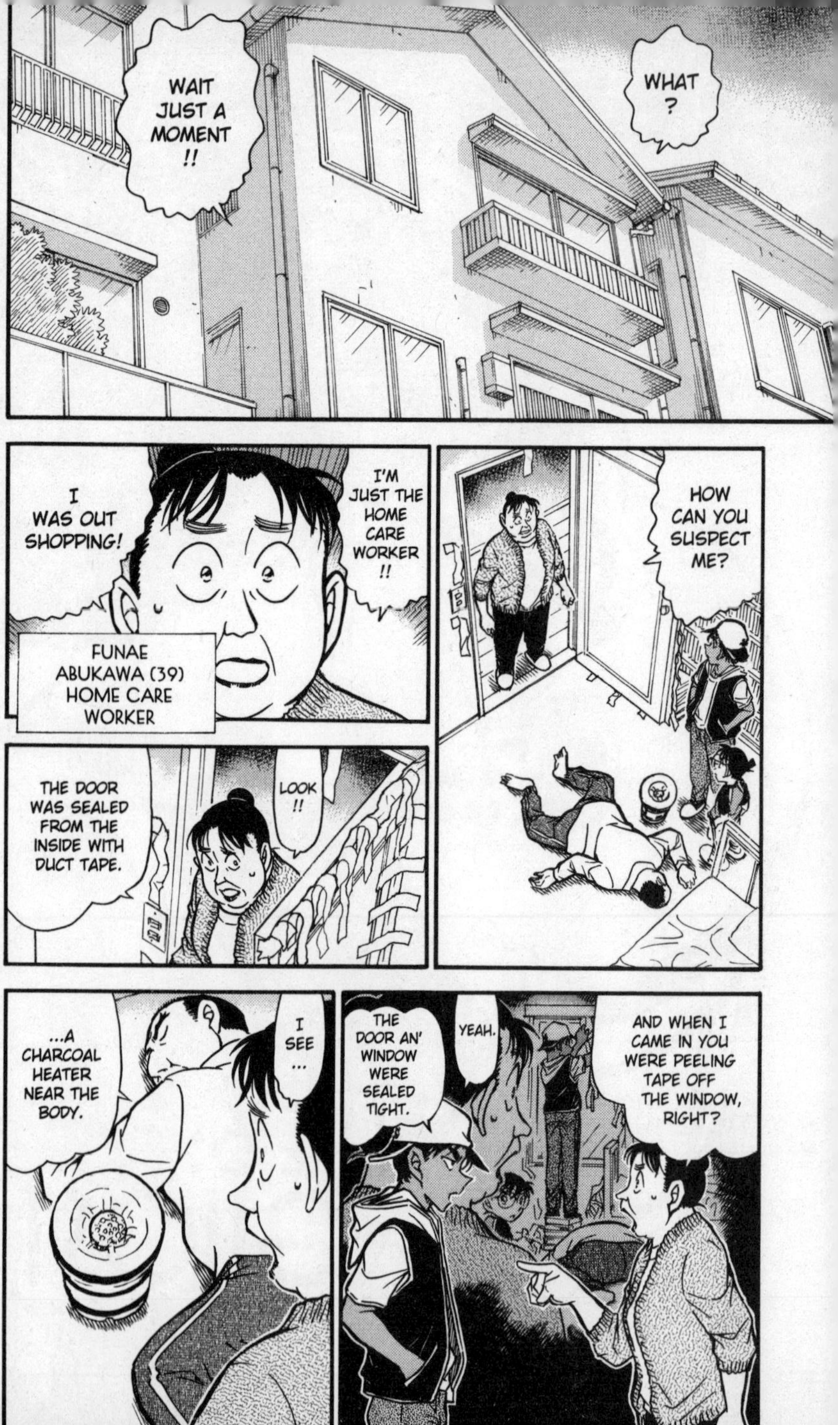
WHAT ?
WAIT JUST A MOMENT !!
HOW CAN YOU SUSPECT ME?
I'M JUST THE HOME CARE WORKER !!
I WAS OUT SHOPPING!
FUNAE ABUKAWA (39) HOME CARE WORKER
LOOK !!
THE DOOR WAS SEALED FROM THE INSIDE WITH DUCT TAPE.
AND WHEN I CAME IN YOU WERE PEELING TAPE OFF THE WINDOW, RIGHT?
YEAH.
THE DOOR AN' WINDOW WERE SEALED TIGHT.
I SEE ...
...A CHARCOAL HEATER NEAR THE BODY.

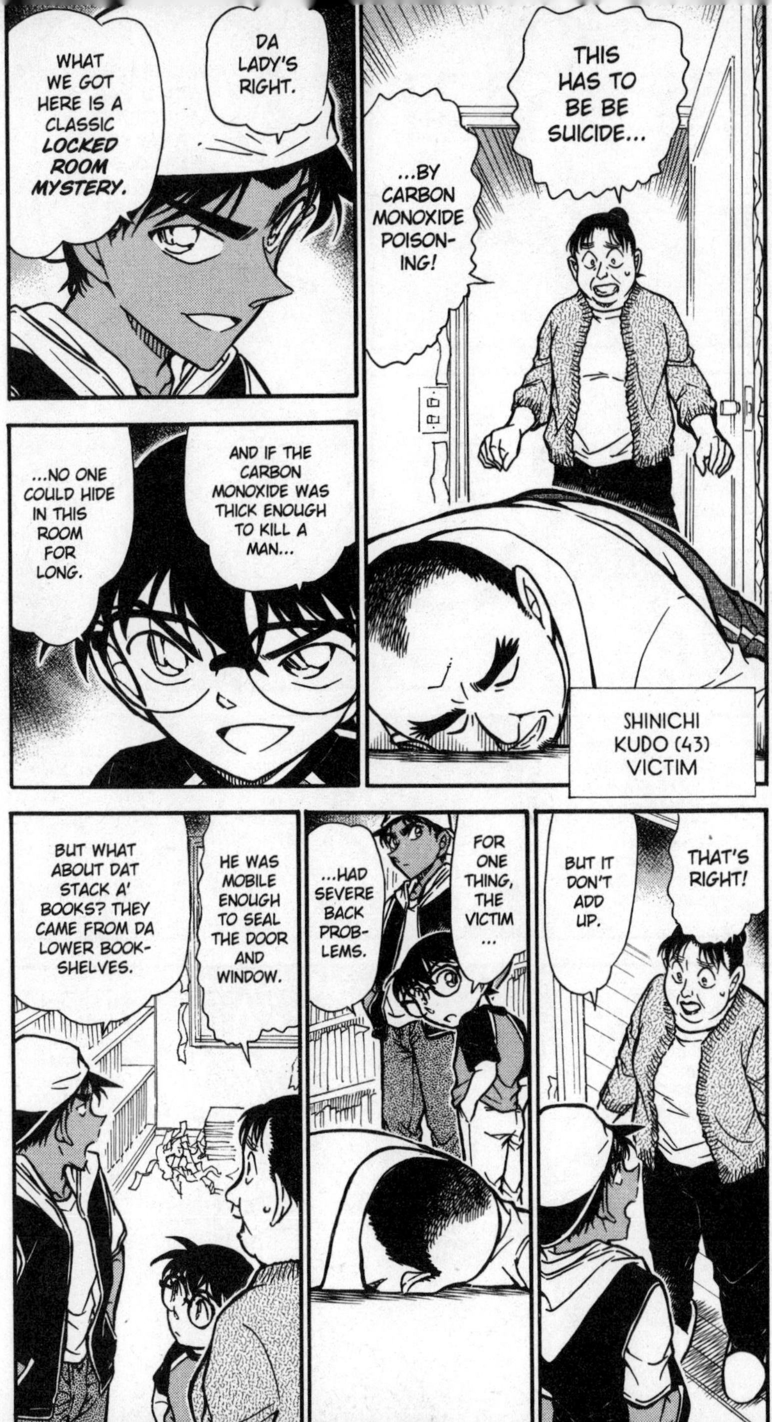
THIS HAS TO BE BE SUICIDE...
...BY CARBON MONOXIDE POISON-ING!
DA LADY'S RIGHT.
WHAT WE GOT HERE IS A CLASSIC **LOCKED ROOM MYSTERY.**
SHINICHI KUDO (43) VICTIM
AND IF THE CARBON MONOXIDE WAS THICK ENOUGH TO KILL A MAN...
...NO ONE COULD HIDE IN THIS ROOM FOR LONG.
THAT'S RIGHT!
BUT IT DON'T ADD UP.
FOR ONE THING, THE VICTIM...
...HAD SEVERE BACK PROB-LEMS.
HE WAS MOBILE ENOUGH TO SEAL THE DOOR AND WINDOW.
BUT WHAT ABOUT DAT STACK A' BOOKS? THEY CAME FROM DA LOWER BOOK-SHELVES.

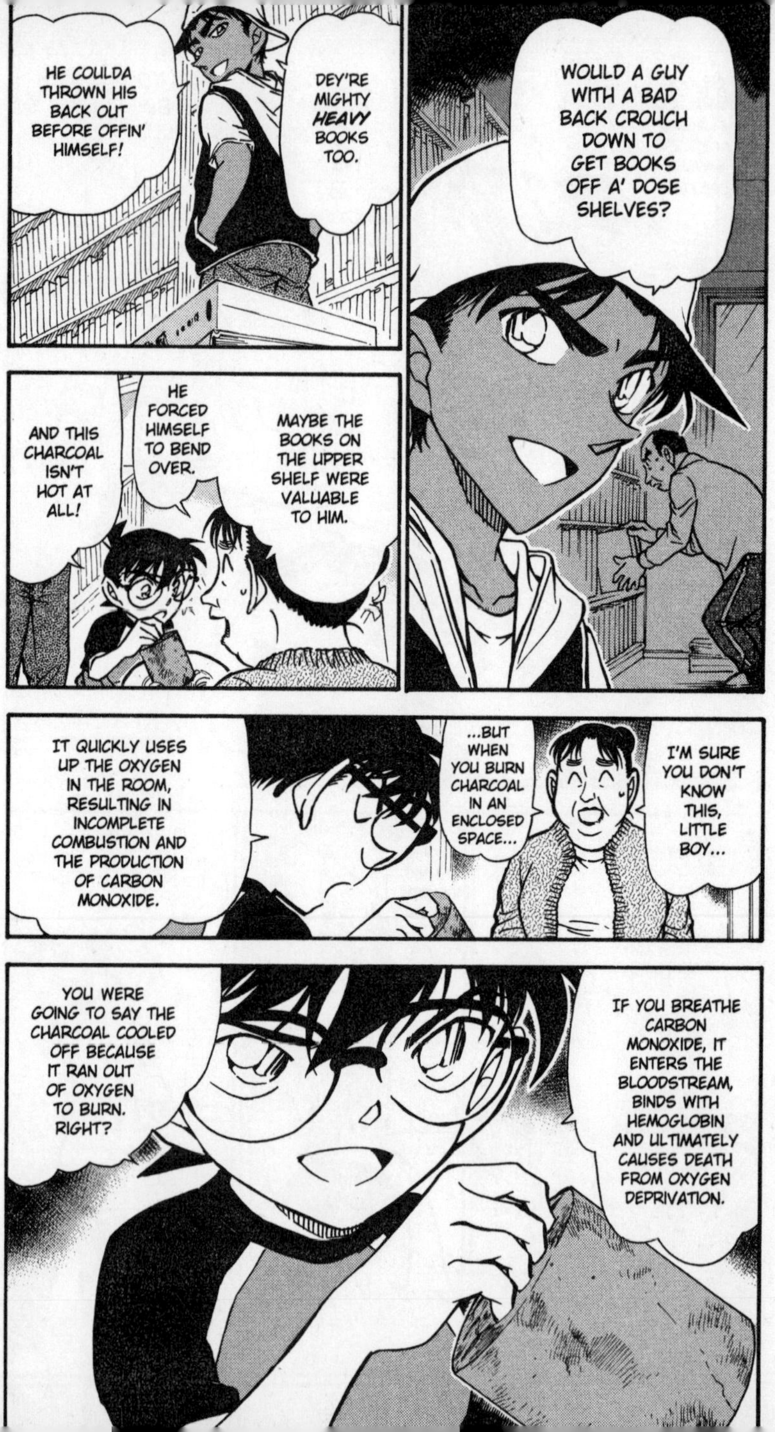
WOULD A GUY WITH A BAD BACK CROUCH DOWN TO GET BOOKS OFF A' DOSE SHELVES?
DEY'RE MIGHTY *HEAVY* BOOKS TOO.
HE COULDA THROWN HIS BACK OUT BEFORE OFFIN' HIMSELF!
MAYBE THE BOOKS ON THE UPPER SHELF WERE VALUABLE TO HIM.
HE FORCED HIMSELF TO BEND OVER.
AND THIS CHARCOAL ISN'T HOT AT ALL!
I'M SURE YOU DON'T KNOW THIS, LITTLE BOY...
...BUT WHEN YOU BURN CHARCOAL IN AN ENCLOSED SPACE...
IT QUICKLY USES UP THE OXYGEN IN THE ROOM, RESULTING IN INCOMPLETE COMBUSTION AND THE PRODUCTION OF CARBON MONOXIDE.
IF YOU BREATHE CARBON MONOXIDE, IT ENTERS THE BLOODSTREAM, BINDS WITH HEMOGLOBIN AND ULTIMATELY CAUSES DEATH FROM OXYGEN DEPRIVATION.
YOU WERE GOING TO SAY THE CHARCOAL COOLED OFF BECAUSE IT RAN OUT OF OXYGEN TO BURN. RIGHT?

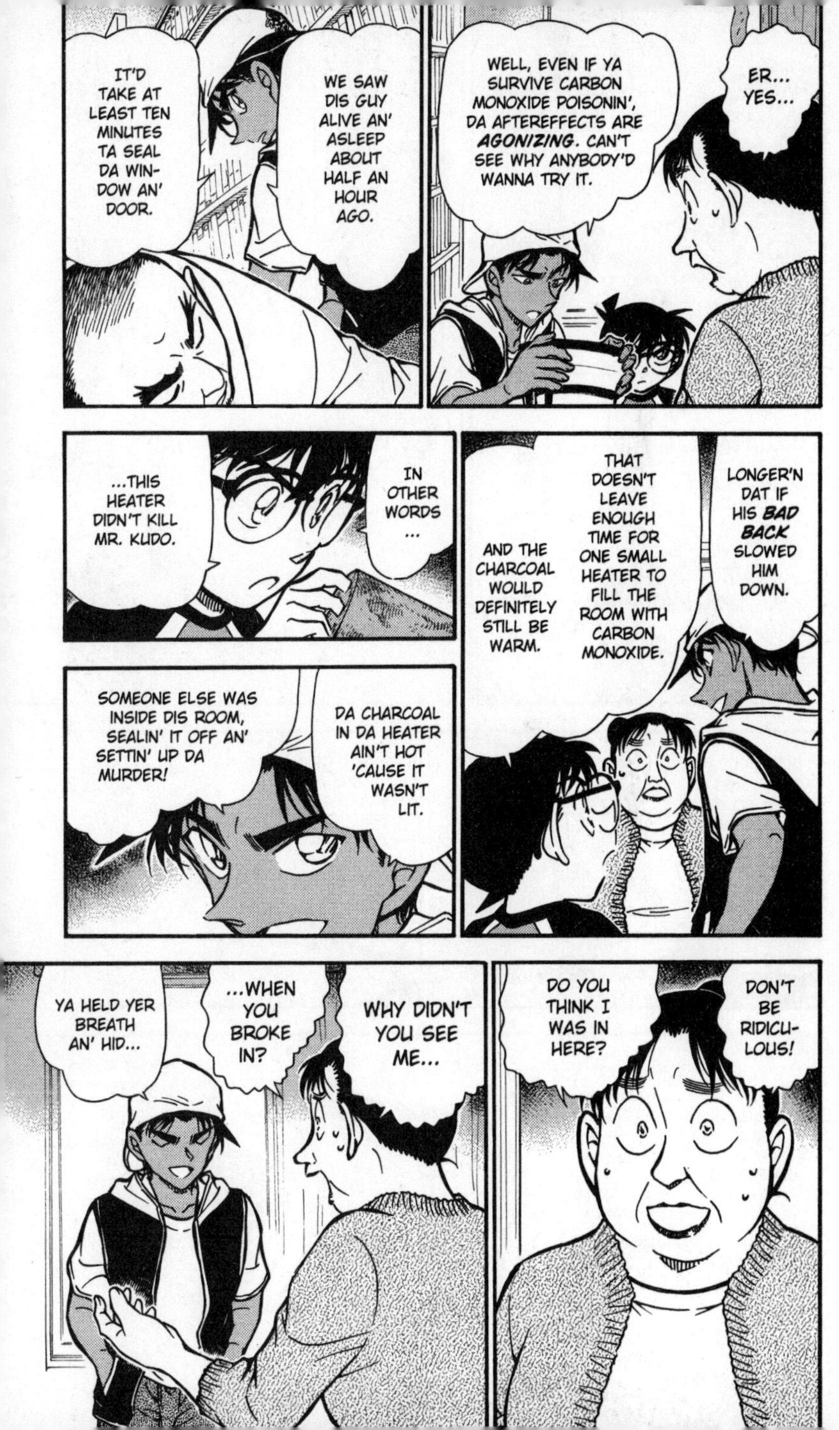
ER... YES...
WELL, EVEN IF YA SURVIVE CARBON MONOXIDE POISONIN', DA AFTEREFFECTS ARE ***AGONIZING***. CAN'T SEE WHY ANYBODY'D WANNA TRY IT.
WE SAW DIS GUY ALIVE AN' ASLEEP ABOUT HALF AN HOUR AGO.
IT'D TAKE AT LEAST TEN MINUTES TA SEAL DA WINDOW AN' DOOR.
LONGER'N DAT IF HIS ***BAD BACK*** SLOWED HIM DOWN.
THAT DOESN'T LEAVE ENOUGH TIME FOR ONE SMALL HEATER TO FILL THE ROOM WITH CARBON MONOXIDE.
AND THE CHARCOAL WOULD DEFINITELY STILL BE WARM.
IN OTHER WORDS ...
...THIS HEATER DIDN'T KILL MR. KUDO.
DA CHARCOAL IN DA HEATER AIN'T HOT 'CAUSE IT WASN'T LIT.
SOMEONE ELSE WAS INSIDE DIS ROOM, SEALIN' IT OFF AN' SETTIN' UP DA MURDER!
DON'T BE RIDICULOUS!
DO YOU THINK I WAS IN HERE?
WHY DIDN'T YOU SEE ME...
...WHEN YOU BROKE IN?
YA HELD YER BREATH AN' HID...

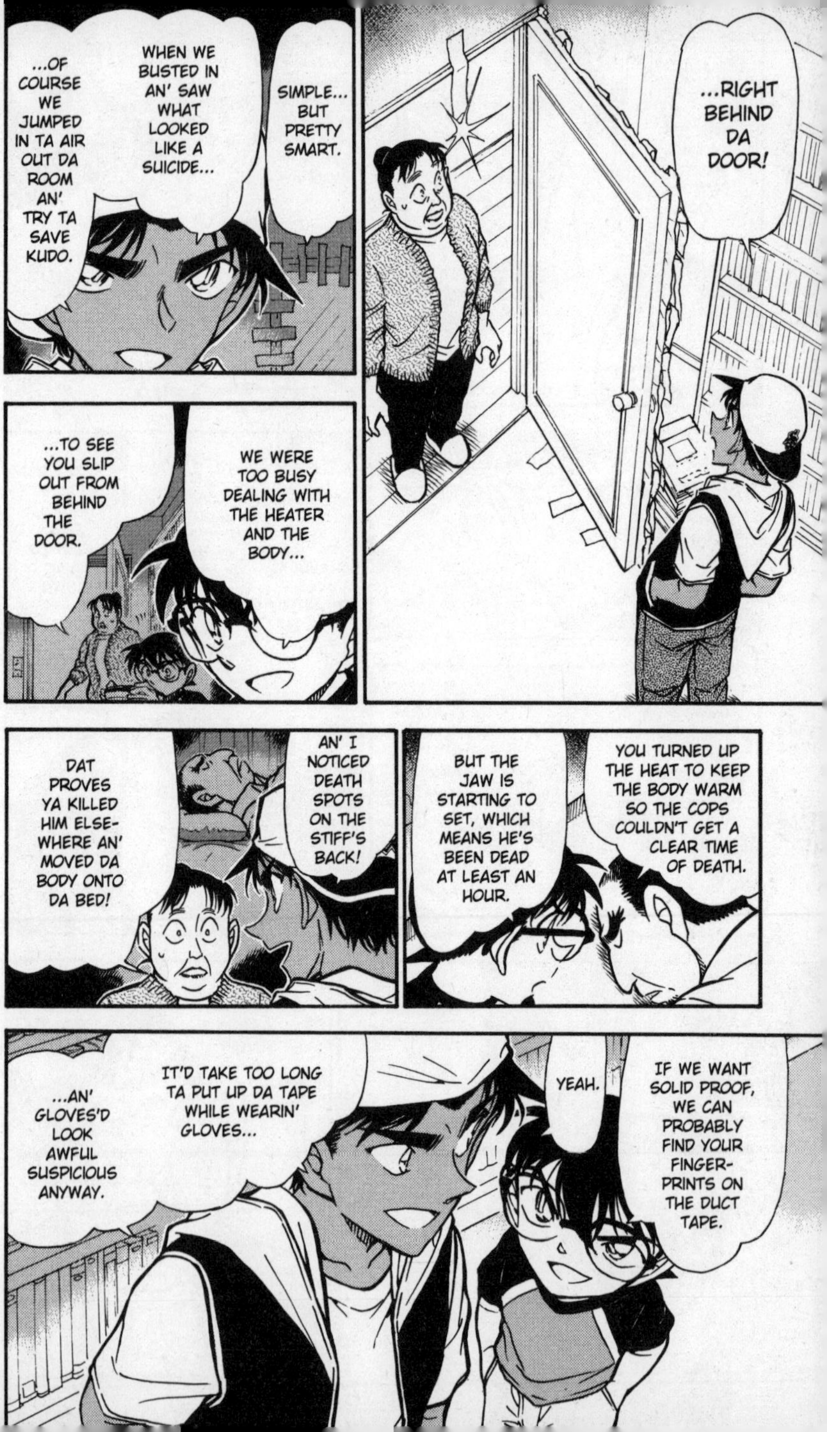
...RIGHT BEHIND DA DOOR!
SIMPLE... BUT PRETTY SMART.
WHEN WE BUSTED IN AN' SAW WHAT LOOKED LIKE A SUICIDE...
...OF COURSE WE JUMPED IN TA AIR OUT DA ROOM AN' TRY TA SAVE KUDO.
WE WERE TOO BUSY DEALING WITH THE HEATER AND THE BODY...
...TO SEE YOU SLIP OUT FROM BEHIND THE DOOR.
YOU TURNED UP THE HEAT TO KEEP THE BODY WARM SO THE COPS COULDN'T GET A CLEAR TIME OF DEATH.
BUT THE JAW IS STARTING TO SET, WHICH MEANS HE'S BEEN DEAD AT LEAST AN HOUR.
AN' I NOTICED DEATH SPOTS ON THE STIFF'S BACK!
DAT PROVES YA KILLED HIM ELSE-WHERE AN' MOVED DA BODY ONTO DA BED!
IF WE WANT SOLID PROOF, WE CAN PROBABLY FIND YOUR FINGER-PRINTS ON THE DUCT TAPE.
YEAH.
IT'D TAKE TOO LONG TA PUT UP DA TAPE WHILE WEARIN' GLOVES...
...AN' GLOVES'D LOOK AWFUL SUSPICIOUS ANYWAY.

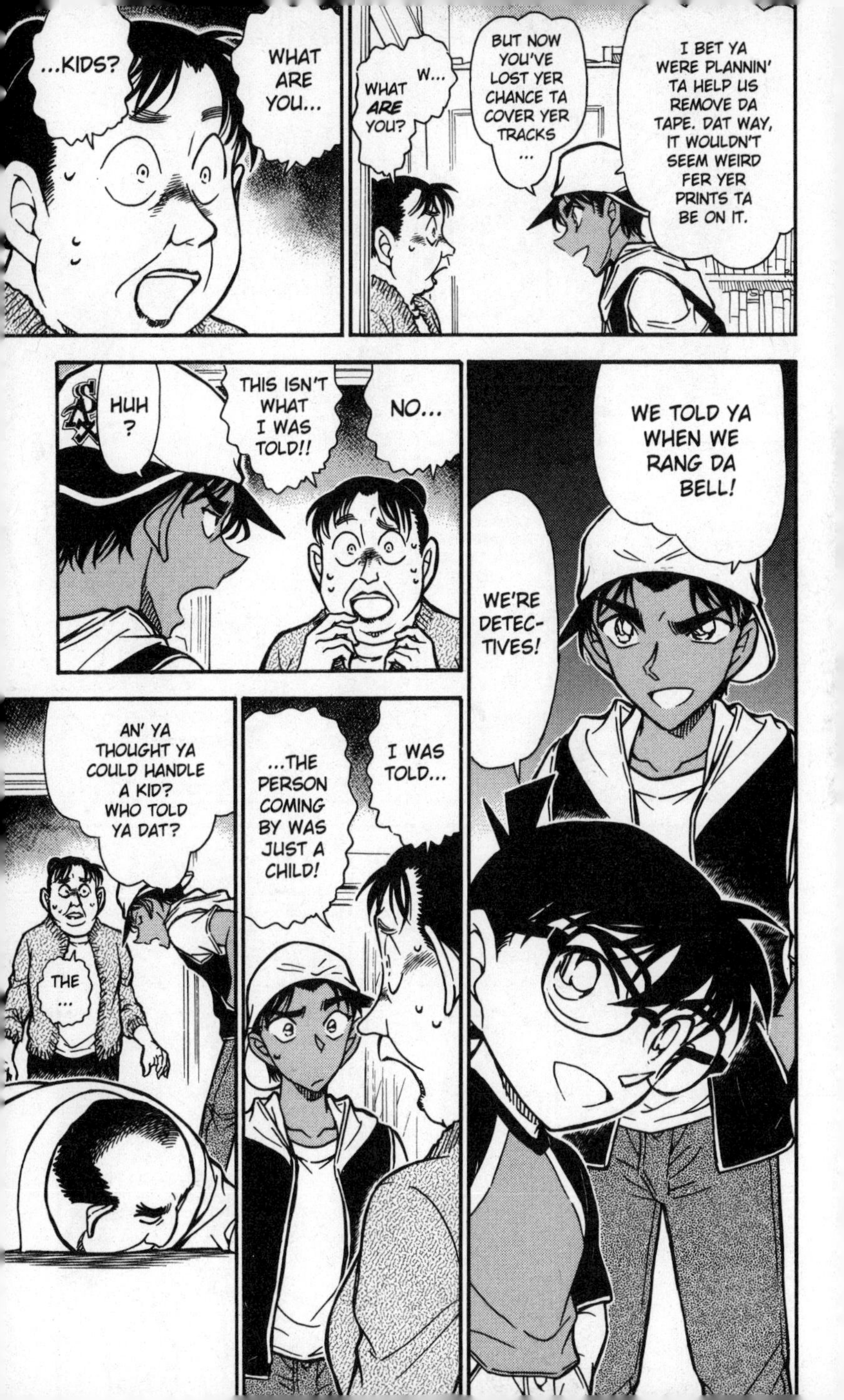
I BET YA WERE PLANNIN' TA HELP US REMOVE DA TAPE. DAT WAY, IT WOULDN'T SEEM WEIRD FER YER PRINTS TA BE ON IT.
BUT NOW YOU'VE LOST YER CHANCE TA COVER YER TRACKS ...
W... WHAT *ARE* YOU?
WHAT ARE YOU...
...KIDS?
WE TOLD YA WHEN WE RANG DA BELL!
WE'RE DETEC-TIVES!
NO...
THIS ISN'T WHAT I WAS TOLD!!
HUH?
I WAS TOLD...
...THE PERSON COMING BY WAS JUST A CHILD!
AN' YA THOUGHT YA COULD HANDLE A KID? WHO TOLD YA DAT?
THE ...

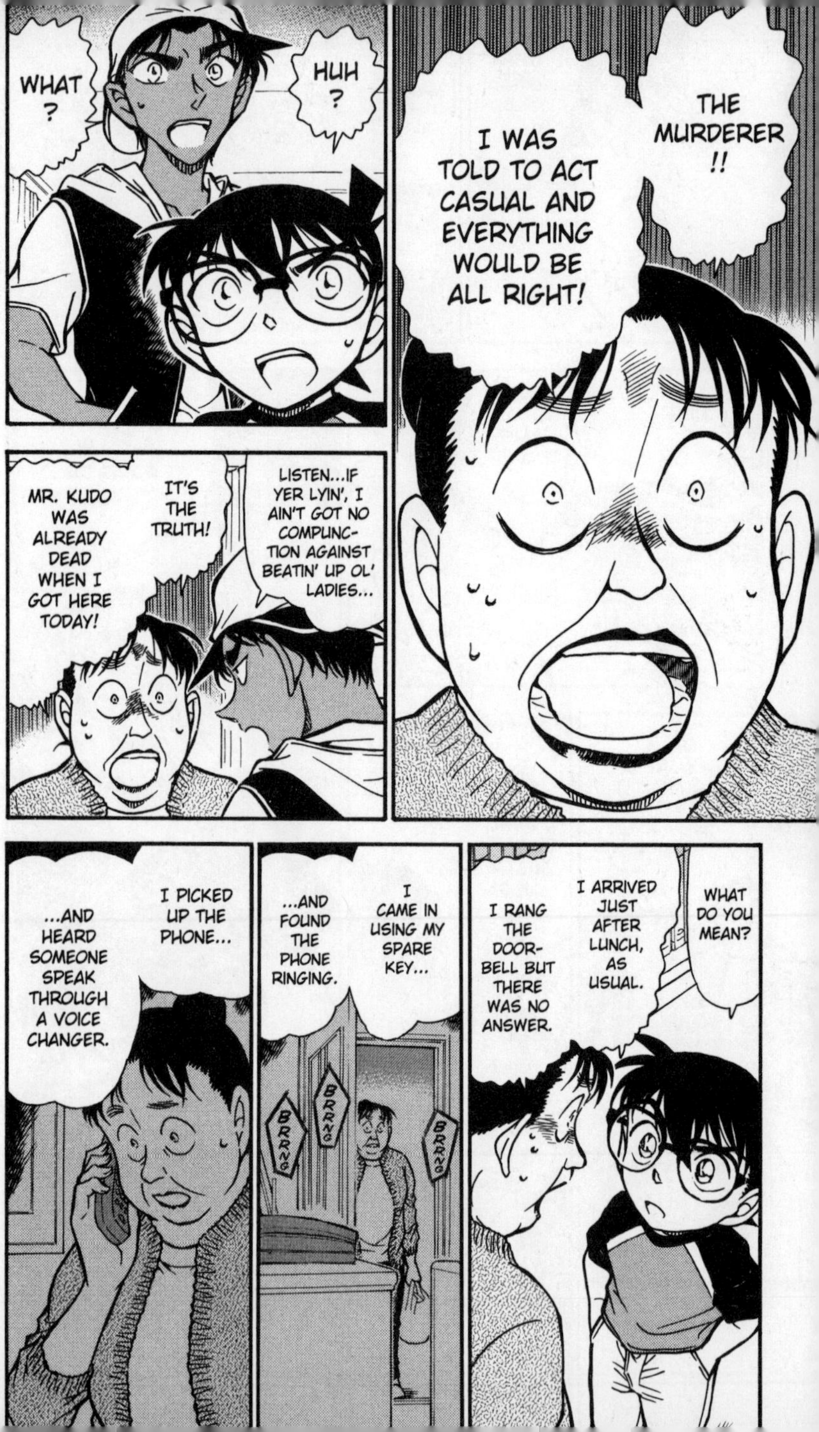
THE MURDERER!!
I WAS TOLD TO ACT CASUAL AND EVERYTHING WOULD BE ALL RIGHT!
HUH?
WHAT?
LISTEN...IF YER LYIN', I AIN'T GOT NO COMPUNC-TION AGAINST BEATIN' UP OL' LADIES...
IT'S THE TRUTH!
MR. KUDO WAS ALREADY DEAD WHEN I GOT HERE TODAY!
WHAT DO YOU MEAN?
I ARRIVED JUST AFTER LUNCH, AS USUAL.
I RANG THE DOOR-BELL BUT THERE WAS NO ANSWER.
I CAME IN USING MY SPARE KEY...
...AND FOUND THE PHONE RINGING.
BRRRNG
BRRRNG
BRRRNG
I PICKED UP THE PHONE...
...AND HEARD SOMEONE SPEAK THROUGH A VOICE CHANGER.

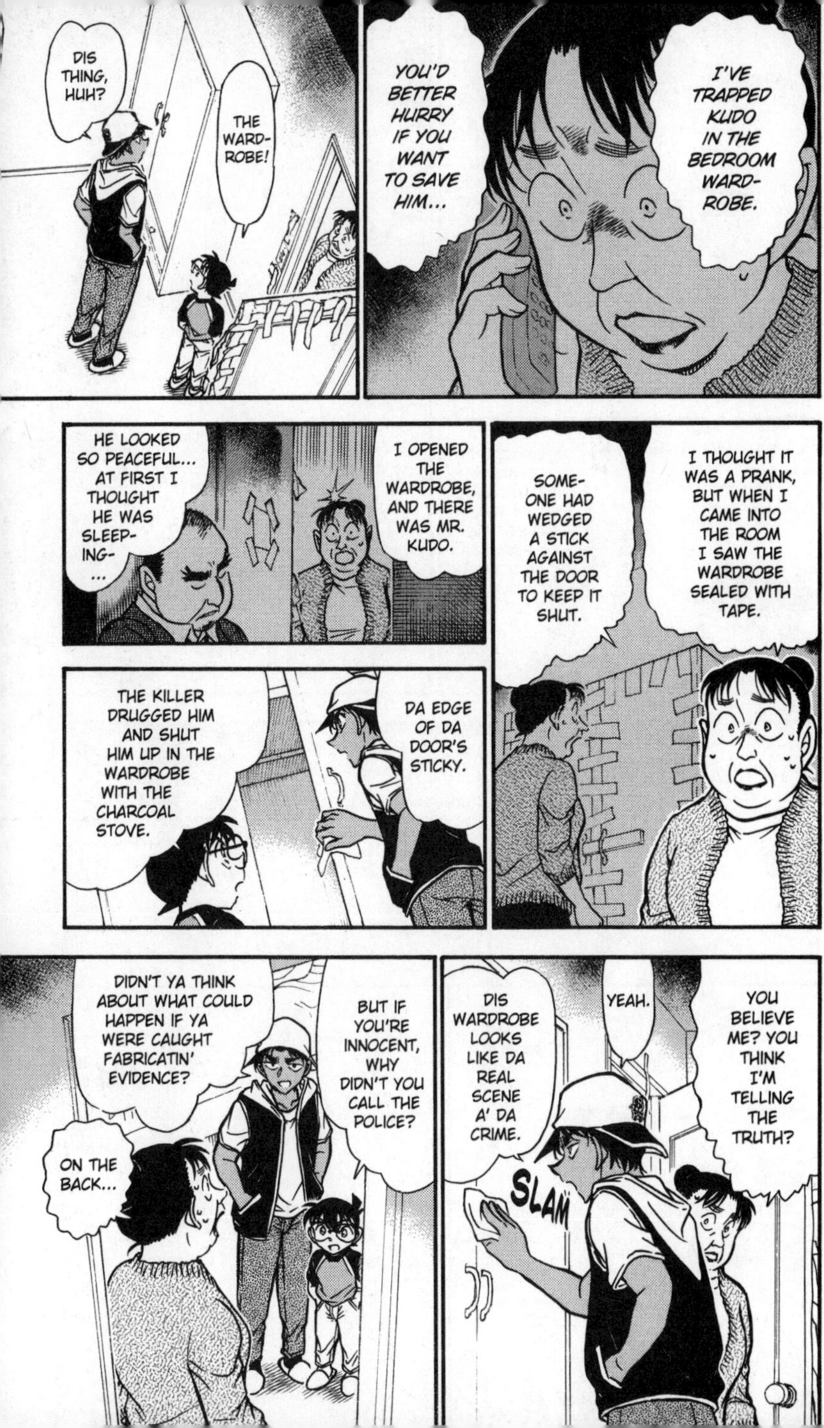
I'VE TRAPPED KUDO IN THE BEDROOM WARDROBE.
YOU'D BETTER HURRY IF YOU WANT TO SAVE HIM...
THE WARDROBE!
DIS THING, HUH?
I THOUGHT IT WAS A PRANK, BUT WHEN I CAME INTO THE ROOM I SAW THE WARDROBE SEALED WITH TAPE.
SOMEONE HAD WEDGED A STICK AGAINST THE DOOR TO KEEP IT SHUT.
I OPENED THE WARDROBE, AND THERE WAS MR. KUDO.
HE LOOKED SO PEACEFUL... AT FIRST I THOUGHT HE WAS SLEEPING-...
DA EDGE OF DA DOOR'S STICKY.
THE KILLER DRUGGED HIM AND SHUT HIM UP IN THE WARDROBE WITH THE CHARCOAL STOVE.
YOU BELIEVE ME? YOU THINK I'M TELLING THE TRUTH?
YEAH.
DIS WARDROBE LOOKS LIKE DA REAL SCENE A' DA CRIME.
SLAM
BUT IF YOU'RE INNOCENT, WHY DIDN'T YOU CALL THE POLICE?
DIDN'T YA THINK ABOUT WHAT COULD HAPPEN IF YA WERE CAUGHT FABRICATIN' EVIDENCE?
ON THE BACK...

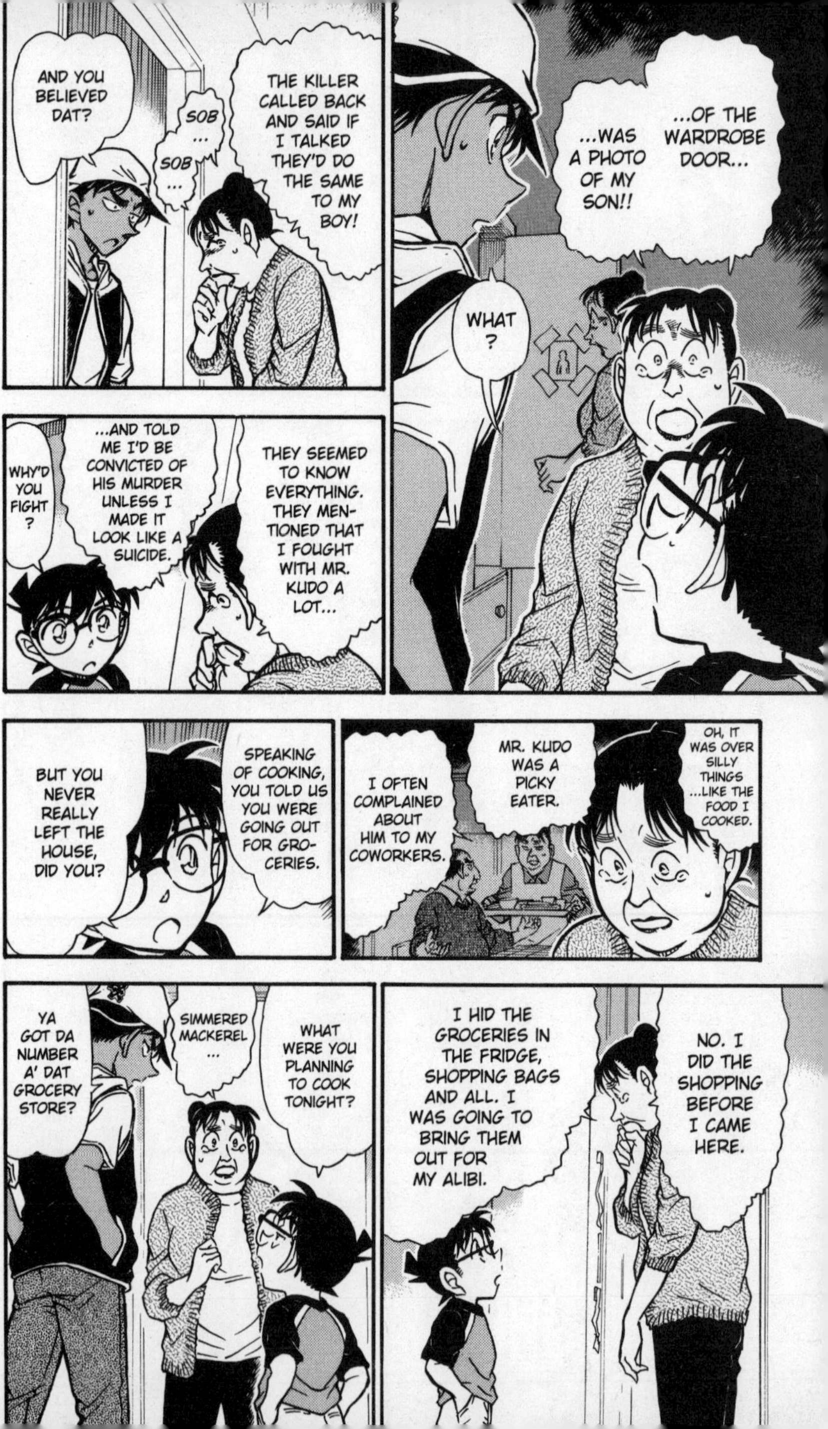
...OF THE WARDROBE DOOR...
...WAS A PHOTO OF MY SON!!
WHAT?
THE KILLER CALLED BACK AND SAID IF I TALKED THEY'D DO THE SAME TO MY BOY!
SOB ... SOB ...
AND YOU BELIEVED DAT?
...AND TOLD ME I'D BE CONVICTED OF HIS MURDER UNLESS I MADE IT LOOK LIKE A SUICIDE.
THEY SEEMED TO KNOW EVERYTHING. THEY MENTIONED THAT I FOUGHT WITH MR. KUDO A LOT...
WHY'D YOU FIGHT?
OH, IT WAS OVER SILLY THINGS ...LIKE THE FOOD I COOKED.
MR. KUDO WAS A PICKY EATER.
I OFTEN COMPLAINED ABOUT HIM TO MY COWORKERS.
SPEAKING OF COOKING, YOU TOLD US YOU WERE GOING OUT FOR GROCERIES.
BUT YOU NEVER REALLY LEFT THE HOUSE, DID YOU?
NO. I DID THE SHOPPING BEFORE I CAME HERE.
I HID THE GROCERIES IN THE FRIDGE, SHOPPING BAGS AND ALL. I WAS GOING TO BRING THEM OUT FOR MY ALIBI.
WHAT WERE YOU PLANNING TO COOK TONIGHT?
SIMMERED MACKEREL ...
YA GOT DA NUMBER A' DAT GROCERY STORE?

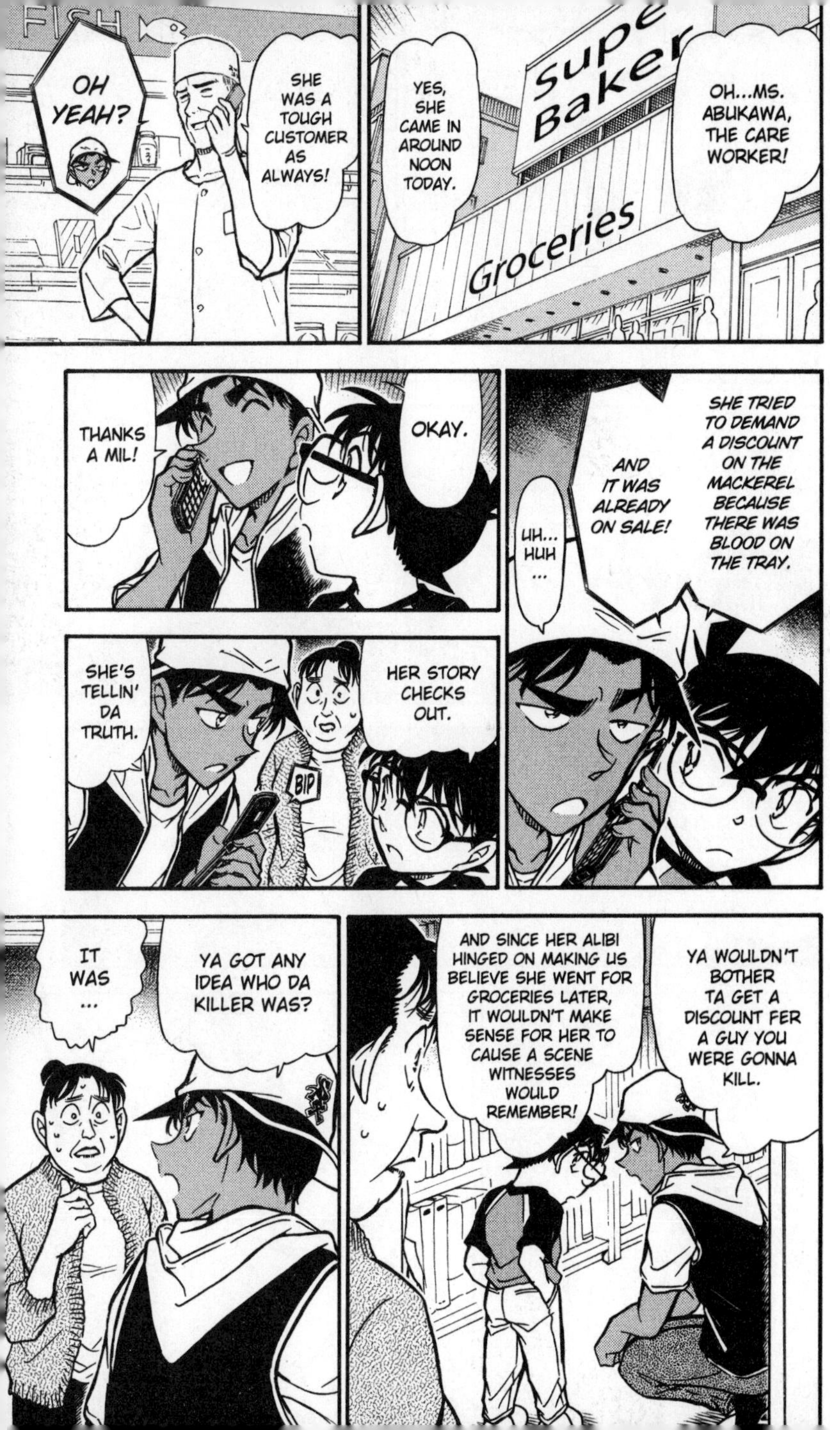

Supe
Baker
Groceries
OH...MS. ABUKAWA, THE CARE WORKER!
YES, SHE CAME IN AROUND NOON TODAY.
FISH
SHE WAS A TOUGH CUSTOMER AS ALWAYS!
OH YEAH?
SHE TRIED TO DEMAND A DISCOUNT ON THE MACKEREL BECAUSE THERE WAS BLOOD ON THE TRAY.
AND IT WAS ALREADY ON SALE!
UH... HUH ...
OKAY.
THANKS A MIL!
HER STORY CHECKS OUT.
BIP
SHE'S TELLIN' DA TRUTH.
YA WOULDN'T BOTHER TA GET A DISCOUNT FER A GUY YOU WERE GONNA KILL.
AND SINCE HER ALIBI HINGED ON MAKING US BELIEVE SHE WENT FOR GROCERIES LATER, IT WOULDN'T MAKE SENSE FOR HER TO CAUSE A SCENE WITNESSES WOULD REMEMBER!
YA GOT ANY IDEA WHO DA KILLER WAS?
IT WAS ...

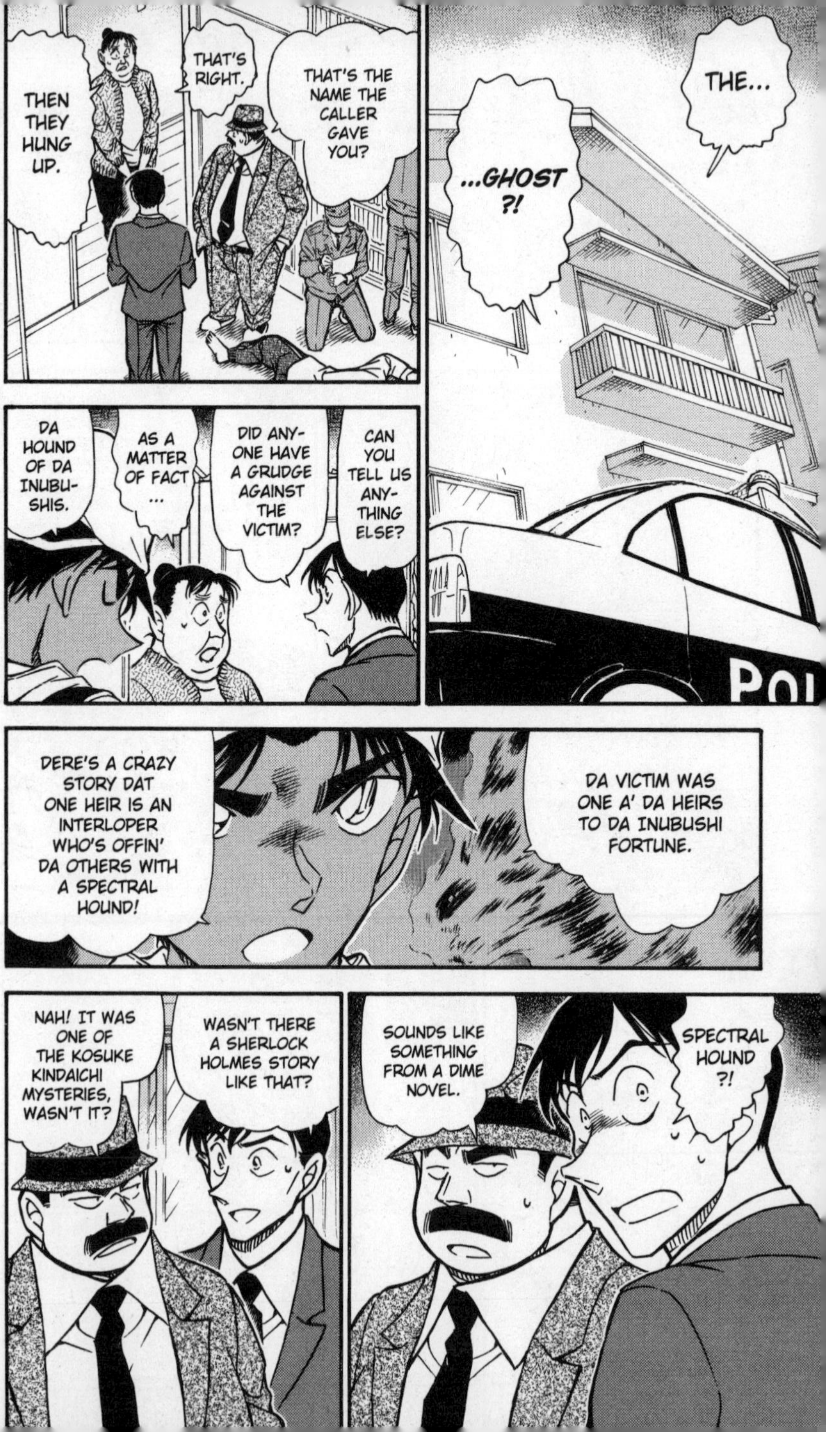
THE...
...GHOST ?!
THAT'S THE NAME THE CALLER GAVE YOU?
THAT'S RIGHT.
THEN THEY HUNG UP.
CAN YOU TELL US ANY-THING ELSE?
DID ANY-ONE HAVE A GRUDGE AGAINST THE VICTIM?
AS A MATTER OF FACT ...
DA HOUND OF DA INUBU-SHIS.
DA VICTIM WAS ONE A' DA HEIRS TO DA INUBUSHI FORTUNE.
DERE'S A CRAZY STORY DAT ONE HEIR IS AN INTERLOPER WHO'S OFFIN' DA OTHERS WITH A SPECTRAL HOUND!
SPECTRAL HOUND ?!
SOUNDS LIKE SOMETHING FROM A DIME NOVEL.
WASN'T THERE A SHERLOCK HOLMES STORY LIKE THAT?
NAH! IT WAS ONE OF THE KOSUKE KINDAICHI MYSTERIES, WASN'T IT?

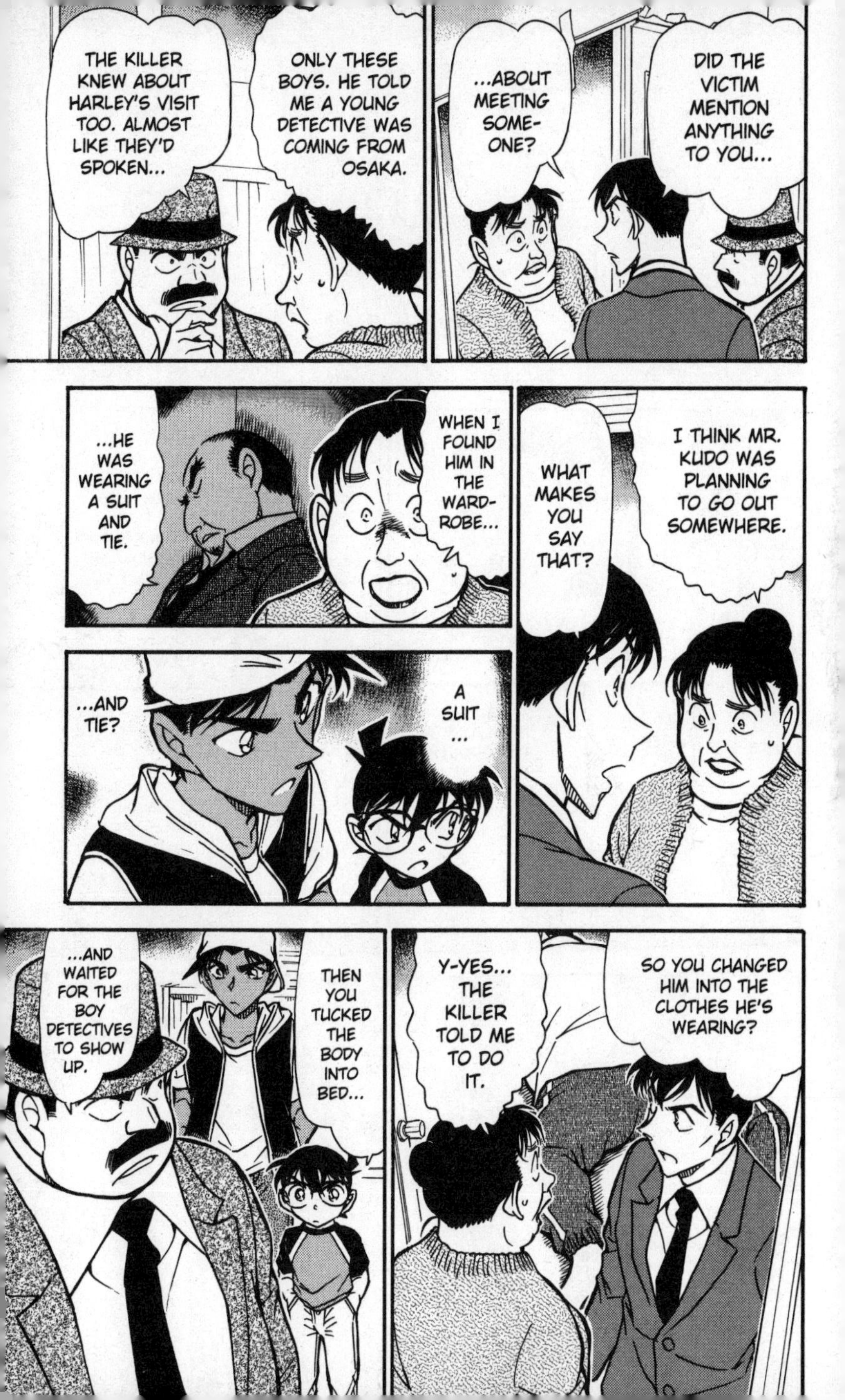
DID THE VICTIM MENTION ANYTHING TO YOU...
...ABOUT MEETING SOME-ONE?
ONLY THESE BOYS. HE TOLD ME A YOUNG DETECTIVE WAS COMING FROM OSAKA.
THE KILLER KNEW ABOUT HARLEY'S VISIT TOO. ALMOST LIKE THEY'D SPOKEN...
I THINK MR. KUDO WAS PLANNING TO GO OUT SOMEWHERE.
WHAT MAKES YOU SAY THAT?
WHEN I FOUND HIM IN THE WARD-ROBE...
...HE WAS WEARING A SUIT AND TIE.
A SUIT...
...AND TIE?
SO YOU CHANGED HIM INTO THE CLOTHES HE'S WEARING?
Y-YES... THE KILLER TOLD ME TO DO IT.
THEN YOU TUCKED THE BODY INTO BED...
...AND WAITED FOR THE BOY DETECTIVES TO SHOW UP.

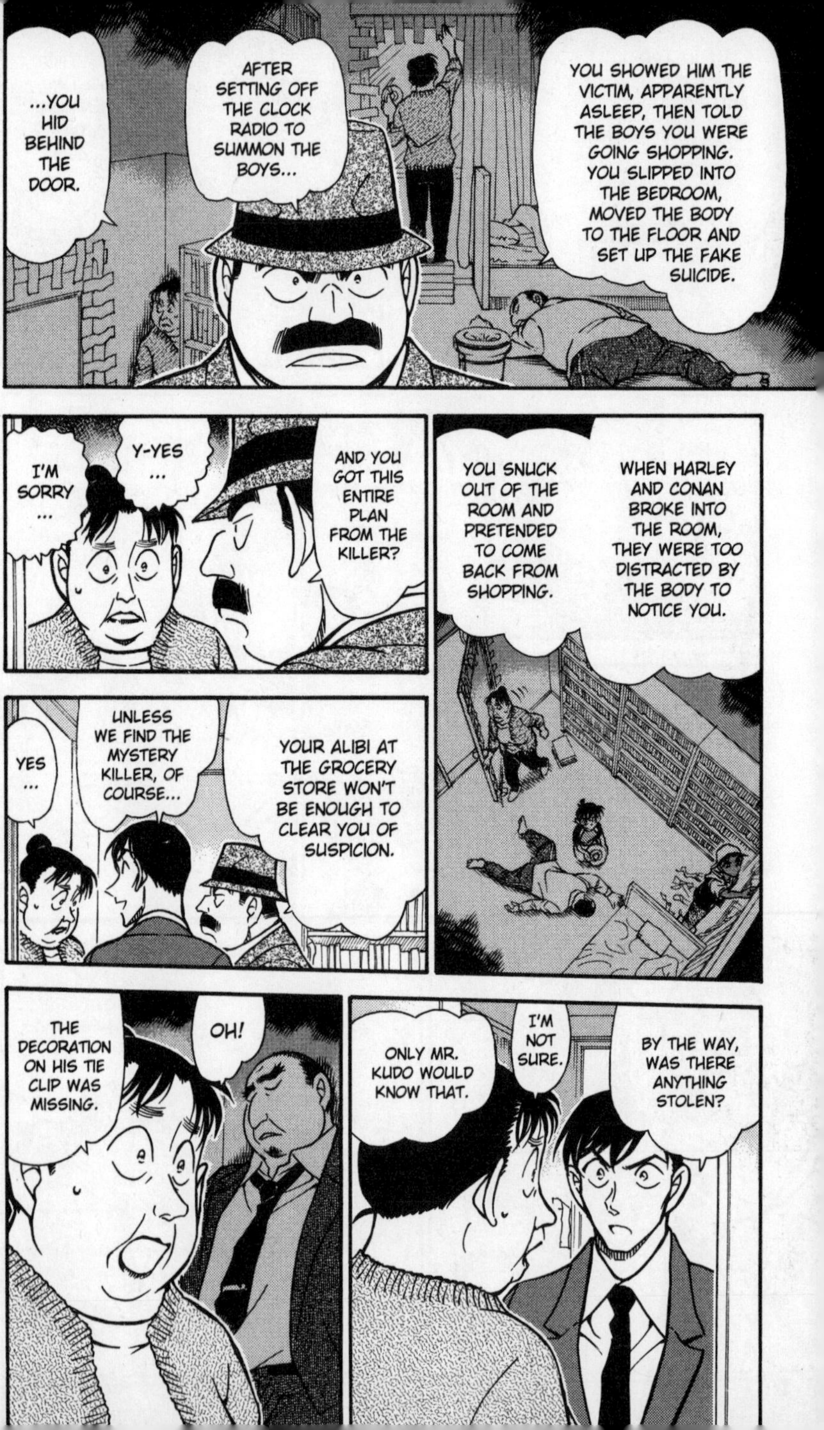
YOU SHOWED HIM THE VICTIM, APPARENTLY ASLEEP, THEN TOLD THE BOYS YOU WERE GOING SHOPPING. YOU SLIPPED INTO THE BEDROOM, MOVED THE BODY TO THE FLOOR AND SET UP THE FAKE SUICIDE.
AFTER SETTING OFF THE CLOCK RADIO TO SUMMON THE BOYS...
...YOU HID BEHIND THE DOOR.
WHEN HARLEY AND CONAN BROKE INTO THE ROOM, THEY WERE TOO DISTRACTED BY THE BODY TO NOTICE YOU.
YOU SNUCK OUT OF THE ROOM AND PRETENDED TO COME BACK FROM SHOPPING.
AND YOU GOT THIS ENTIRE PLAN FROM THE KILLER?
Y-YES...
I'M SORRY...
YOUR ALIBI AT THE GROCERY STORE WON'T BE ENOUGH TO CLEAR YOU OF SUSPICION.
UNLESS WE FIND THE MYSTERY KILLER, OF COURSE...
YES...
BY THE WAY, WAS THERE ANYTHING STOLEN?
I'M NOT SURE.
ONLY MR. KUDO WOULD KNOW THAT.
OH!
THE DECORATION ON HIS TIE CLIP WAS MISSING.

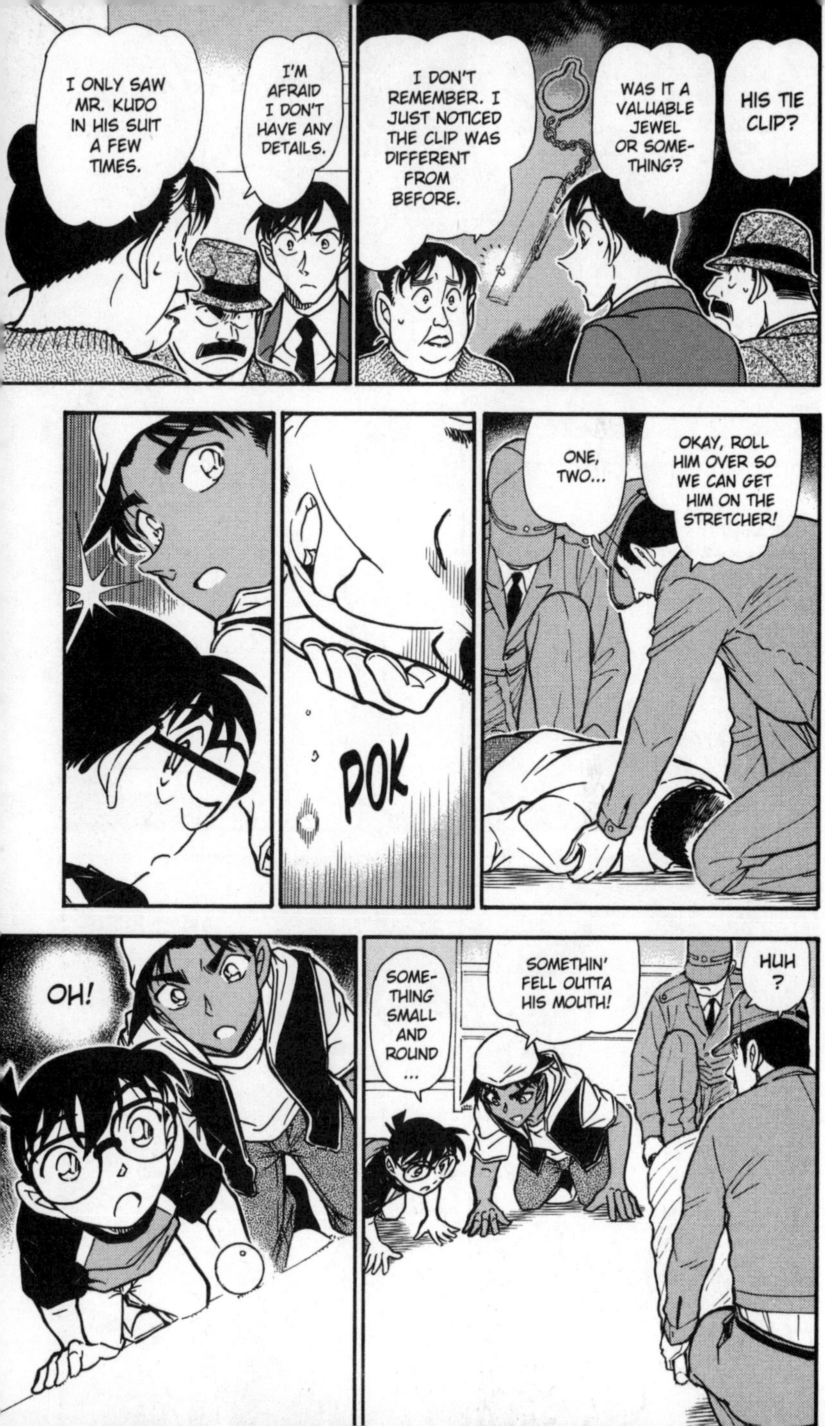
HIS TIE CLIP?
WAS IT A VALUABLE JEWEL OR SOMETHING?
I DON'T REMEMBER. I JUST NOTICED THE CLIP WAS DIFFERENT FROM BEFORE.
I'M AFRAID I DON'T HAVE ANY DETAILS.
I ONLY SAW MR. KUDO IN HIS SUIT A FEW TIMES.
OKAY, ROLL HIM OVER SO WE CAN GET HIM ON THE STRETCHER!
ONE, TWO...
POK
HUH?
SOMETHIN' FELL OUTTA HIS MOUTH!
SOMETHING SMALL AND ROUND...
OH!

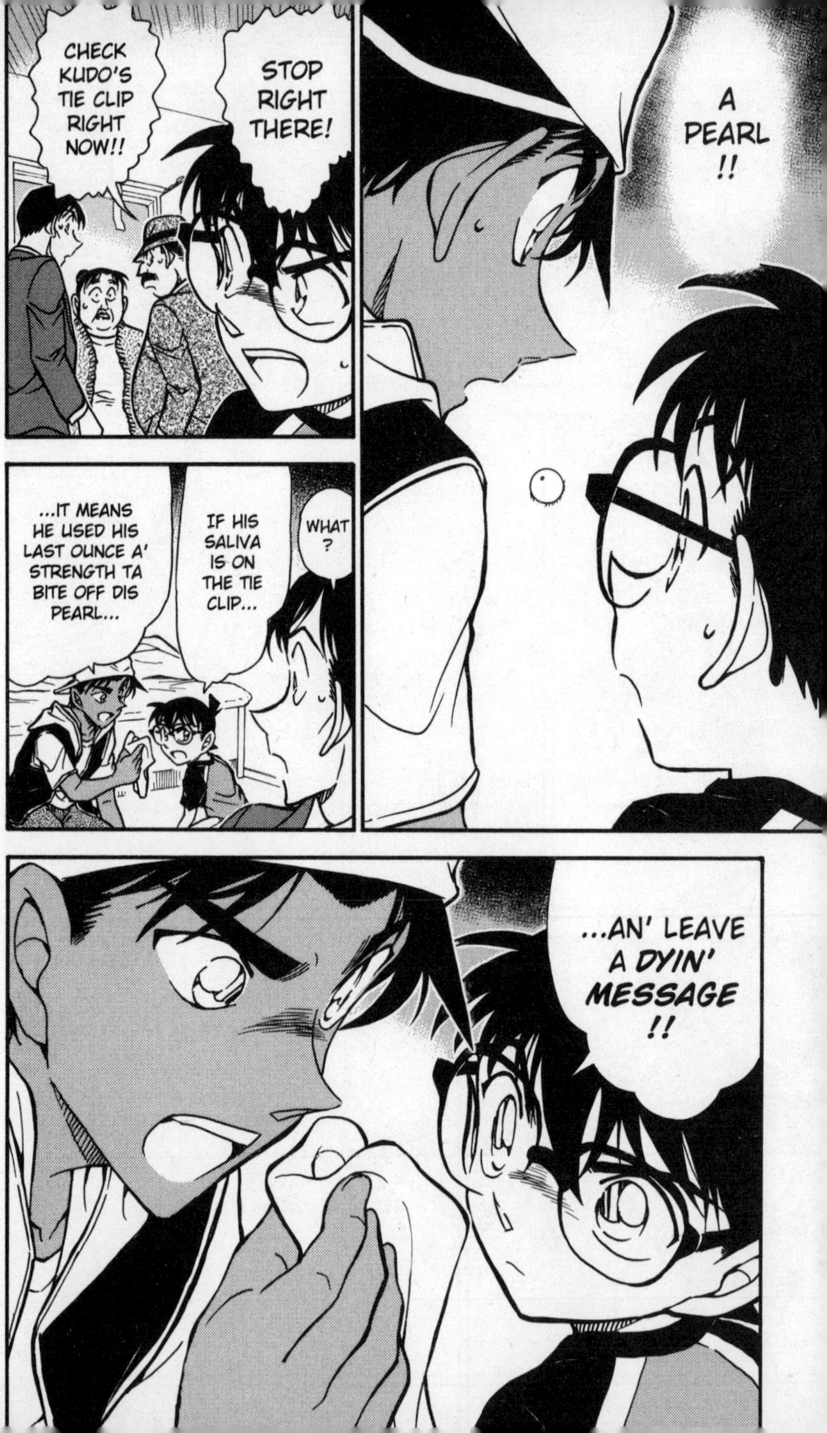
A PEARL !!
STOP RIGHT THERE!
CHECK KUDO'S TIE CLIP RIGHT NOW!!
WHAT ?
IF HIS SALIVA IS ON THE TIE CLIP...
...IT MEANS HE USED HIS LAST OUNCE A' STRENGTH TA BITE OFF DIS PEARL...
...AN' LEAVE A *DYIN'* MESSAGE !!

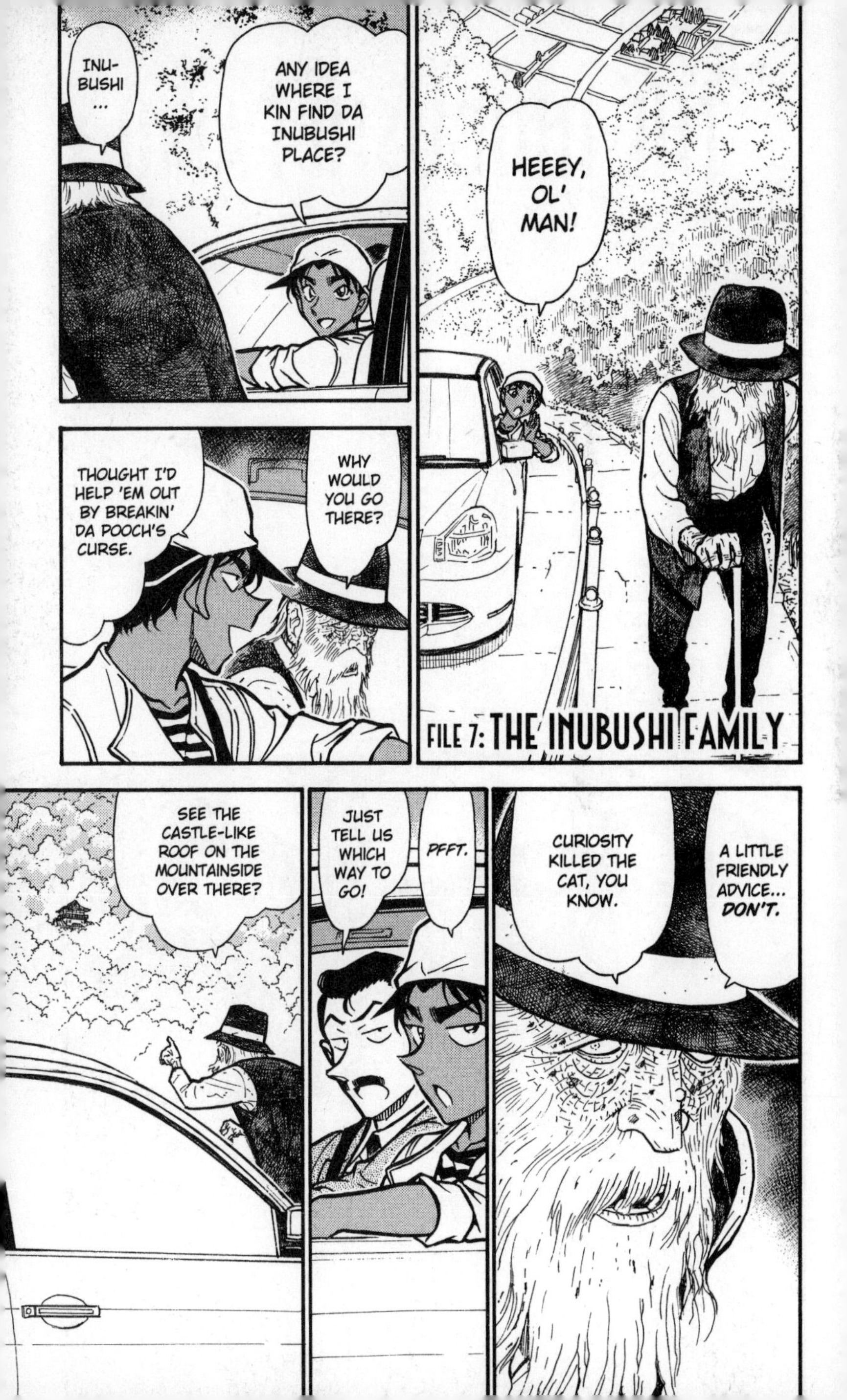
HEEEY, OL' MAN!
FILE 7: THE INUBUSHI FAMILY
ANY IDEA WHERE I KIN FIND DA INUBUSHI PLACE?
INU-BUSHI ...
WHY WOULD YOU GO THERE?
THOUGHT I'D HELP 'EM OUT BY BREAKIN' DA POOCH'S CURSE.
A LITTLE FRIENDLY ADVICE... *DON'T.*
CURIOSITY KILLED THE CAT, YOU KNOW.
PFFT.
JUST TELL US WHICH WAY TO GO!
SEE THE CASTLE-LIKE ROOF ON THE MOUNTAINSIDE OVER THERE?

FILE 7: THE INUBUSHI FAMILY

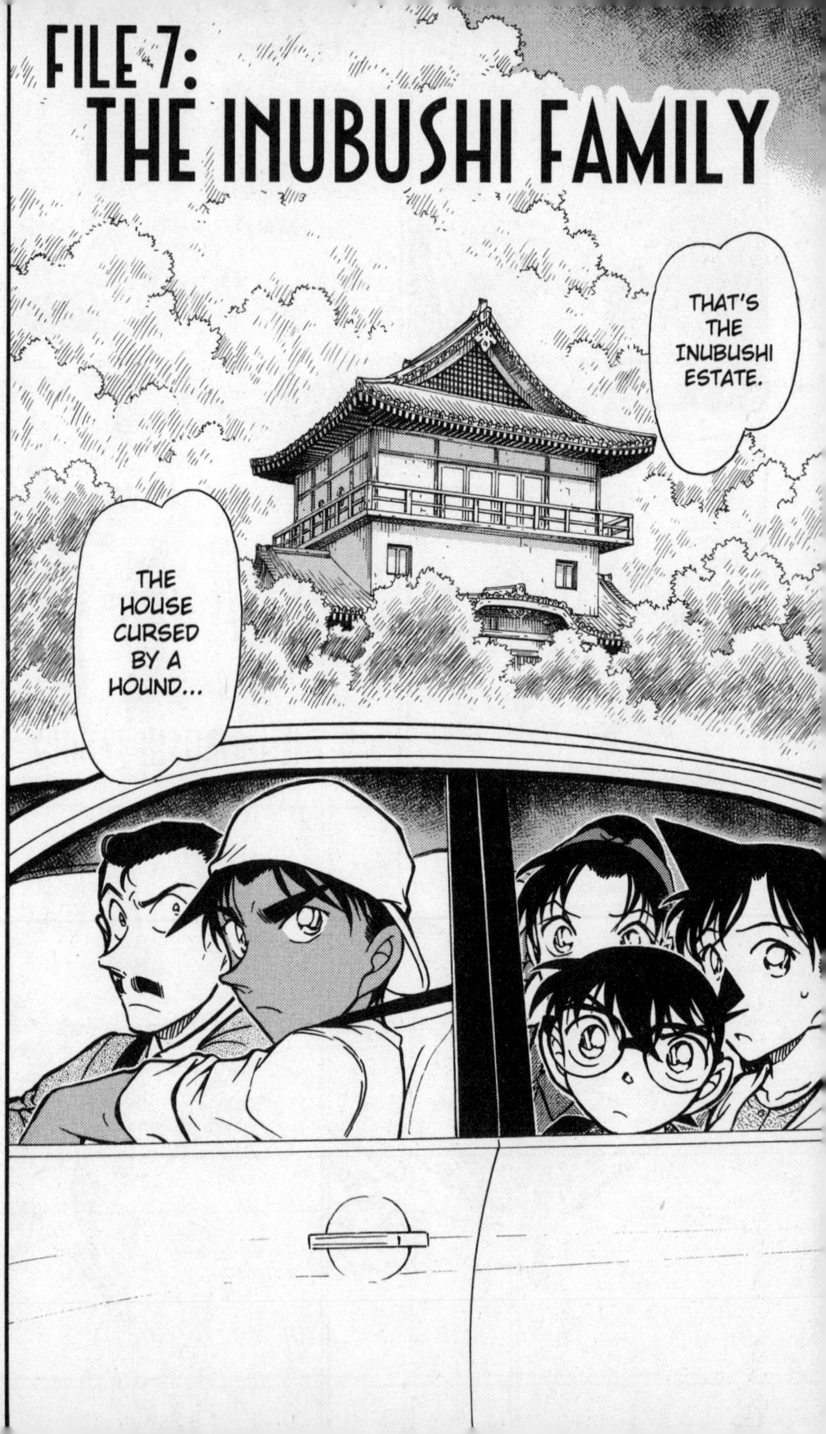
THAT'S THE INUBUSHI ESTATE.
THE HOUSE CURSED BY A HOUND...

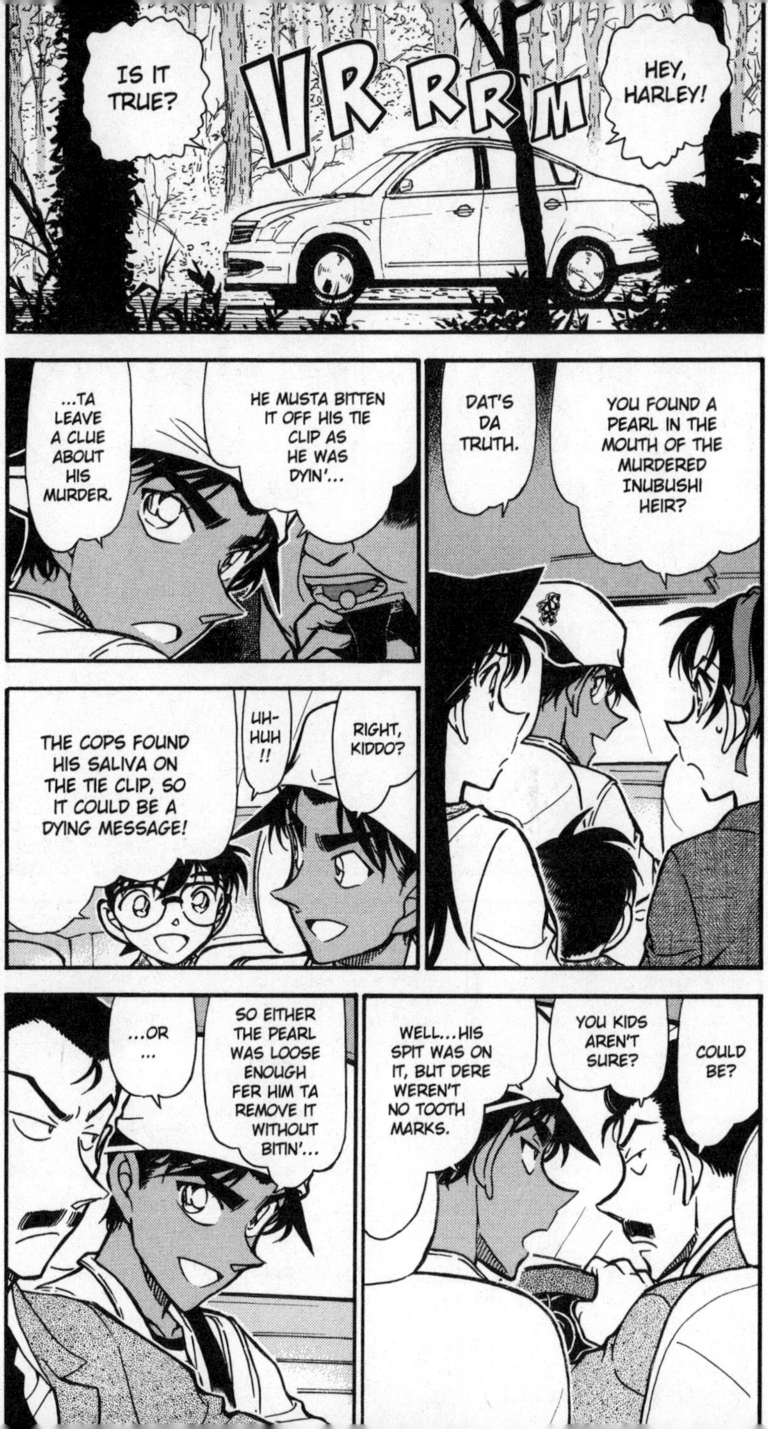
HEY, HARLEY!
VRRRM
IS IT TRUE?
YOU FOUND A PEARL IN THE MOUTH OF THE MURDERED INUBUSHI HEIR?
DAT'S DA TRUTH.
HE MUSTA BITTEN IT OFF HIS TIE CLIP AS HE WAS DYIN'...
...TA LEAVE A CLUE ABOUT HIS MURDER.
RIGHT, KIDDO?
UH-HUH!!
THE COPS FOUND HIS SALIVA ON THE TIE CLIP, SO IT COULD BE A DYING MESSAGE!
COULD BE?
YOU KIDS AREN'T SURE?
WELL...HIS SPIT WAS ON IT, BUT DERE WEREN'T NO TOOTH MARKS.
SO EITHER THE PEARL WAS LOOSE ENOUGH FER HIM TA REMOVE IT WITHOUT BITIN'...
...OR ...

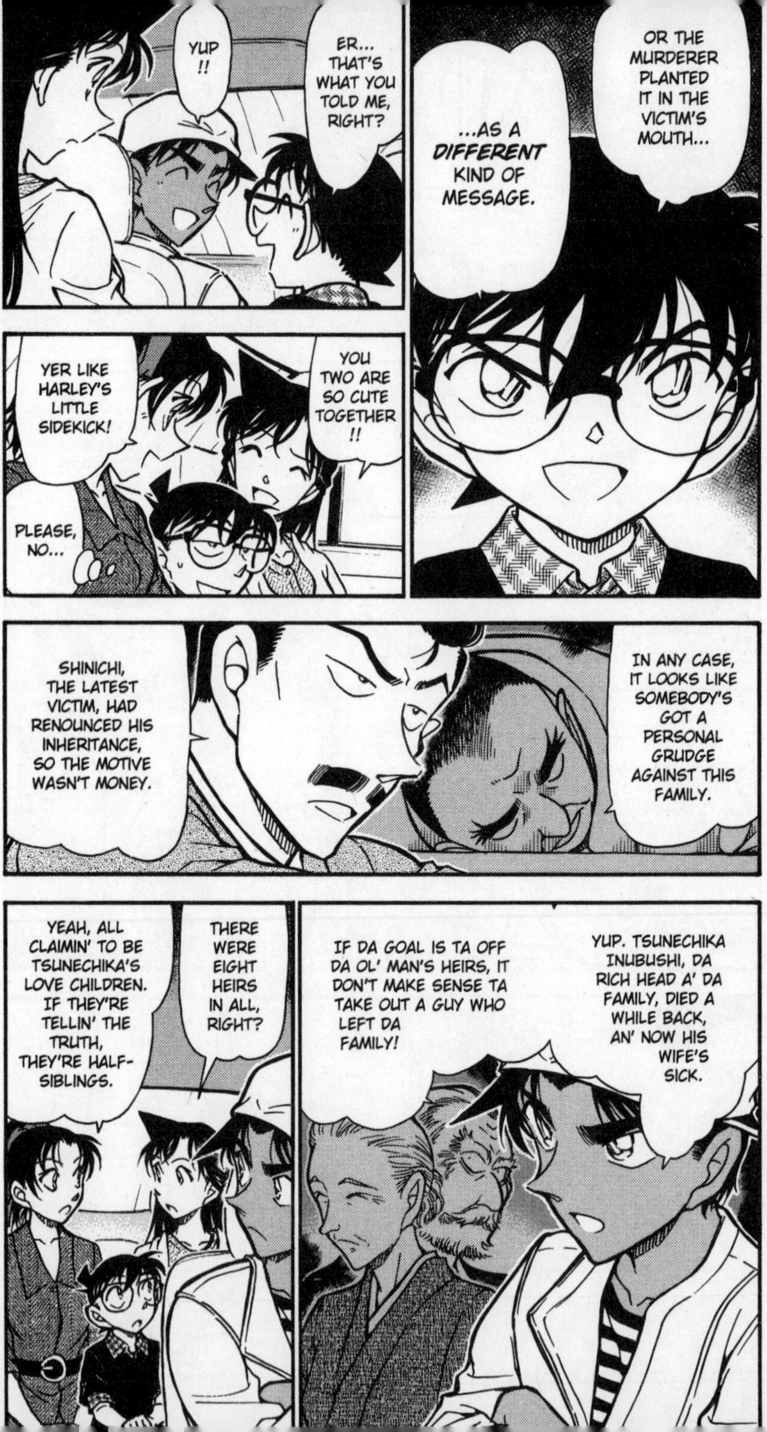
OR THE MURDERER PLANTED IT IN THE VICTIM'S MOUTH...
...AS A ***DIFFERENT*** KIND OF MESSAGE.
ER... THAT'S WHAT YOU TOLD ME, RIGHT?
YUP!!
YOU TWO ARE SO CUTE TOGETHER!!
YER LIKE HARLEY'S LITTLE SIDEKICK!
PLEASE, NO...
IN ANY CASE, IT LOOKS LIKE SOMEBODY'S GOT A PERSONAL GRUDGE AGAINST THIS FAMILY.
SHINICHI, THE LATEST VICTIM, HAD RENOUNCED HIS INHERITANCE, SO THE MOTIVE WASN'T MONEY.
YUP. TSUNECHIKA INUBUSHI, DA RICH HEAD A' DA FAMILY, DIED A WHILE BACK, AN' NOW HIS WIFE'S SICK.
IF DA GOAL IS TA OFF DA OL' MAN'S HEIRS, IT DON'T MAKE SENSE TA TAKE OUT A GUY WHO LEFT DA FAMILY!
THERE WERE EIGHT HEIRS IN ALL, RIGHT?
YEAH, ALL CLAIMIN' TO BE TSUNECHIKA'S LOVE CHILDREN. IF THEY'RE TELLIN' THE TRUTH, THEY'RE HALF-SIBLINGS.

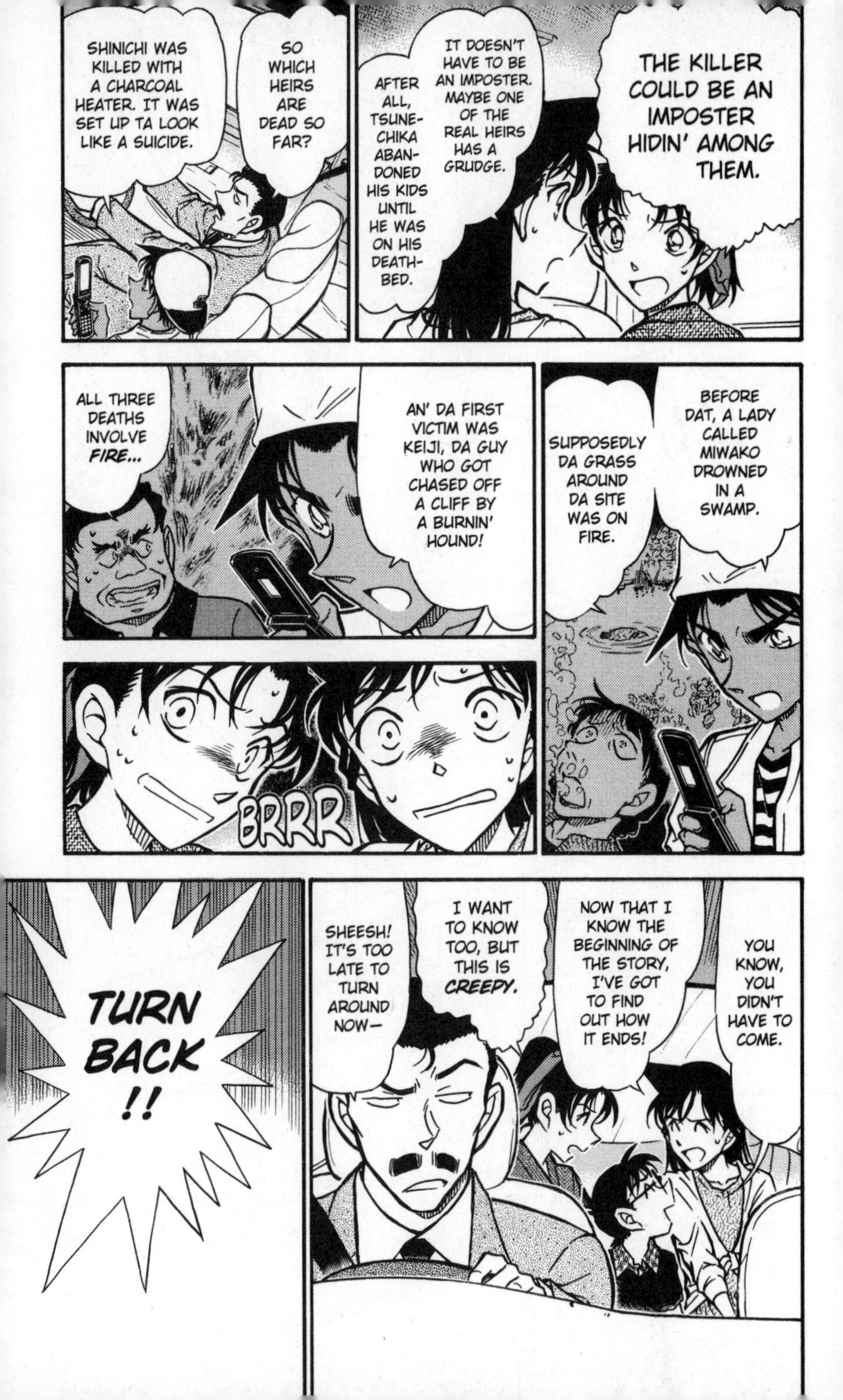
THE KILLER COULD BE AN IMPOSTER HIDIN' AMONG THEM.
IT DOESN'T HAVE TO BE AN IMPOSTER. MAYBE ONE OF THE REAL HEIRS HAS A GRUDGE.
AFTER ALL, TSUNE-CHIKA ABAN-DONED HIS KIDS UNTIL HE WAS ON HIS DEATH-BED.
SO WHICH HEIRS ARE DEAD SO FAR?
SHINICHI WAS KILLED WITH A CHARCOAL HEATER. IT WAS SET UP TA LOOK LIKE A SUICIDE.
BEFORE DAT, A LADY CALLED MIWAKO DROWNED IN A SWAMP.
SUPPOSEDLY DA GRASS AROUND DA SITE WAS ON FIRE.
AN' DA FIRST VICTIM WAS KEIJI, DA GUY WHO GOT CHASED OFF A CLIFF BY A BURNIN' HOUND!
ALL THREE DEATHS INVOLVE *FIRE...*
BRRR
YOU KNOW, YOU DIDN'T HAVE TO COME.
NOW THAT I KNOW THE BEGINNING OF THE STORY, I'VE GOT TO FIND OUT HOW IT ENDS!
I WANT TO KNOW TOO, BUT THIS IS *CREEPY.*
SHEESH! IT'S TOO LATE TO TURN AROUND NOW—
TURN BACK !!

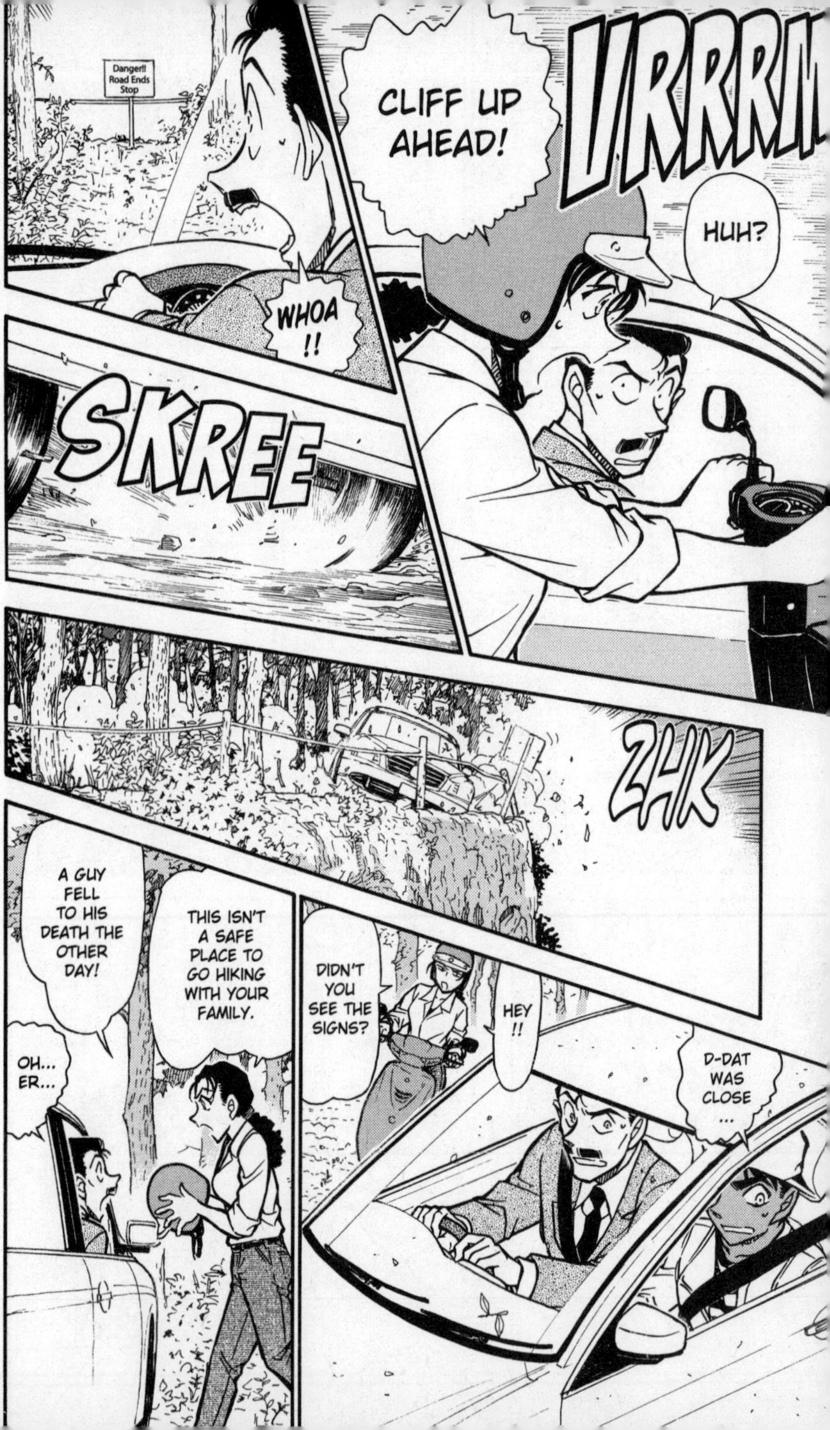
URRRM
CLIFF UP AHEAD!
HUH?
Danger!! Road Ends Stop
WHOA !!
SKREE
ZHK
D-DAT WAS CLOSE ...
HEY !!
DIDN'T YOU SEE THE SIGNS?
THIS ISN'T A SAFE PLACE TO GO HIKING WITH YOUR FAMILY.
A GUY FELL TO HIS DEATH THE OTHER DAY!
OH... ER...

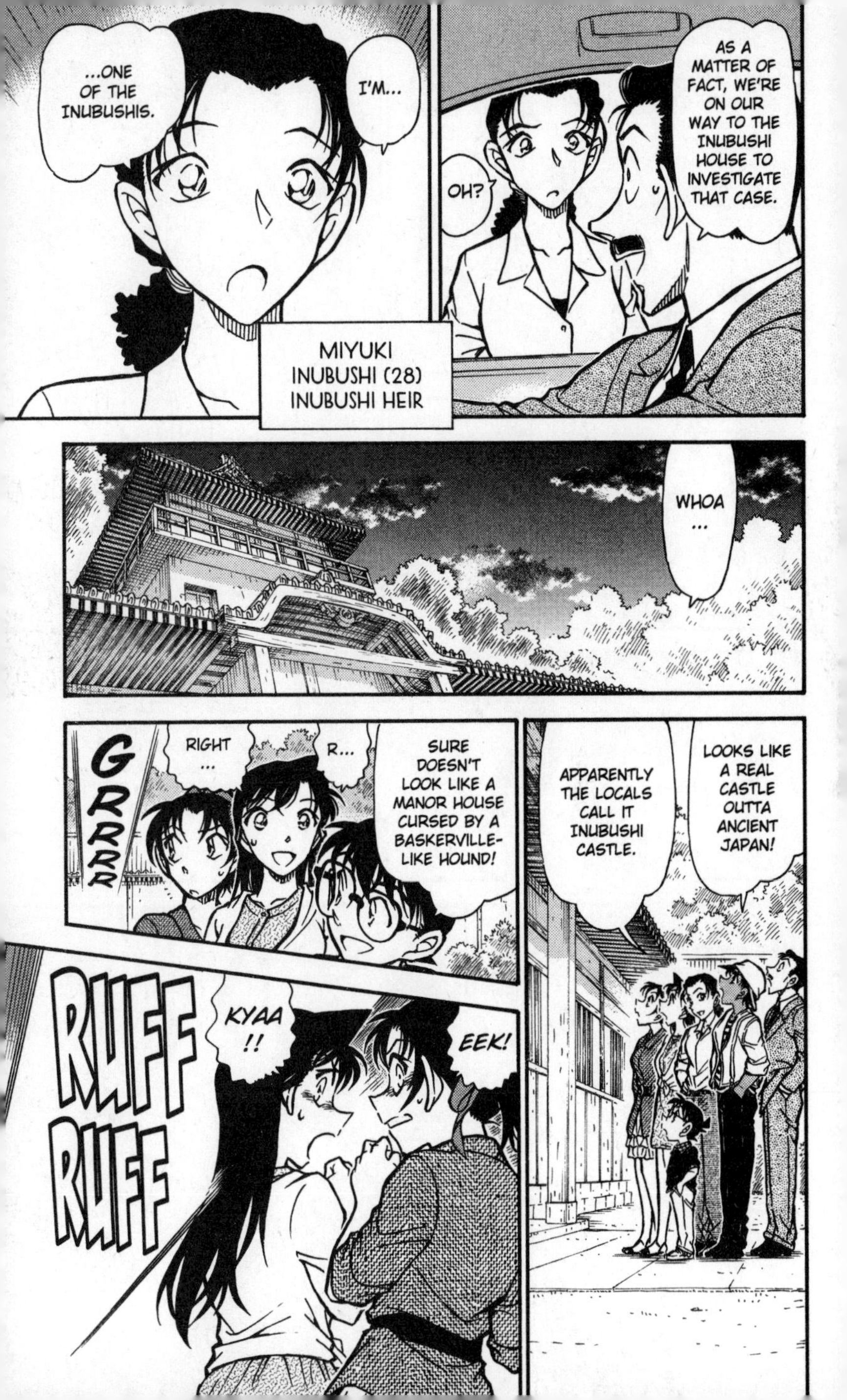
AS A MATTER OF FACT, WE'RE ON OUR WAY TO THE INUBUSHI HOUSE TO INVESTIGATE THAT CASE.
OH?
I'M...
...ONE OF THE INUBUSHIS.
MIYUKI INUBUSHI (28) INUBUSHI HEIR
WHOA ...
LOOKS LIKE A REAL CASTLE OUTTA ANCIENT JAPAN!
APPARENTLY THE LOCALS CALL IT INUBUSHI CASTLE.
SURE DOESN'T LOOK LIKE A MANOR HOUSE CURSED BY A BASKERVILLE-LIKE HOUND!
R...
RIGHT ...
GRRRR
EEK!
KYAA !!
RUFF RUFF

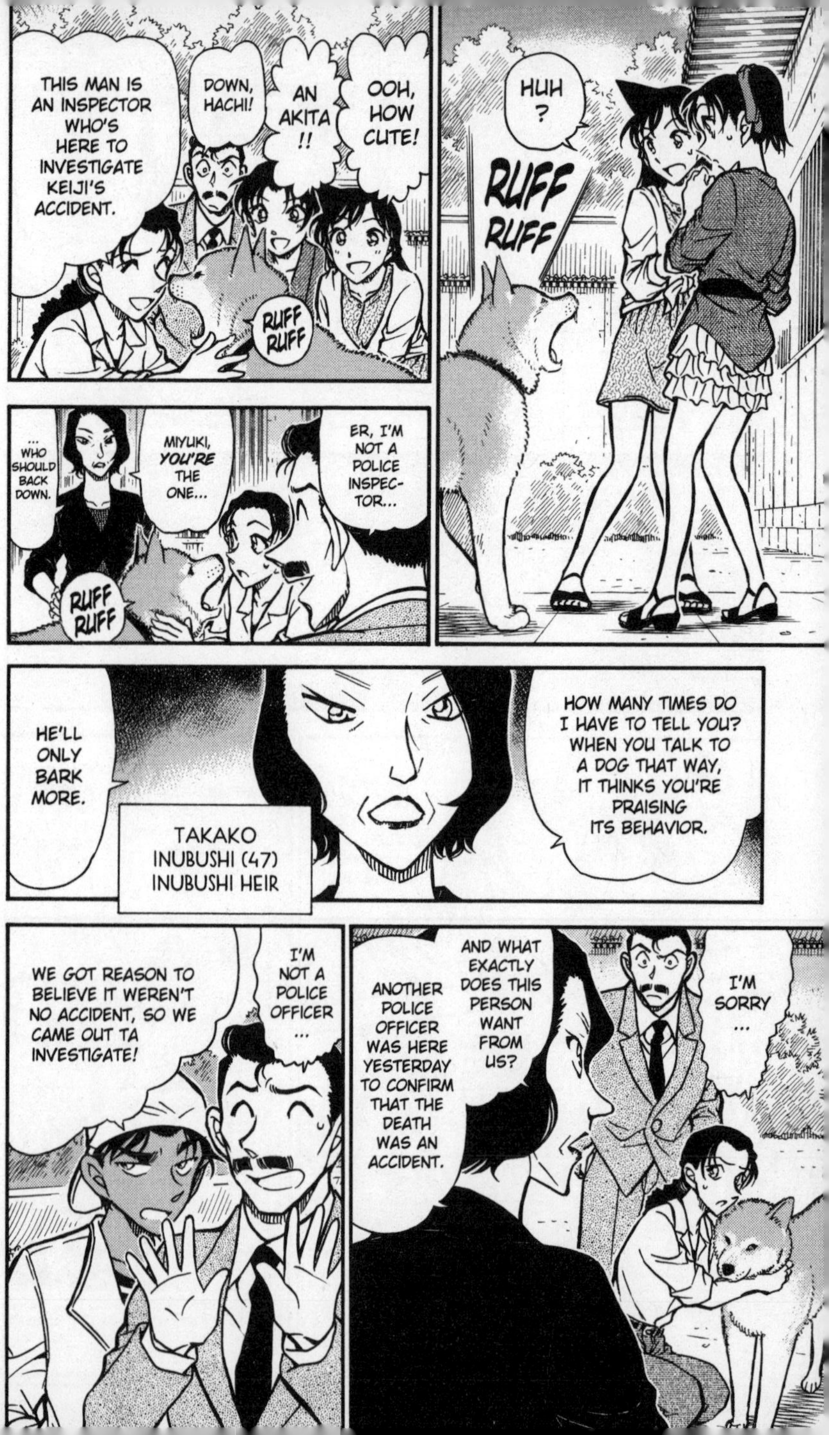
HUH ?
RUFF RUFF
OOH, HOW CUTE!
AN AKITA !!
DOWN, HACHI!
THIS MAN IS AN INSPECTOR WHO'S HERE TO INVESTIGATE KEIJI'S ACCIDENT.
RUFF RUFF
ER, I'M NOT A POLICE INSPECTOR...
MIYUKI, YOU'RE THE ONE...
... WHO SHOULD BACK DOWN.
RUFF RUFF
HOW MANY TIMES DO I HAVE TO TELL YOU? WHEN YOU TALK TO A DOG THAT WAY, IT THINKS YOU'RE PRAISING ITS BEHAVIOR.
TAKAKO INUBUSHI (47) INUBUSHI HEIR
HE'LL ONLY BARK MORE.
I'M SORRY ...
AND WHAT EXACTLY DOES THIS PERSON WANT FROM US?
ANOTHER POLICE OFFICER WAS HERE YESTERDAY TO CONFIRM THAT THE DEATH WAS AN ACCIDENT.
I'M NOT A POLICE OFFICER ...
WE GOT REASON TO BELIEVE IT WEREN'T NO ACCIDENT, SO WE CAME OUT TA INVESTIGATE!

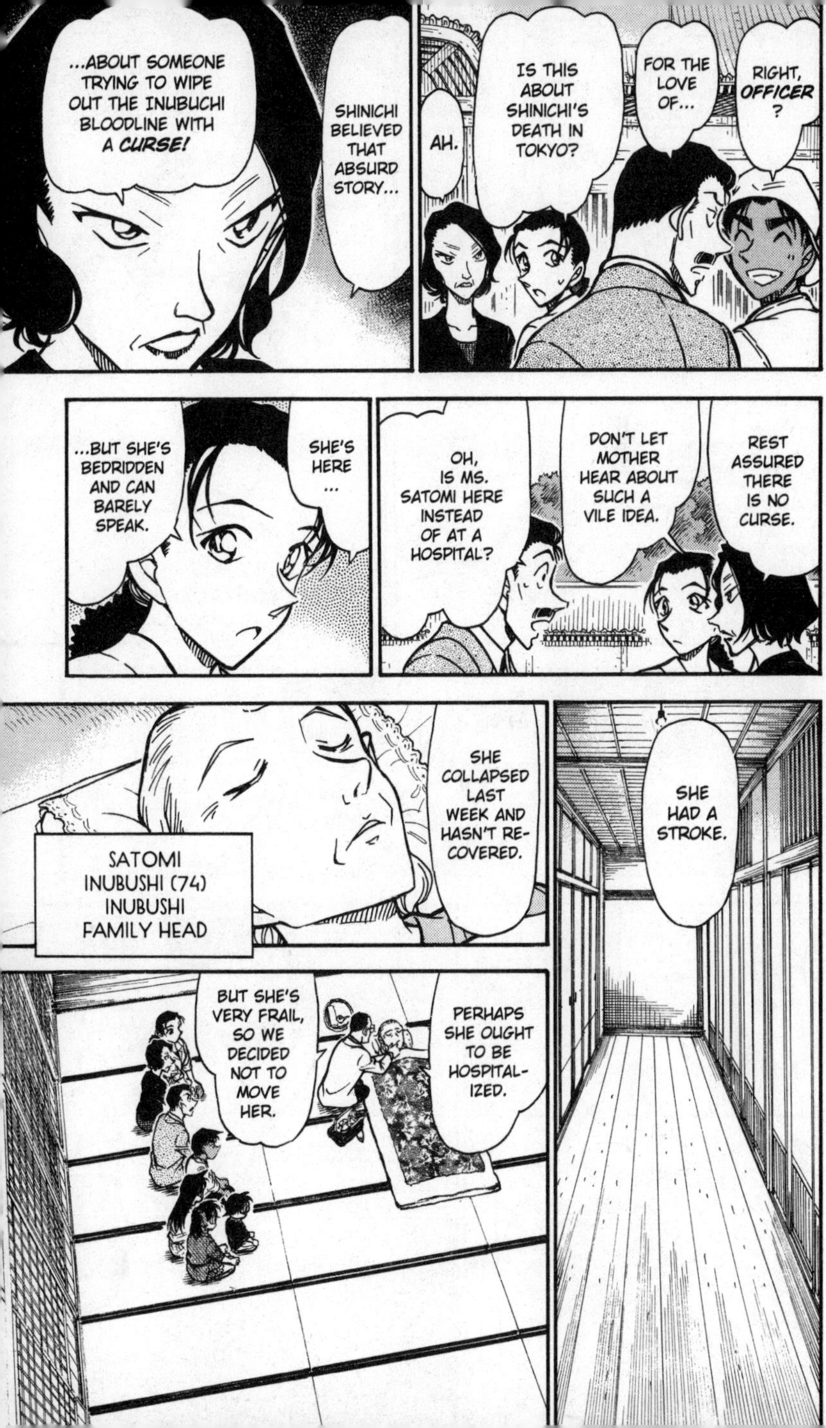
RIGHT, OFFICER?
FOR THE LOVE OF...
IS THIS ABOUT SHINICHI'S DEATH IN TOKYO?
AH.
SHINICHI BELIEVED THAT ABSURD STORY...
...ABOUT SOMEONE TRYING TO WIPE OUT THE INUBUCHI BLOODLINE WITH A CURSE!
REST ASSURED THERE IS NO CURSE.
DON'T LET MOTHER HEAR ABOUT SUCH A VILE IDEA.
OH, IS MS. SATOMI HERE INSTEAD OF AT A HOSPITAL?
SHE'S HERE ...
...BUT SHE'S BEDRIDDEN AND CAN BARELY SPEAK.
SHE HAD A STROKE.
SHE COLLAPSED LAST WEEK AND HASN'T RE-COVERED.
SATOMI INUBUSHI (74) INUBUSHI FAMILY HEAD
PERHAPS SHE OUGHT TO BE HOSPITAL-IZED.
BUT SHE'S VERY FRAIL, SO WE DECIDED NOT TO MOVE HER.

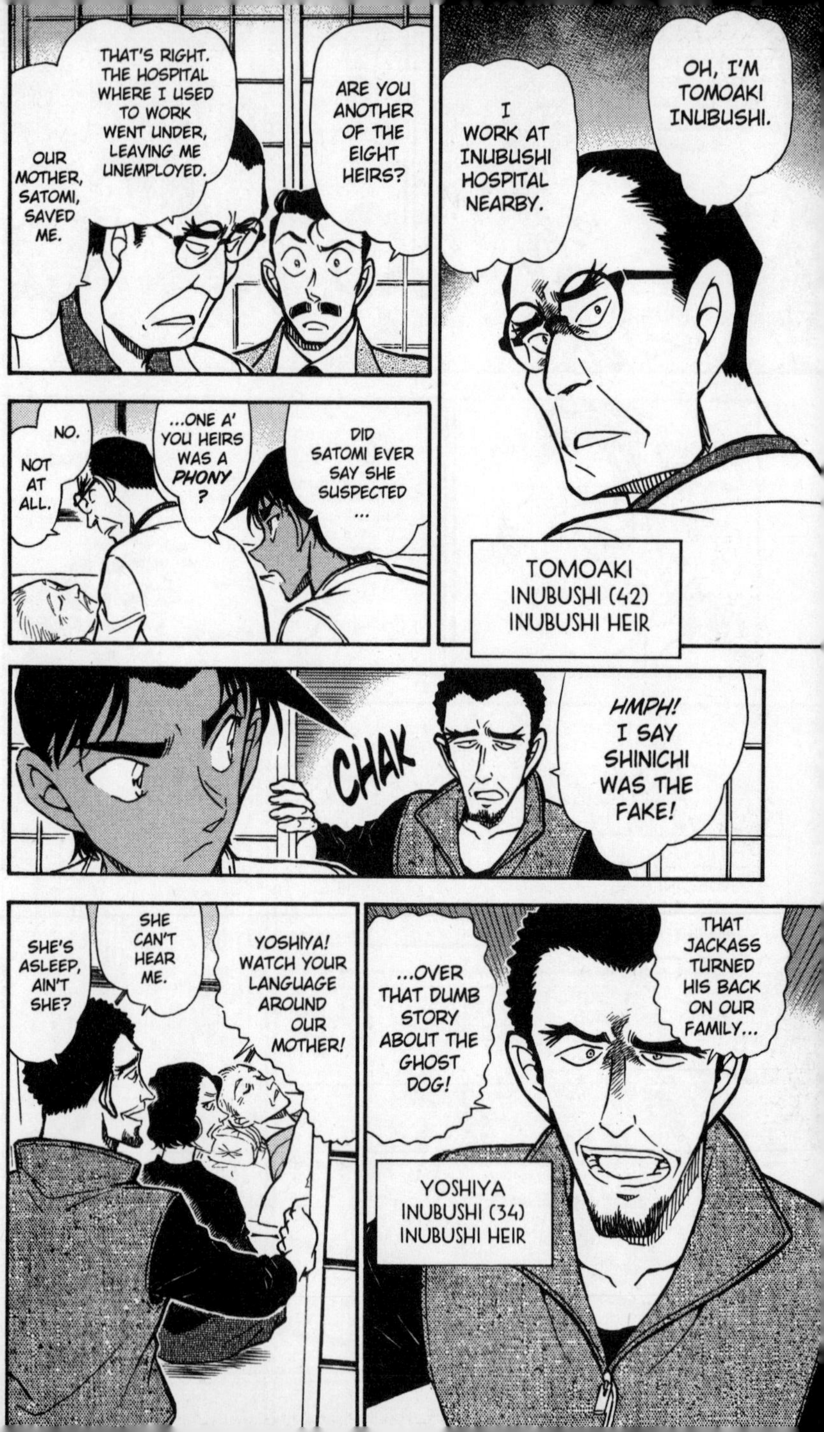
OH, I'M TOMOAKI INUBUSHI.
I WORK AT INUBUSHI HOSPITAL NEARBY.
TOMOAKI INUBUSHI (42) INUBUSHI HEIR
ARE YOU ANOTHER OF THE EIGHT HEIRS?
THAT'S RIGHT. THE HOSPITAL WHERE I USED TO WORK WENT UNDER, LEAVING ME UNEMPLOYED.
OUR MOTHER, SATOMI, SAVED ME.
DID SATOMI EVER SAY SHE SUSPECTED...
...ONE A' YOU HEIRS WAS A *PHONY*?
NO.
NOT AT ALL.
HMPH! I SAY SHINICHI WAS THE FAKE!
CHAK
THAT JACKASS TURNED HIS BACK ON OUR FAMILY...
...OVER THAT DUMB STORY ABOUT THE GHOST DOG!
YOSHIYA INUBUSHI (34) INUBUSHI HEIR
YOSHIYA! WATCH YOUR LANGUAGE AROUND OUR MOTHER!
SHE CAN'T HEAR ME.
SHE'S ASLEEP, AIN'T SHE?

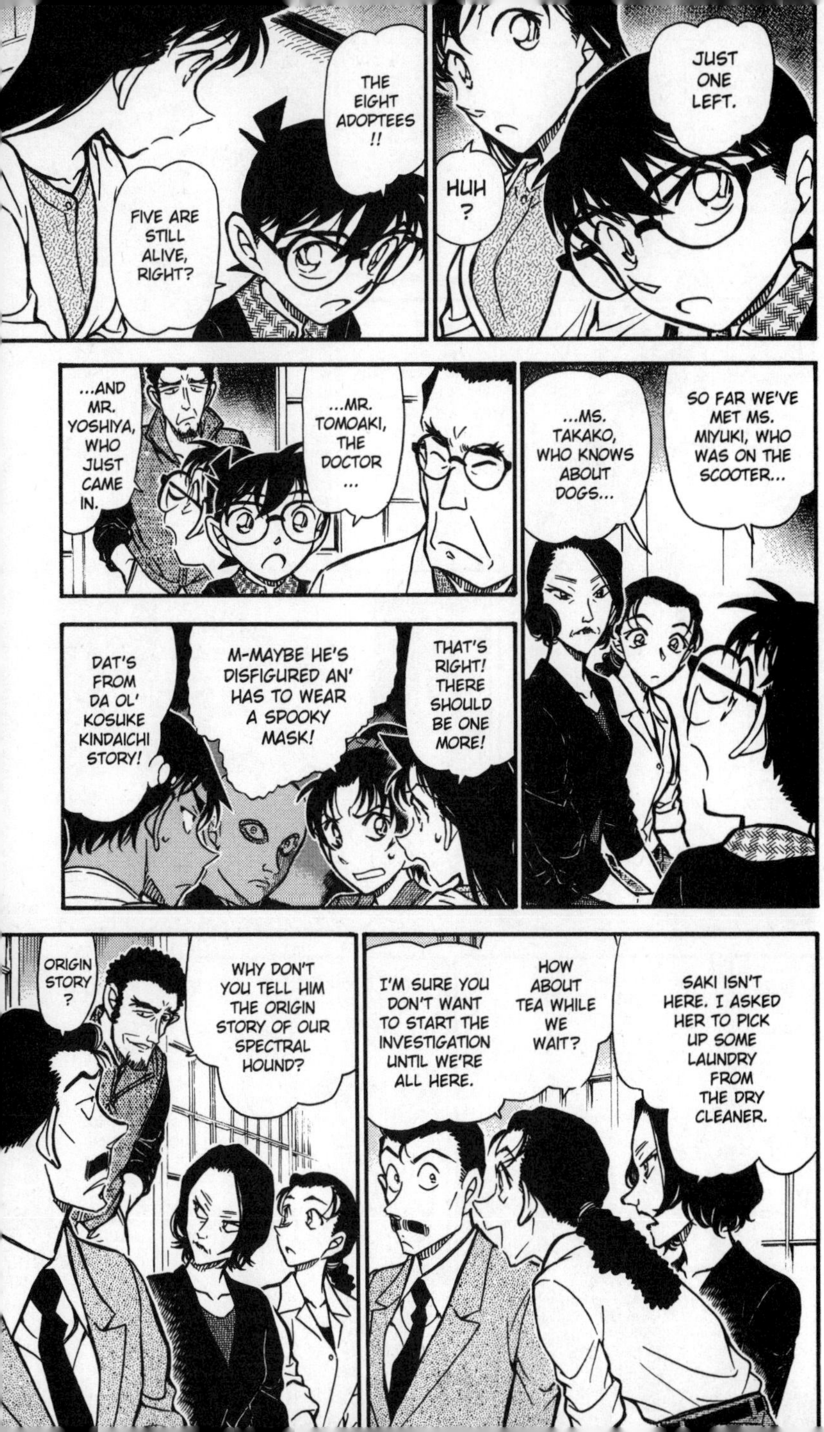
JUST ONE LEFT.
HUH?
THE EIGHT ADOPTEES!!
FIVE ARE STILL ALIVE, RIGHT?
SO FAR WE'VE MET MS. MIYUKI, WHO WAS ON THE SCOOTER...
...MS. TAKAKO, WHO KNOWS ABOUT DOGS...
...MR. TOMOAKI, THE DOCTOR...
...AND MR. YOSHIYA, WHO JUST CAME IN.
THAT'S RIGHT! THERE SHOULD BE ONE MORE!
M-MAYBE HE'S DISFIGURED AN' HAS TO WEAR A SPOOKY MASK!
DAT'S FROM DA OL' KOSUKE KINDAICHI STORY!
SAKI ISN'T HERE. I ASKED HER TO PICK UP SOME LAUNDRY FROM THE DRY CLEANER.
HOW ABOUT TEA WHILE WE WAIT?
I'M SURE YOU DON'T WANT TO START THE INVESTIGATION UNTIL WE'RE ALL HERE.
WHY DON'T YOU TELL HIM THE ORIGIN STORY OF OUR SPECTRAL HOUND?
ORIGIN STORY?

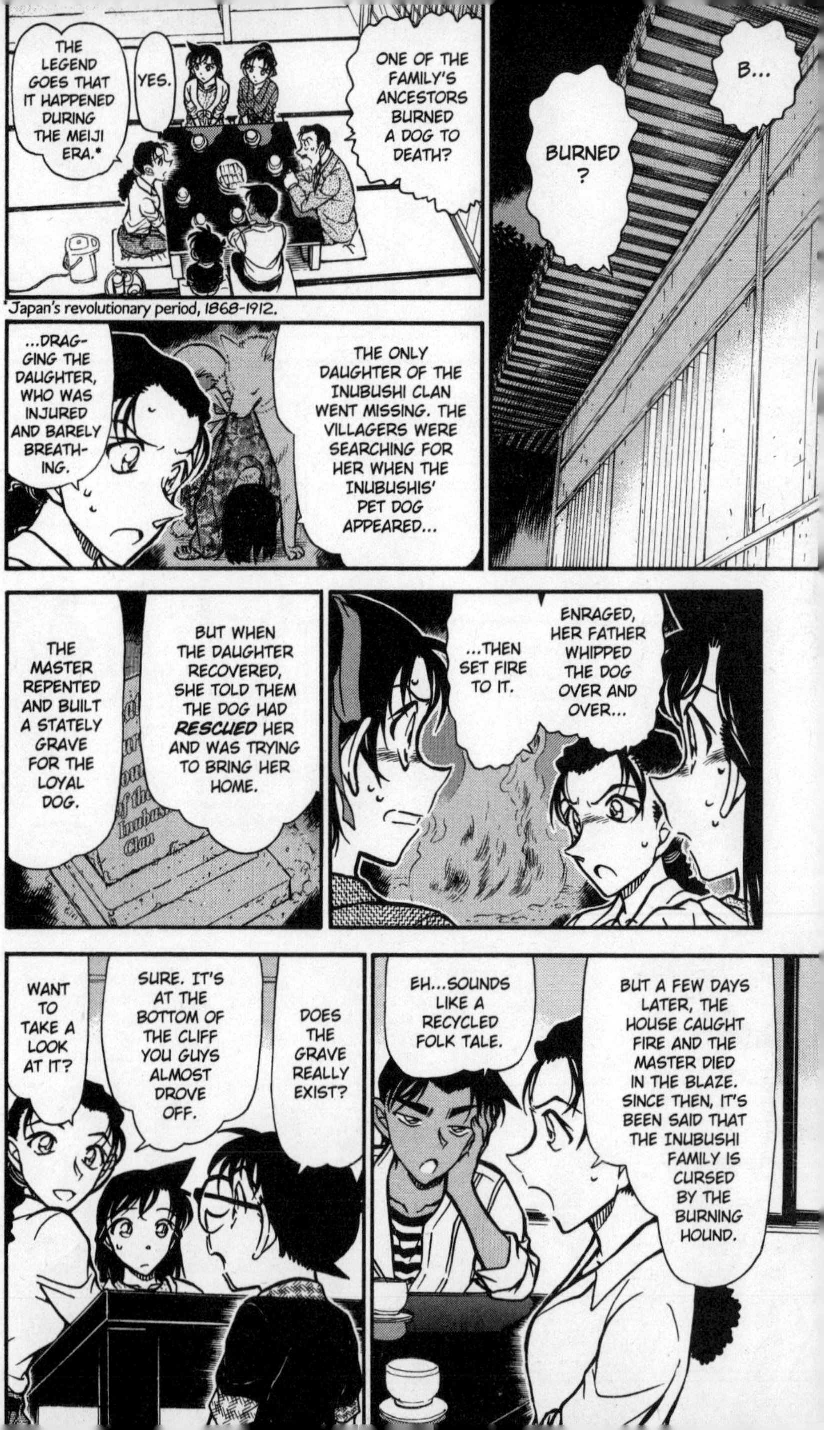
B...
BURNED?
ONE OF THE FAMILY'S ANCESTORS BURNED A DOG TO DEATH?
YES.
THE LEGEND GOES THAT IT HAPPENED DURING THE MEIJI ERA.*
THE ONLY DAUGHTER OF THE INUBUSHI CLAN WENT MISSING. THE VILLAGERS WERE SEARCHING FOR HER WHEN THE INUBUSHIS' PET DOG APPEARED...
...DRAGGING THE DAUGHTER, WHO WAS INJURED AND BARELY BREATHING.
ENRAGED, HER FATHER WHIPPED THE DOG OVER AND OVER...
...THEN SET FIRE TO IT.
BUT WHEN THE DAUGHTER RECOVERED, SHE TOLD THEM THE DOG HAD ***RESCUED*** HER AND WAS TRYING TO BRING HER HOME.
THE MASTER REPENTED AND BUILT A STATELY GRAVE FOR THE LOYAL DOG.
BUT A FEW DAYS LATER, THE HOUSE CAUGHT FIRE AND THE MASTER DIED IN THE BLAZE. SINCE THEN, IT'S BEEN SAID THAT THE INUBUSHI FAMILY IS CURSED BY THE BURNING HOUND.
EH...SOUNDS LIKE A RECYCLED FOLK TALE.
DOES THE GRAVE REALLY EXIST?
SURE. IT'S AT THE BOTTOM OF THE CLIFF YOU GUYS ALMOST DROVE OFF.
WANT TO TAKE A LOOK AT IT?
*Japan's revolutionary period, 1868-1912.

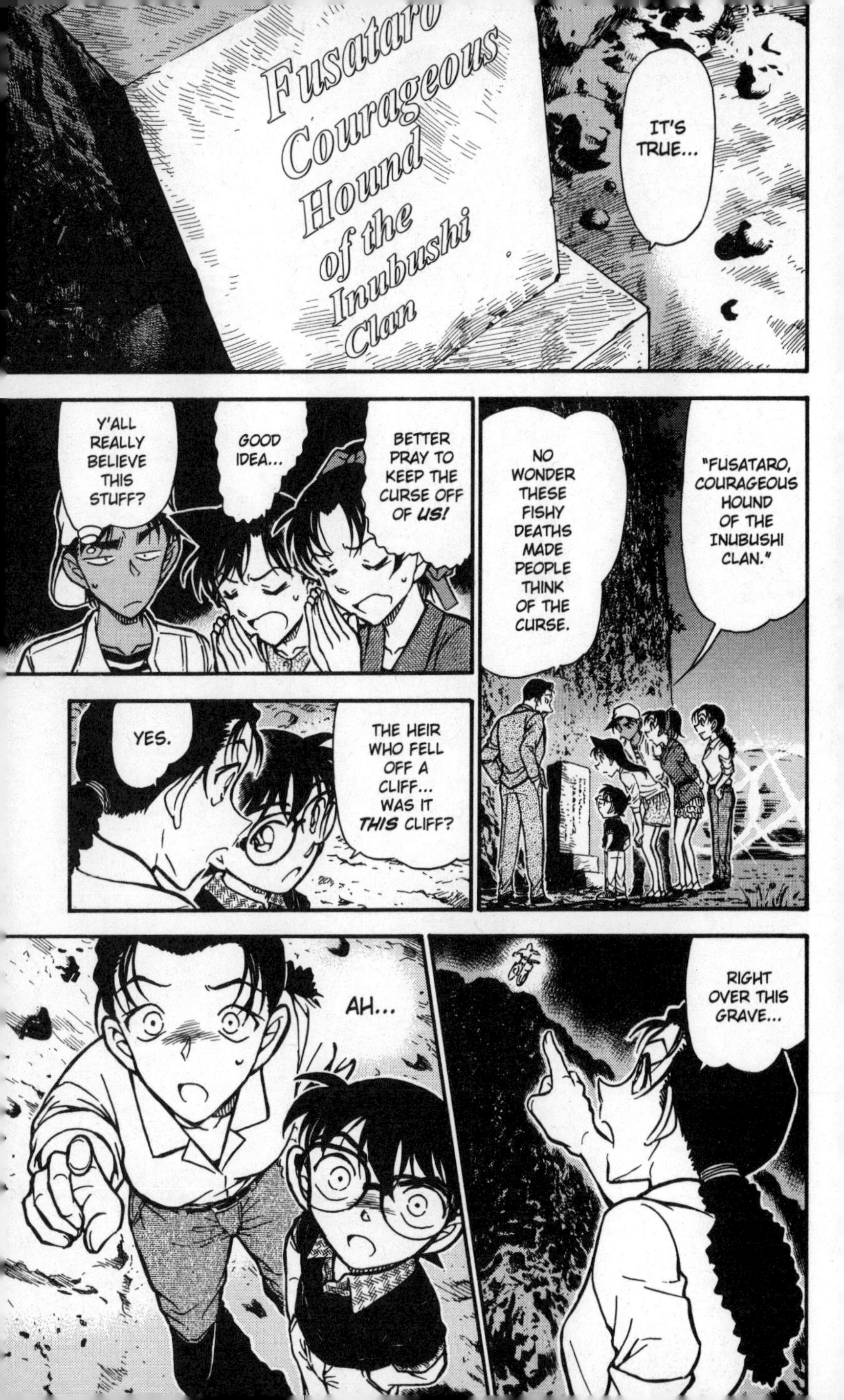
IT'S TRUE...
Fusataro Courageous Hound of the Inubushi Clan
"FUSATARO, COURAGEOUS HOUND OF THE INUBUSHI CLAN."
NO WONDER THESE FISHY DEATHS MADE PEOPLE THINK OF THE CURSE.
BETTER PRAY TO KEEP THE CURSE OFF OF *US!*
GOOD IDEA...
Y'ALL REALLY BELIEVE THIS STUFF?
THE HEIR WHO FELL OFF A CLIFF... WAS IT *THIS* CLIFF?
YES.
RIGHT OVER THIS GRAVE...
AH...

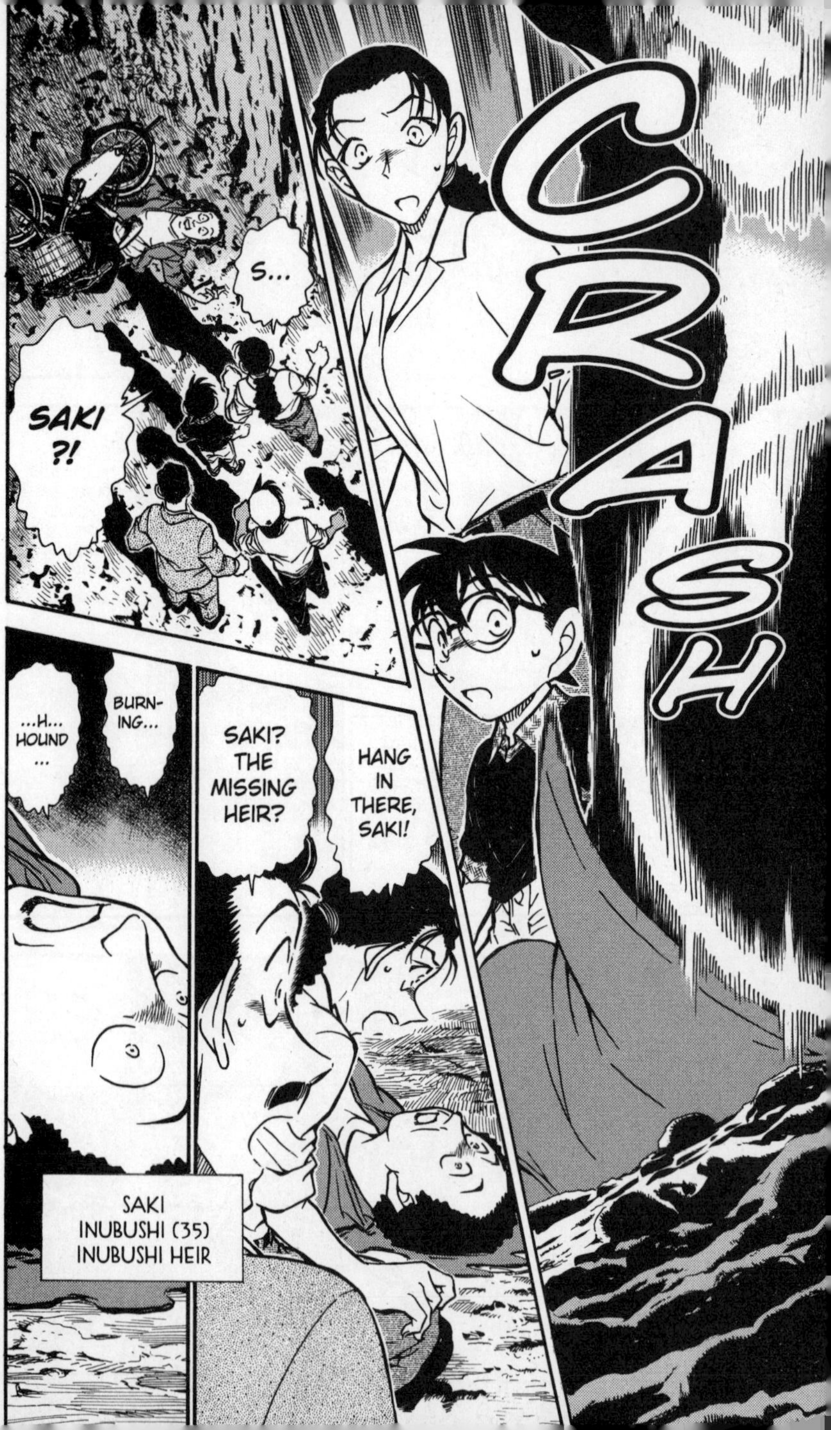
CRASH
S...
SAKI ?!
HANG IN THERE, SAKI!
SAKI? THE MISSING HEIR?
BURNING...
...H... HOUND ...
SAKI INUBUSHI (35) INUBUSHI HEIR

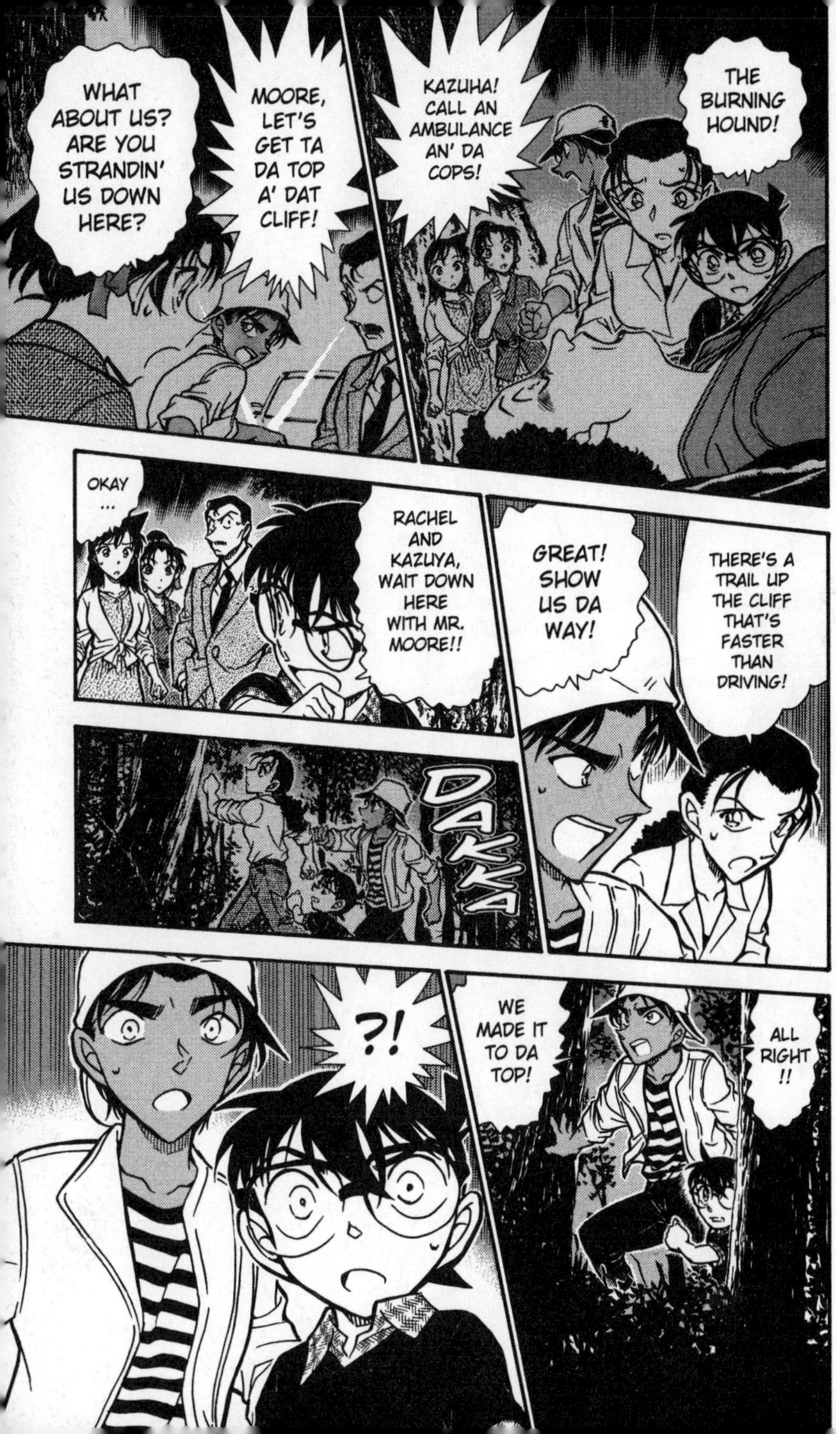
THE BURNING HOUND!
KAZUHA! CALL AN AMBULANCE AN' DA COPS!
MOORE, LET'S GET TA DA TOP A' DAT CLIFF!
WHAT ABOUT US? ARE YOU STRANDIN' US DOWN HERE?
THERE'S A TRAIL UP THE CLIFF THAT'S FASTER THAN DRIVING!
GREAT! SHOW US DA WAY!
RACHEL AND KAZUYA, WAIT DOWN HERE WITH MR. MOORE!!
OKAY ...
DAKKA
ALL RIGHT !!
WE MADE IT TO DA TOP!
?!

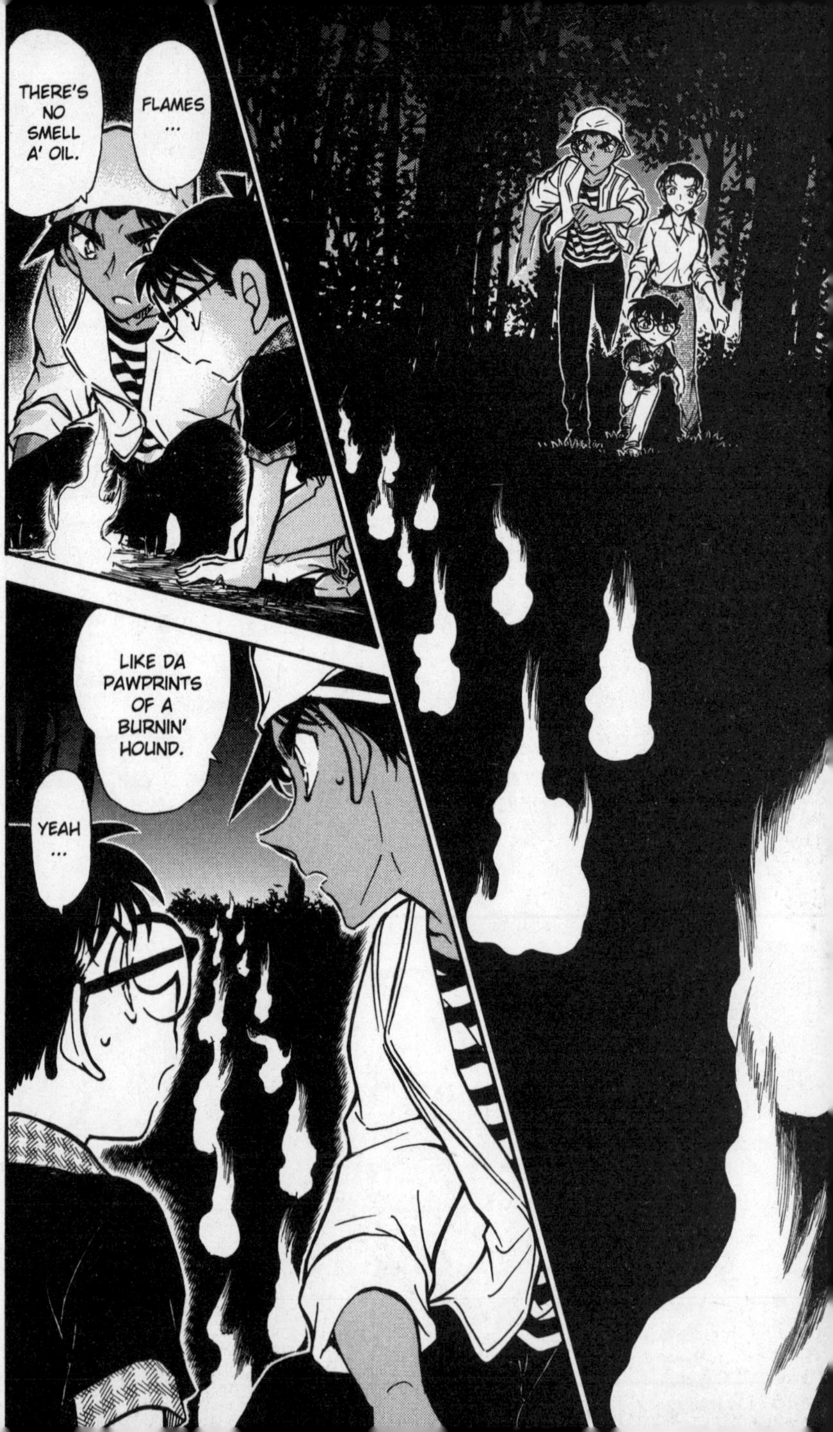
FLAMES ...
THERE'S NO SMELL A' OIL.
LIKE DA PAWPRINTS OF A BURNIN' HOUND.
YEAH ...

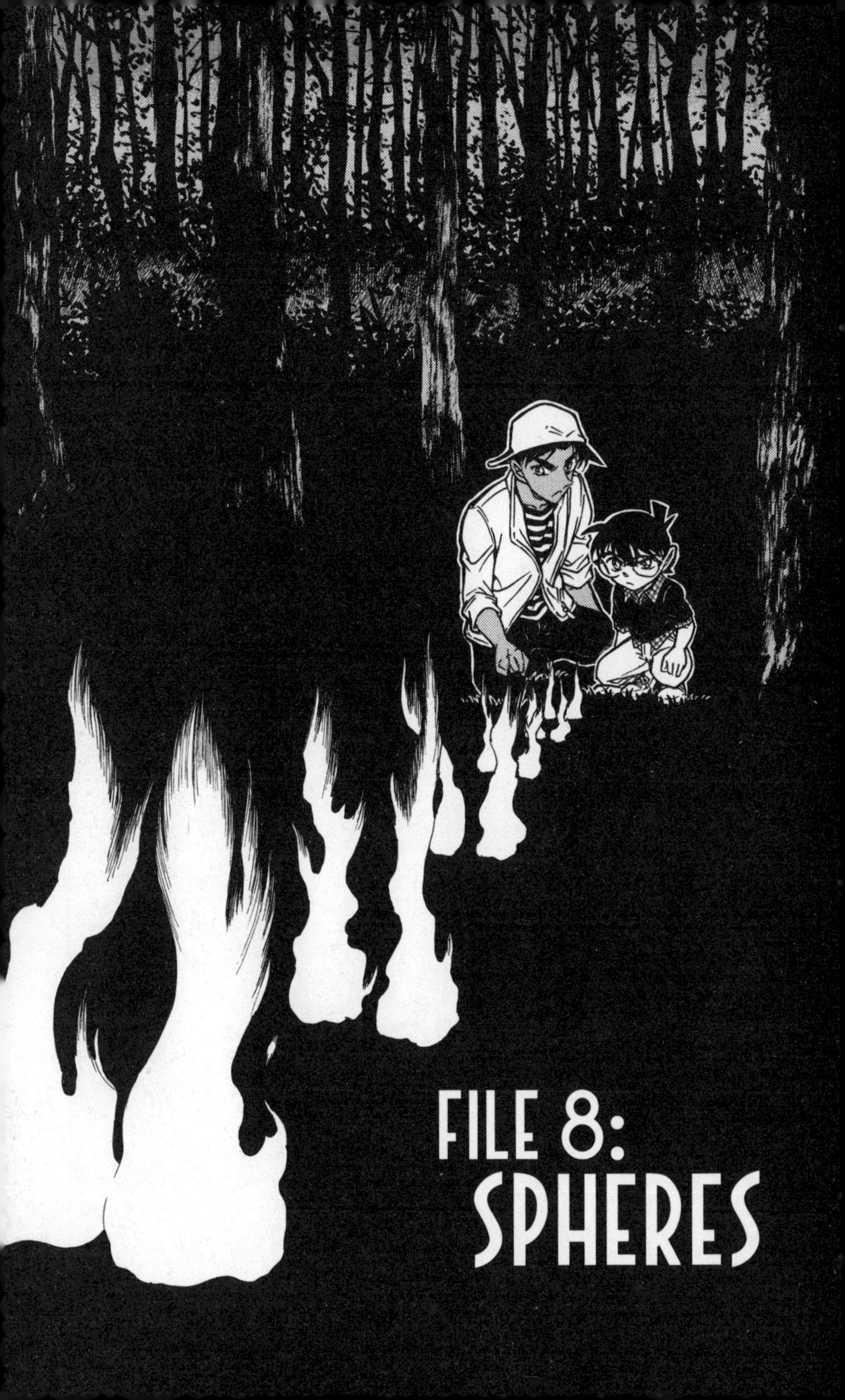
FILE 8:
SPHERES

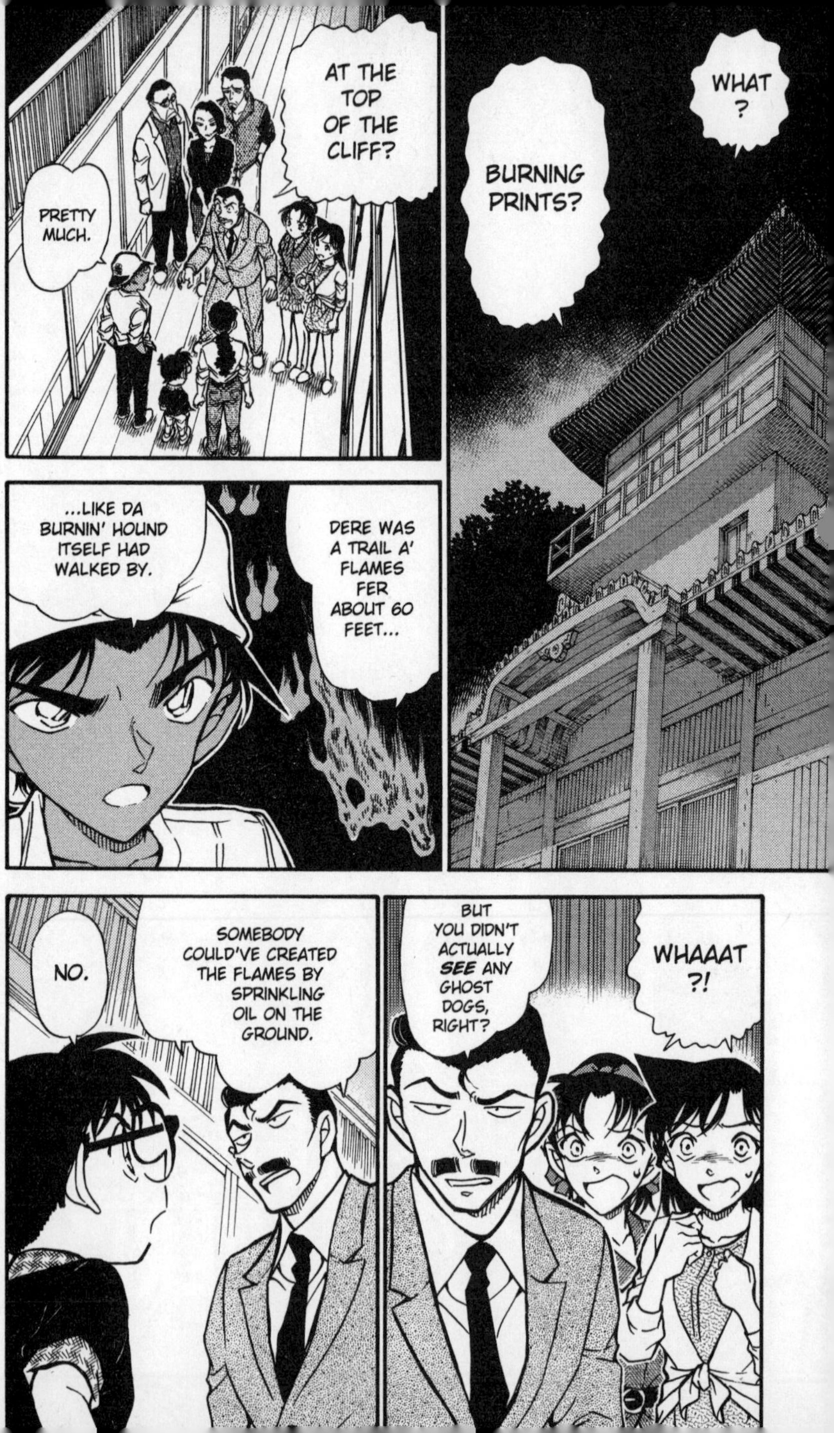
WHAT ?
BURNING PRINTS?
AT THE TOP OF THE CLIFF?
PRETTY MUCH.
DERE WAS A TRAIL A' FLAMES FER ABOUT 60 FEET...
...LIKE DA BURNIN' HOUND ITSELF HAD WALKED BY.
BUT YOU DIDN'T ACTUALLY SEE ANY GHOST DOGS, RIGHT?
WHAAAT ?!
SOMEBODY COULD'VE CREATED THE FLAMES BY SPRINKLING OIL ON THE GROUND.
NO.

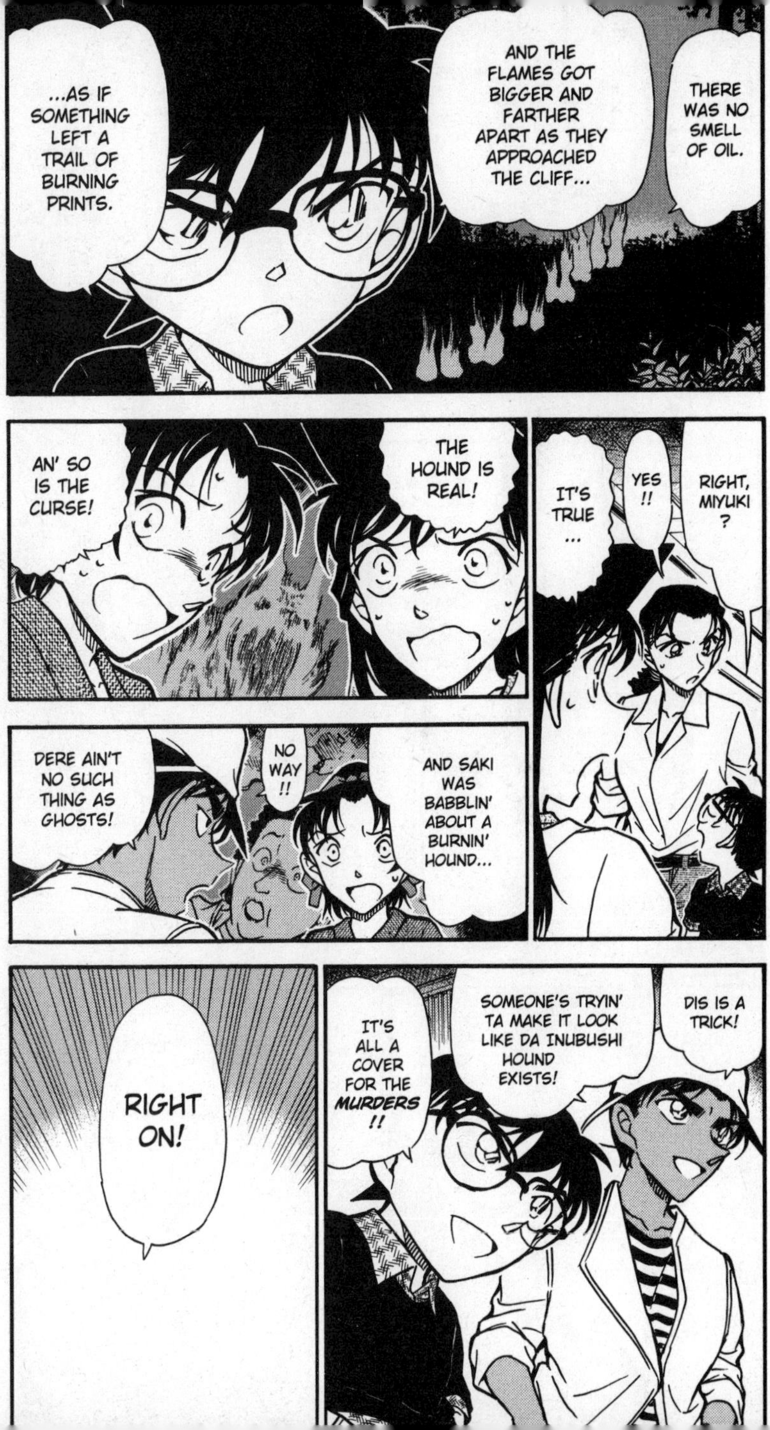
THERE WAS NO SMELL OF OIL.
AND THE FLAMES GOT BIGGER AND FARTHER APART AS THEY APPROACHED THE CLIFF...
...AS IF SOMETHING LEFT A TRAIL OF BURNING PRINTS.
RIGHT, MIYUKI?
YES!!
IT'S TRUE...
THE HOUND IS REAL!
AN' SO IS THE CURSE!
AND SAKI WAS BABBLIN' ABOUT A BURNIN' HOUND...
NO WAY!!
DERE AIN'T NO SUCH THING AS GHOSTS!
DIS IS A TRICK!
SOMEONE'S TRYIN' TA MAKE IT LOOK LIKE DA INUBUSHI HOUND EXISTS!
IT'S ALL A COVER FOR THE *MURDERS*!!
RIGHT ON!

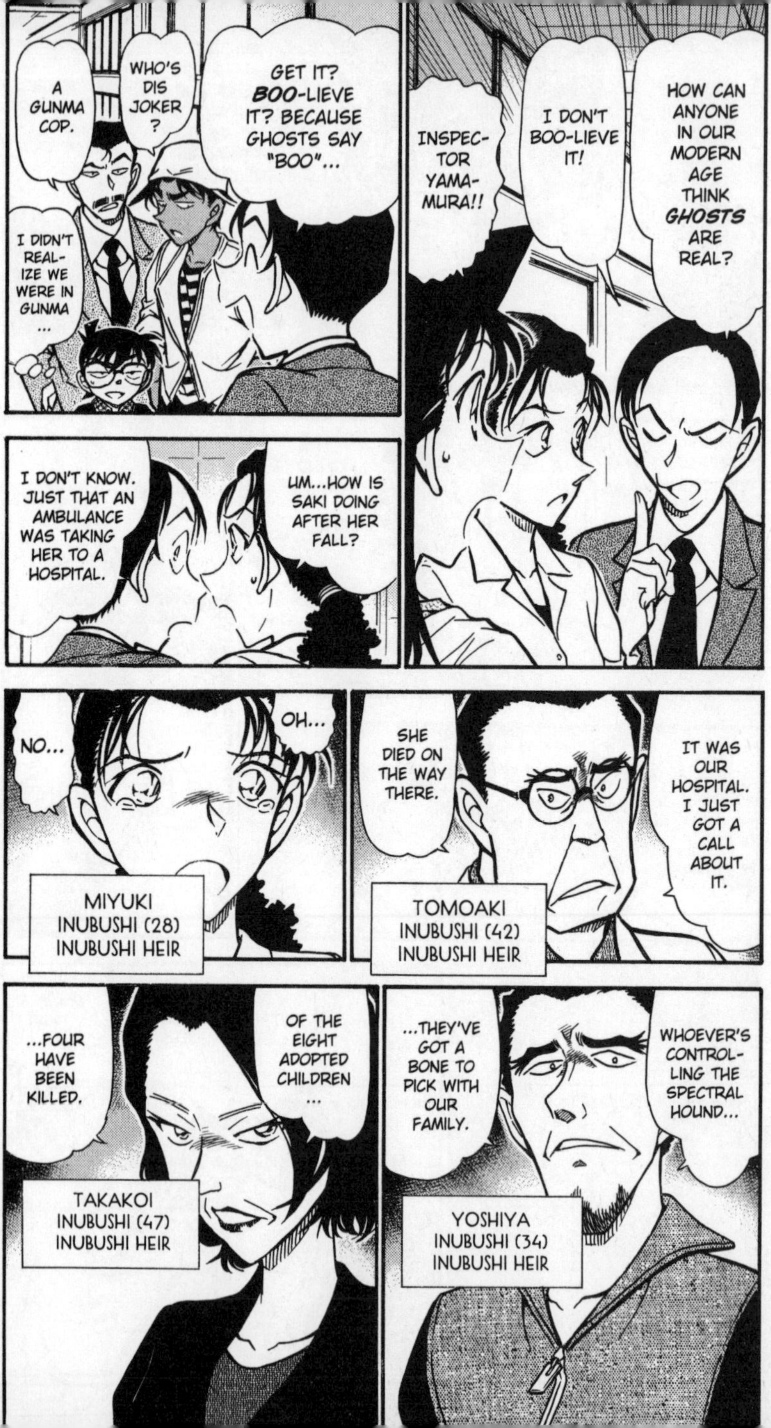
HOW CAN ANYONE IN OUR MODERN AGE THINK **GHOSTS** ARE REAL?
I DON'T BOO-LIEVE IT!
INSPECTOR YAMAMURA!!
GET IT? **BOO**-LIEVE IT? BECAUSE GHOSTS SAY "BOO"...
WHO'S DIS JOKER?
A GUNMA COP.
I DIDN'T REALIZE WE WERE IN GUNMA...
UM...HOW IS SAKI DOING AFTER HER FALL?
I DON'T KNOW. JUST THAT AN AMBULANCE WAS TAKING HER TO A HOSPITAL.
IT WAS OUR HOSPITAL. I JUST GOT A CALL ABOUT IT.
SHE DIED ON THE WAY THERE.
TOMOAKI INUBUSHI (42) INUBUSHI HEIR
OH...
NO...
MIYUKI INUBUSHI (28) INUBUSHI HEIR
WHOEVER'S CONTROLLING THE SPECTRAL HOUND...
...THEY'VE GOT A BONE TO PICK WITH OUR FAMILY.
YOSHIYA INUBUSHI (34) INUBUSHI HEIR
OF THE EIGHT ADOPTED CHILDREN...
...FOUR HAVE BEEN KILLED.
TAKAKOI INUBUSHI (47) INUBUSHI HEIR

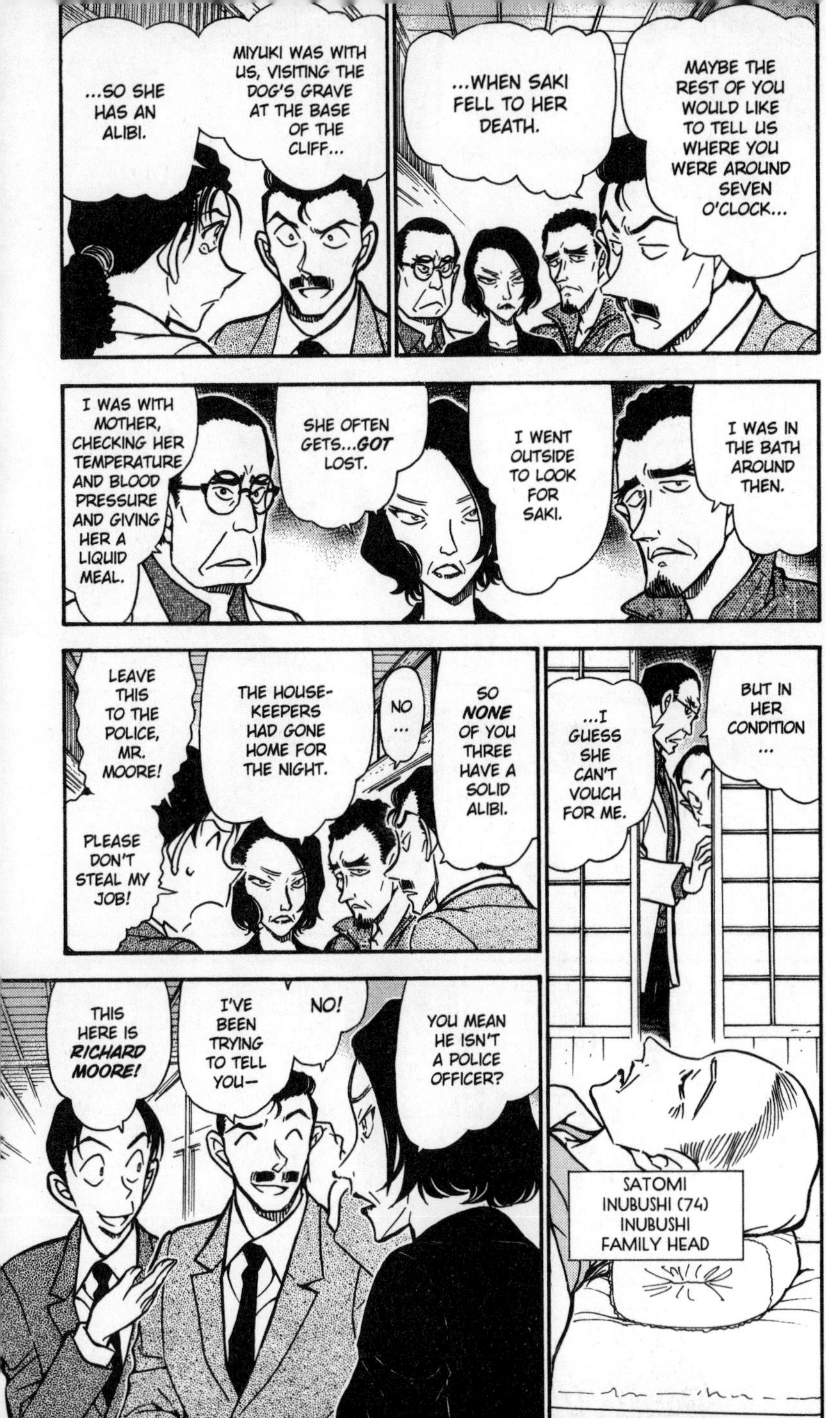
MAYBE THE REST OF YOU WOULD LIKE TO TELL US WHERE YOU WERE AROUND SEVEN O'CLOCK...
...WHEN SAKI FELL TO HER DEATH.
MIYUKI WAS WITH US, VISITING THE DOG'S GRAVE AT THE BASE OF THE CLIFF...
...SO SHE HAS AN ALIBI.
I WAS IN THE BATH AROUND THEN.
I WENT OUTSIDE TO LOOK FOR SAKI.
SHE OFTEN GETS...**GOT** LOST.
I WAS WITH MOTHER, CHECKING HER TEMPERATURE AND BLOOD PRESSURE AND GIVING HER A LIQUID MEAL.
BUT IN HER CONDITION...
...I GUESS SHE CAN'T VOUCH FOR ME.
SATOMI INUBUSHI (74) INUBUSHI FAMILY HEAD
SO ***NONE*** OF YOU THREE HAVE A SOLID ALIBI.
NO...
THE HOUSE-KEEPERS HAD GONE HOME FOR THE NIGHT.
LEAVE THIS TO THE POLICE, MR. MOORE!
PLEASE DON'T STEAL MY JOB!
YOU MEAN HE ISN'T A POLICE OFFICER?
NO!
I'VE BEEN TRYING TO TELL YOU—
THIS HERE IS ***RICHARD MOORE!***

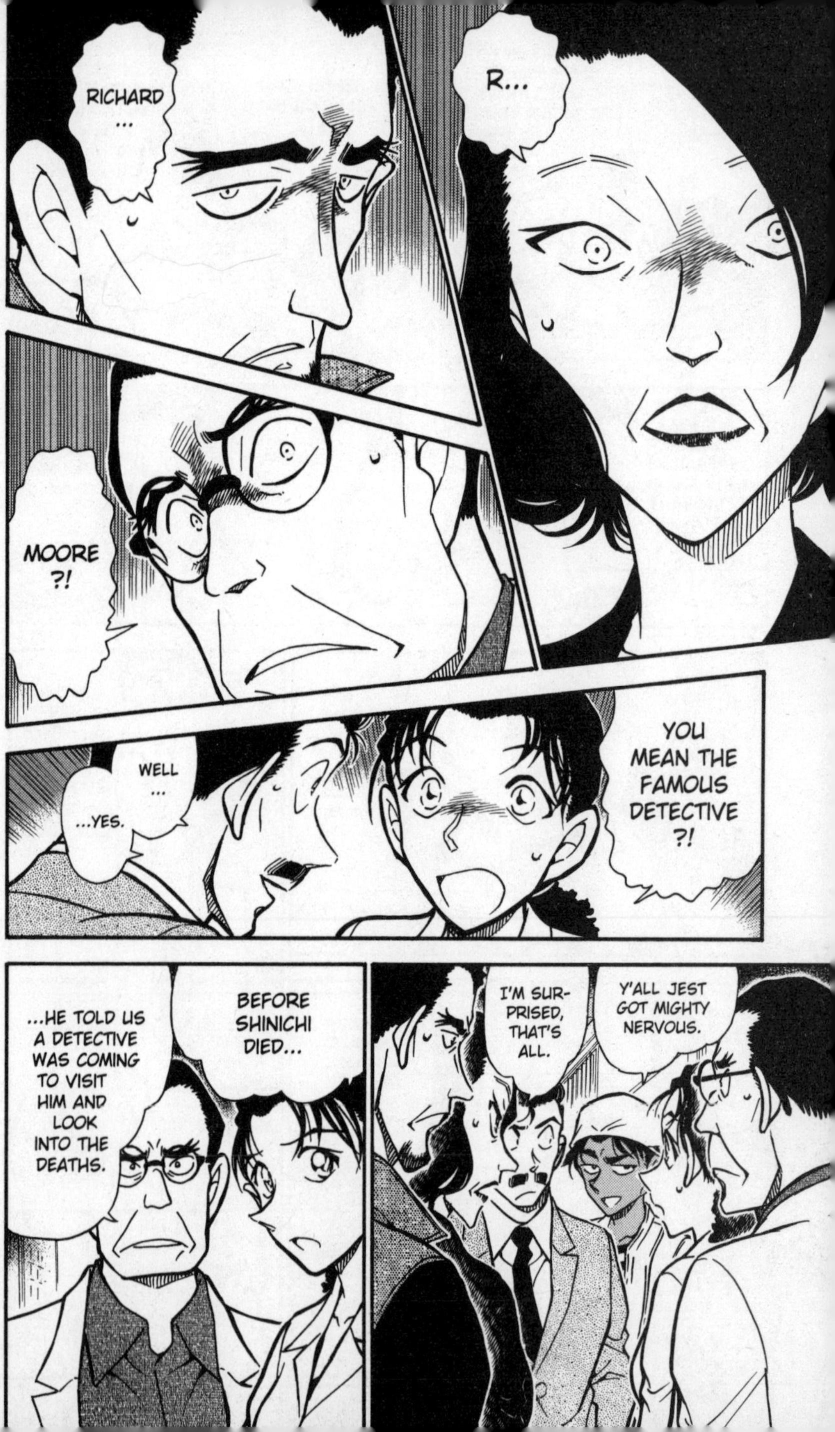
R...
RICHARD ...
MOORE ?!
YOU MEAN THE FAMOUS DETECTIVE ?!
WELL ...
...YES.
Y'ALL JEST GOT MIGHTY NERVOUS.
I'M SUR-PRISED, THAT'S ALL.
BEFORE SHINICHI DIED...
...HE TOLD US A DETECTIVE WAS COMING TO VISIT HIM AND LOOK INTO THE DEATHS.

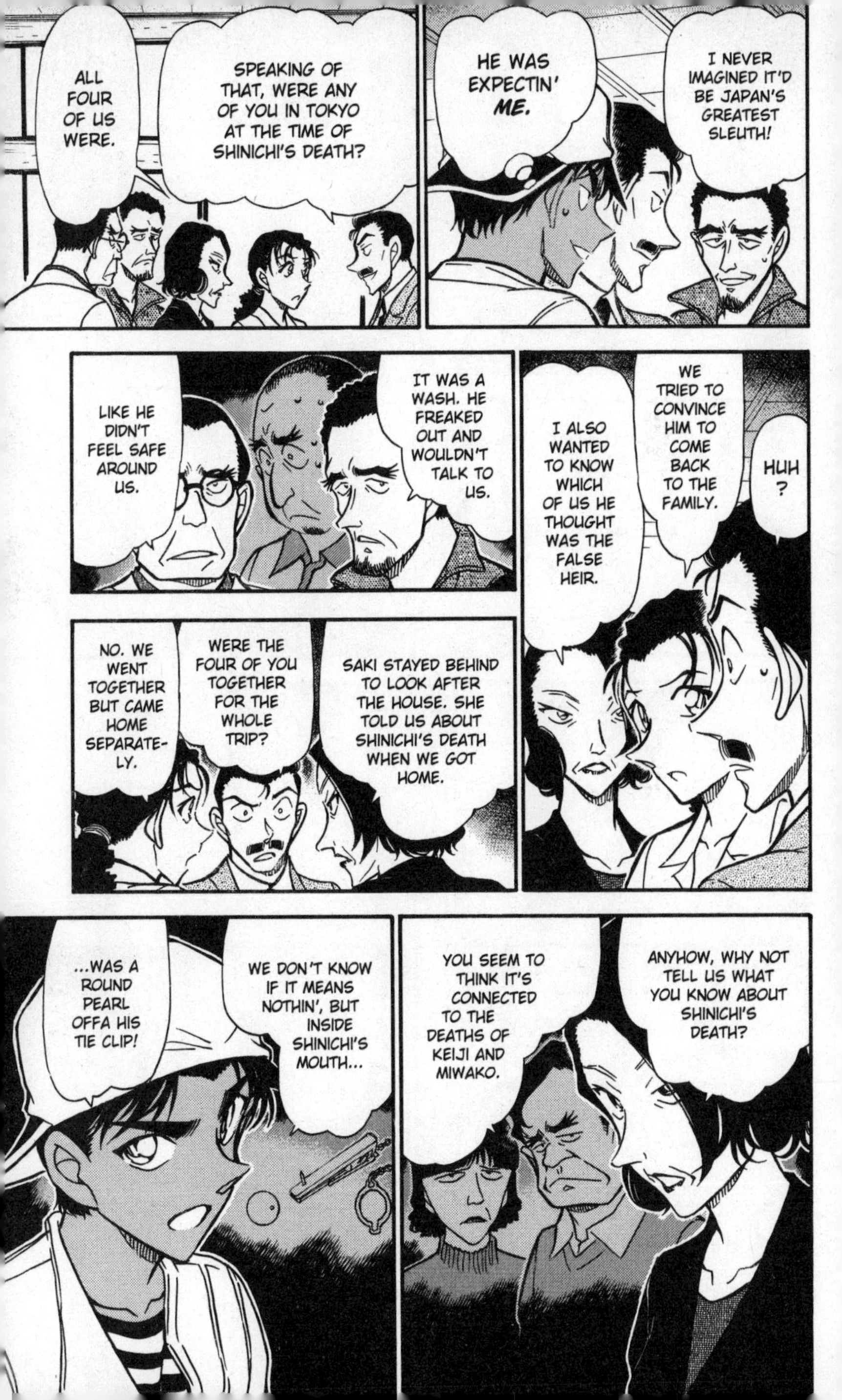
I NEVER IMAGINED IT'D BE JAPAN'S GREATEST SLEUTH!
HE WAS EXPECTIN' *ME.*
SPEAKING OF THAT, WERE ANY OF YOU IN TOKYO AT THE TIME OF SHINICHI'S DEATH?
ALL FOUR OF US WERE.
HUH?
WE TRIED TO CONVINCE HIM TO COME BACK TO THE FAMILY.
I ALSO WANTED TO KNOW WHICH OF US HE THOUGHT WAS THE FALSE HEIR.
IT WAS A WASH. HE FREAKED OUT AND WOULDN'T TALK TO US.
LIKE HE DIDN'T FEEL SAFE AROUND US.
SAKI STAYED BEHIND TO LOOK AFTER THE HOUSE. SHE TOLD US ABOUT SHINICHI'S DEATH WHEN WE GOT HOME.
WERE THE FOUR OF YOU TOGETHER FOR THE WHOLE TRIP?
NO. WE WENT TOGETHER BUT CAME HOME SEPARATE-LY.
ANYHOW, WHY NOT TELL US WHAT YOU KNOW ABOUT SHINICHI'S DEATH?
YOU SEEM TO THINK IT'S CONNECTED TO THE DEATHS OF KEIJI AND MIWAKO.
WE DON'T KNOW IF IT MEANS NOTHIN', BUT INSIDE SHINICHI'S MOUTH...
...WAS A ROUND PEARL OFFA HIS TIE CLIP!

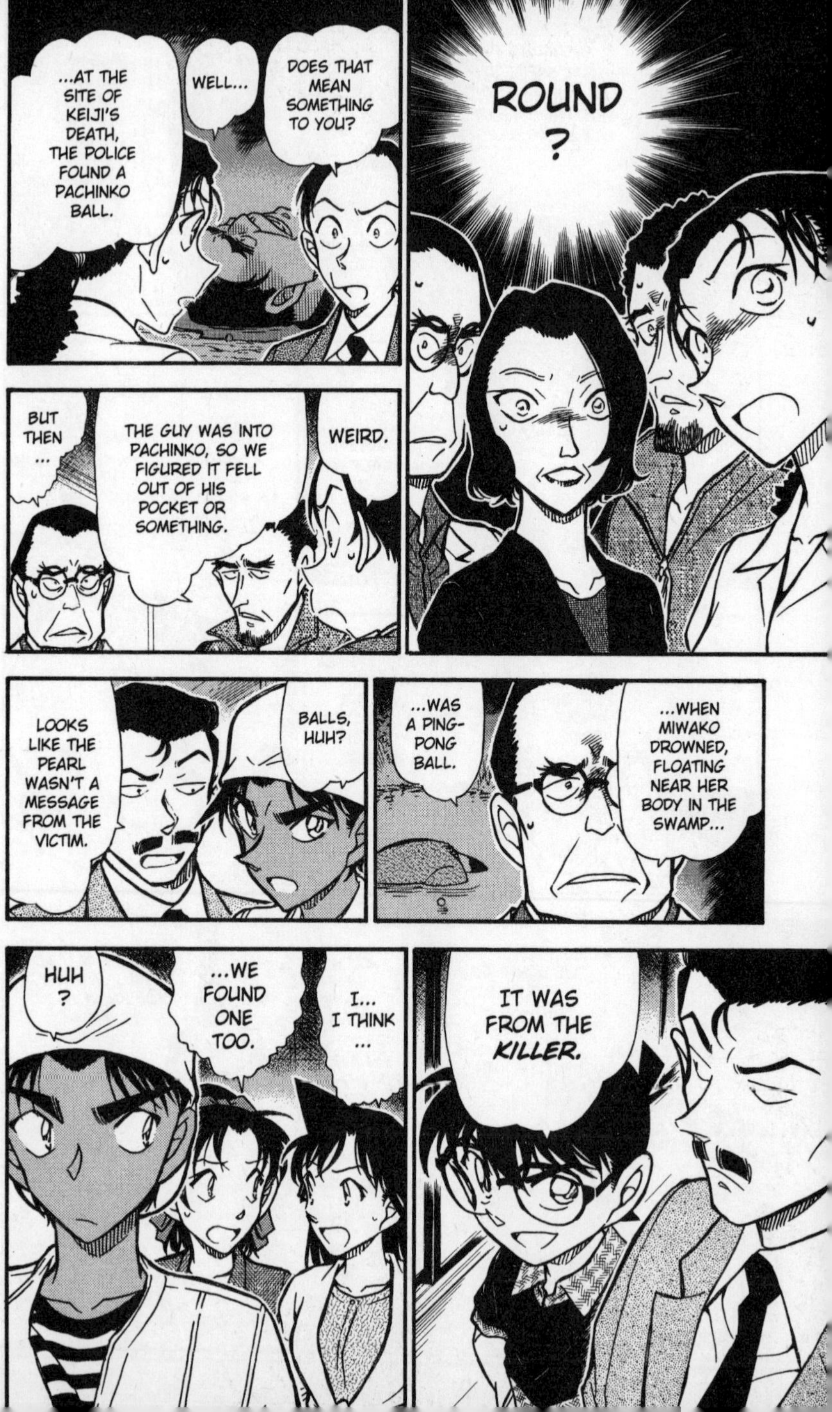
ROUND ?
DOES THAT MEAN SOMETHING TO YOU?
WELL...
...AT THE SITE OF KEIJI'S DEATH, THE POLICE FOUND A PACHINKO BALL.
WEIRD.
THE GUY WAS INTO PACHINKO, SO WE FIGURED IT FELL OUT OF HIS POCKET OR SOMETHING.
BUT THEN ...
...WHEN MIWAKO DROWNED, FLOATING NEAR HER BODY IN THE SWAMP...
...WAS A PING-PONG BALL.
BALLS, HUH?
LOOKS LIKE THE PEARL WASN'T A MESSAGE FROM THE VICTIM.
IT WAS FROM THE *KILLER.*
I... I THINK ...
...WE FOUND ONE TOO.
HUH ?

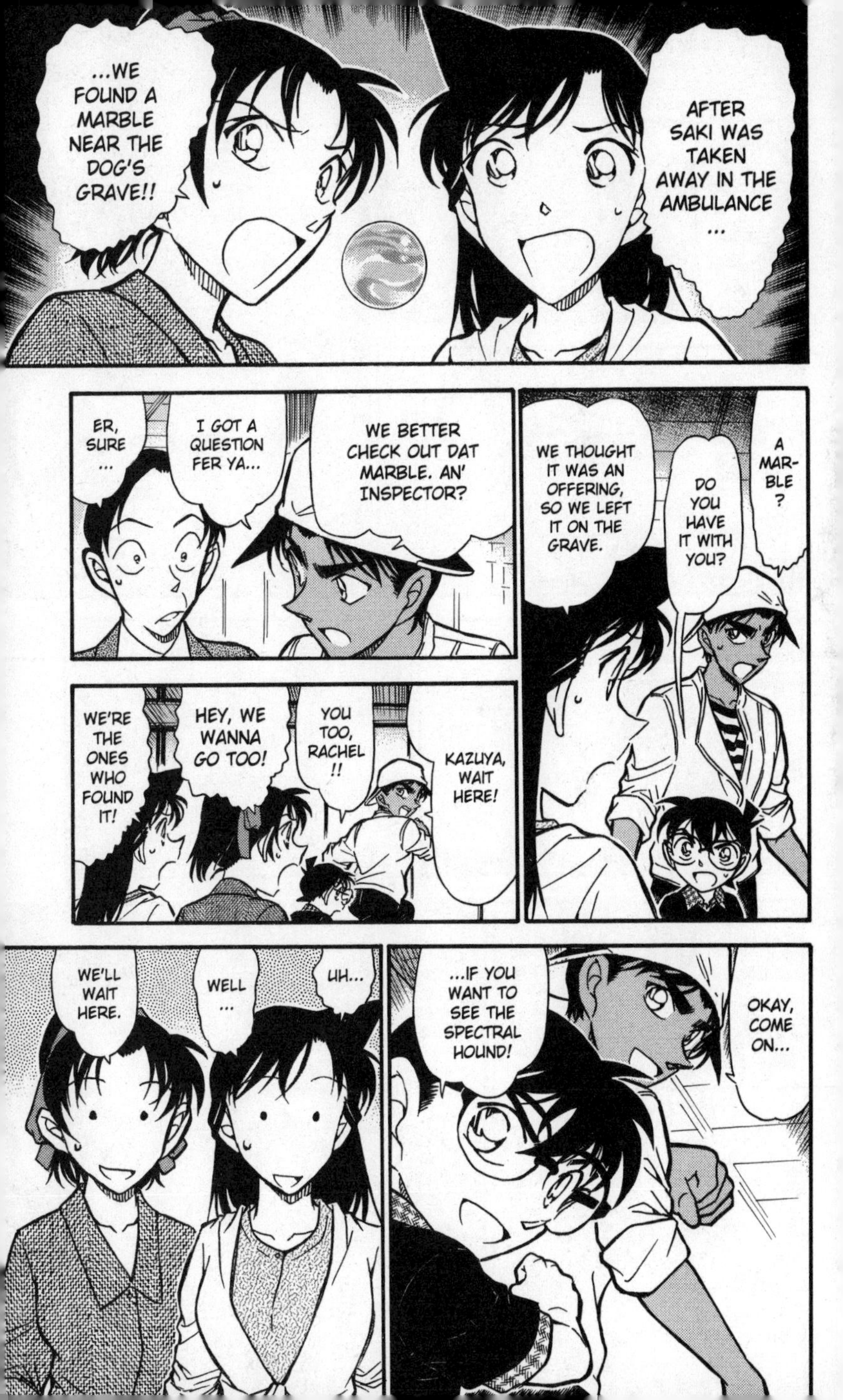
AFTER SAKI WAS TAKEN AWAY IN THE AMBULANCE ...
...WE FOUND A MARBLE NEAR THE DOG'S GRAVE!!
A MARBLE?
DO YOU HAVE IT WITH YOU?
WE THOUGHT IT WAS AN OFFERING, SO WE LEFT IT ON THE GRAVE.
WE BETTER CHECK OUT DAT MARBLE. AN' INSPECTOR?
I GOT A QUESTION FER YA...
ER, SURE ...
KAZUYA, WAIT HERE!
YOU TOO, RACHEL !!
HEY, WE WANNA GO TOO!
WE'RE THE ONES WHO FOUND IT!
OKAY, COME ON...
...IF YOU WANT TO SEE THE SPECTRAL HOUND!
UH...
WELL ...
WE'LL WAIT HERE.

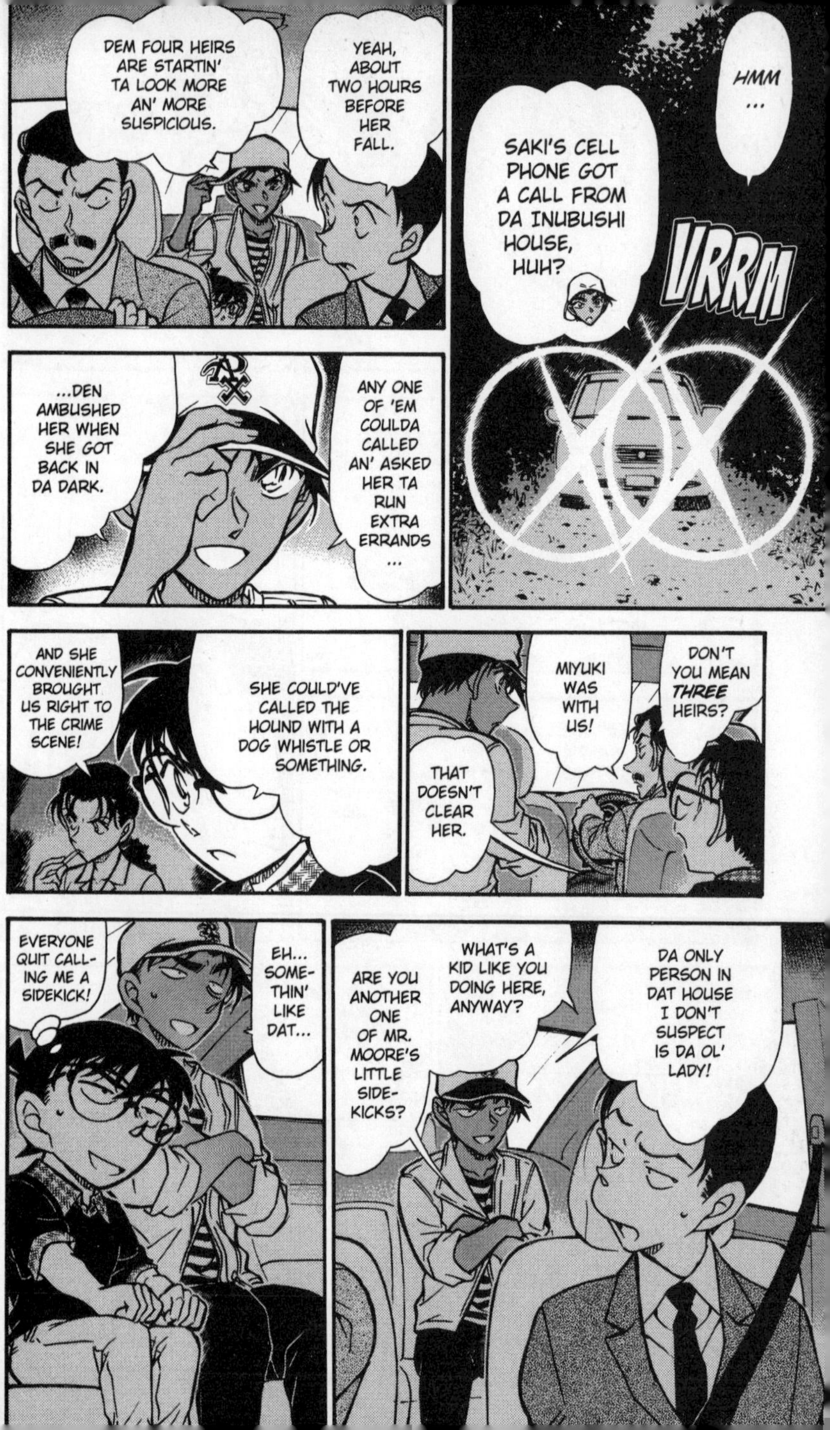
HMM ...
SAKI'S CELL PHONE GOT A CALL FROM DA INUBUSHI HOUSE, HUH?
URRM
YEAH, ABOUT TWO HOURS BEFORE HER FALL.
DEM FOUR HEIRS ARE STARTIN' TA LOOK MORE AN' MORE SUSPICIOUS.
ANY ONE OF 'EM COULDA CALLED AN' ASKED HER TA RUN EXTRA ERRANDS ...
...DEN AMBUSHED HER WHEN SHE GOT BACK IN DA DARK.
DON'T YOU MEAN *THREE* HEIRS?
MIYUKI WAS WITH US!
THAT DOESN'T CLEAR HER.
SHE COULD'VE CALLED THE HOUND WITH A DOG WHISTLE OR SOMETHING.
AND SHE CONVENIENTLY BROUGHT US RIGHT TO THE CRIME SCENE!
DA ONLY PERSON IN DAT HOUSE I DON'T SUSPECT IS DA OL' LADY!
WHAT'S A KID LIKE YOU DOING HERE, ANYWAY?
ARE YOU ANOTHER ONE OF MR. MOORE'S LITTLE SIDE-KICKS?
EH... SOME-THIN' LIKE DAT...
EVERYONE QUIT CALL-ING ME A SIDEKICK!

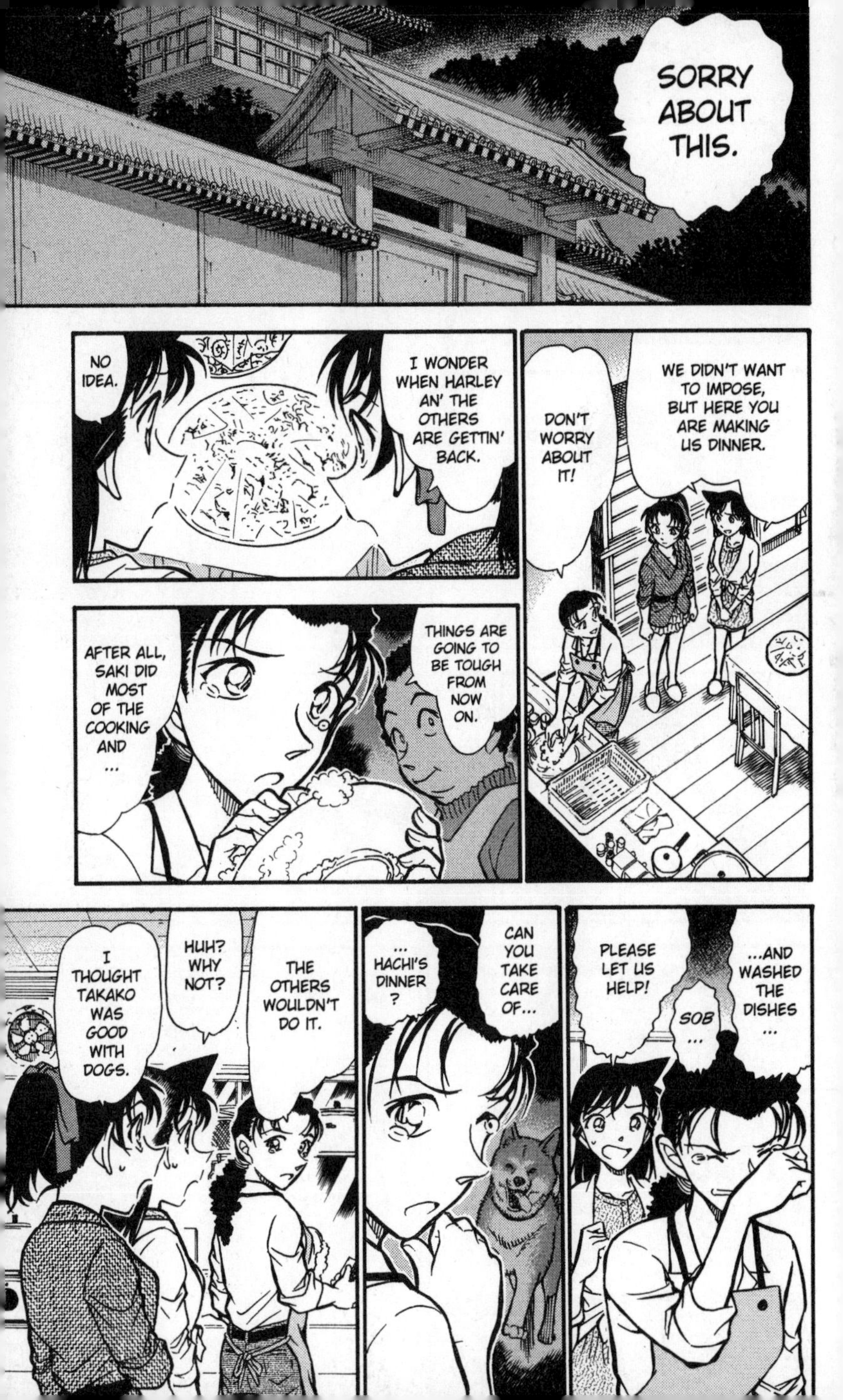
SORRY ABOUT THIS.
WE DIDN'T WANT TO IMPOSE, BUT HERE YOU ARE MAKING US DINNER.
DON'T WORRY ABOUT IT!
I WONDER WHEN HARLEY AN' THE OTHERS ARE GETTIN' BACK.
NO IDEA.
THINGS ARE GOING TO BE TOUGH FROM NOW ON.
AFTER ALL, SAKI DID MOST OF THE COOKING AND ...
...AND WASHED THE DISHES ...
SOB ...
PLEASE LET US HELP!
CAN YOU TAKE CARE OF...
... HACHI'S DINNER ?
THE OTHERS WOULDN'T DO IT.
HUH? WHY NOT?
I THOUGHT TAKAKO WAS GOOD WITH DOGS.

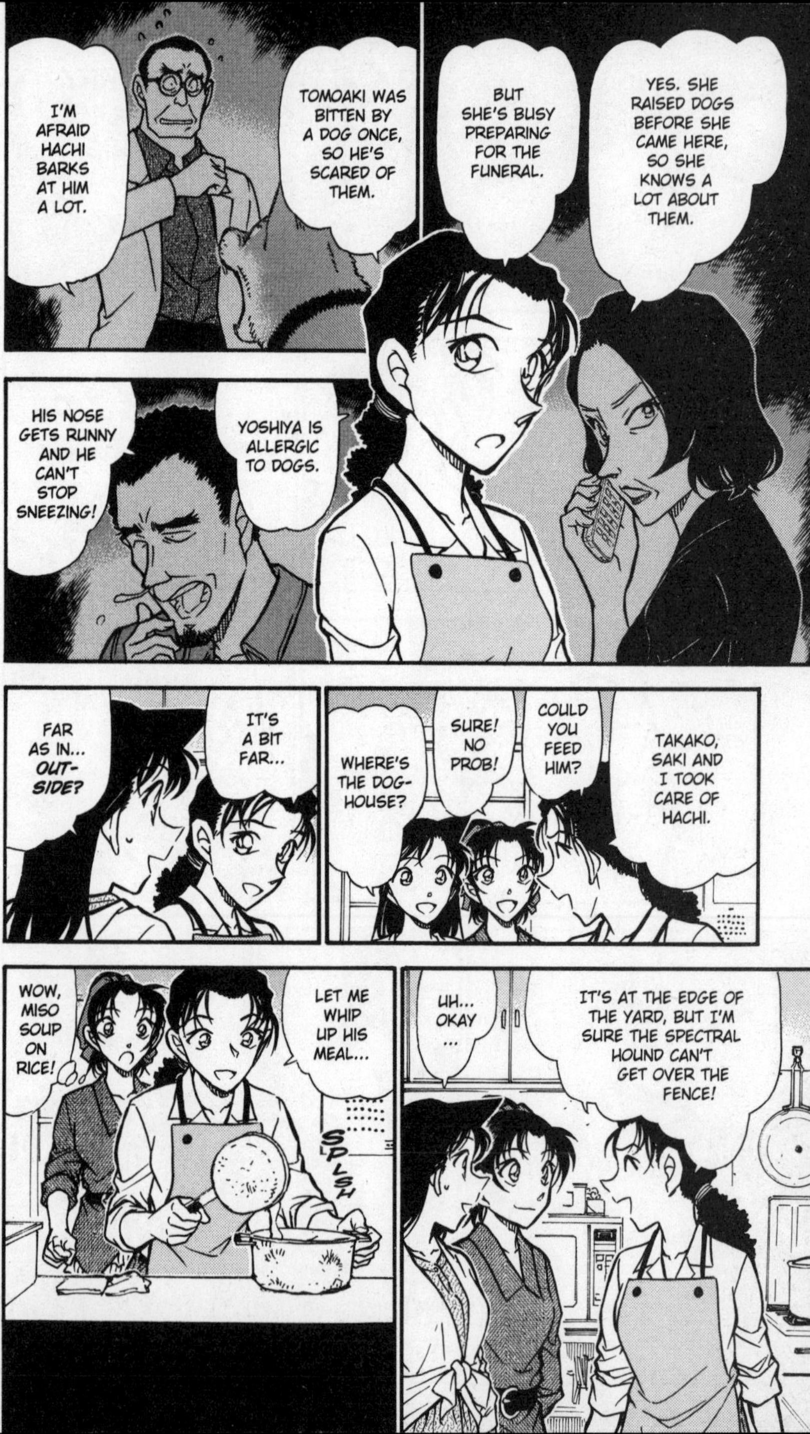

YES. SHE RAISED DOGS BEFORE SHE CAME HERE, SO SHE KNOWS A LOT ABOUT THEM.
BUT SHE'S BUSY PREPARING FOR THE FUNERAL.
TOMOAKI WAS BITTEN BY A DOG ONCE, SO HE'S SCARED OF THEM.
I'M AFRAID HACHI BARKS AT HIM A LOT.
YOSHIYA IS ALLERGIC TO DOGS.
HIS NOSE GETS RUNNY AND HE CAN'T STOP SNEEZING!
TAKAKO, SAKI AND I TOOK CARE OF HACHI.
COULD YOU FEED HIM?
SURE! NO PROB!
WHERE'S THE DOG-HOUSE?
IT'S A BIT FAR...
FAR AS IN... ***OUT-SIDE?***
IT'S AT THE EDGE OF THE YARD, BUT I'M SURE THE SPECTRAL HOUND CAN'T GET OVER THE FENCE!
UH... OKAY ...
LET ME WHIP UP HIS MEAL...
SPLSH
WOW, MISO SOUP ON RICE!

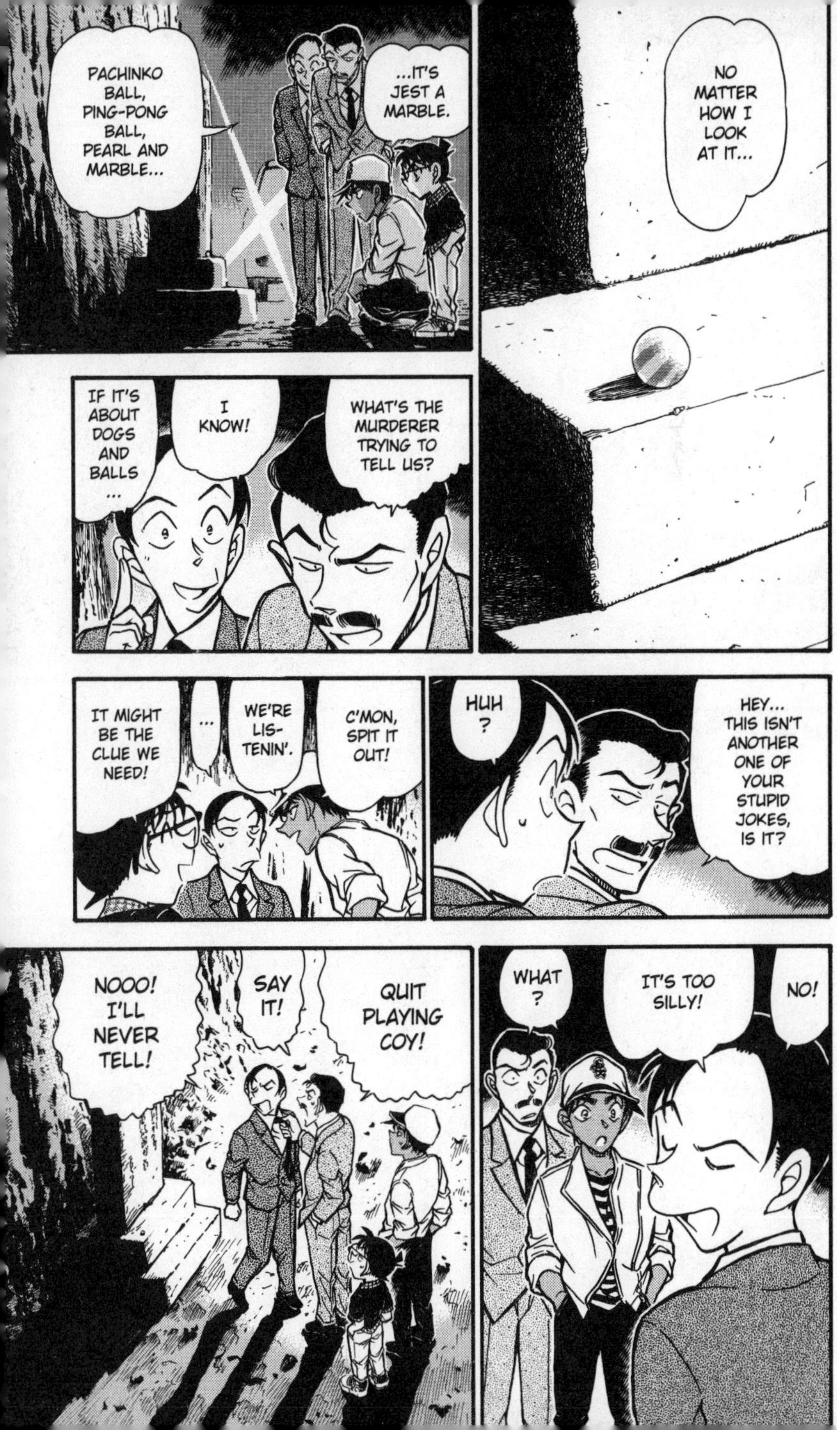
NO MATTER HOW I LOOK AT IT...
...IT'S JEST A MARBLE.
PACHINKO BALL, PING-PONG BALL, PEARL AND MARBLE...
WHAT'S THE MURDERER TRYING TO TELL US?
I KNOW!
IF IT'S ABOUT DOGS AND BALLS...
HEY... THIS ISN'T ANOTHER ONE OF YOUR STUPID JOKES, IS IT?
HUH?
C'MON, SPIT IT OUT!
WE'RE LIS-TENIN'.
...
IT MIGHT BE THE CLUE WE NEED!
NO!
IT'S TOO SILLY!
WHAT?
QUIT PLAYING COY!
SAY IT!
NOOO! I'LL NEVER TELL!

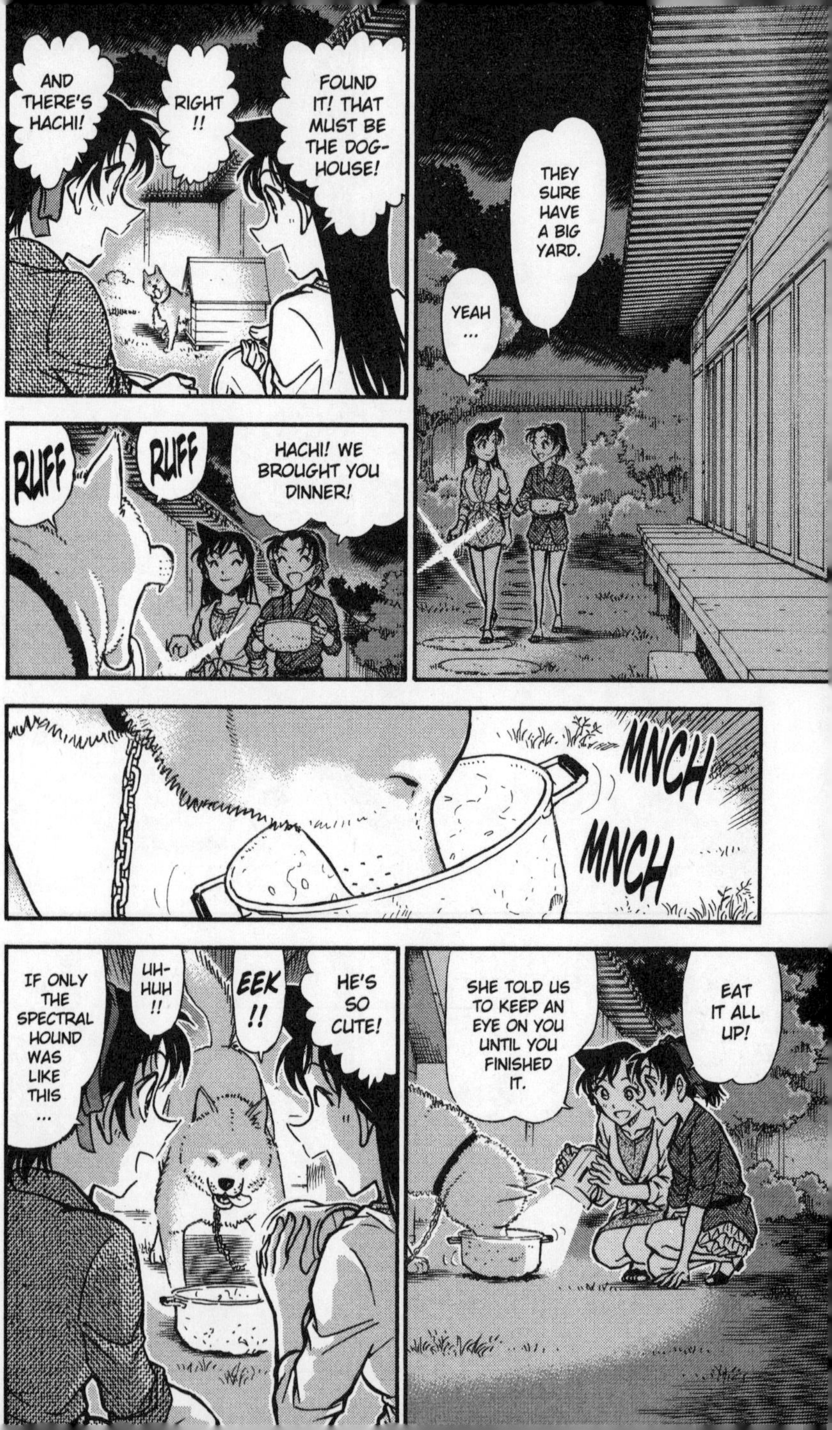
THEY SURE HAVE A BIG YARD.
YEAH...
FOUND IT! THAT MUST BE THE DOG-HOUSE!
RIGHT!!
AND THERE'S HACHI!
HACHI! WE BROUGHT YOU DINNER!
RUFF
RUFF
MNCH
MNCH
EAT IT ALL UP!
SHE TOLD US TO KEEP AN EYE ON YOU UNTIL YOU FINISHED IT.
HE'S SO CUTE!
EEK!!
UH-HUH!!
IF ONLY THE SPECTRAL HOUND WAS LIKE THIS...

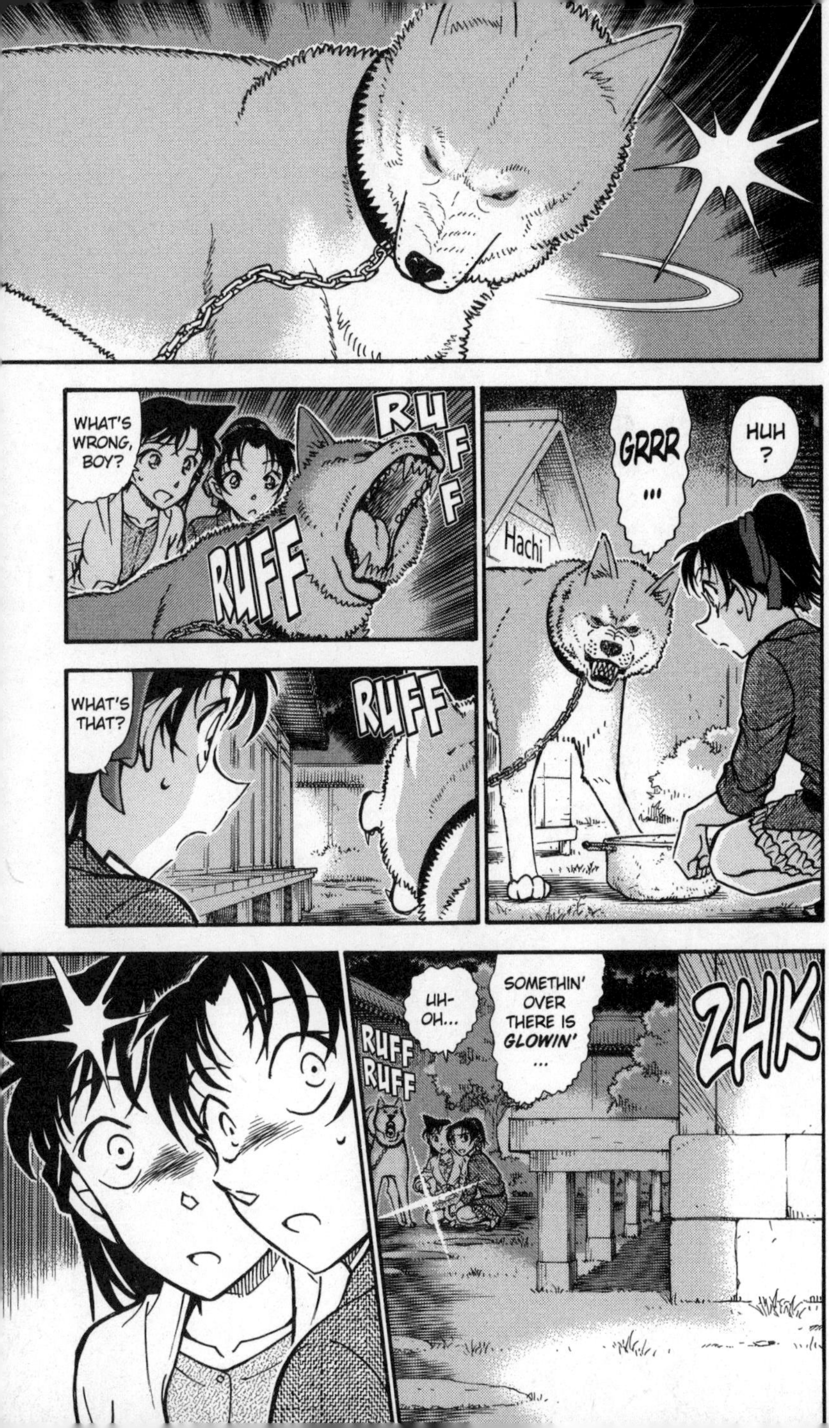
HUH?
GRRR ...
Hachi
RUFF
WHAT'S WRONG, BOY?
RUFF
RUFF
WHAT'S THAT?
ZHK
SOMETHIN' OVER THERE IS *GLOWIN'* ...
UH-OH...
RUFF RUFF

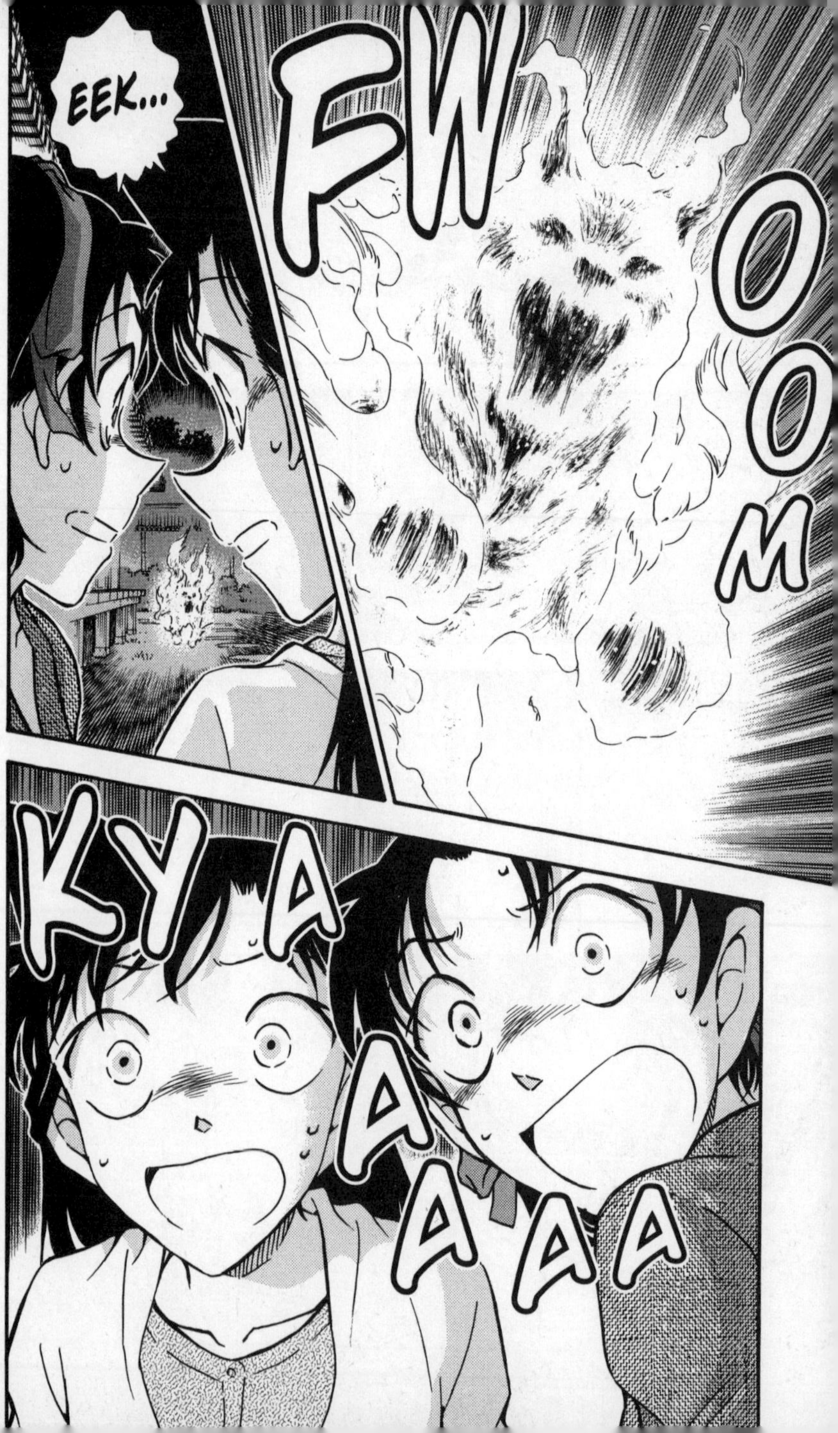
FWOOOM
EEK...
KYAAAAA

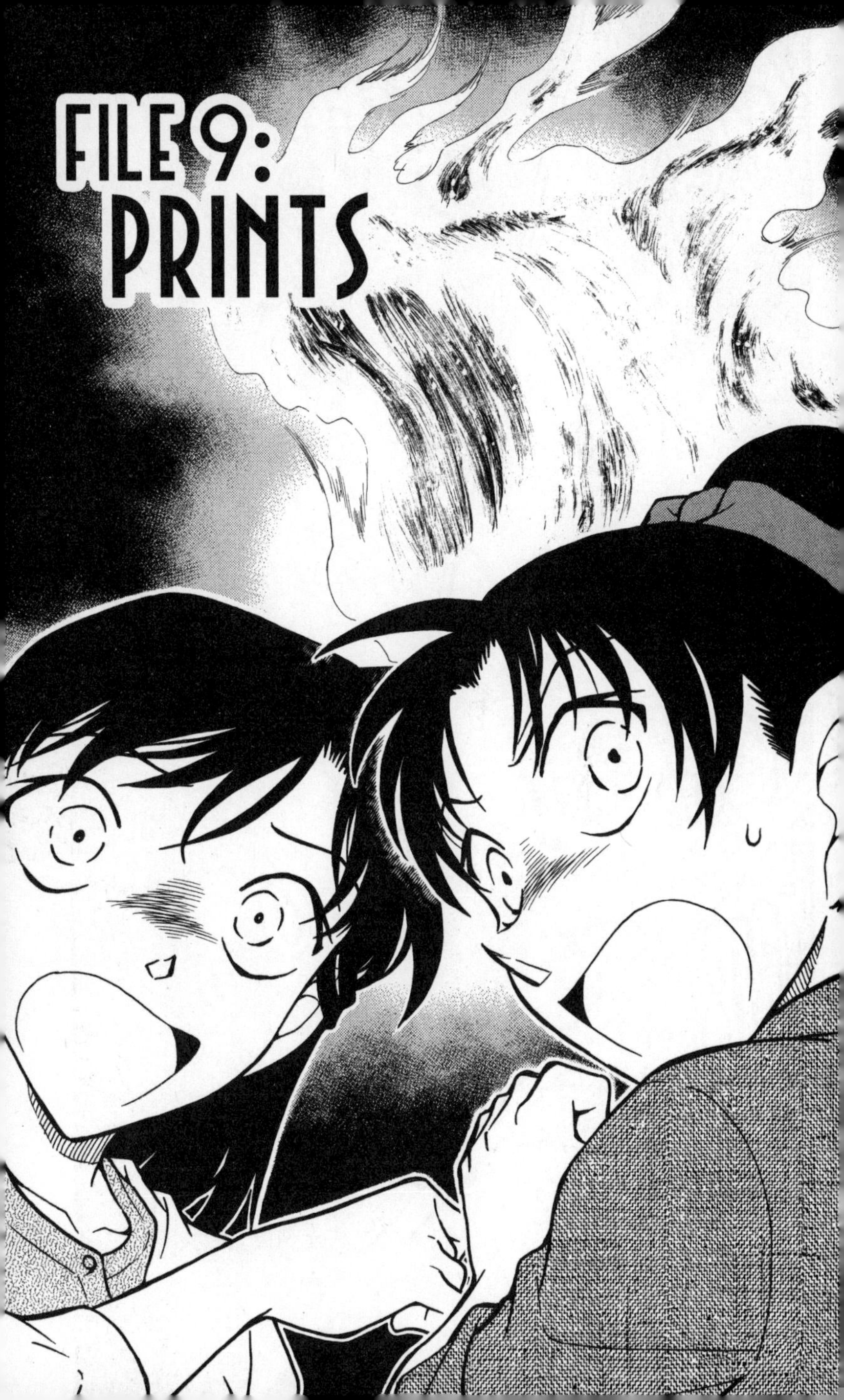
FILE 9:
PRINTS

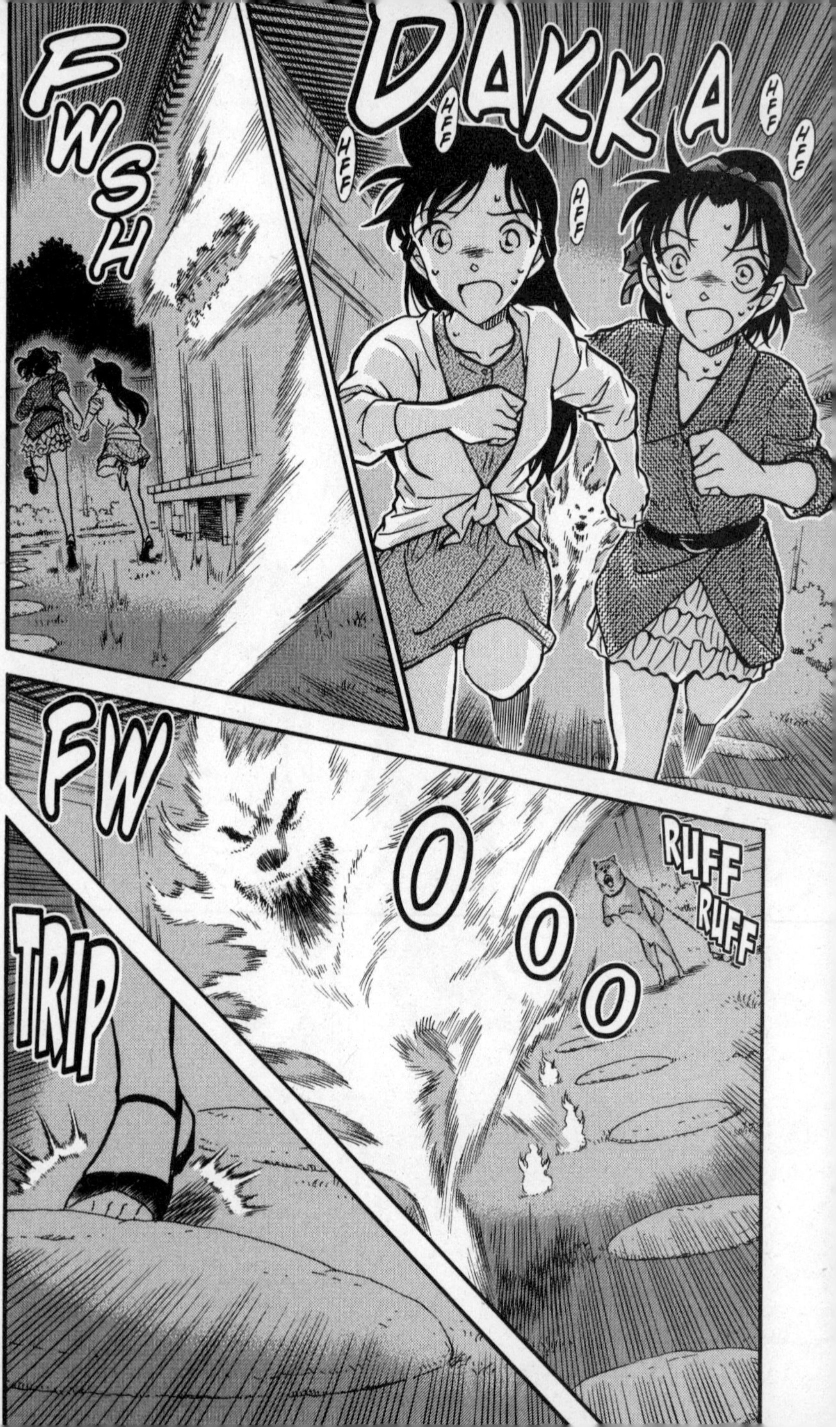
DAKKA
HFF HFF
HFF HFF
HFF HFF
FWSH
FWOOOO
RUFF RUFF
TRIP

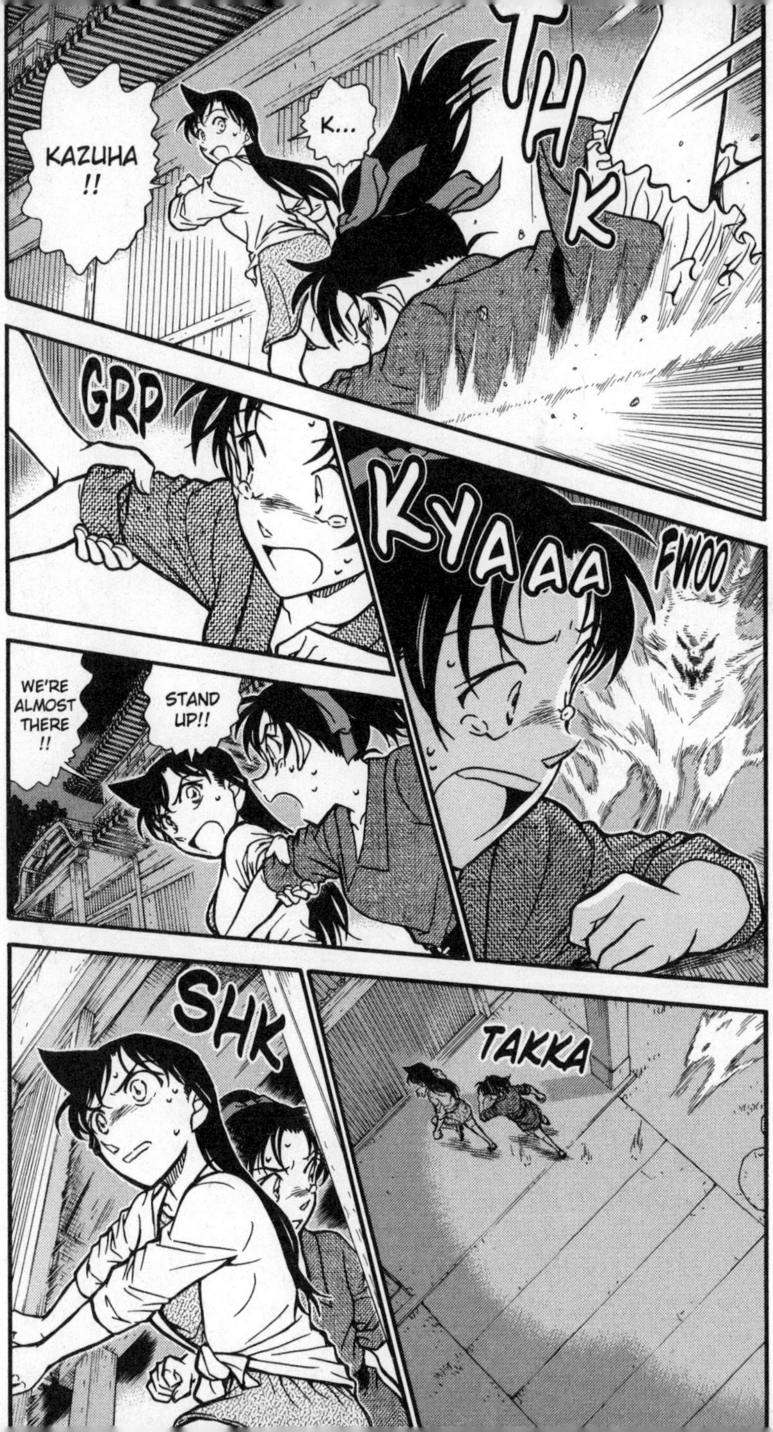
THK
K...
KAZUHA!!
KYAAA
FWOO
GRP
STAND UP!!
WE'RE ALMOST THERE!!
TAKKA
SHK

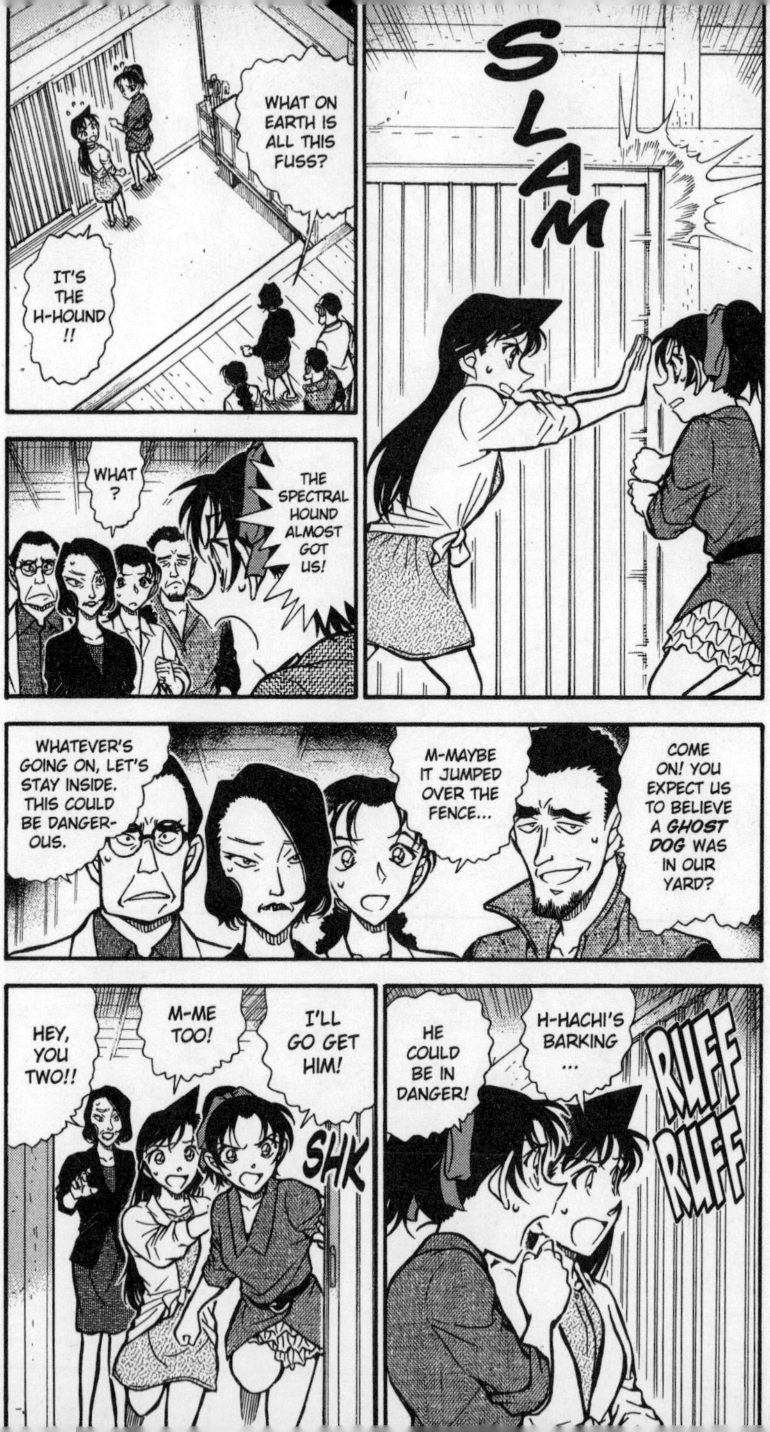
SLAM
WHAT ON EARTH IS ALL THIS FUSS?
IT'S THE H-HOUND!!
THE SPECTRAL HOUND ALMOST GOT US!
WHAT?
COME ON! YOU EXPECT US TO BELIEVE A *GHOST DOG* WAS IN OUR YARD?
M-MAYBE IT JUMPED OVER THE FENCE...
WHATEVER'S GOING ON, LET'S STAY INSIDE. THIS COULD BE DANGER-OUS.
RUFF RUFF
H-HACHI'S BARKING...
HE COULD BE IN DANGER!
I'LL GO GET HIM!
SHK
M-ME TOO!
HEY, YOU TWO!!

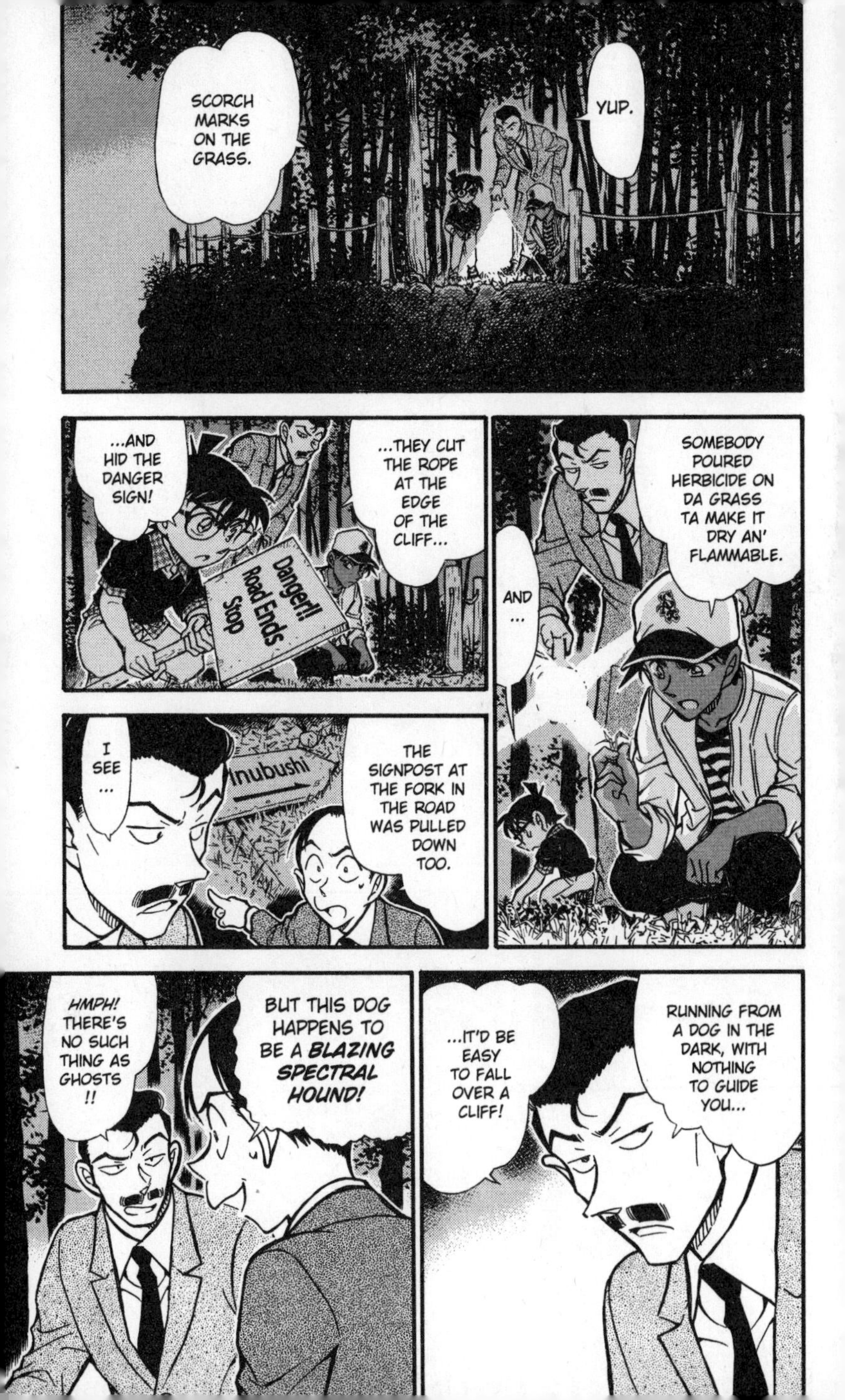
SCORCH MARKS ON THE GRASS.
YUP.
SOMEBODY POURED HERBICIDE ON DA GRASS TA MAKE IT DRY AN' FLAMMABLE.
AND ...
...THEY CUT THE ROPE AT THE EDGE OF THE CLIFF...
...AND HID THE DANGER SIGN!
Danger!! Road Ends Stop
THE SIGNPOST AT THE FORK IN THE ROAD WAS PULLED DOWN TOO.
Inubushi
I SEE ...
RUNNING FROM A DOG IN THE DARK, WITH NOTHING TO GUIDE YOU...
...IT'D BE EASY TO FALL OVER A CLIFF!
BUT THIS DOG HAPPENS TO BE A *BLAZING SPECTRAL HOUND!*
HMPH! THERE'S NO SUCH THING AS GHOSTS!!

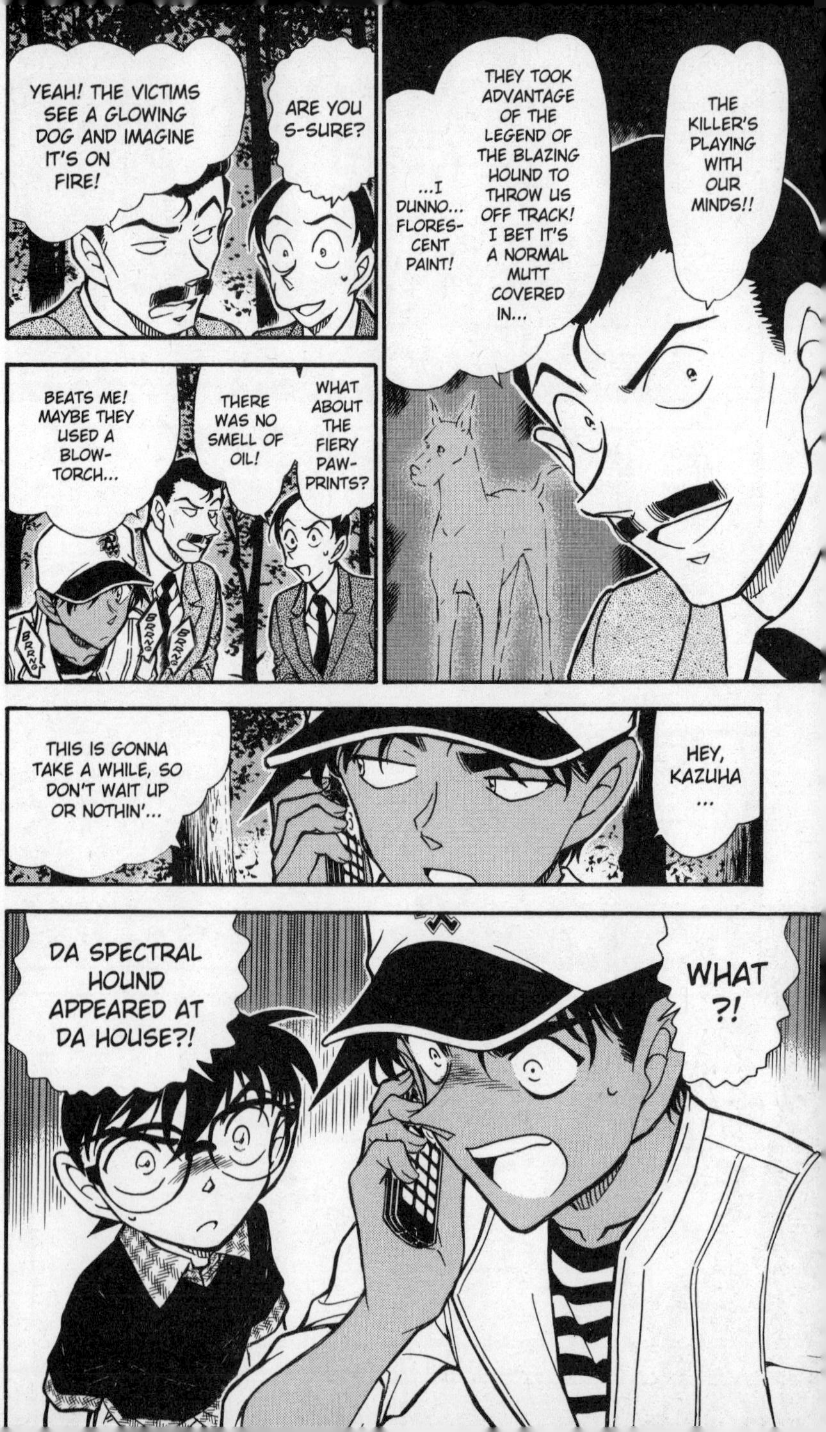
THE KILLER'S PLAYING WITH OUR MINDS!!
THEY TOOK ADVANTAGE OF THE LEGEND OF THE BLAZING HOUND TO THROW US OFF TRACK! I BET IT'S A NORMAL MUTT COVERED IN...
...I DUNNO... FLORES-CENT PAINT!
ARE YOU S-SURE?
YEAH! THE VICTIMS SEE A GLOWING DOG AND IMAGINE IT'S ON FIRE!
WHAT ABOUT THE FIERY PAW-PRINTS?
THERE WAS NO SMELL OF OIL!
BEATS ME! MAYBE THEY USED A BLOW-TORCH...
BRRRNG
BRRRNG
BRRRNG
HEY, KAZUHA ...
THIS IS GONNA TAKE A WHILE, SO DON'T WAIT UP OR NOTHIN'...
WHAT ?!
DA SPECTRAL HOUND APPEARED AT DA HOUSE?!

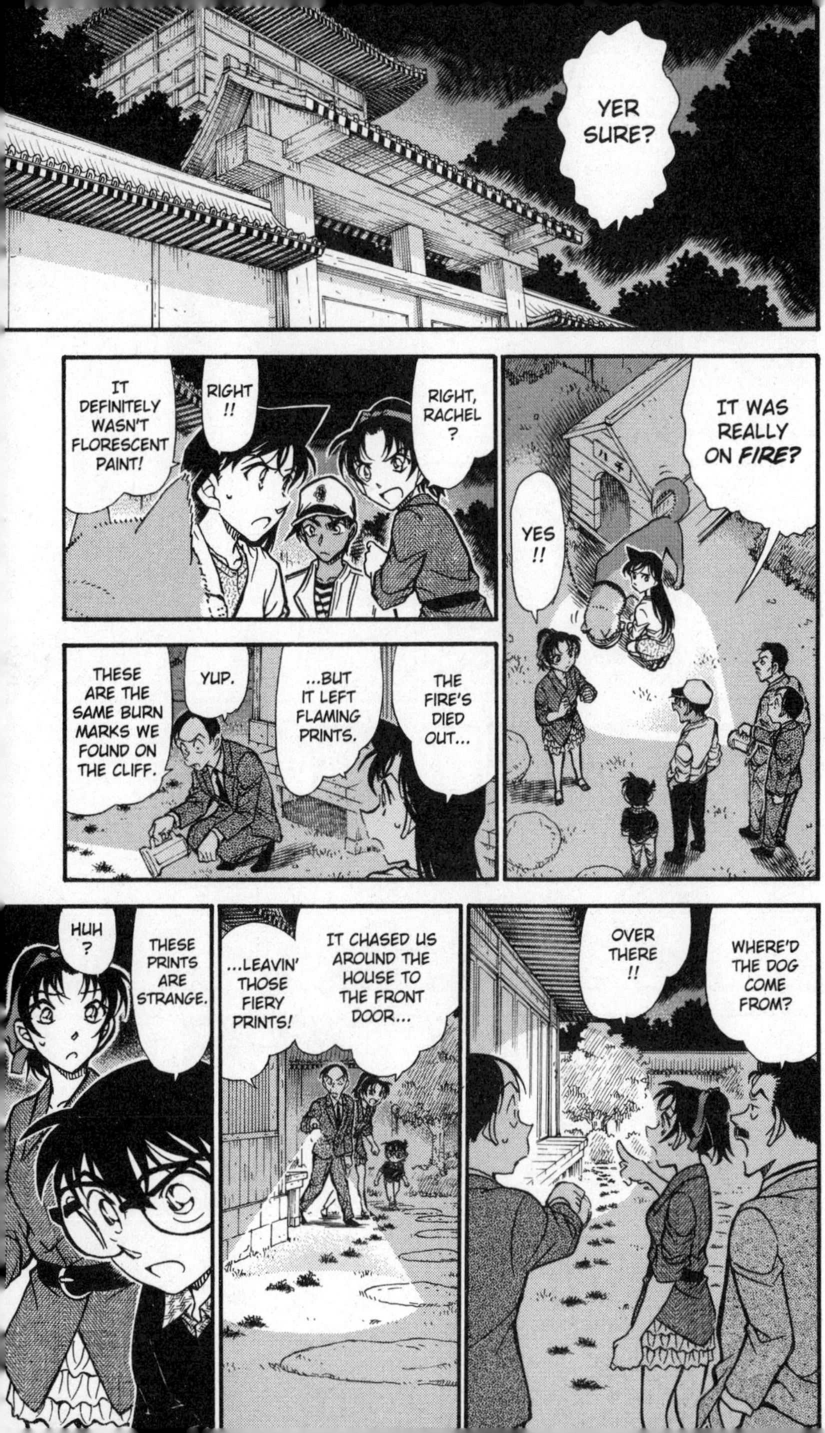
YER SURE?
IT WAS REALLY ON *FIRE?*
YES!!
RIGHT, RACHEL?
RIGHT!!
IT DEFINITELY WASN'T FLORESCENT PAINT!
THE FIRE'S DIED OUT...
...BUT IT LEFT FLAMING PRINTS.
YUP.
THESE ARE THE SAME BURN MARKS WE FOUND ON THE CLIFF.
WHERE'D THE DOG COME FROM?
OVER THERE!!
IT CHASED US AROUND THE HOUSE TO THE FRONT DOOR...
...LEAVIN' THOSE FIERY PRINTS!
THESE PRINTS ARE STRANGE.
HUH?

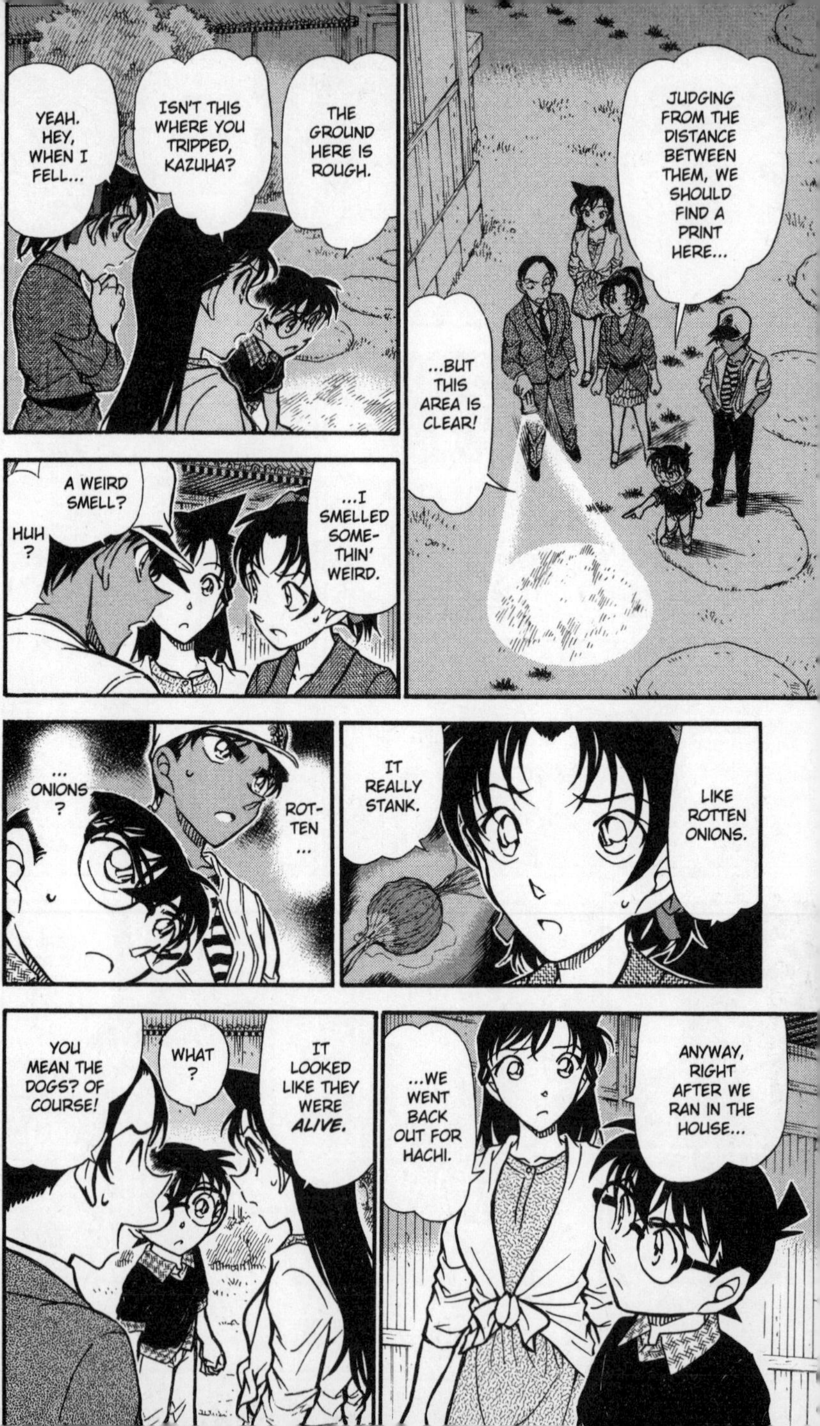
JUDGING FROM THE DISTANCE BETWEEN THEM, WE SHOULD FIND A PRINT HERE...
...BUT THIS AREA IS CLEAR!
THE GROUND HERE IS ROUGH.
ISN'T THIS WHERE YOU TRIPPED, KAZUHA?
YEAH. HEY, WHEN I FELL...
...I SMELLED SOME-THIN' WEIRD.
A WEIRD SMELL?
HUH?
LIKE ROTTEN ONIONS.
IT REALLY STANK.
ROT-TEN...
...ONIONS?
ANYWAY, RIGHT AFTER WE RAN IN THE HOUSE...
...WE WENT BACK OUT FOR HACHI.
IT LOOKED LIKE THEY WERE *ALIVE.*
WHAT?
YOU MEAN THE DOGS? OF COURSE!

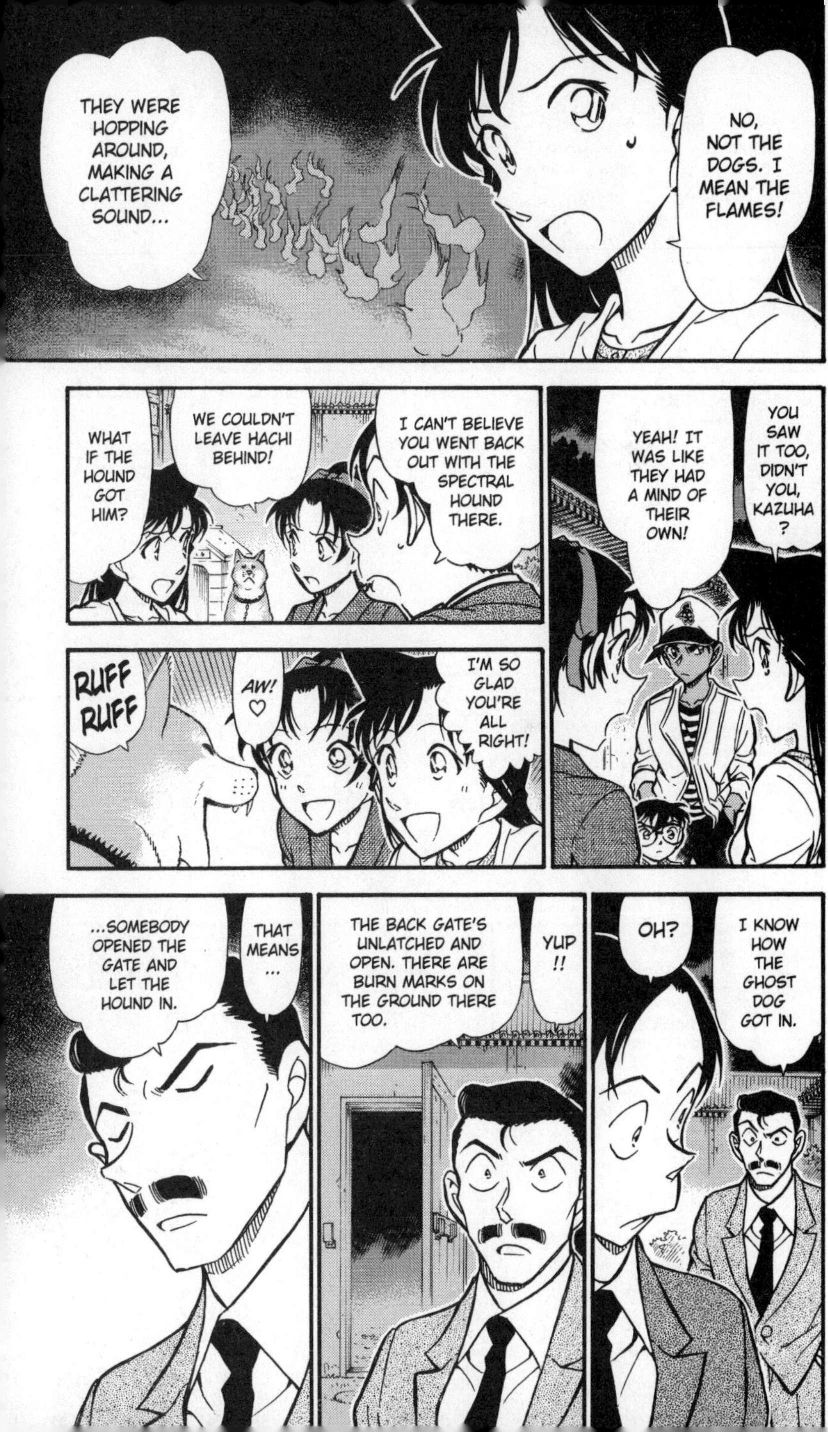
NO, NOT THE DOGS. I MEAN THE FLAMES!
THEY WERE HOPPING AROUND, MAKING A CLATTERING SOUND...
YOU SAW IT TOO, DIDN'T YOU, KAZUHA?
YEAH! IT WAS LIKE THEY HAD A MIND OF THEIR OWN!
I CAN'T BELIEVE YOU WENT BACK OUT WITH THE SPECTRAL HOUND THERE.
WE COULDN'T LEAVE HACHI BEHIND!
WHAT IF THE HOUND GOT HIM?
I'M SO GLAD YOU'RE ALL RIGHT!
AW! ♡
RUFF RUFF
I KNOW HOW THE GHOST DOG GOT IN.
OH?
YUP!!
THE BACK GATE'S UNLATCHED AND OPEN. THERE ARE BURN MARKS ON THE GROUND THERE TOO.
THAT MEANS...
...SOMEBODY OPENED THE GATE AND LET THE HOUND IN.

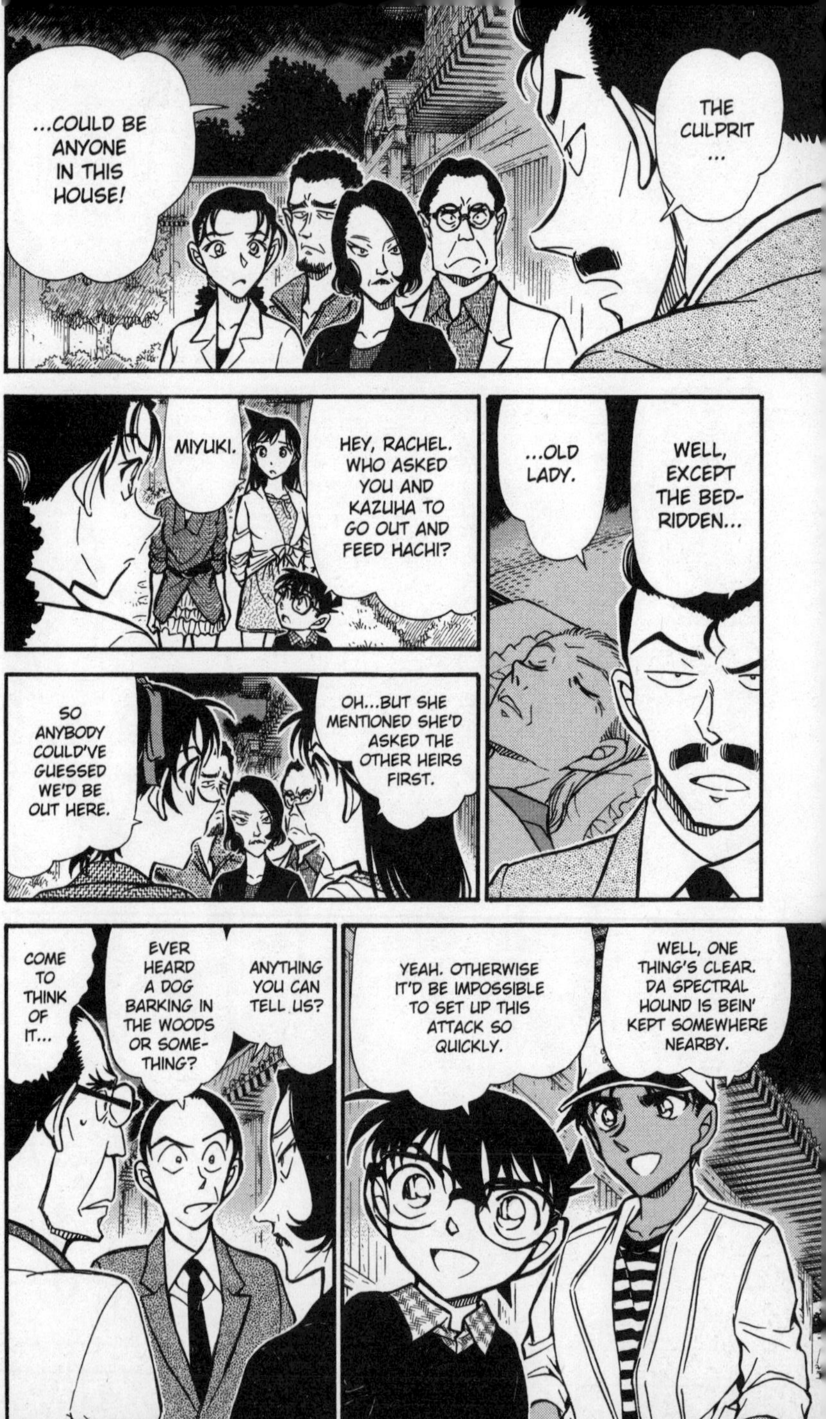
THE CULPRIT...
...COULD BE ANYONE IN THIS HOUSE!
WELL, EXCEPT THE BED-RIDDEN...
...OLD LADY.
HEY, RACHEL. WHO ASKED YOU AND KAZUHA TO GO OUT AND FEED HACHI?
MIYUKI.
OH...BUT SHE MENTIONED SHE'D ASKED THE OTHER HEIRS FIRST.
SO ANYBODY COULD'VE GUESSED WE'D BE OUT HERE.
WELL, ONE THING'S CLEAR. DA SPECTRAL HOUND IS BEIN' KEPT SOMEWHERE NEARBY.
YEAH. OTHERWISE IT'D BE IMPOSSIBLE TO SET UP THIS ATTACK SO QUICKLY.
ANYTHING YOU CAN TELL US?
EVER HEARD A DOG BARKING IN THE WOODS OR SOME-THING?
COME TO THINK OF IT...

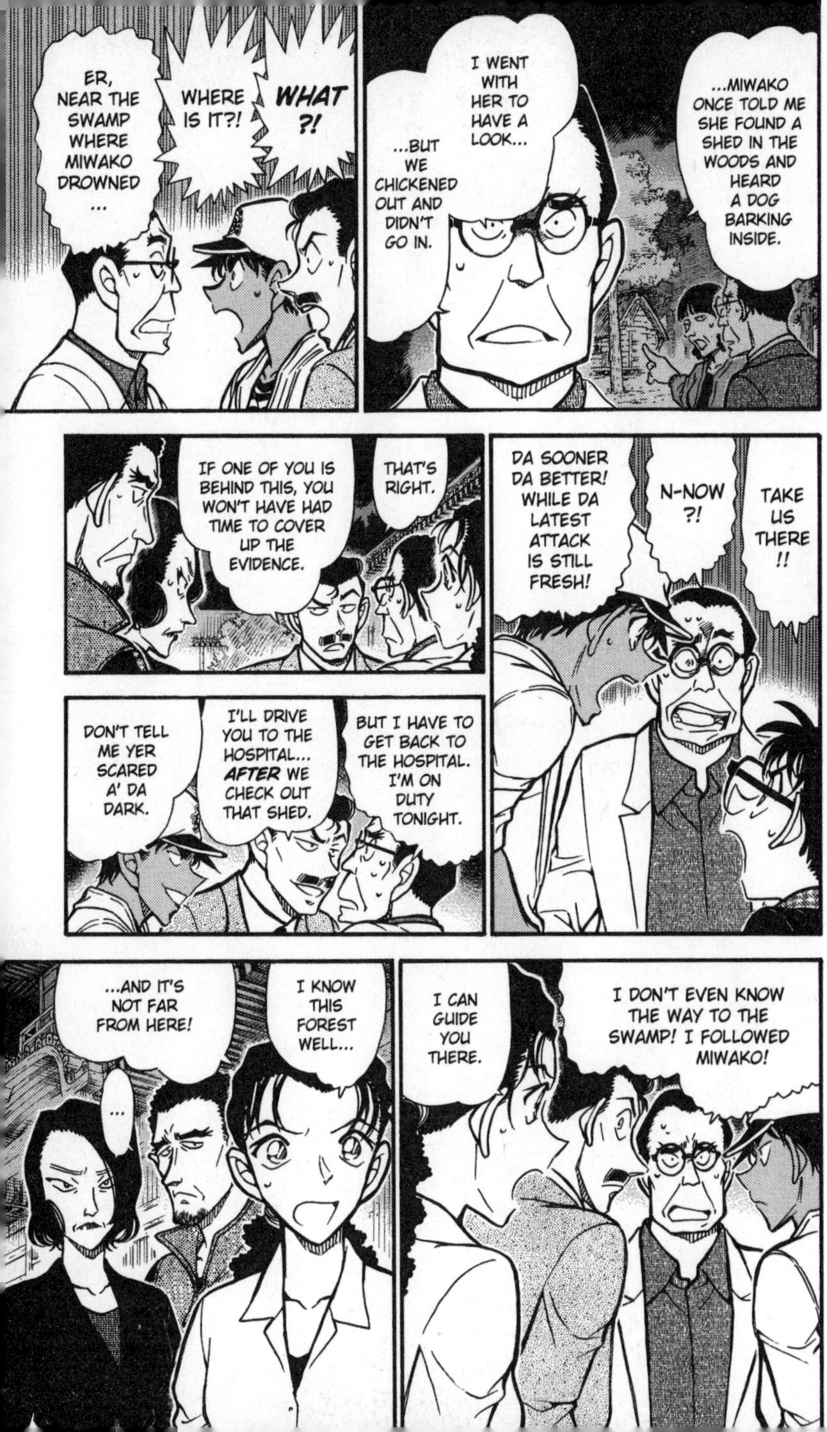
...MIWAKO ONCE TOLD ME SHE FOUND A SHED IN THE WOODS AND HEARD A DOG BARKING INSIDE.
I WENT WITH HER TO HAVE A LOOK...
...BUT WE CHICKENED OUT AND DIDN'T GO IN.
WHAT?!
WHERE IS IT?!
ER, NEAR THE SWAMP WHERE MIWAKO DROWNED...
TAKE US THERE!!
N-NOW?!
DA SOONER DA BETTER! WHILE DA LATEST ATTACK IS STILL FRESH!
THAT'S RIGHT.
IF ONE OF YOU IS BEHIND THIS, YOU WON'T HAVE HAD TIME TO COVER UP THE EVIDENCE.
BUT I HAVE TO GET BACK TO THE HOSPITAL. I'M ON DUTY TONIGHT.
I'LL DRIVE YOU TO THE HOSPITAL... AFTER WE CHECK OUT THAT SHED.
DON'T TELL ME YER SCARED A' DA DARK.
I DON'T EVEN KNOW THE WAY TO THE SWAMP! I FOLLOWED MIWAKO!
I CAN GUIDE YOU THERE.
I KNOW THIS FOREST WELL...
...AND IT'S NOT FAR FROM HERE!
...

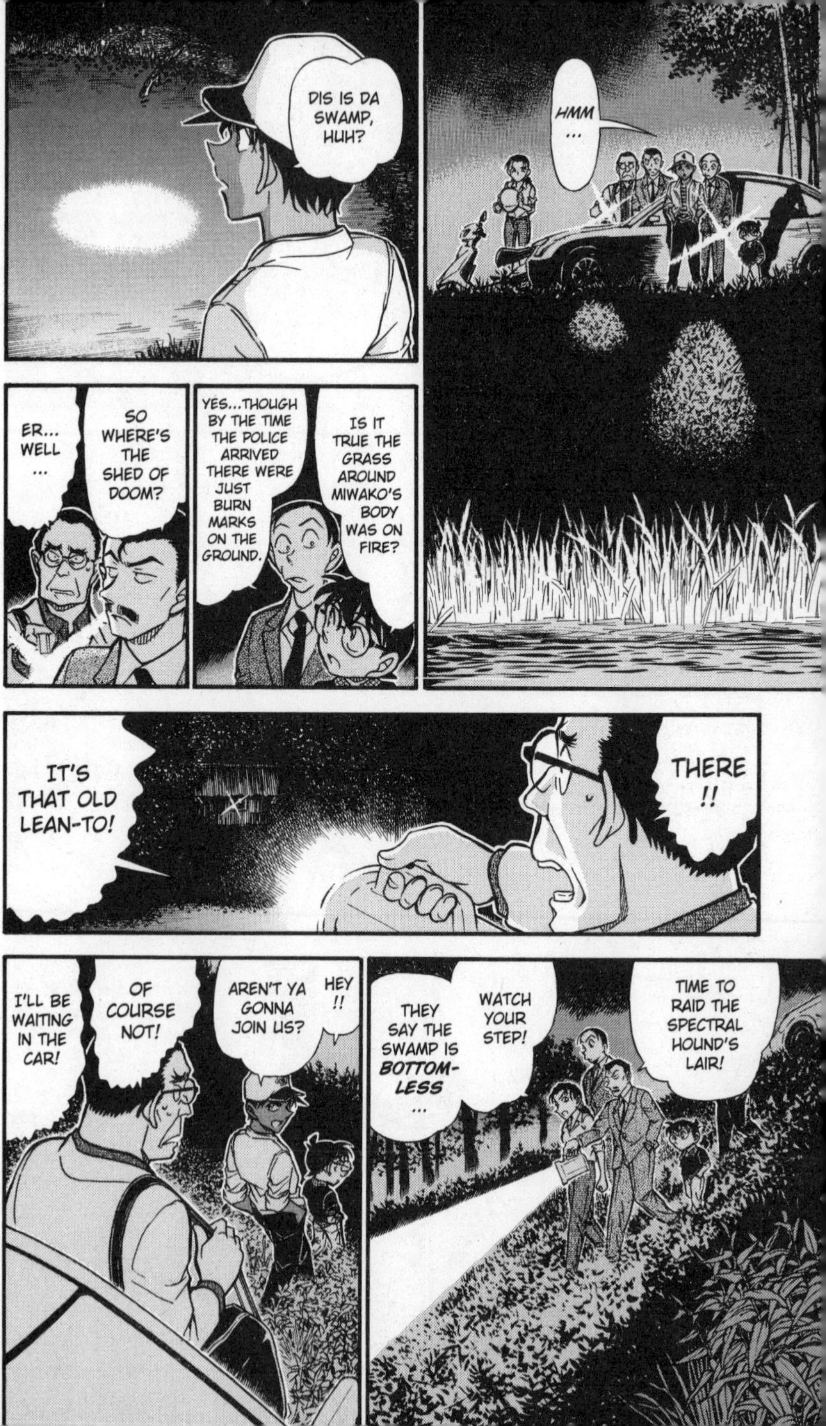
HMM ...
DIS IS DA SWAMP, HUH?
IS IT TRUE THE GRASS AROUND MIWAKO'S BODY WAS ON FIRE?
YES...THOUGH BY THE TIME THE POLICE ARRIVED THERE WERE JUST BURN MARKS ON THE GROUND.
SO WHERE'S THE SHED OF DOOM?
ER... WELL ...
THERE !!
IT'S THAT OLD LEAN-TO!
TIME TO RAID THE SPECTRAL HOUND'S LAIR!
WATCH YOUR STEP!
THEY SAY THE SWAMP IS BOTTOMLESS ...
HEY !!
AREN'T YA GONNA JOIN US?
OF COURSE NOT!
I'LL BE WAITING IN THE CAR!

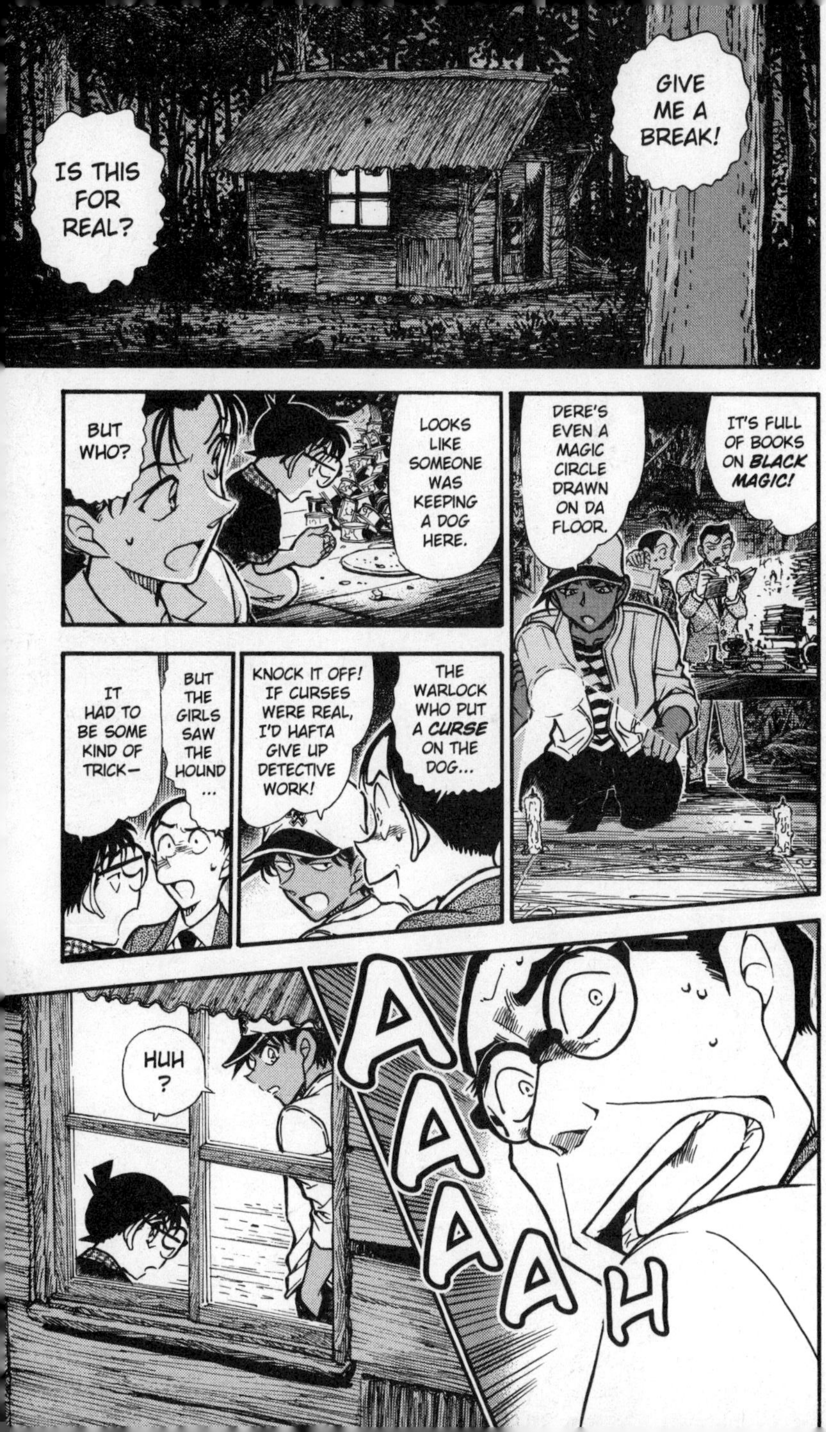

GIVE ME A BREAK!
IS THIS FOR REAL?
IT'S FULL OF BOOKS ON ***BLACK MAGIC!***
DERE'S EVEN A MAGIC CIRCLE DRAWN ON DA FLOOR.
LOOKS LIKE SOMEONE WAS KEEPING A DOG HERE.
BUT WHO?
THE WARLOCK WHO PUT A ***CURSE*** ON THE DOG...
KNOCK IT OFF! IF CURSES WERE REAL, I'D HAFTA GIVE UP DETECTIVE WORK!
BUT THE GIRLS SAW THE HOUND ...
IT HAD TO BE SOME KIND OF TRICK—
AAAAAH
HUH ?

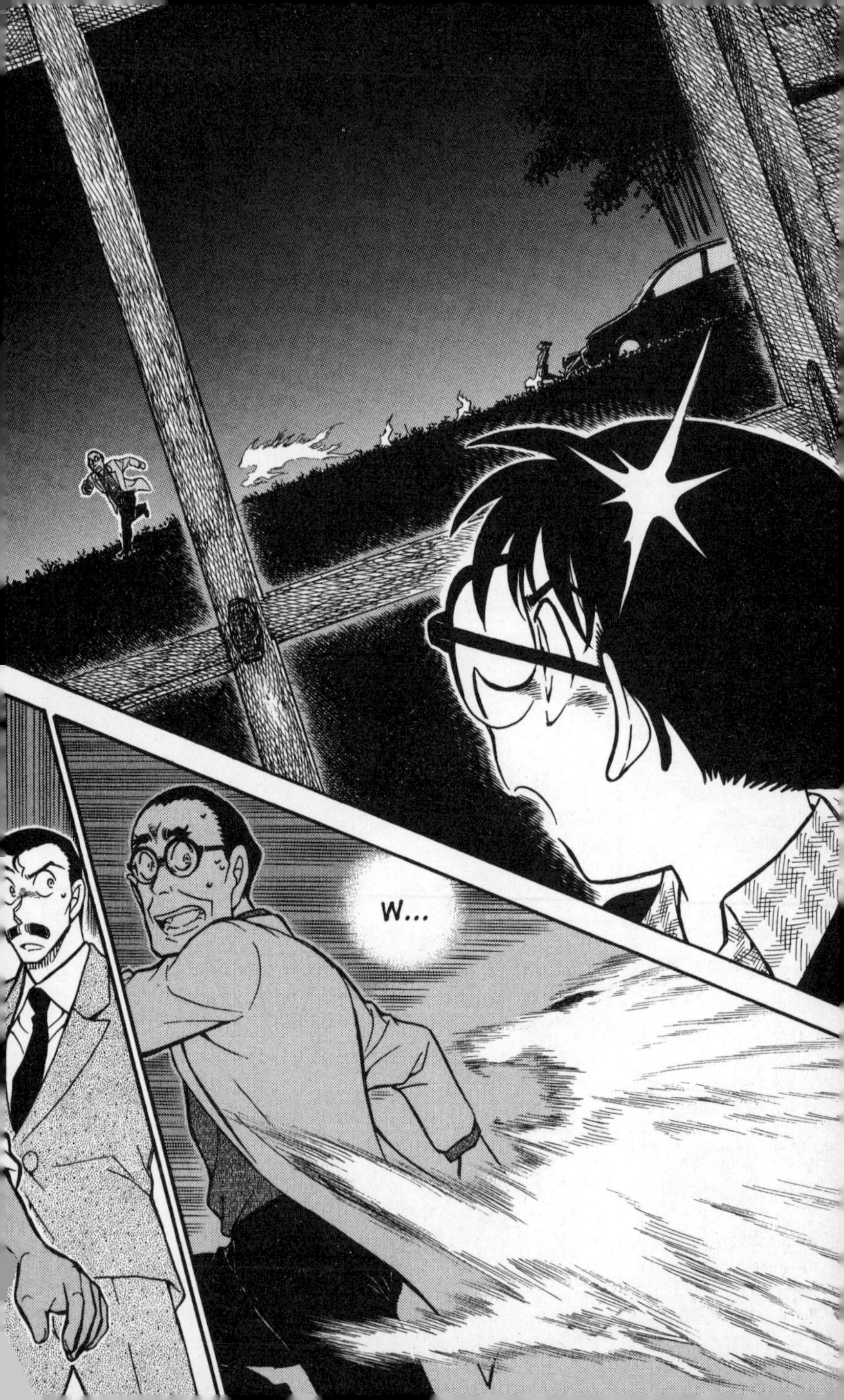
W...

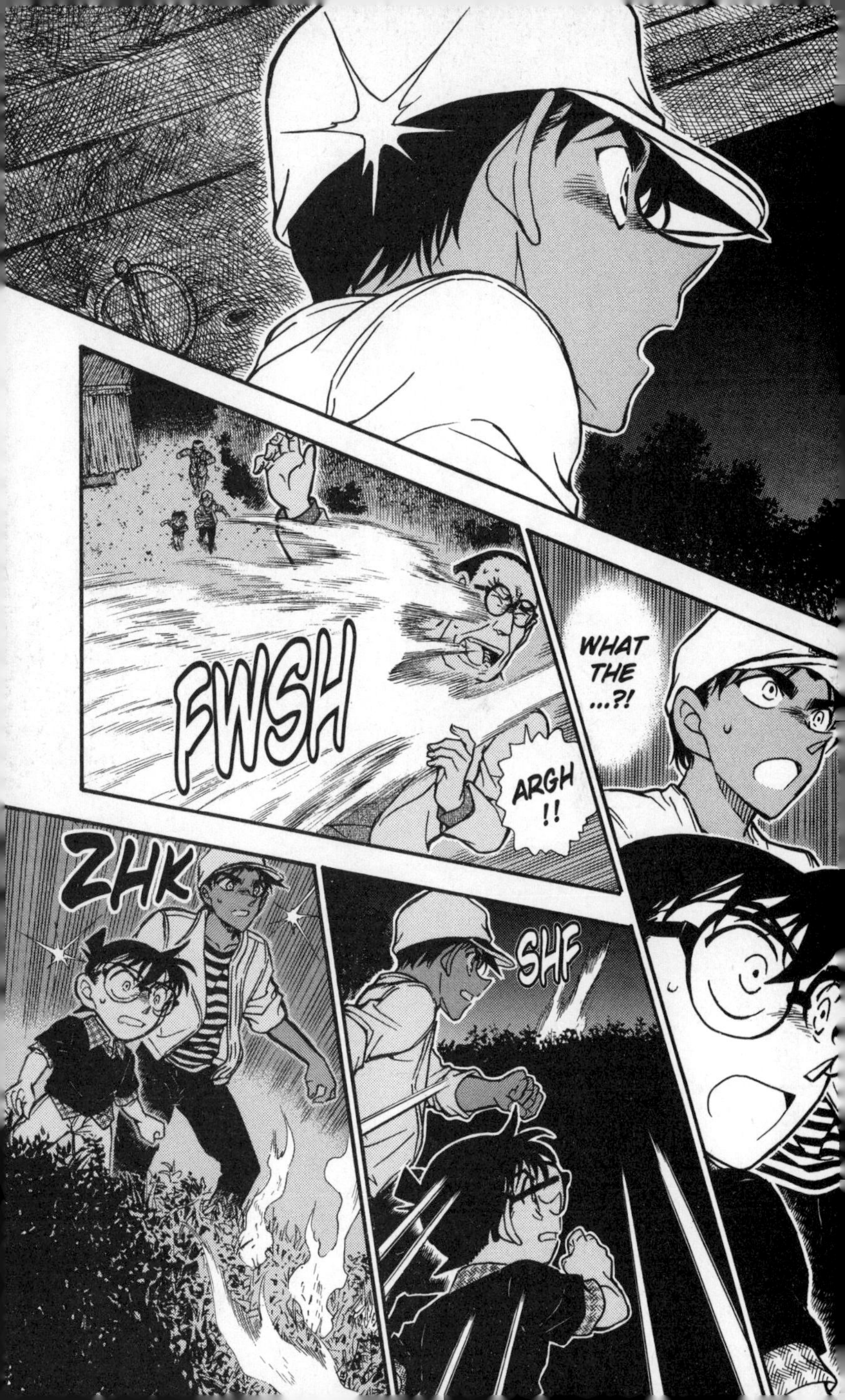
FWSH
ARGH !!
WHAT THE ...?!
SHF
ZHK

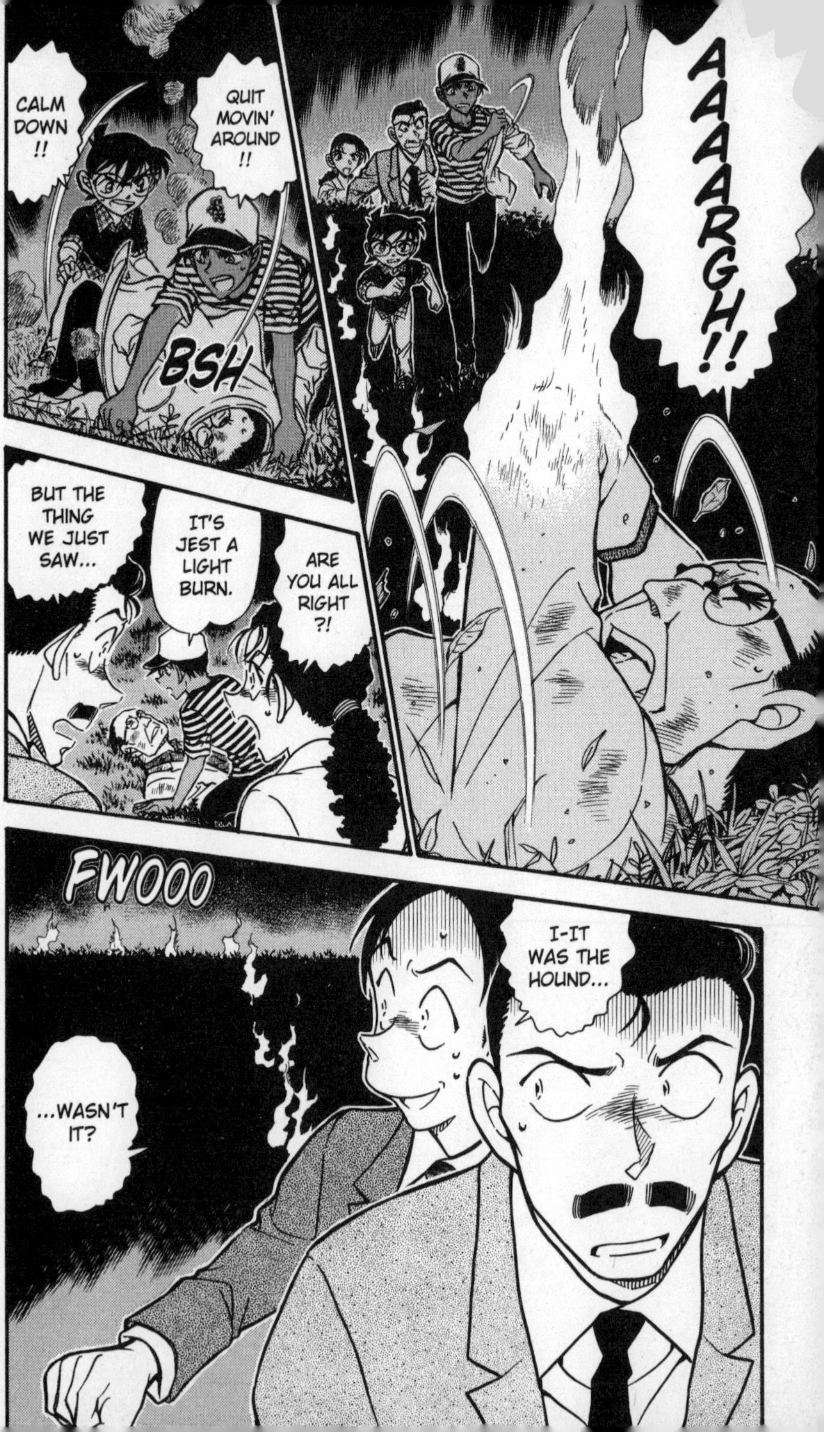
AAAARGH!!
QUIT MOVIN' AROUND !!
CALM DOWN !!
BSH
ARE YOU ALL RIGHT ?!
IT'S JEST A LIGHT BURN.
BUT THE THING WE JUST SAW...
I-IT WAS THE HOUND...
FWOOO
...WASN'T IT?

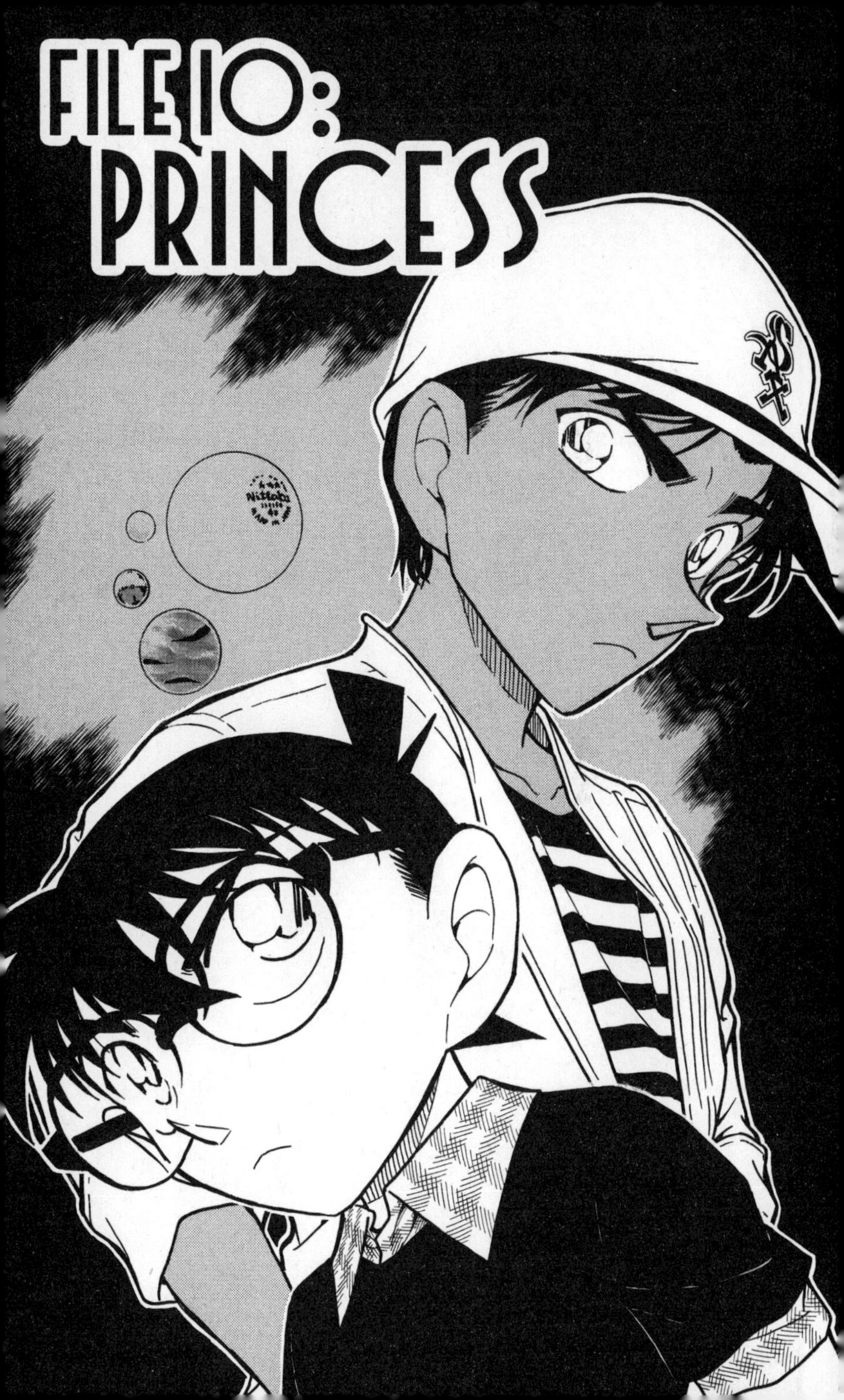
FILE 10:
PRINCESS

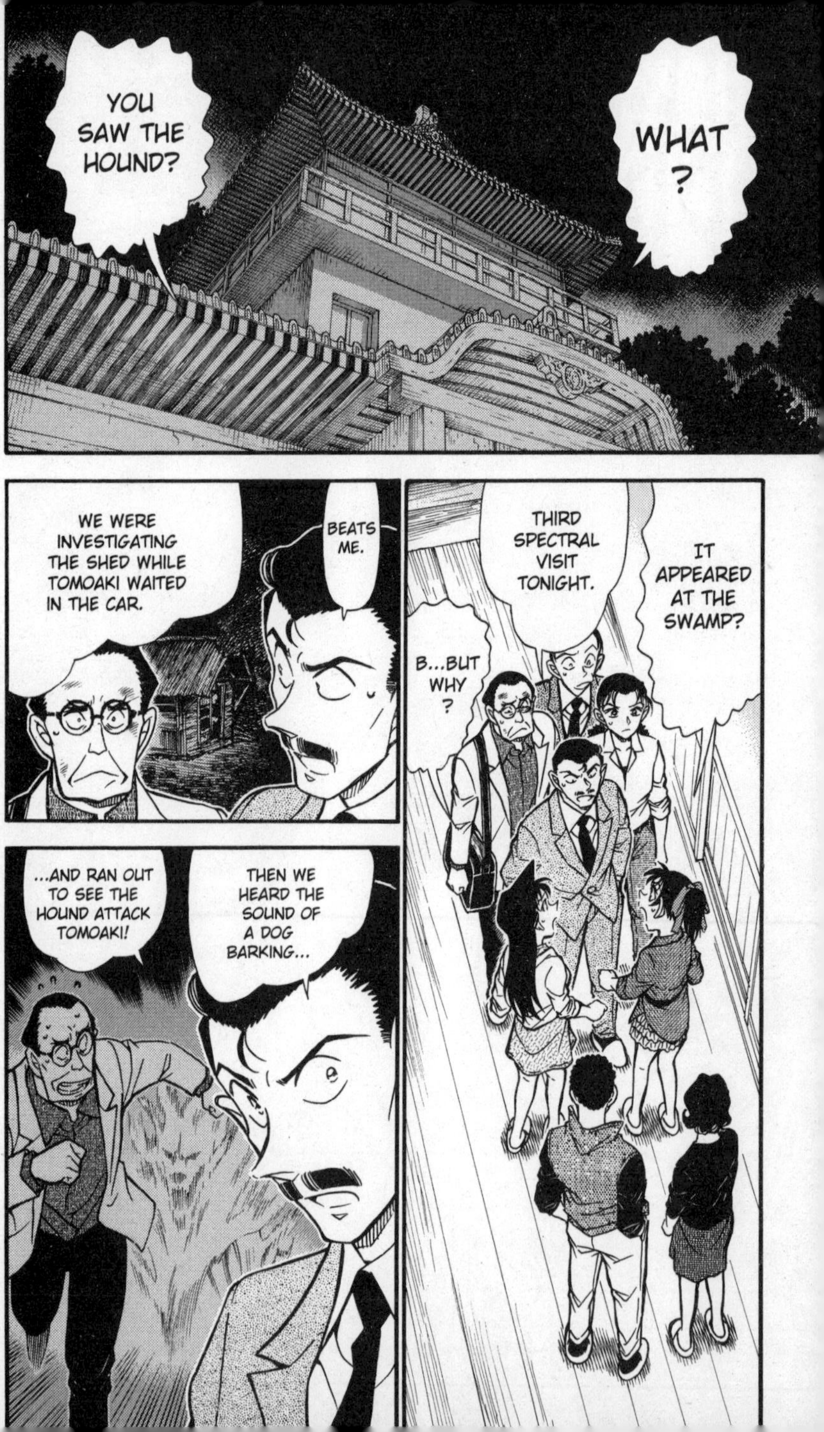
WHAT?
YOU SAW THE HOUND?
IT APPEARED AT THE SWAMP?
THIRD SPECTRAL VISIT TONIGHT.
B...BUT WHY?
BEATS ME.
WE WERE INVESTIGATING THE SHED WHILE TOMOAKI WAITED IN THE CAR.
THEN WE HEARD THE SOUND OF A DOG BARKING...
...AND RAN OUT TO SEE THE HOUND ATTACK TOMOAKI!

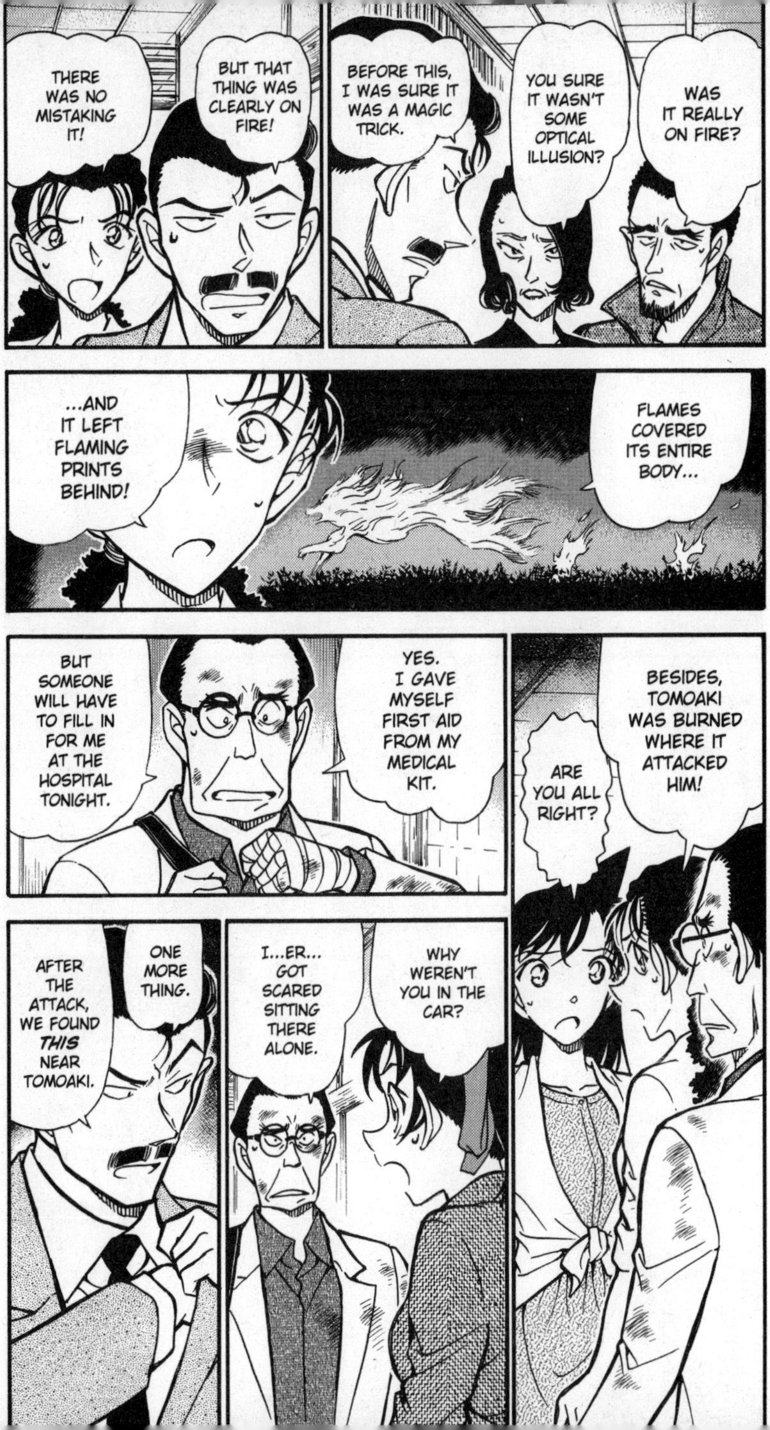
WAS IT REALLY ON FIRE?
YOU SURE IT WASN'T SOME OPTICAL ILLUSION?
BEFORE THIS, I WAS SURE IT WAS A MAGIC TRICK.
BUT THAT THING WAS CLEARLY ON FIRE!
THERE WAS NO MISTAKING IT!
FLAMES COVERED ITS ENTIRE BODY...
...AND IT LEFT FLAMING PRINTS BEHIND!
BESIDES, TOMOAKI WAS BURNED WHERE IT ATTACKED HIM!
ARE YOU ALL RIGHT?
YES. I GAVE MYSELF FIRST AID FROM MY MEDICAL KIT.
BUT SOMEONE WILL HAVE TO FILL IN FOR ME AT THE HOSPITAL TONIGHT.
WHY WEREN'T YOU IN THE CAR?
I...ER... GOT SCARED SITTING THERE ALONE.
ONE MORE THING.
AFTER THE ATTACK, WE FOUND *THIS* NEAR TOMOAKI.

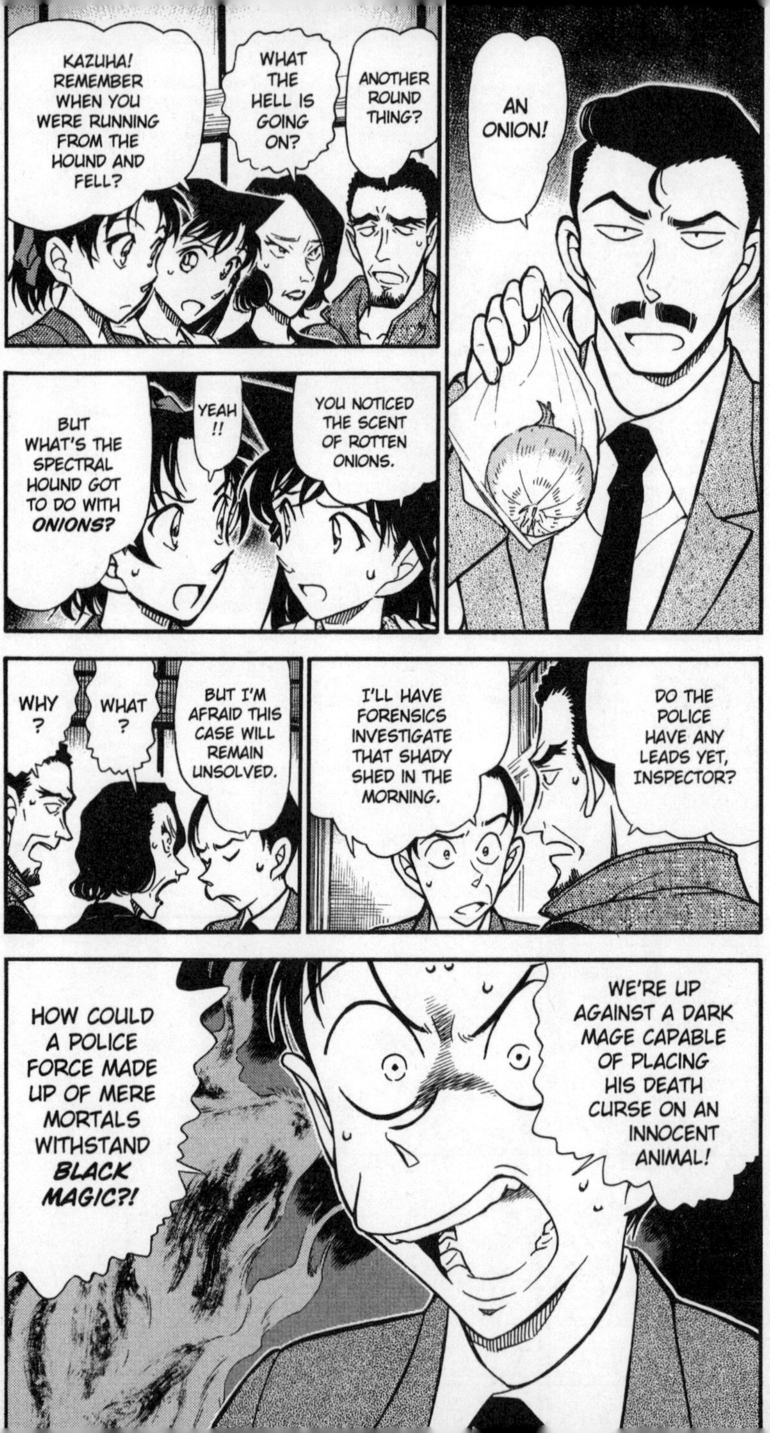
AN ONION!
ANOTHER ROUND THING?
WHAT THE HELL IS GOING ON?
KAZUHA! REMEMBER WHEN YOU WERE RUNNING FROM THE HOUND AND FELL?
YOU NOTICED THE SCENT OF ROTTEN ONIONS.
YEAH!!
BUT WHAT'S THE SPECTRAL HOUND GOT TO DO WITH *ONIONS?*
DO THE POLICE HAVE ANY LEADS YET, INSPECTOR?
I'LL HAVE FORENSICS INVESTIGATE THAT SHADY SHED IN THE MORNING.
BUT I'M AFRAID THIS CASE WILL REMAIN UNSOLVED.
WHAT?
WHY?
WE'RE UP AGAINST A DARK MAGE CAPABLE OF PLACING HIS DEATH CURSE ON AN INNOCENT ANIMAL!
HOW COULD A POLICE FORCE MADE UP OF MERE MORTALS WITHSTAND *BLACK MAGIC?!*

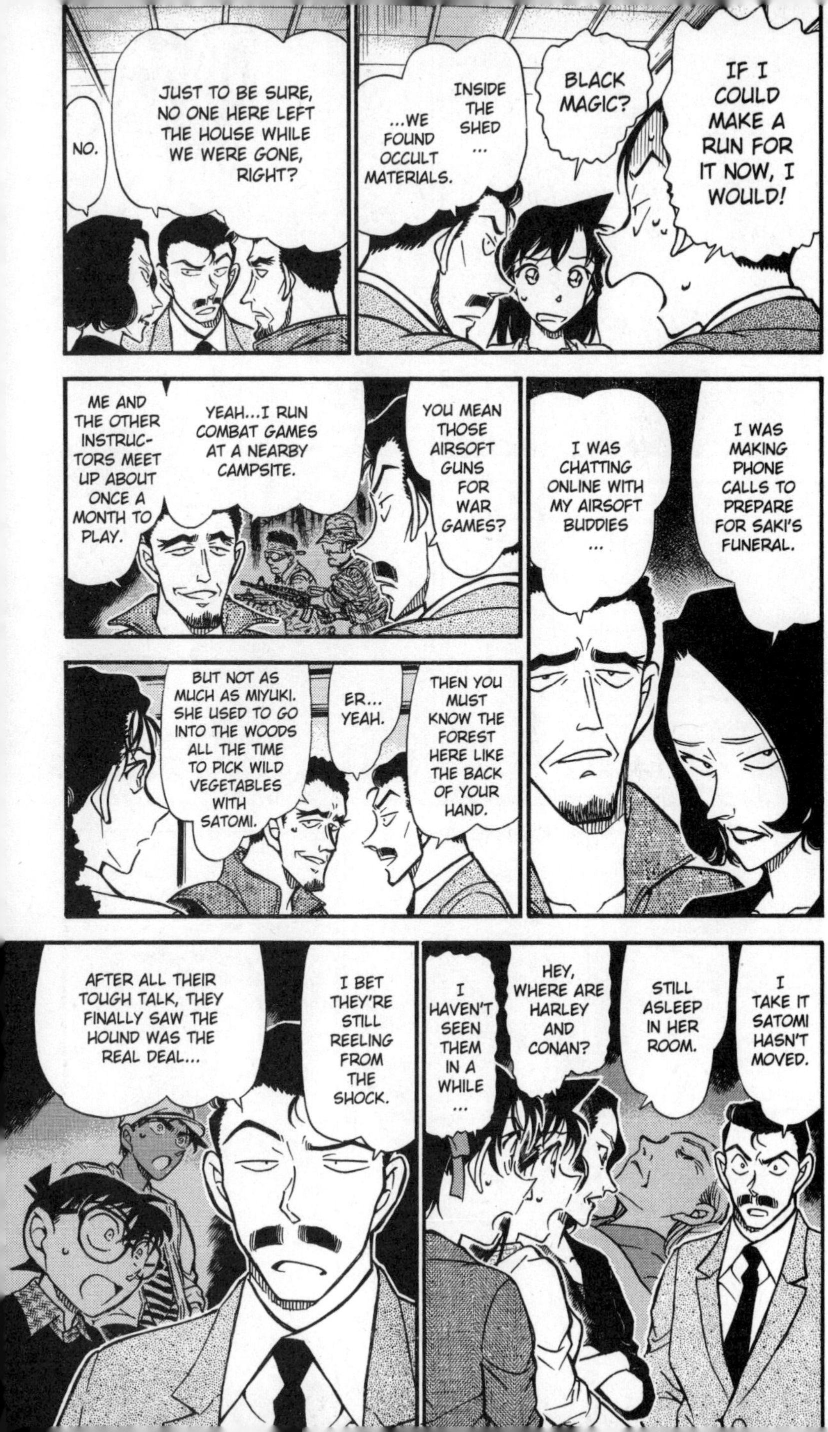
IF I COULD MAKE A RUN FOR IT NOW, I WOULD!
BLACK MAGIC?
INSIDE THE SHED ...
...WE FOUND OCCULT MATERIALS.
JUST TO BE SURE, NO ONE HERE LEFT THE HOUSE WHILE WE WERE GONE, RIGHT?
NO.
I WAS MAKING PHONE CALLS TO PREPARE FOR SAKI'S FUNERAL.
I WAS CHATTING ONLINE WITH MY AIRSOFT BUDDIES ...
YOU MEAN THOSE AIRSOFT GUNS FOR WAR GAMES?
YEAH...I RUN COMBAT GAMES AT A NEARBY CAMPSITE.
ME AND THE OTHER INSTRUC-TORS MEET UP ABOUT ONCE A MONTH TO PLAY.
THEN YOU MUST KNOW THE FOREST HERE LIKE THE BACK OF YOUR HAND.
ER... YEAH.
BUT NOT AS MUCH AS MIYUKI. SHE USED TO GO INTO THE WOODS ALL THE TIME TO PICK WILD VEGETABLES WITH SATOMI.
I TAKE IT SATOMI HASN'T MOVED.
STILL ASLEEP IN HER ROOM.
HEY, WHERE ARE HARLEY AND CONAN?
I HAVEN'T SEEN THEM IN A WHILE ...
I BET THEY'RE STILL REELING FROM THE SHOCK.
AFTER ALL THEIR TOUGH TALK, THEY FINALLY SAW THE HOUND WAS THE REAL DEAL...

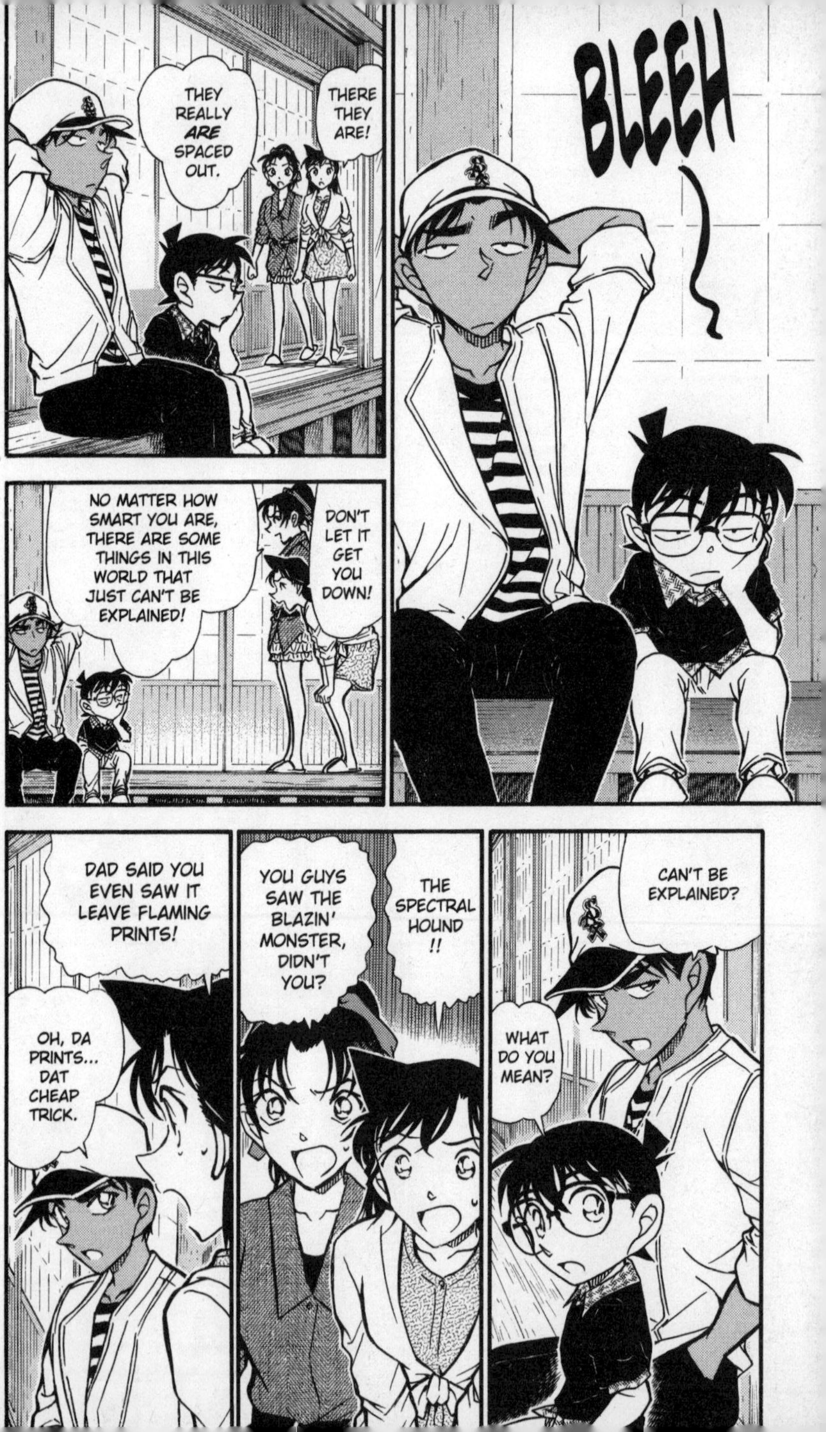
BLEEH
THERE THEY ARE!
THEY REALLY *ARE* SPACED OUT.
DON'T LET IT GET YOU DOWN!
NO MATTER HOW SMART YOU ARE, THERE ARE SOME THINGS IN THIS WORLD THAT JUST CAN'T BE EXPLAINED!
CAN'T BE EXPLAINED?
WHAT DO YOU MEAN?
THE SPECTRAL HOUND !!
YOU GUYS SAW THE BLAZIN' MONSTER, DIDN'T YOU?
DAD SAID YOU EVEN SAW IT LEAVE FLAMING PRINTS!
OH, DA PRINTS... DAT CHEAP TRICK.

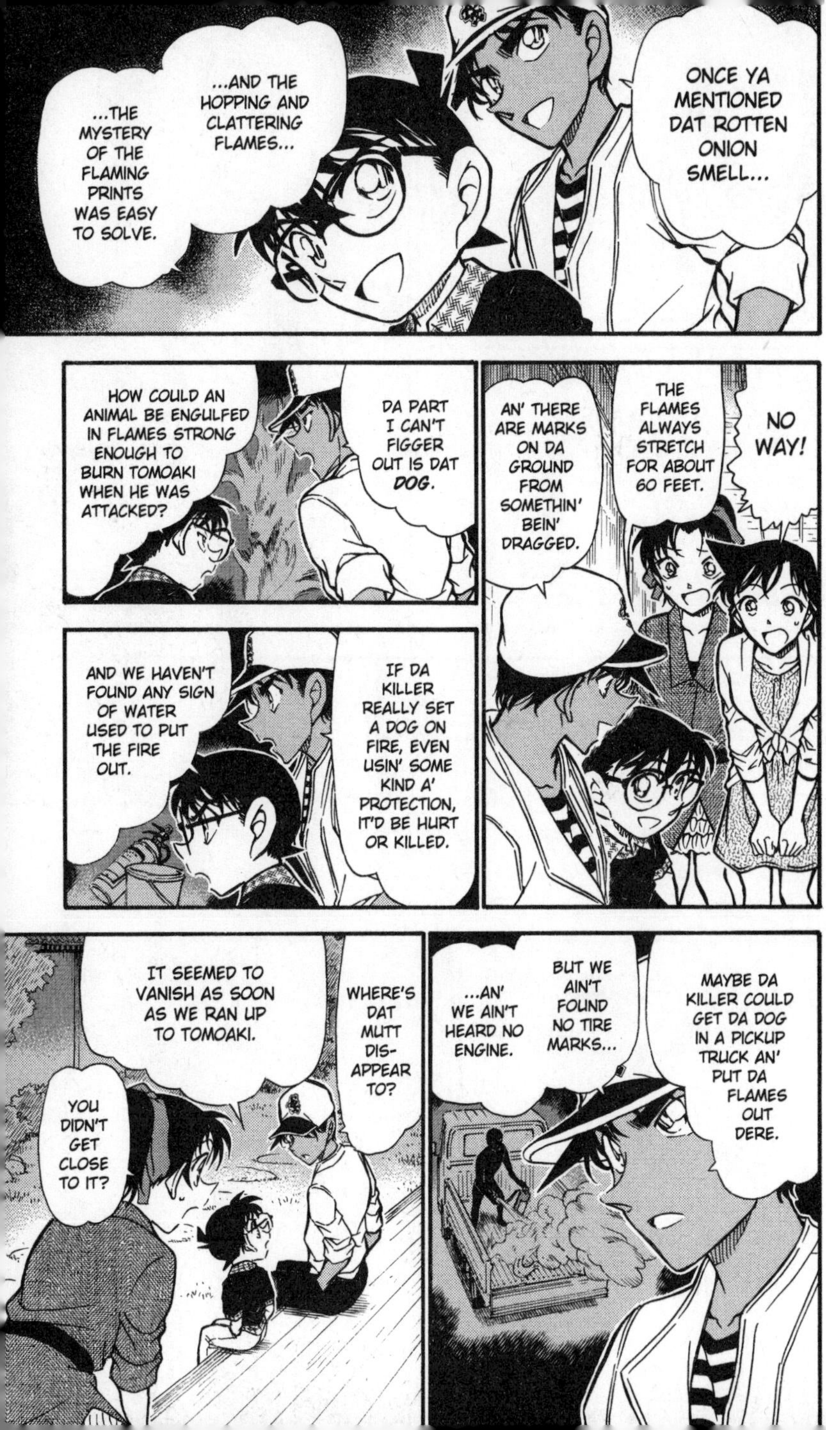
ONCE YA MENTIONED DAT ROTTEN ONION SMELL...
...AND THE HOPPING AND CLATTERING FLAMES...
...THE MYSTERY OF THE FLAMING PRINTS WAS EASY TO SOLVE.
NO WAY!
THE FLAMES ALWAYS STRETCH FOR ABOUT 60 FEET.
AN' THERE ARE MARKS ON DA GROUND FROM SOMETHIN' BEIN' DRAGGED.
DA PART I CAN'T FIGGER OUT IS DAT **DOG**.
HOW COULD AN ANIMAL BE ENGULFED IN FLAMES STRONG ENOUGH TO BURN TOMOAKI WHEN HE WAS ATTACKED?
IF DA KILLER REALLY SET A DOG ON FIRE, EVEN USIN' SOME KIND A' PROTECTION, IT'D BE HURT OR KILLED.
AND WE HAVEN'T FOUND ANY SIGN OF WATER USED TO PUT THE FIRE OUT.
MAYBE DA KILLER COULD GET DA DOG IN A PICKUP TRUCK AN' PUT DA FLAMES OUT DERE.
BUT WE AIN'T FOUND NO TIRE MARKS...
...AN' WE AIN'T HEARD NO ENGINE.
WHERE'S DAT MUTT DIS-APPEAR TO?
IT SEEMED TO VANISH AS SOON AS WE RAN UP TO TOMOAKI.
YOU DIDN'T GET CLOSE TO IT?

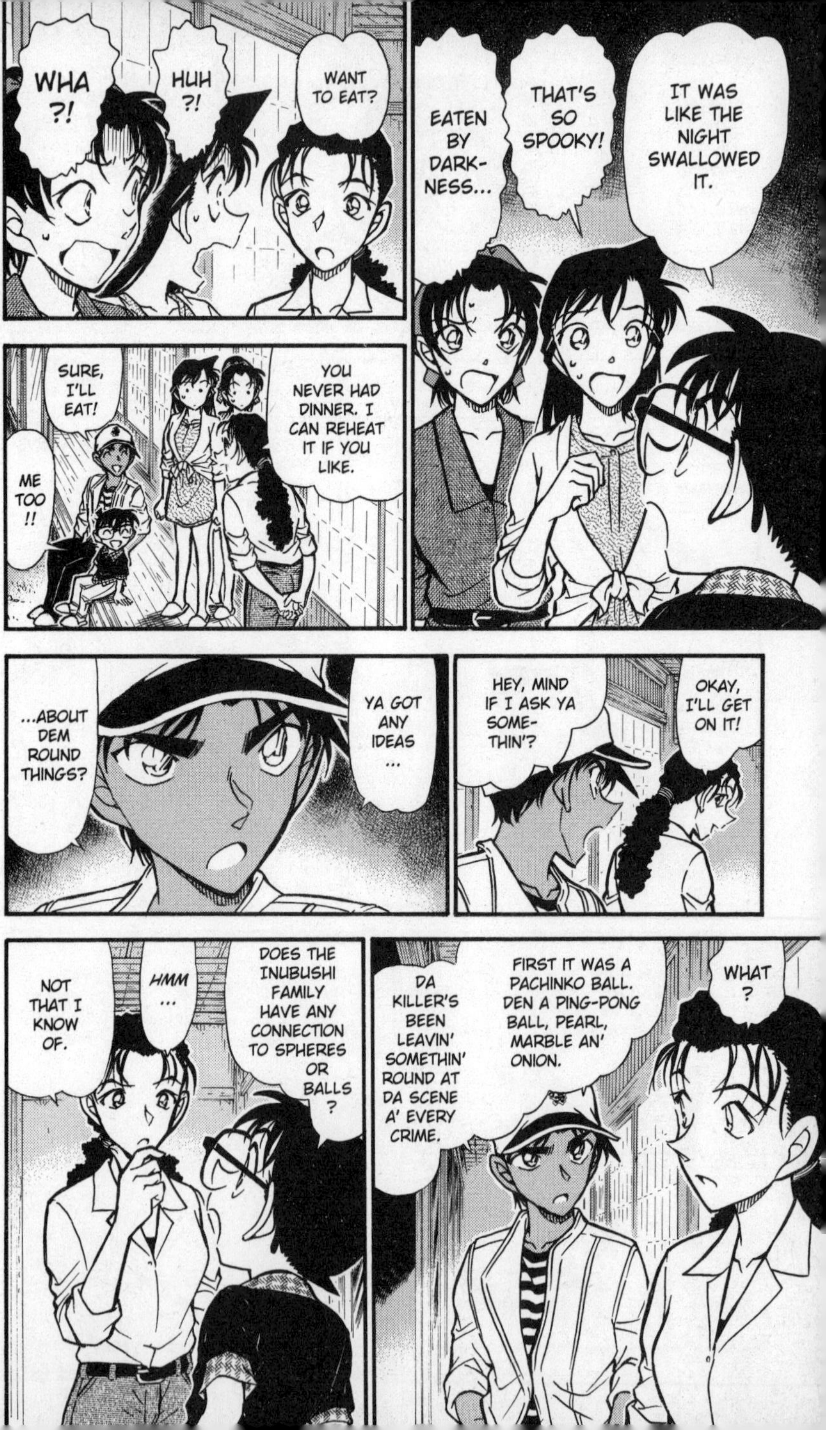
IT WAS LIKE THE NIGHT SWALLOWED IT.
THAT'S SO SPOOKY!
EATEN BY DARKNESS...
WANT TO EAT?
HUH?!
WHA?!
YOU NEVER HAD DINNER. I CAN REHEAT IT IF YOU LIKE.
SURE, I'LL EAT!
ME TOO!!
OKAY, I'LL GET ON IT!
HEY, MIND IF I ASK YA SOMETHIN'?
YA GOT ANY IDEAS...
...ABOUT DEM ROUND THINGS?
WHAT?
FIRST IT WAS A PACHINKO BALL. DEN A PING-PONG BALL, PEARL, MARBLE AN' ONION.
DA KILLER'S BEEN LEAVIN' SOMETHIN' ROUND AT DA SCENE A' EVERY CRIME.
DOES THE INUBUSHI FAMILY HAVE ANY CONNECTION TO SPHERES OR BALLS?
HMM...
NOT THAT I KNOW OF.

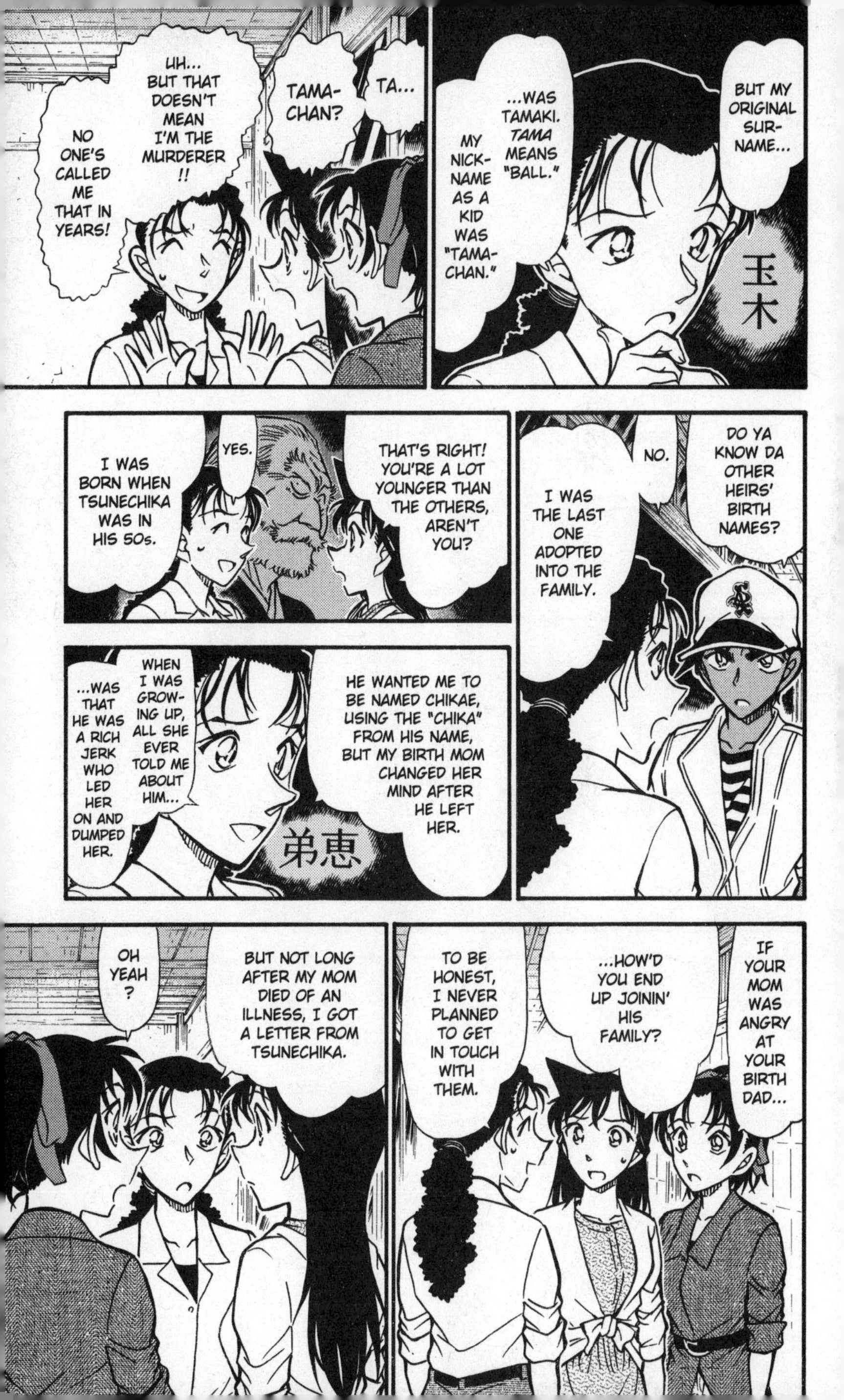
BUT MY ORIGINAL SUR-NAME...
...WAS TAMAKI. *TAMA* MEANS "BALL."
MY NICK-NAME AS A KID WAS "TAMA-CHAN."
玉木
TA...
TAMA-CHAN?
UH... BUT THAT DOESN'T MEAN I'M THE MURDERER !!
NO ONE'S CALLED ME THAT IN YEARS!
DO YA KNOW DA OTHER HEIRS' BIRTH NAMES?
NO.
I WAS THE LAST ONE ADOPTED INTO THE FAMILY.
THAT'S RIGHT! YOU'RE A LOT YOUNGER THAN THE OTHERS, AREN'T YOU?
YES.
I WAS BORN WHEN TSUNECHIKA WAS IN HIS 50s.
HE WANTED ME TO BE NAMED CHIKAE, USING THE "CHIKA" FROM HIS NAME, BUT MY BIRTH MOM CHANGED HER MIND AFTER HE LEFT HER.
弟恵
WHEN I WAS GROWING UP, ALL SHE EVER TOLD ME ABOUT HIM...
...WAS THAT HE WAS A RICH JERK WHO LED HER ON AND DUMPED HER.
IF YOUR MOM WAS ANGRY AT YOUR BIRTH DAD...
...HOW'D YOU END UP JOININ' HIS FAMILY?
TO BE HONEST, I NEVER PLANNED TO GET IN TOUCH WITH THEM.
BUT NOT LONG AFTER MY MOM DIED OF AN ILLNESS, I GOT A LETTER FROM TSUNECHIKA.
OH YEAH?

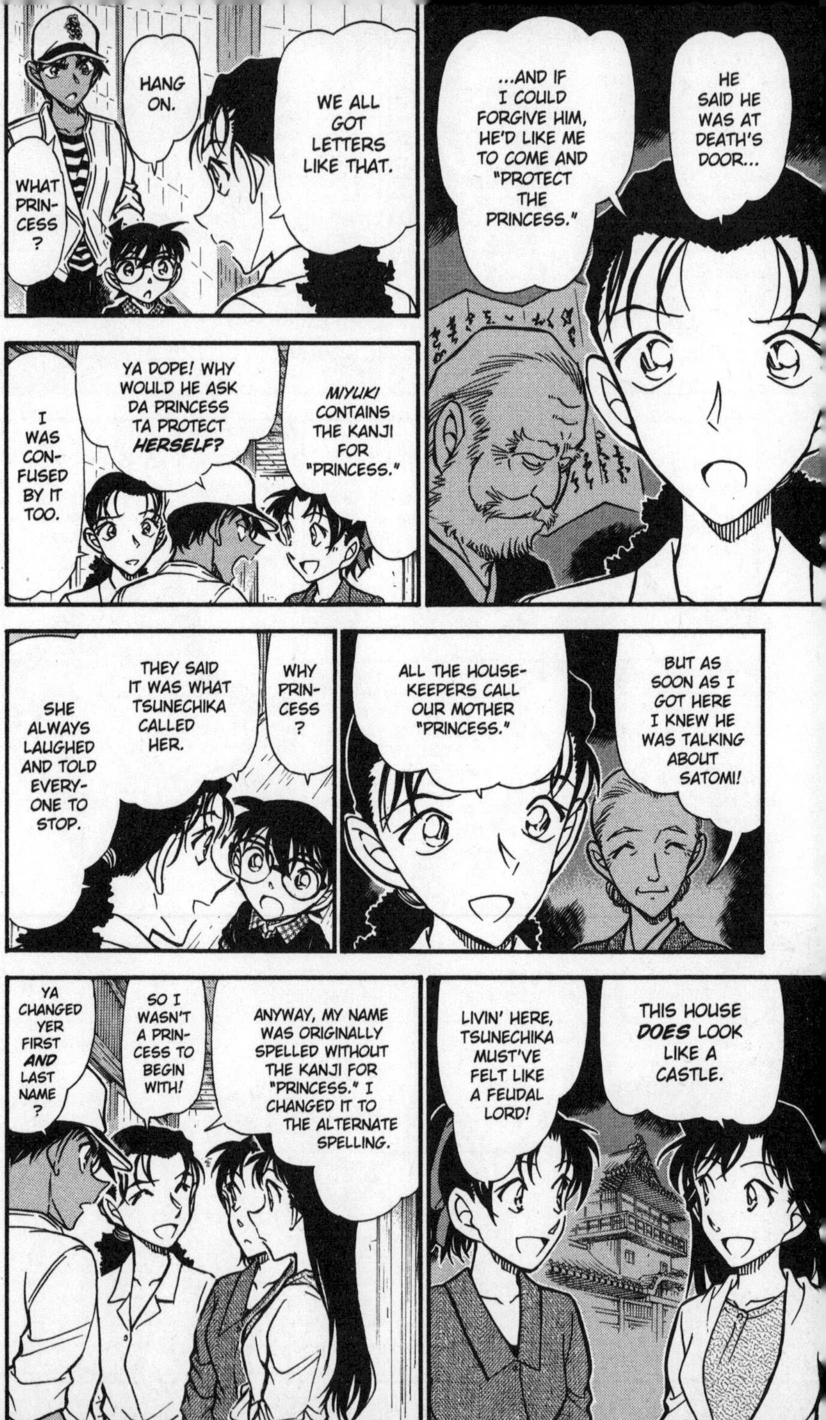
HE SAID HE WAS AT DEATH'S DOOR...
...AND IF I COULD FORGIVE HIM, HE'D LIKE ME TO COME AND "PROTECT THE PRINCESS."
WE ALL GOT LETTERS LIKE THAT.
HANG ON.
WHAT PRINCESS?
MIYUKI CONTAINS THE KANJI FOR "PRINCESS."
YA DOPE! WHY WOULD HE ASK DA PRINCESS TA PROTECT ***HERSELF?***
I WAS CONFUSED BY IT TOO.
BUT AS SOON AS I GOT HERE I KNEW HE WAS TALKING ABOUT SATOMI!
ALL THE HOUSEKEEPERS CALL OUR MOTHER "PRINCESS."
WHY PRINCESS?
THEY SAID IT WAS WHAT TSUNECHIKA CALLED HER.
SHE ALWAYS LAUGHED AND TOLD EVERYONE TO STOP.
THIS HOUSE ***DOES*** LOOK LIKE A CASTLE.
LIVIN' HERE, TSUNECHIKA MUST'VE FELT LIKE A FEUDAL LORD!
ANYWAY, MY NAME WAS ORIGINALLY SPELLED WITHOUT THE KANJI FOR "PRINCESS." I CHANGED IT TO THE ALTERNATE SPELLING.
SO I WASN'T A PRINCESS TO BEGIN WITH!
YA CHANGED YER FIRST ***AND*** LAST NAME?

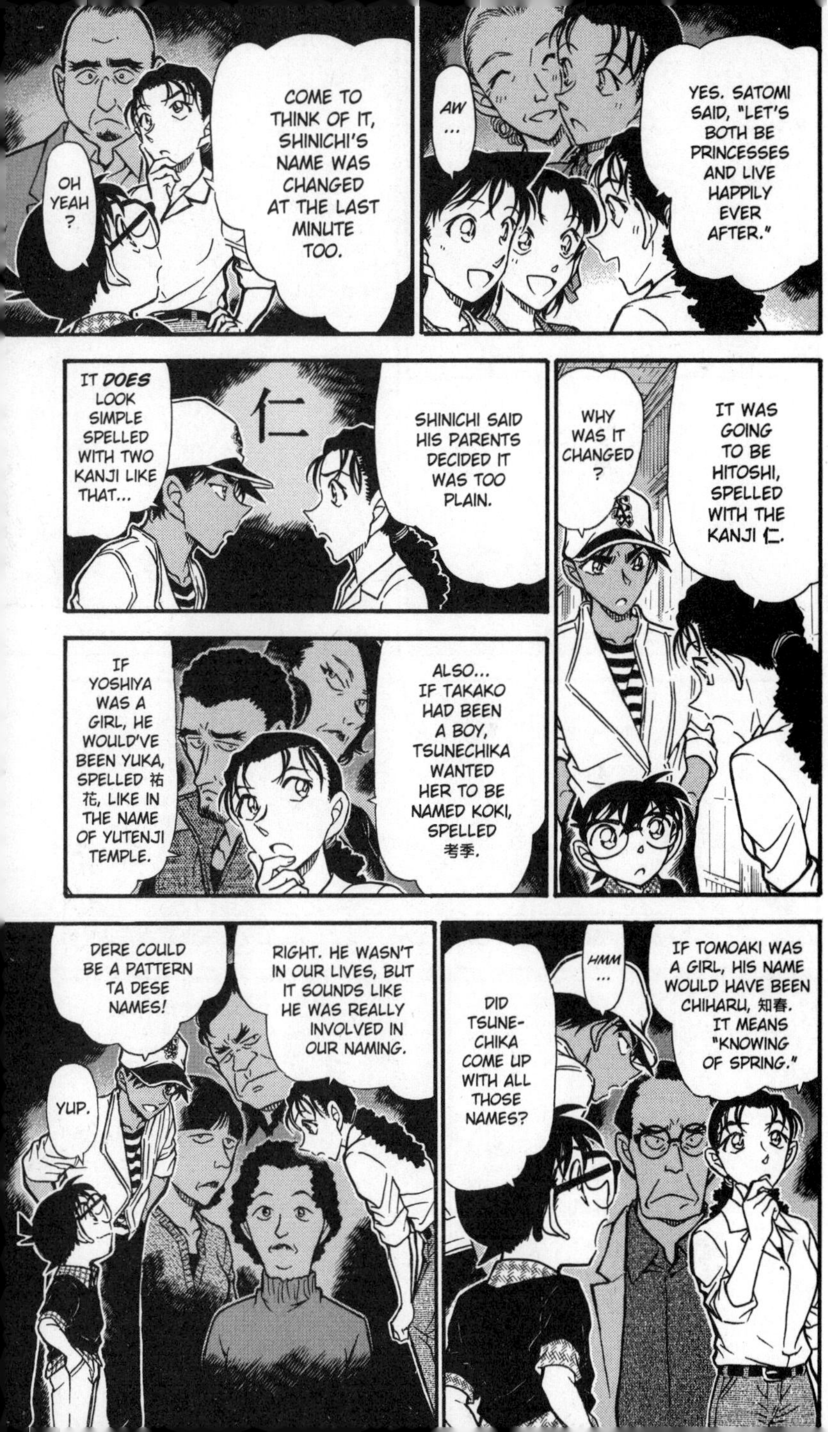
YES. SATOMI SAID, "LET'S BOTH BE PRINCESSES AND LIVE HAPPILY EVER AFTER."
AW...
COME TO THINK OF IT, SHINICHI'S NAME WAS CHANGED AT THE LAST MINUTE TOO.
OH YEAH?
IT WAS GOING TO BE HITOSHI, SPELLED WITH THE KANJI 仁.
WHY WAS IT CHANGED?
SHINICHI SAID HIS PARENTS DECIDED IT WAS TOO PLAIN.
仁
IT *DOES* LOOK SIMPLE SPELLED WITH TWO KANJI LIKE THAT...
ALSO... IF TAKAKO HAD BEEN A BOY, TSUNECHIKA WANTED HER TO BE NAMED KOKI, SPELLED 考季.
IF YOSHIYA WAS A GIRL, HE WOULD'VE BEEN YUKA, SPELLED 祐花, LIKE IN THE NAME OF YUTENJI TEMPLE.
IF TOMOAKI WAS A GIRL, HIS NAME WOULD HAVE BEEN CHIHARU, 知春. IT MEANS "KNOWING OF SPRING."
HMM...
DID TSUNE-CHIKA COME UP WITH ALL THOSE NAMES?
RIGHT. HE WASN'T IN OUR LIVES, BUT IT SOUNDS LIKE HE WAS REALLY INVOLVED IN OUR NAMING.
DERE COULD BE A PATTERN TA DESE NAMES!
YUP.

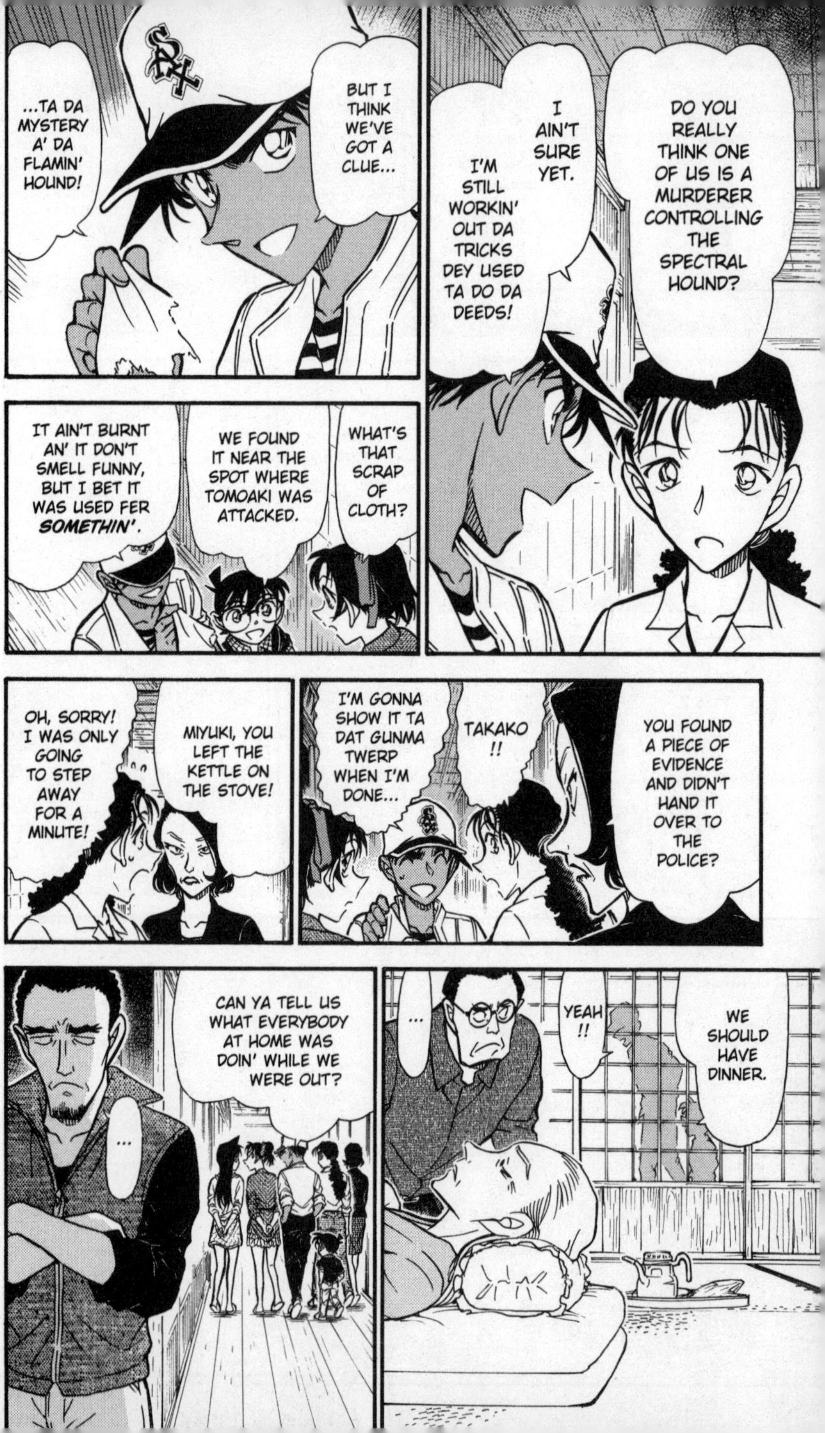

DO YOU REALLY THINK ONE OF US IS A MURDERER CONTROLLING THE SPECTRAL HOUND?
I AIN'T SURE YET.
I'M STILL WORKIN' OUT DA TRICKS DEY USED TA DO DA DEEDS!
BUT I THINK WE'VE GOT A CLUE...
...TA DA MYSTERY A' DA FLAMIN' HOUND!
WHAT'S THAT SCRAP OF CLOTH?
WE FOUND IT NEAR THE SPOT WHERE TOMOAKI WAS ATTACKED.
IT AIN'T BURNT AN' IT DON'T SMELL FUNNY, BUT I BET IT WAS USED FER ***SOMETHIN'***.
YOU FOUND A PIECE OF EVIDENCE AND DIDN'T HAND IT OVER TO THE POLICE?
TAKAKO !!
I'M GONNA SHOW IT TA DAT GUNMA TWERP WHEN I'M DONE...
MIYUKI, YOU LEFT THE KETTLE ON THE STOVE!
OH, SORRY! I WAS ONLY GOING TO STEP AWAY FOR A MINUTE!
WE SHOULD HAVE DINNER.
YEAH !!
...
CAN YA TELL US WHAT EVERYBODY AT HOME WAS DOIN' WHILE WE WERE OUT?
...

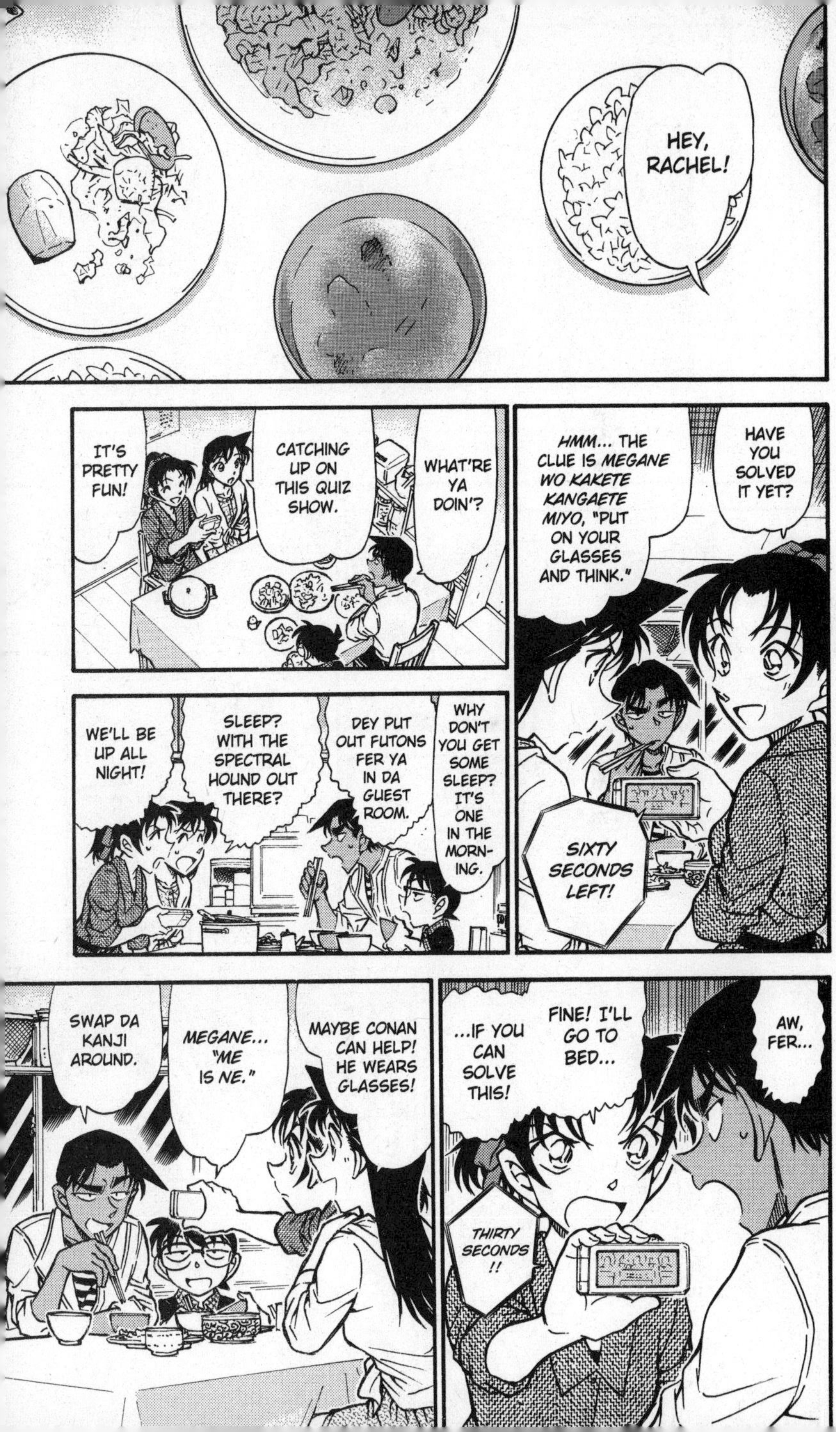
HEY, RACHEL!
HAVE YOU SOLVED IT YET?
HMM... THE CLUE IS *MEGANE WO KAKETE KANGAETE MIYO*, "PUT ON YOUR GLASSES AND THINK."
SIXTY SECONDS LEFT!
WHAT'RE YA DOIN'?
CATCHING UP ON THIS QUIZ SHOW.
IT'S PRETTY FUN!
WHY DON'T YOU GET SOME SLEEP? IT'S ONE IN THE MORN-ING.
DEY PUT OUT FUTONS FER YA IN DA GUEST ROOM.
SLEEP? WITH THE SPECTRAL HOUND OUT THERE?
WE'LL BE UP ALL NIGHT!
AW, FER...
FINE! I'LL GO TO BED...
...IF YOU CAN SOLVE THIS!
THIRTY SECONDS!!
MAYBE CONAN CAN HELP! HE WEARS GLASSES!
MEGANE... "*ME* IS *NE*."
SWAP DA KANJI AROUND.

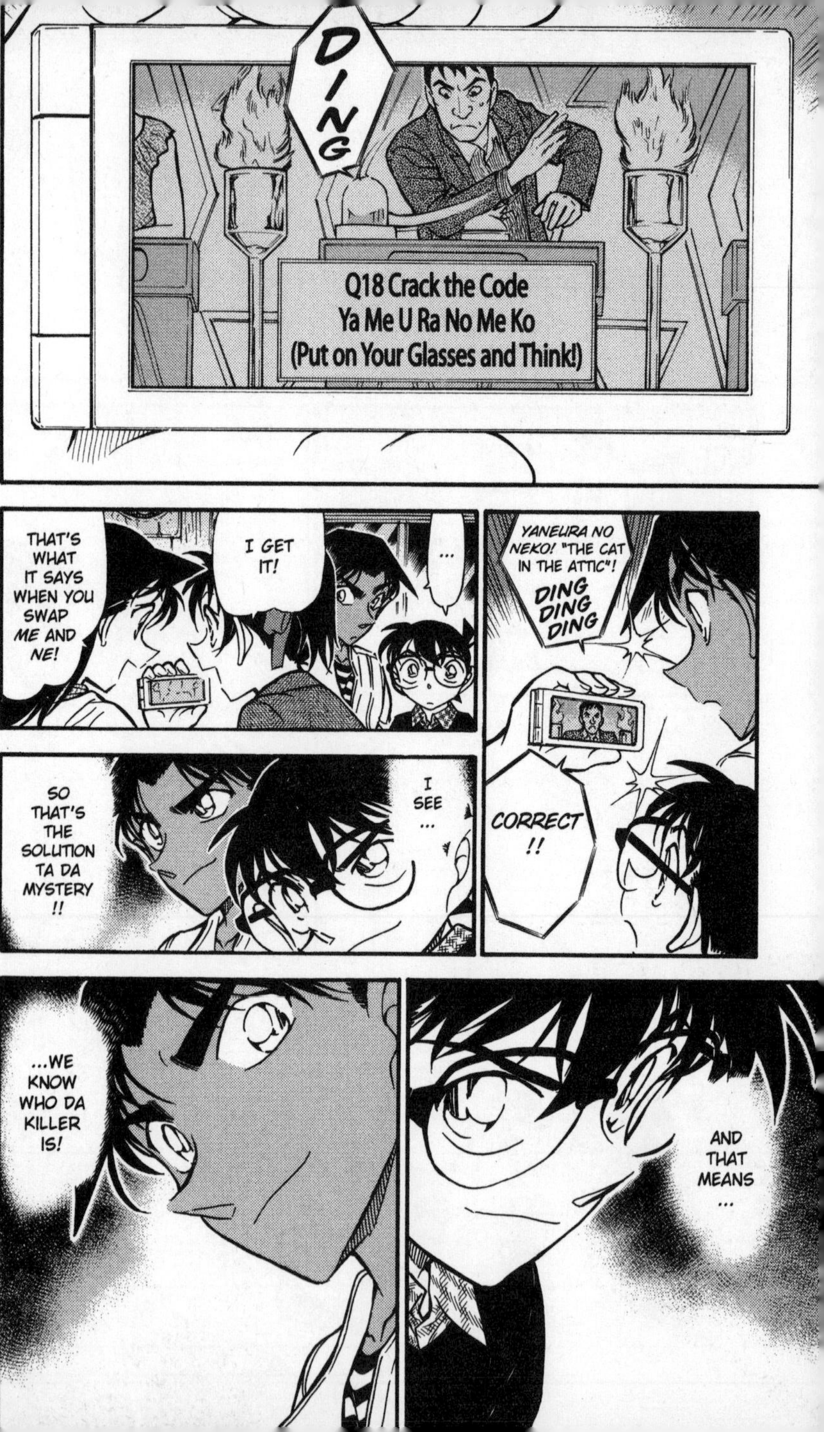
DING
Q18 Crack the Code
Ya Me U Ra No Me Ko
(Put on Your Glasses and Think!)
YANEURA NO NEKO! "THE CAT IN THE ATTIC"!
DING DING DING
CORRECT!!
...
I GET IT!
THAT'S WHAT IT SAYS WHEN YOU SWAP *ME* AND *NE*!
I SEE...
SO THAT'S THE SOLUTION TA DA MYSTERY!!
AND THAT MEANS...
...WE KNOW WHO DA KILLER IS!

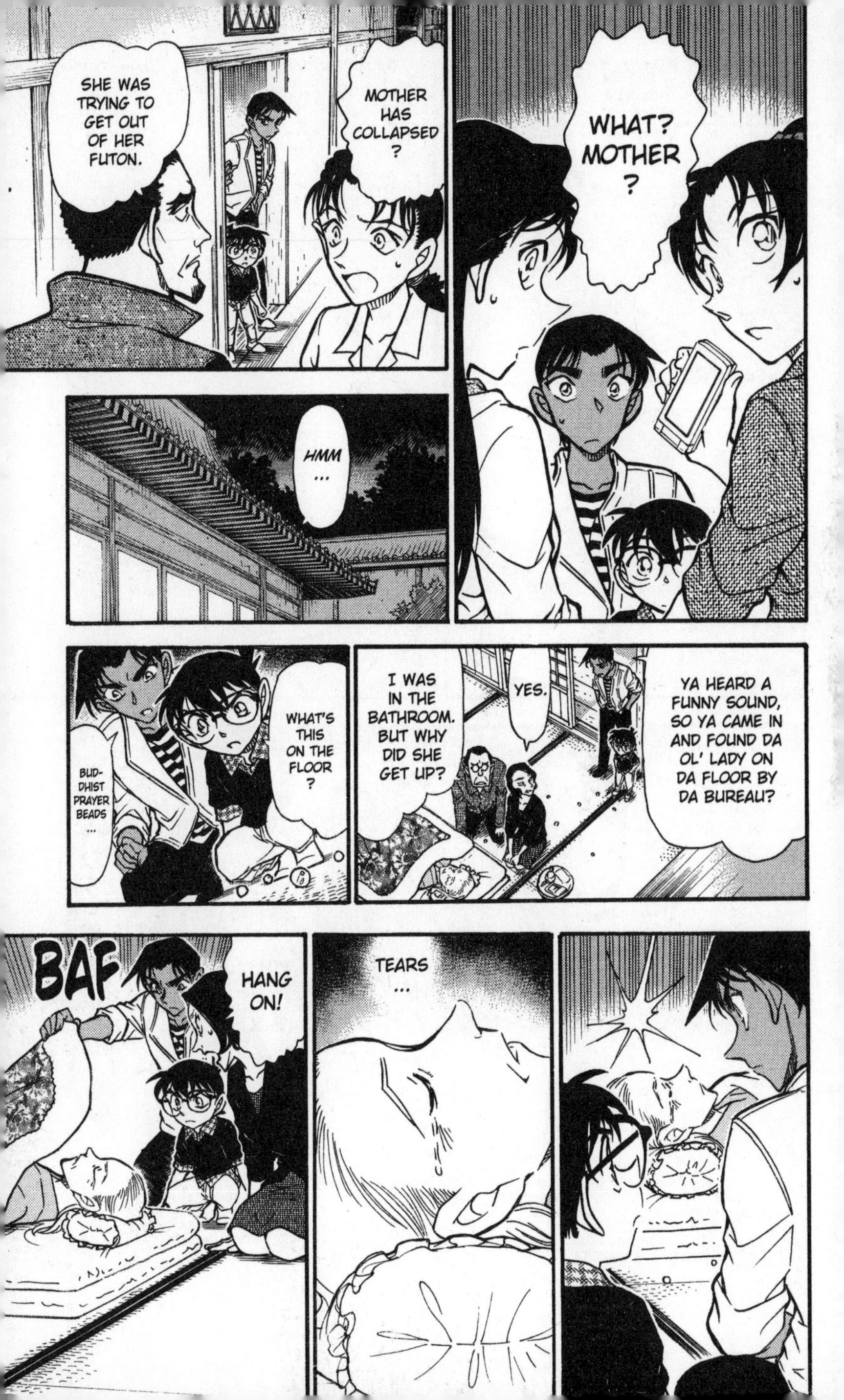
WHAT? MOTHER ?
MOTHER HAS COLLAPSED ?
SHE WAS TRYING TO GET OUT OF HER FUTON.
HMM ...
YA HEARD A FUNNY SOUND, SO YA CAME IN AND FOUND DA OL' LADY ON DA FLOOR BY DA BUREAU?
YES.
I WAS IN THE BATHROOM. BUT WHY DID SHE GET UP?
WHAT'S THIS ON THE FLOOR ?
BUD-DHIST PRAYER BEADS ...
TEARS ...
HANG ON!
BAF

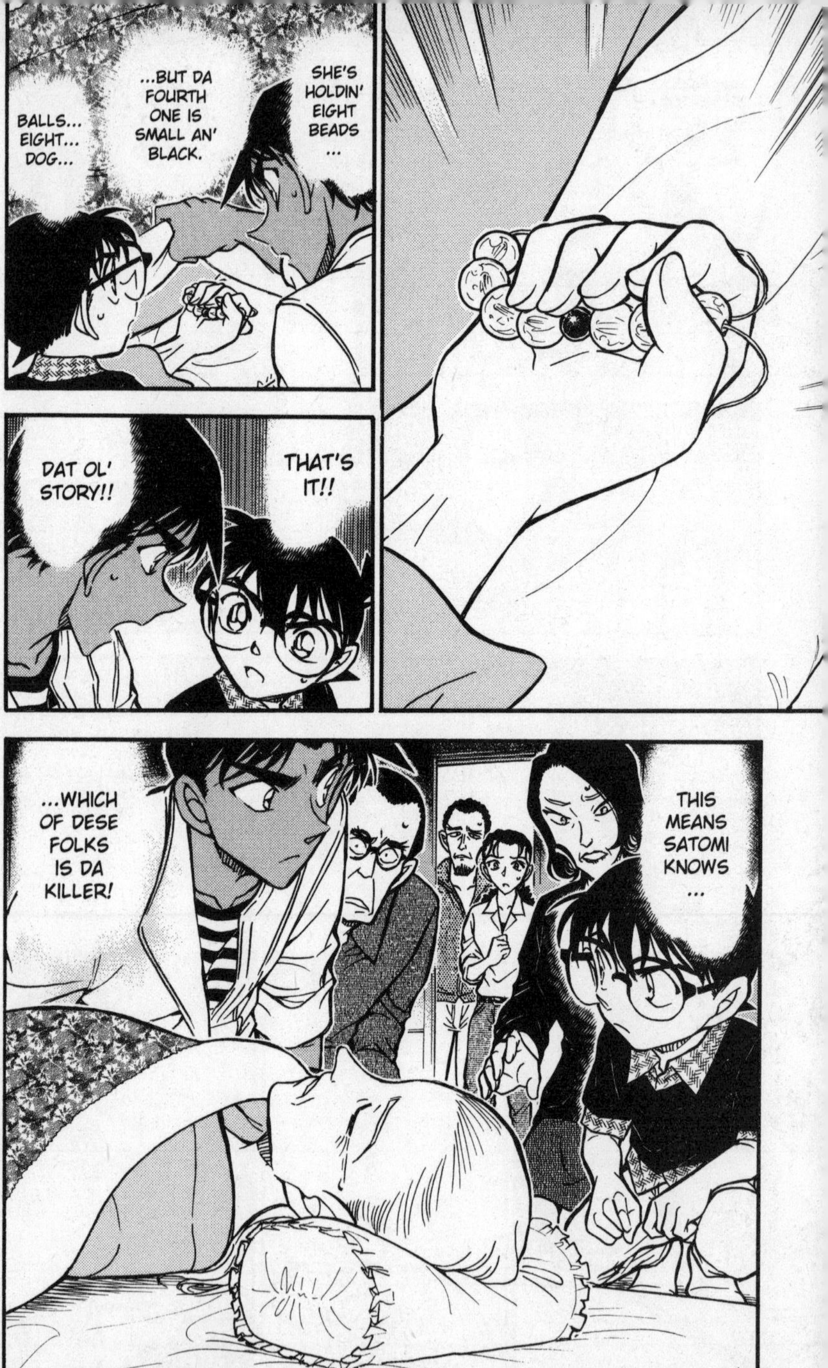
SHE'S HOLDIN' EIGHT BEADS ...
...BUT DA FOURTH ONE IS SMALL AN' BLACK.
BALLS... EIGHT... DOG...
THAT'S IT!!
DAT OL' STORY!!
THIS MEANS SATOMI KNOWS ...
...WHICH OF DESE FOLKS IS DA KILLER!

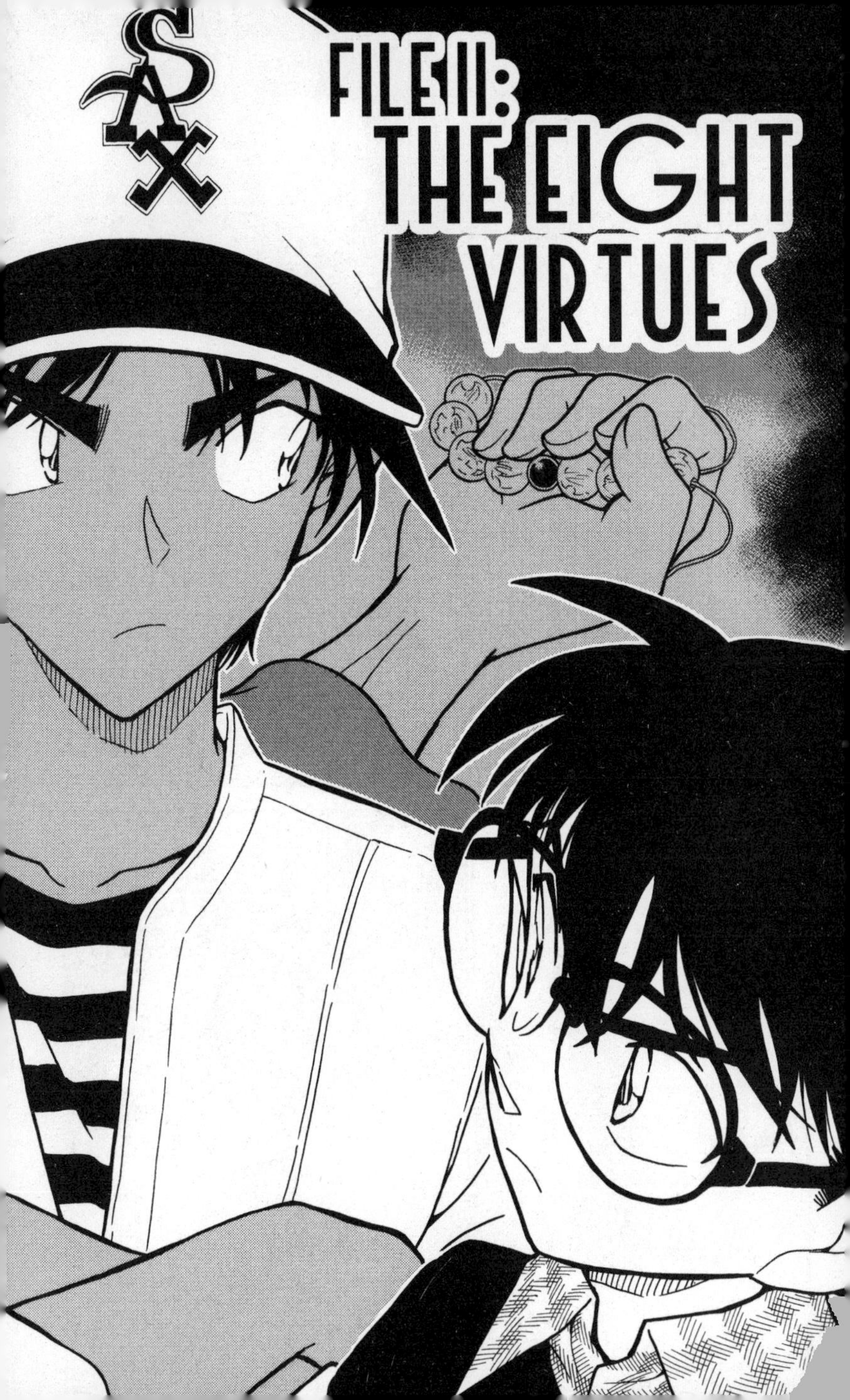
FILE 11:
THE EIGHT VIRTUES

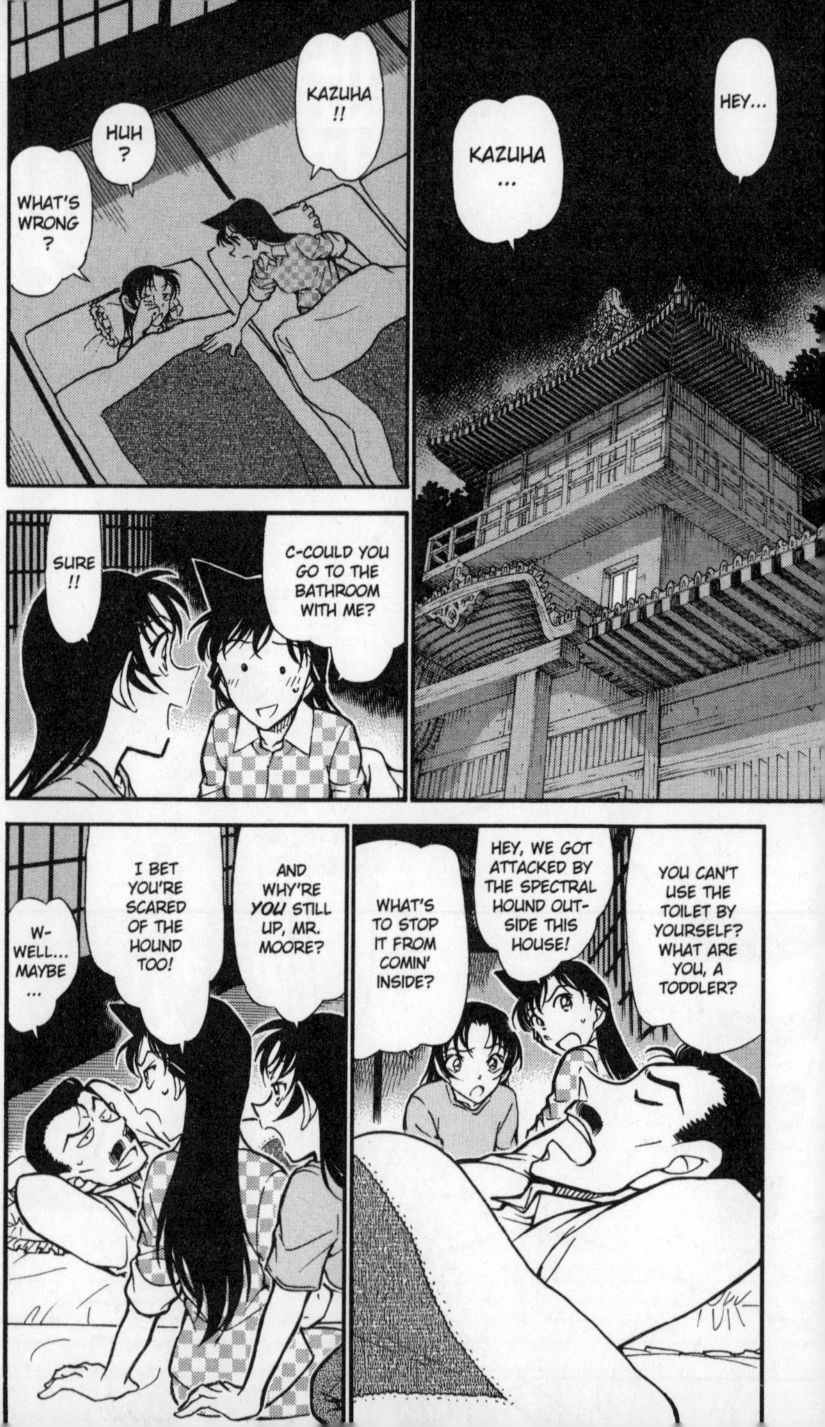
HEY...
KAZUHA...
KAZUHA!!
HUH?
WHAT'S WRONG?
C-COULD YOU GO TO THE BATHROOM WITH ME?
SURE!!
YOU CAN'T USE THE TOILET BY YOURSELF? WHAT ARE YOU, A TODDLER?
HEY, WE GOT ATTACKED BY THE SPECTRAL HOUND OUTSIDE THIS HOUSE!
WHAT'S TO STOP IT FROM COMIN' INSIDE?
AND WHY'RE YOU STILL UP, MR. MOORE?
I BET YOU'RE SCARED OF THE HOUND TOO!
W-WELL... MAYBE...

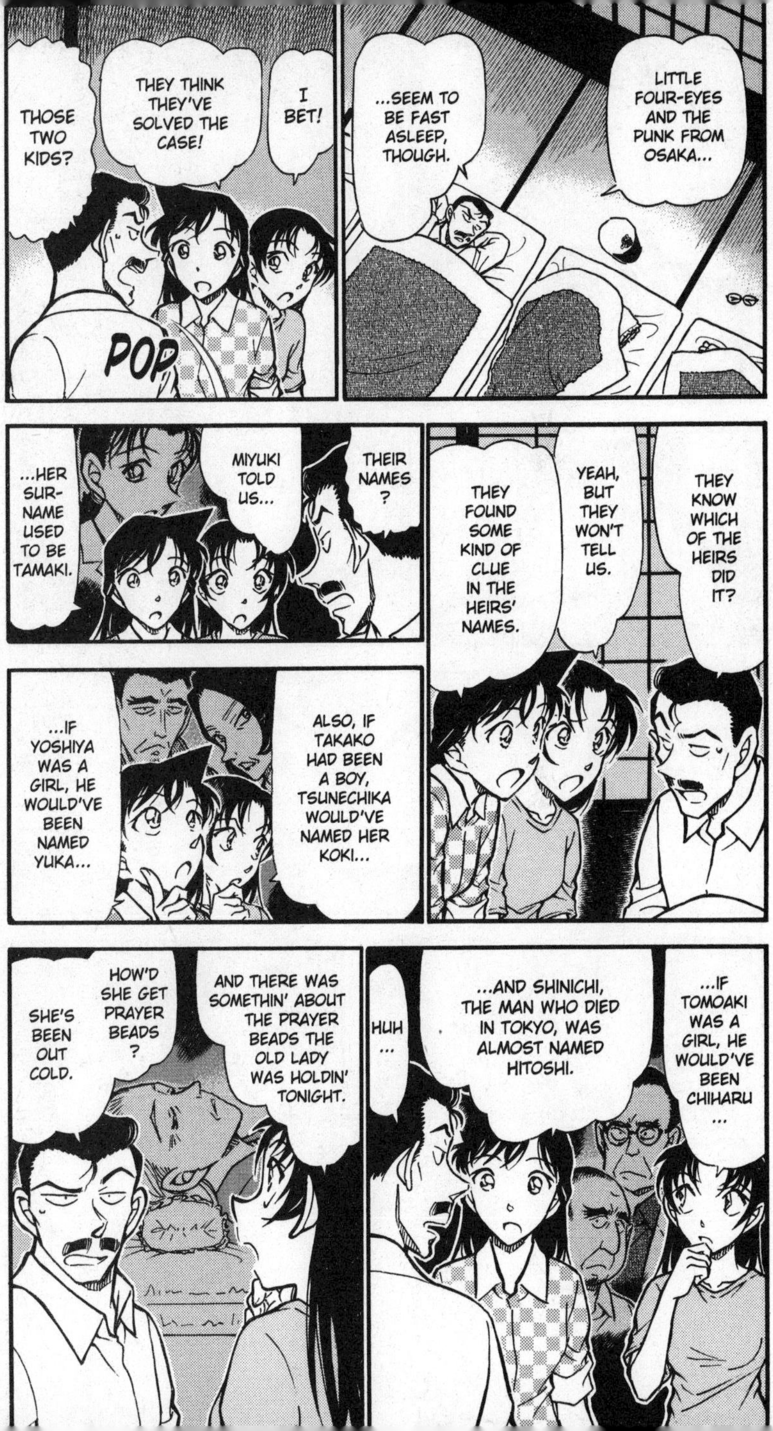
LITTLE FOUR-EYES AND THE PUNK FROM OSAKA...
...SEEM TO BE FAST ASLEEP, THOUGH.
I BET!
THEY THINK THEY'VE SOLVED THE CASE!
THOSE TWO KIDS?
POP
THEY KNOW WHICH OF THE HEIRS DID IT?
YEAH, BUT THEY WON'T TELL US.
THEY FOUND SOME KIND OF CLUE IN THE HEIRS' NAMES.
THEIR NAMES?
MIYUKI TOLD US...
...HER SURNAME USED TO BE TAMAKI.
ALSO, IF TAKAKO HAD BEEN A BOY, TSUNECHIKA WOULD'VE NAMED HER KOKI...
...IF YOSHIYA WAS A GIRL, HE WOULD'VE BEEN NAMED YUKA...
...IF TOMOAKI WAS A GIRL, HE WOULD'VE BEEN CHIHARU...
...AND SHINICHI, THE MAN WHO DIED IN TOKYO, WAS ALMOST NAMED HITOSHI.
HUH...
AND THERE WAS SOMETHIN' ABOUT THE PRAYER BEADS THE OLD LADY WAS HOLDIN' TONIGHT.
HOW'D SHE GET PRAYER BEADS?
SHE'S BEEN OUT COLD.

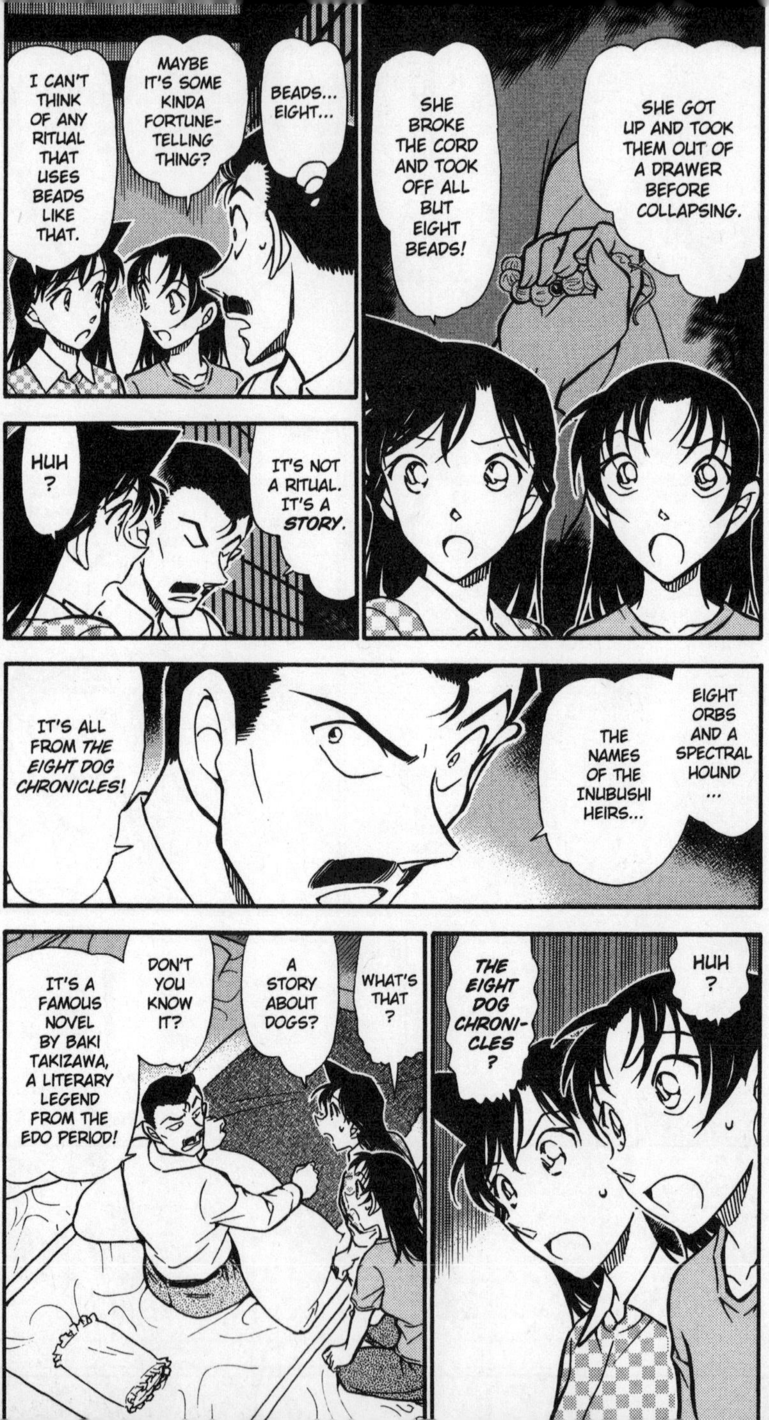
SHE GOT UP AND TOOK THEM OUT OF A DRAWER BEFORE COLLAPSING.
SHE BROKE THE CORD AND TOOK OFF ALL BUT EIGHT BEADS!
BEADS... EIGHT...
MAYBE IT'S SOME KINDA FORTUNE-TELLING THING?
I CAN'T THINK OF ANY RITUAL THAT USES BEADS LIKE THAT.
IT'S NOT A RITUAL. IT'S A *STORY*.
HUH?
EIGHT ORBS AND A SPECTRAL HOUND...
THE NAMES OF THE INUBUSHI HEIRS...
IT'S ALL FROM *THE EIGHT DOG CHRONICLES*!
HUH?
THE EIGHT DOG CHRONICLES?
WHAT'S THAT?
A STORY ABOUT DOGS?
DON'T YOU KNOW IT?
IT'S A FAMOUS NOVEL BY BAKI TAKIZAWA, A LITERARY LEGEND FROM THE EDO PERIOD!

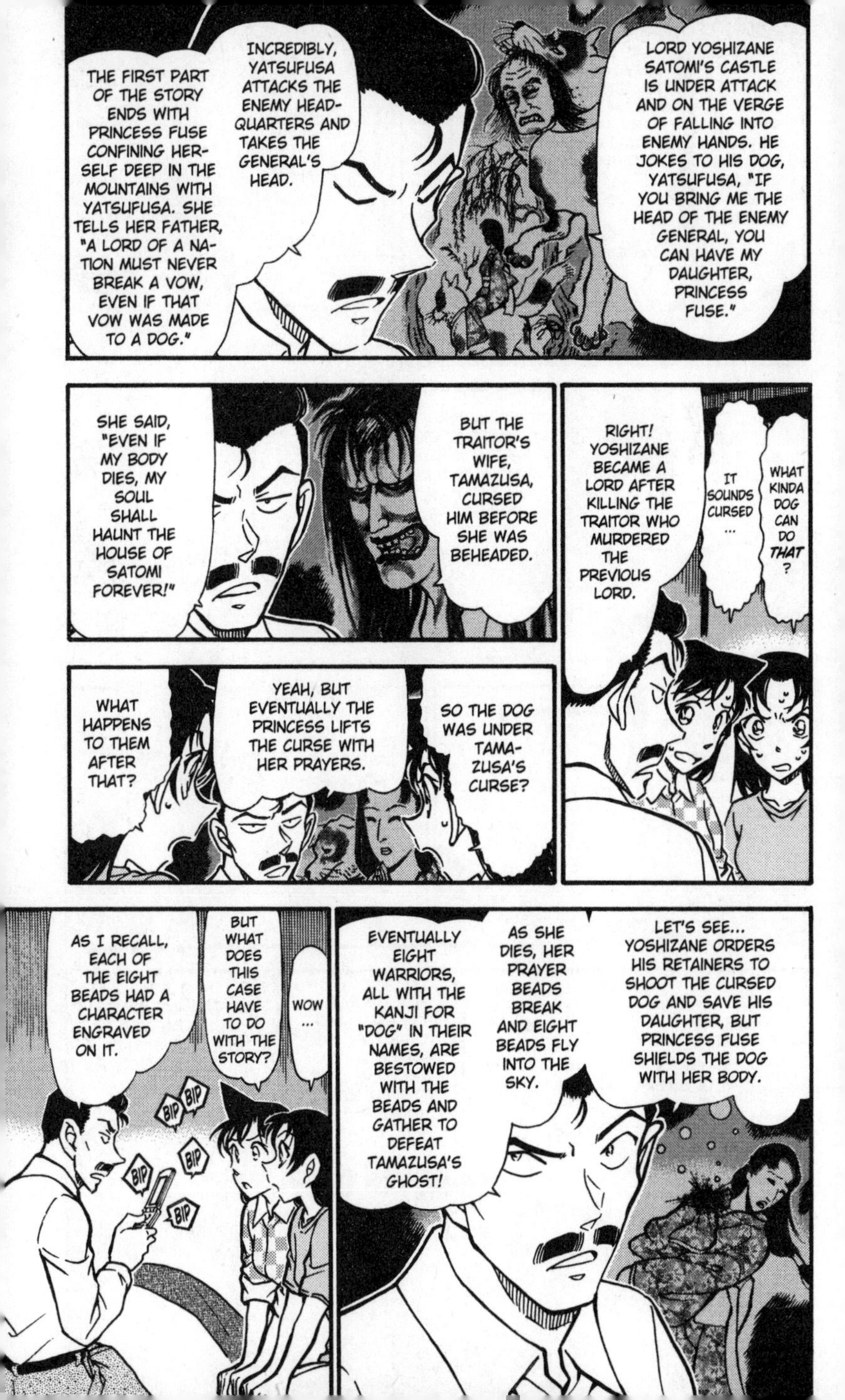

LORD YOSHIZANE SATOMI'S CASTLE IS UNDER ATTACK AND ON THE VERGE OF FALLING INTO ENEMY HANDS. HE JOKES TO HIS DOG, YATSUFUSA, "IF YOU BRING ME THE HEAD OF THE ENEMY GENERAL, YOU CAN HAVE MY DAUGHTER, PRINCESS FUSE."
INCREDIBLY, YATSUFUSA ATTACKS THE ENEMY HEAD-QUARTERS AND TAKES THE GENERAL'S HEAD.
THE FIRST PART OF THE STORY ENDS WITH PRINCESS FUSE CONFINING HER-SELF DEEP IN THE MOUNTAINS WITH YATSUFUSA. SHE TELLS HER FATHER, "A LORD OF A NA-TION MUST NEVER BREAK A VOW, EVEN IF THAT VOW WAS MADE TO A DOG."
WHAT KINDA DOG CAN DO *THAT*?
IT SOUNDS CURSED...
RIGHT! YOSHIZANE BECAME A LORD AFTER KILLING THE TRAITOR WHO MURDERED THE PREVIOUS LORD.
BUT THE TRAITOR'S WIFE, TAMAZUSA, CURSED HIM BEFORE SHE WAS BEHEADED.
SHE SAID, "EVEN IF MY BODY DIES, MY SOUL SHALL HAUNT THE HOUSE OF SATOMI FOREVER!"
SO THE DOG WAS UNDER TAMA-ZUSA'S CURSE?
YEAH, BUT EVENTUALLY THE PRINCESS LIFTS THE CURSE WITH HER PRAYERS.
WHAT HAPPENS TO THEM AFTER THAT?
LET'S SEE... YOSHIZANE ORDERS HIS RETAINERS TO SHOOT THE CURSED DOG AND SAVE HIS DAUGHTER, BUT PRINCESS FUSE SHIELDS THE DOG WITH HER BODY.
AS SHE DIES, HER PRAYER BEADS BREAK AND EIGHT BEADS FLY INTO THE SKY.
EVENTUALLY EIGHT WARRIORS, ALL WITH THE KANJI FOR "DOG" IN THEIR NAMES, ARE BESTOWED WITH THE BEADS AND GATHER TO DEFEAT TAMAZUSA'S GHOST!
WOW...
BUT WHAT DOES THIS CASE HAVE TO DO WITH THE STORY?
AS I RECALL, EACH OF THE EIGHT BEADS HAD A CHARACTER ENGRAVED ON IT.
BIP BIP BIP BIP BIP BIP

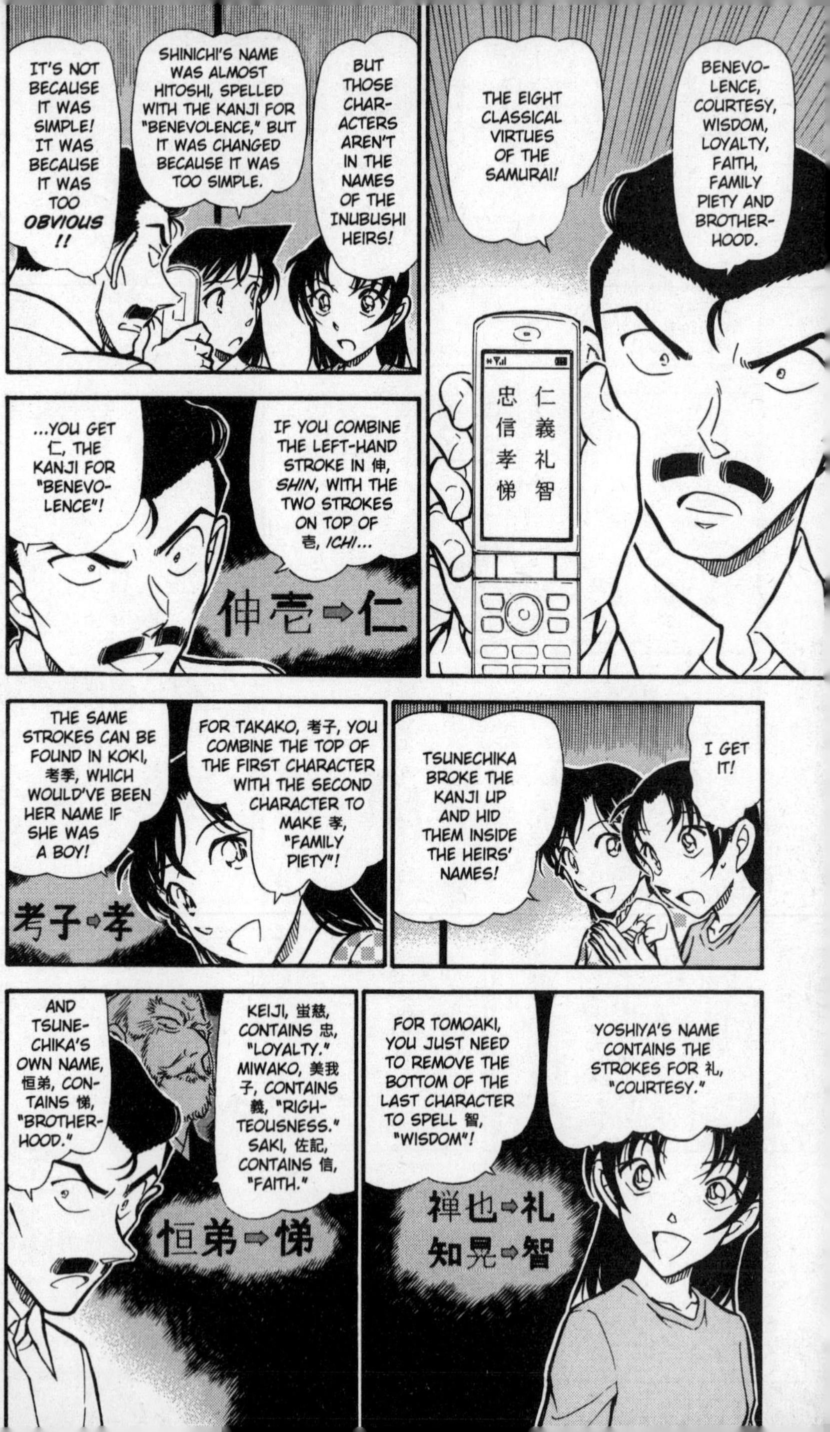
BENEVOLENCE, COURTESY, WISDOM, LOYALTY, FAITH, FAMILY PIETY AND BROTHERHOOD.
THE EIGHT CLASSICAL VIRTUES OF THE SAMURAI!
仁義礼智
忠信孝悌
BUT THOSE CHARACTERS AREN'T IN THE NAMES OF THE INUBUSHI HEIRS!
SHINICHI'S NAME WAS ALMOST HITOSHI, SPELLED WITH THE KANJI FOR "BENEVOLENCE," BUT IT WAS CHANGED BECAUSE IT WAS TOO SIMPLE.
IT'S NOT BECAUSE IT WAS SIMPLE! IT WAS BECAUSE IT WAS TOO *OBVIOUS*!!
IF YOU COMBINE THE LEFT-HAND STROKE IN 伸, *SHIN*, WITH THE TWO STROKES ON TOP OF 壱, *ICHI*...
...YOU GET 仁, THE KANJI FOR "BENEVOLENCE"!
伸壱➡仁
I GET IT!
TSUNECHIKA BROKE THE KANJI UP AND HID THEM INSIDE THE HEIRS' NAMES!
FOR TAKAKO, 考子, YOU COMBINE THE TOP OF THE FIRST CHARACTER WITH THE SECOND CHARACTER TO MAKE 孝, "FAMILY PIETY"!
THE SAME STROKES CAN BE FOUND IN KOKI, 考季, WHICH WOULD'VE BEEN HER NAME IF SHE WAS A BOY!
考子➡孝
YOSHIYA'S NAME CONTAINS THE STROKES FOR 礼, "COURTESY."
FOR TOMOAKI, YOU JUST NEED TO REMOVE THE BOTTOM OF THE LAST CHARACTER TO SPELL 智, "WISDOM"!
禅也➡礼
知晃➡智
KEIJI, 蛍慈, CONTAINS 忠, "LOYALTY." MIWAKO, 美我子, CONTAINS 義, "RIGHTEOUSNESS." SAKI, 佐記, CONTAINS 信, "FAITH."
AND TSUNECHIKA'S OWN NAME, 恒弟, CONTAINS 悌, "BROTHERHOOD."
恒弟➡悌

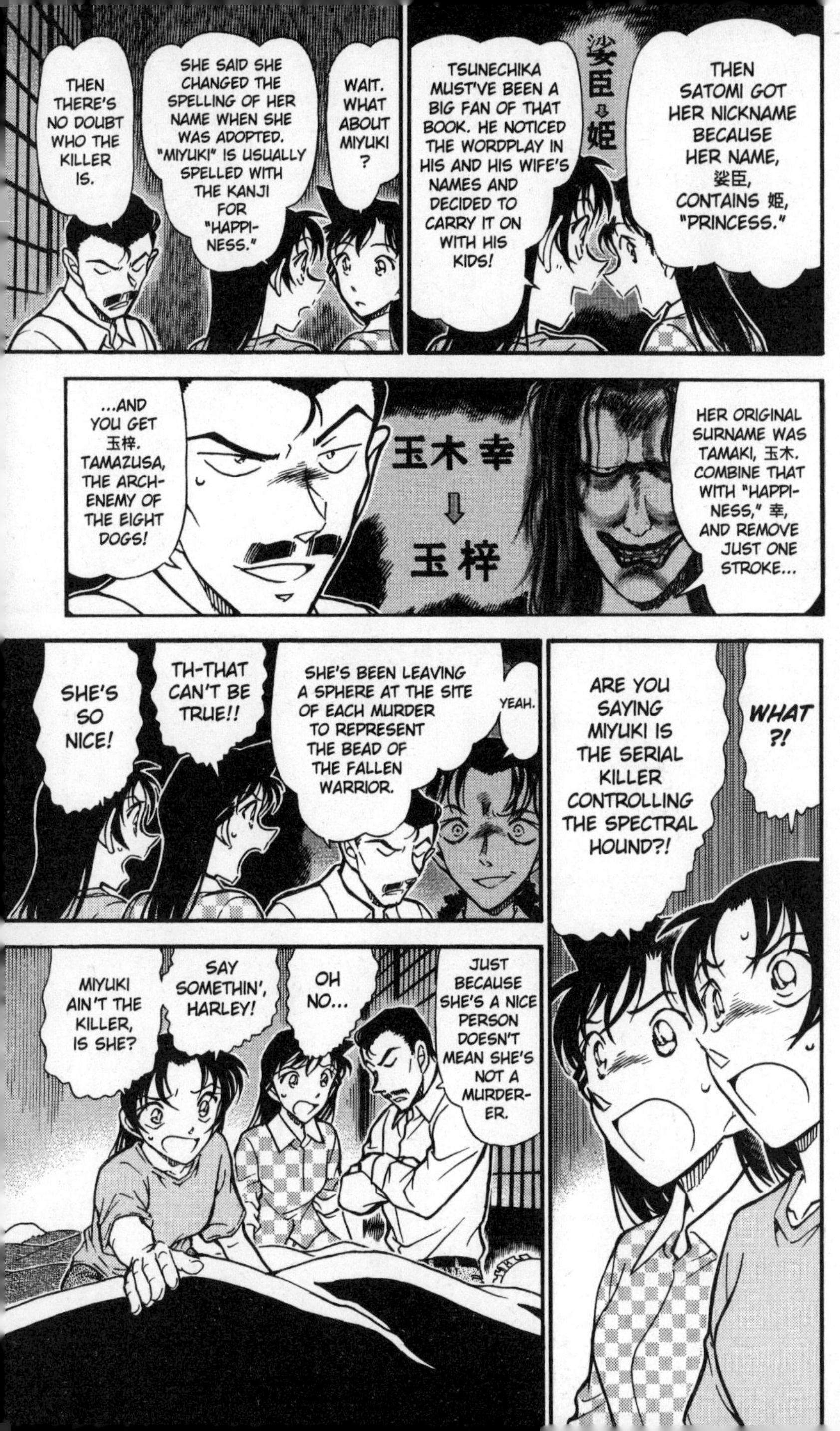
THEN SATOMI GOT HER NICKNAME BECAUSE HER NAME, 娑臣, CONTAINS 姫, "PRINCESS."
娑臣 ⇩ 姫
TSUNECHIKA MUST'VE BEEN A BIG FAN OF THAT BOOK. HE NOTICED THE WORDPLAY IN HIS AND HIS WIFE'S NAMES AND DECIDED TO CARRY IT ON WITH HIS KIDS!
WAIT. WHAT ABOUT MIYUKI?
SHE SAID SHE CHANGED THE SPELLING OF HER NAME WHEN SHE WAS ADOPTED. "MIYUKI" IS USUALLY SPELLED WITH THE KANJI FOR "HAPPINESS."
THEN THERE'S NO DOUBT WHO THE KILLER IS.
HER ORIGINAL SURNAME WAS TAMAKI, 玉木. COMBINE THAT WITH "HAPPINESS," 幸, AND REMOVE JUST ONE STROKE...
玉木 幸 ⇩ 玉梓
...AND YOU GET 玉梓. TAMAZUSA, THE ARCH-ENEMY OF THE EIGHT DOGS!
WHAT?!
ARE YOU SAYING MIYUKI IS THE SERIAL KILLER CONTROLLING THE SPECTRAL HOUND?!
YEAH.
SHE'S BEEN LEAVING A SPHERE AT THE SITE OF EACH MURDER TO REPRESENT THE BEAD OF THE FALLEN WARRIOR.
TH-THAT CAN'T BE TRUE!!
SHE'S SO NICE!
JUST BECAUSE SHE'S A NICE PERSON DOESN'T MEAN SHE'S NOT A MURDERER.
OH NO...
SAY SOMETHIN', HARLEY!
MIYUKI AIN'T THE KILLER, IS SHE?

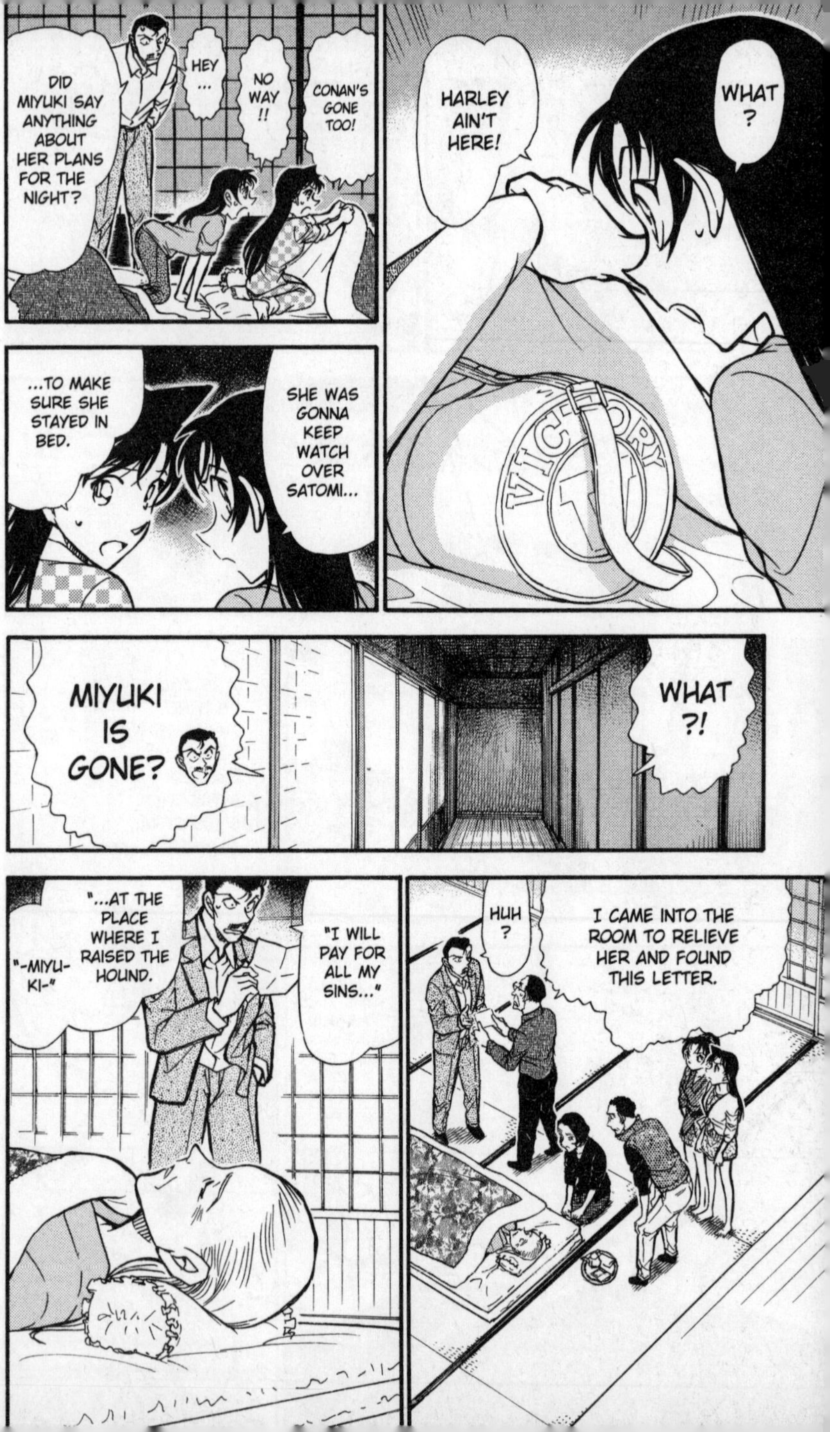
WHAT ?
HARLEY AIN'T HERE!
VICTORY
CONAN'S GONE TOO!
NO WAY !!
HEY ...
DID MIYUKI SAY ANYTHING ABOUT HER PLANS FOR THE NIGHT?
SHE WAS GONNA KEEP WATCH OVER SATOMI...
...TO MAKE SURE SHE STAYED IN BED.
WHAT ?!
MIYUKI IS GONE?
I CAME INTO THE ROOM TO RELIEVE HER AND FOUND THIS LETTER.
HUH ?
"I WILL PAY FOR ALL MY SINS..."
"...AT THE PLACE WHERE I RAISED THE HOUND.
"-MIYU-KI-"

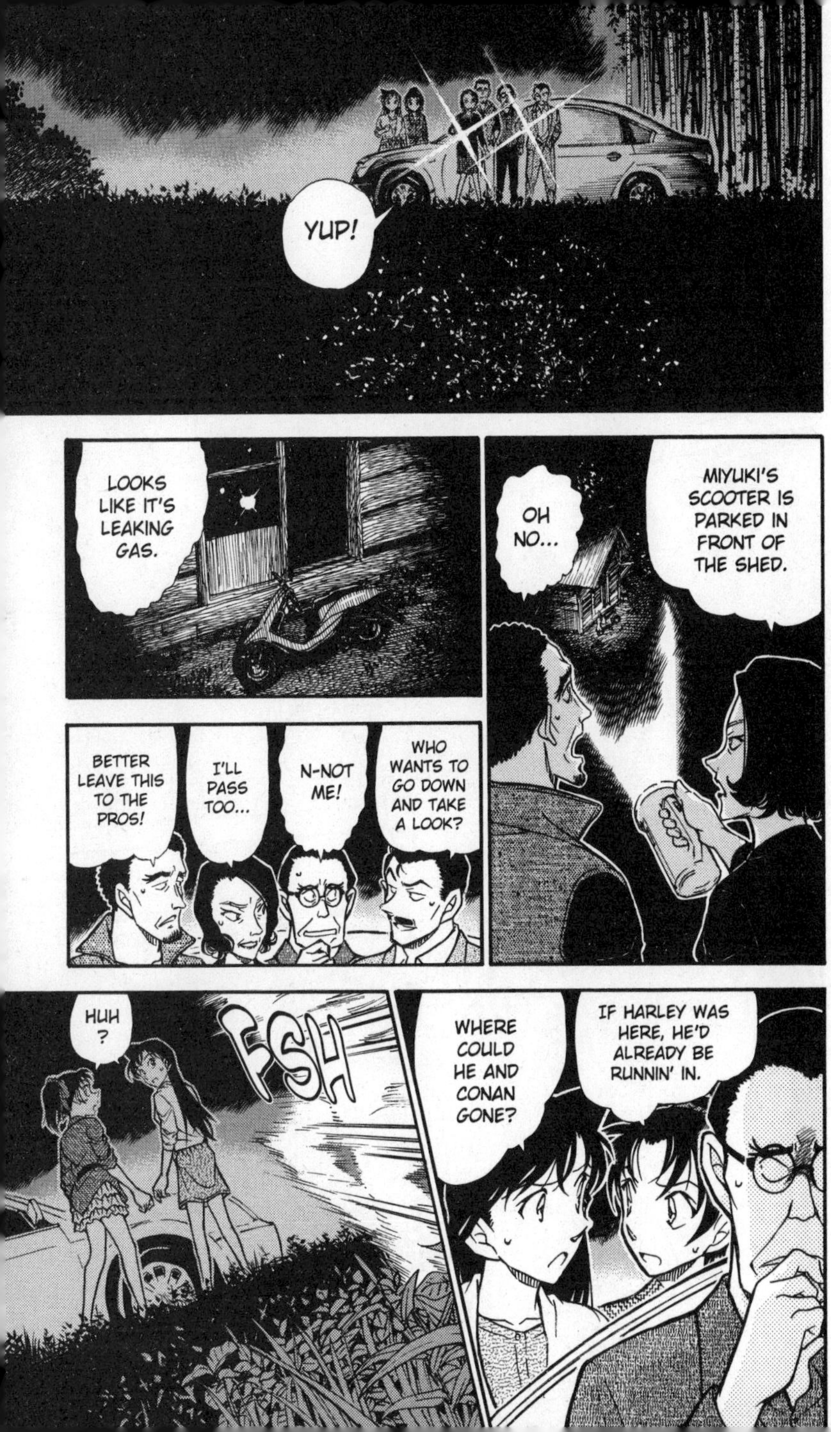
YUP!
MIYUKI'S SCOOTER IS PARKED IN FRONT OF THE SHED.
OH NO...
LOOKS LIKE IT'S LEAKING GAS.
WHO WANTS TO GO DOWN AND TAKE A LOOK?
N-NOT ME!
I'LL PASS TOO...
BETTER LEAVE THIS TO THE PROS!
IF HARLEY WAS HERE, HE'D ALREADY BE RUNNIN' IN.
WHERE COULD HE AND CONAN GONE?
FSH
HUH?

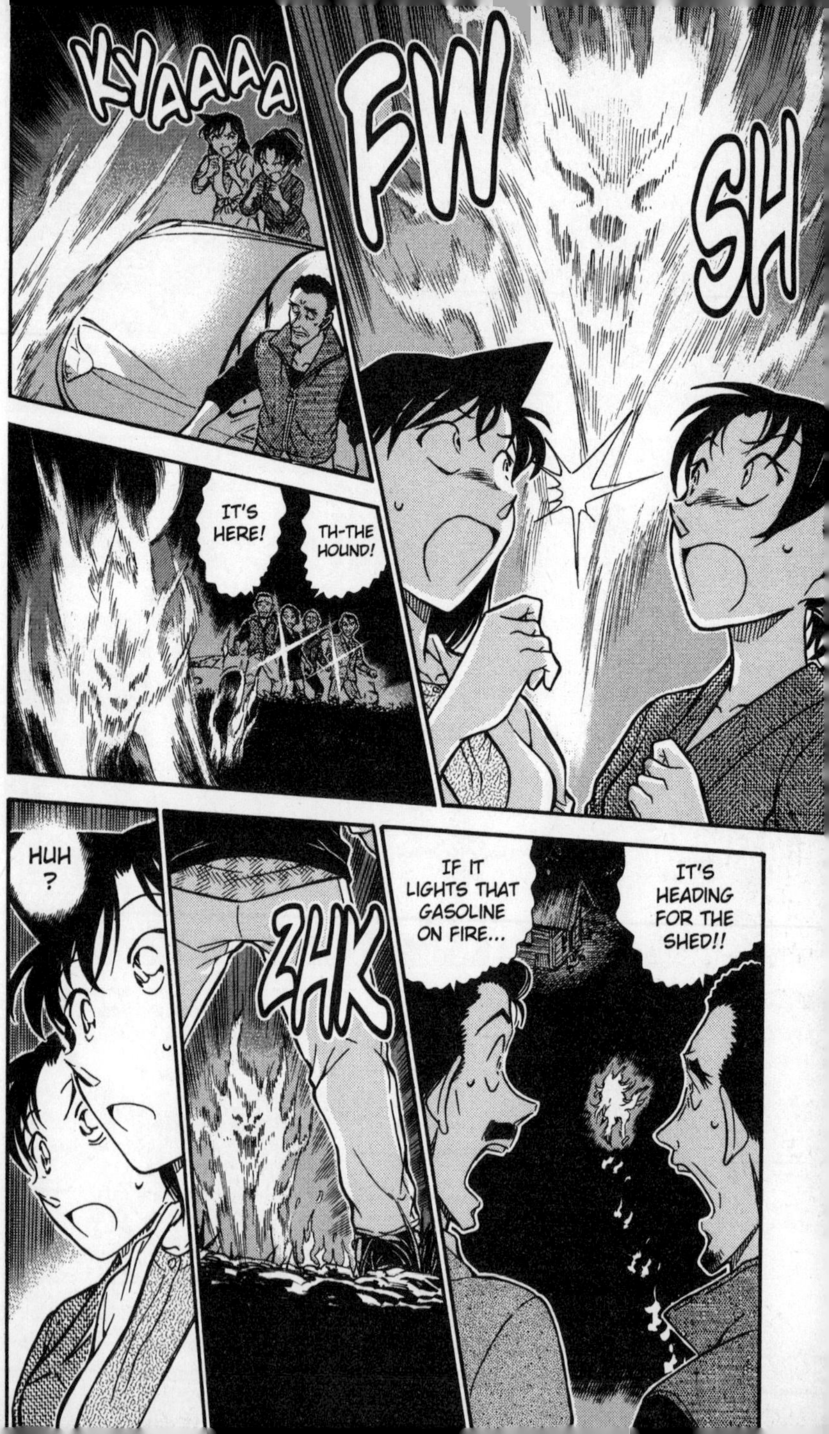
FW
SH
KYAAAA
TH-THE HOUND!
IT'S HERE!
IT'S HEADING FOR THE SHED!!
IF IT LIGHTS THAT GASOLINE ON FIRE...
ZHK
HUH?

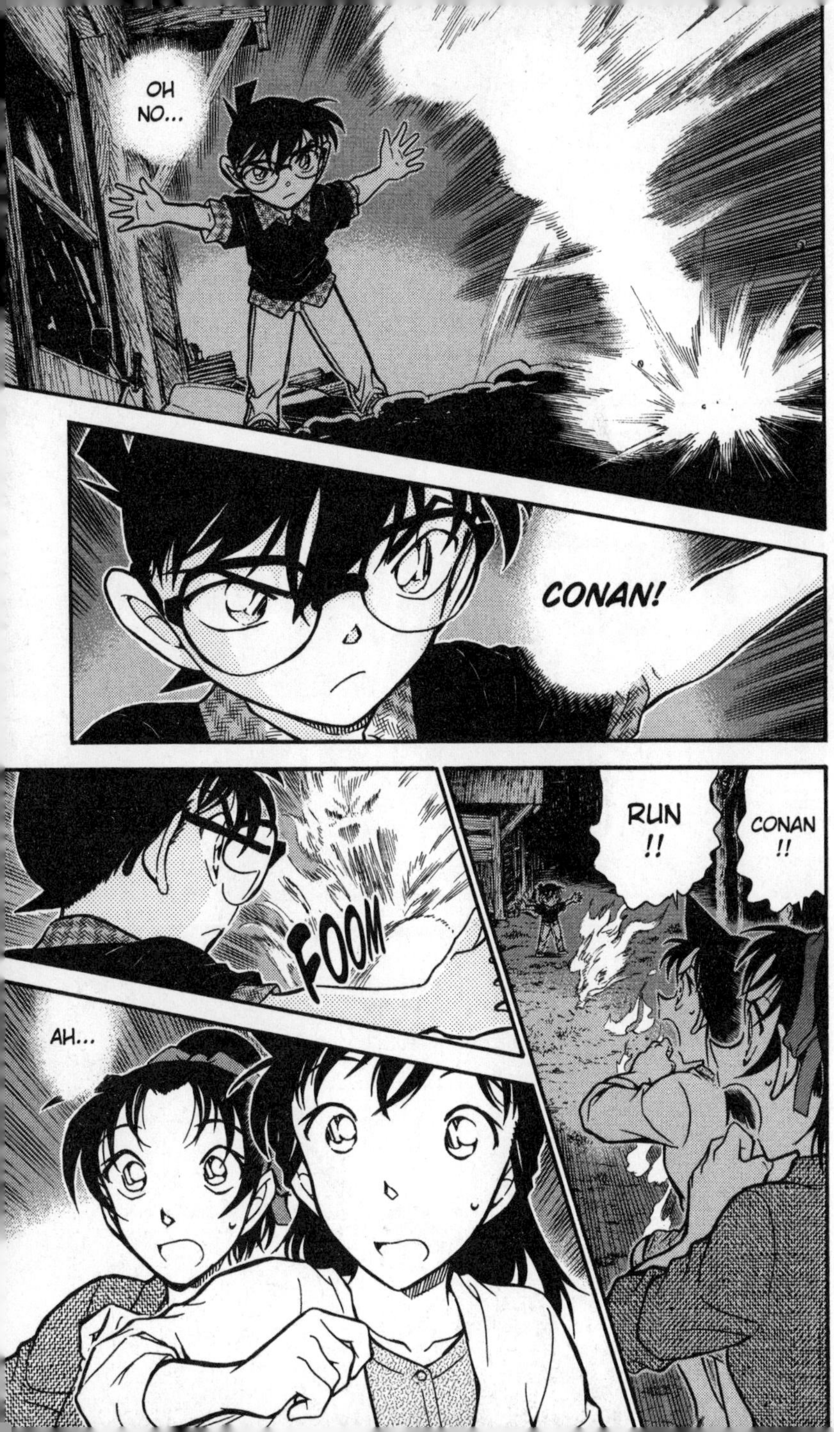
OH NO...
CONAN!
CONAN !!
RUN !!
FOOM
AH...

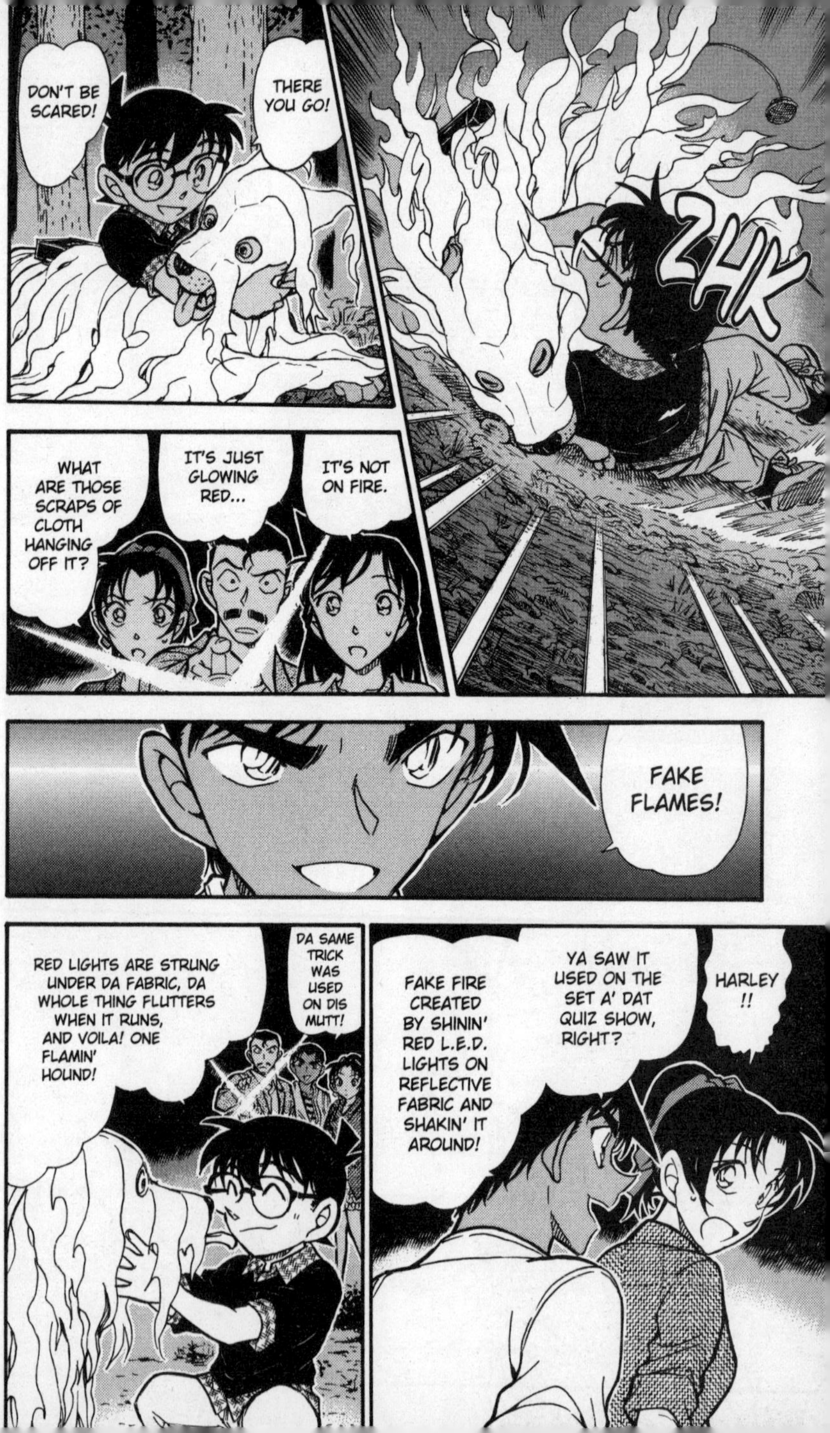
ZHK
THERE YOU GO!
DON'T BE SCARED!
IT'S NOT ON FIRE.
IT'S JUST GLOWING RED...
WHAT ARE THOSE SCRAPS OF CLOTH HANGING OFF IT?
FAKE FLAMES!
HARLEY !!
YA SAW IT USED ON THE SET A' DAT QUIZ SHOW, RIGHT?
FAKE FIRE CREATED BY SHININ' RED L.E.D. LIGHTS ON REFLECTIVE FABRIC AND SHAKIN' IT AROUND!
DA SAME TRICK WAS USED ON DIS MUTT!
RED LIGHTS ARE STRUNG UNDER DA FABRIC, DA WHOLE THING FLUTTERS WHEN IT RUNS, AND VOILA! ONE FLAMIN' HOUND!

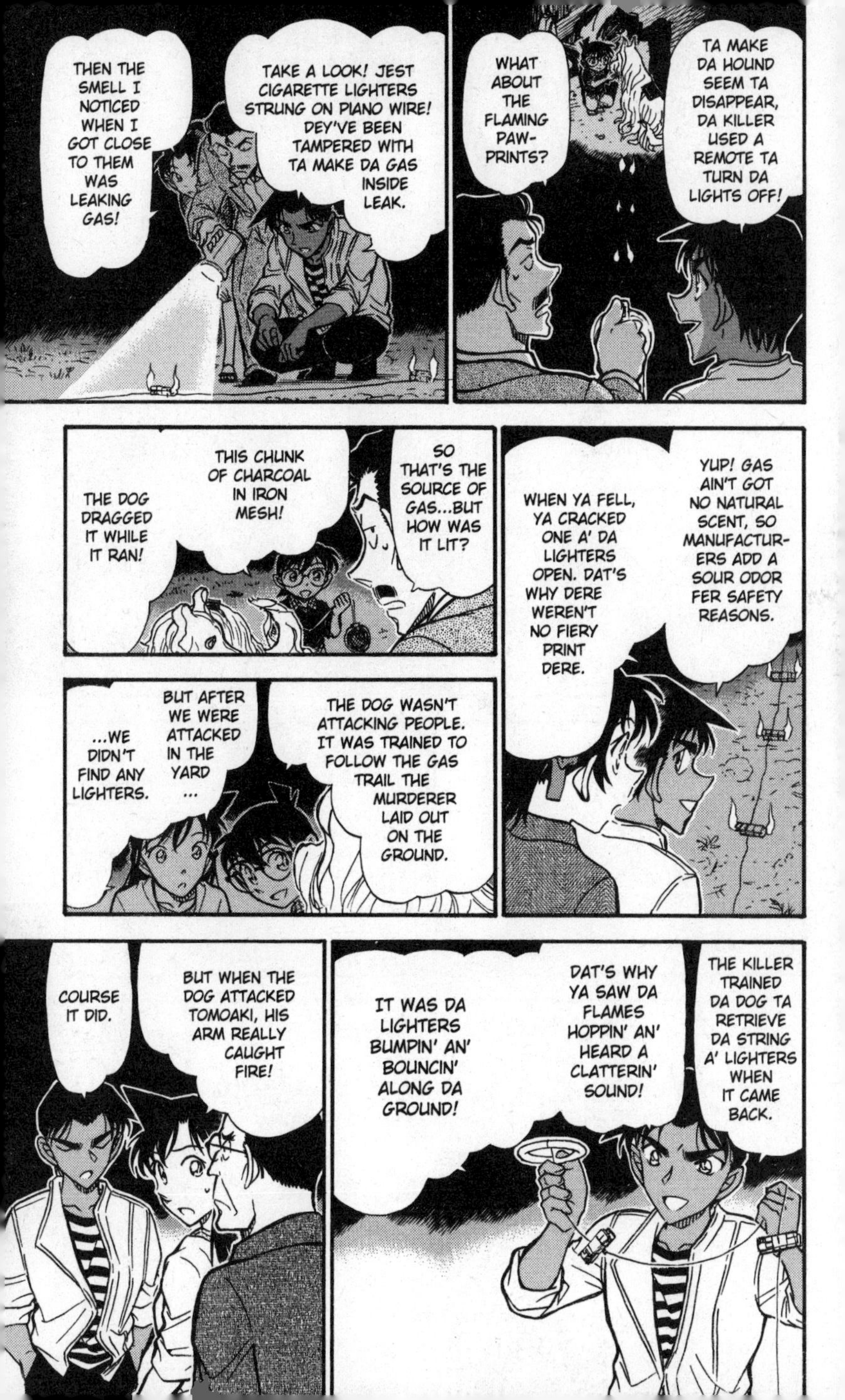
TA MAKE DA HOUND SEEM TA DISAPPEAR, DA KILLER USED A REMOTE TA TURN DA LIGHTS OFF!
WHAT ABOUT THE FLAMING PAW-PRINTS?
TAKE A LOOK! JEST CIGARETTE LIGHTERS STRUNG ON PIANO WIRE! DEY'VE BEEN TAMPERED WITH TA MAKE DA GAS INSIDE LEAK.
THEN THE SMELL I NOTICED WHEN I GOT CLOSE TO THEM WAS LEAKING GAS!
YUP! GAS AIN'T GOT NO NATURAL SCENT, SO MANUFACTURERS ADD A SOUR ODOR FER SAFETY REASONS.
WHEN YA FELL, YA CRACKED ONE A' DA LIGHTERS OPEN. DAT'S WHY DERE WEREN'T NO FIERY PRINT DERE.
SO THAT'S THE SOURCE OF GAS...BUT HOW WAS IT LIT?
THIS CHUNK OF CHARCOAL IN IRON MESH!
THE DOG DRAGGED IT WHILE IT RAN!
THE DOG WASN'T ATTACKING PEOPLE. IT WAS TRAINED TO FOLLOW THE GAS TRAIL THE MURDERER LAID OUT ON THE GROUND.
BUT AFTER WE WERE ATTACKED IN THE YARD ...
...WE DIDN'T FIND ANY LIGHTERS.
THE KILLER TRAINED DA DOG TA RETRIEVE DA STRING A' LIGHTERS WHEN IT CAME BACK.
DAT'S WHY YA SAW DA FLAMES HOPPIN' AN' HEARD A CLATTERIN' SOUND!
IT WAS DA LIGHTERS BUMPIN' AN' BOUNCIN' ALONG DA GROUND!
BUT WHEN THE DOG ATTACKED TOMOAKI, HIS ARM REALLY CAUGHT FIRE!
COURSE IT DID.

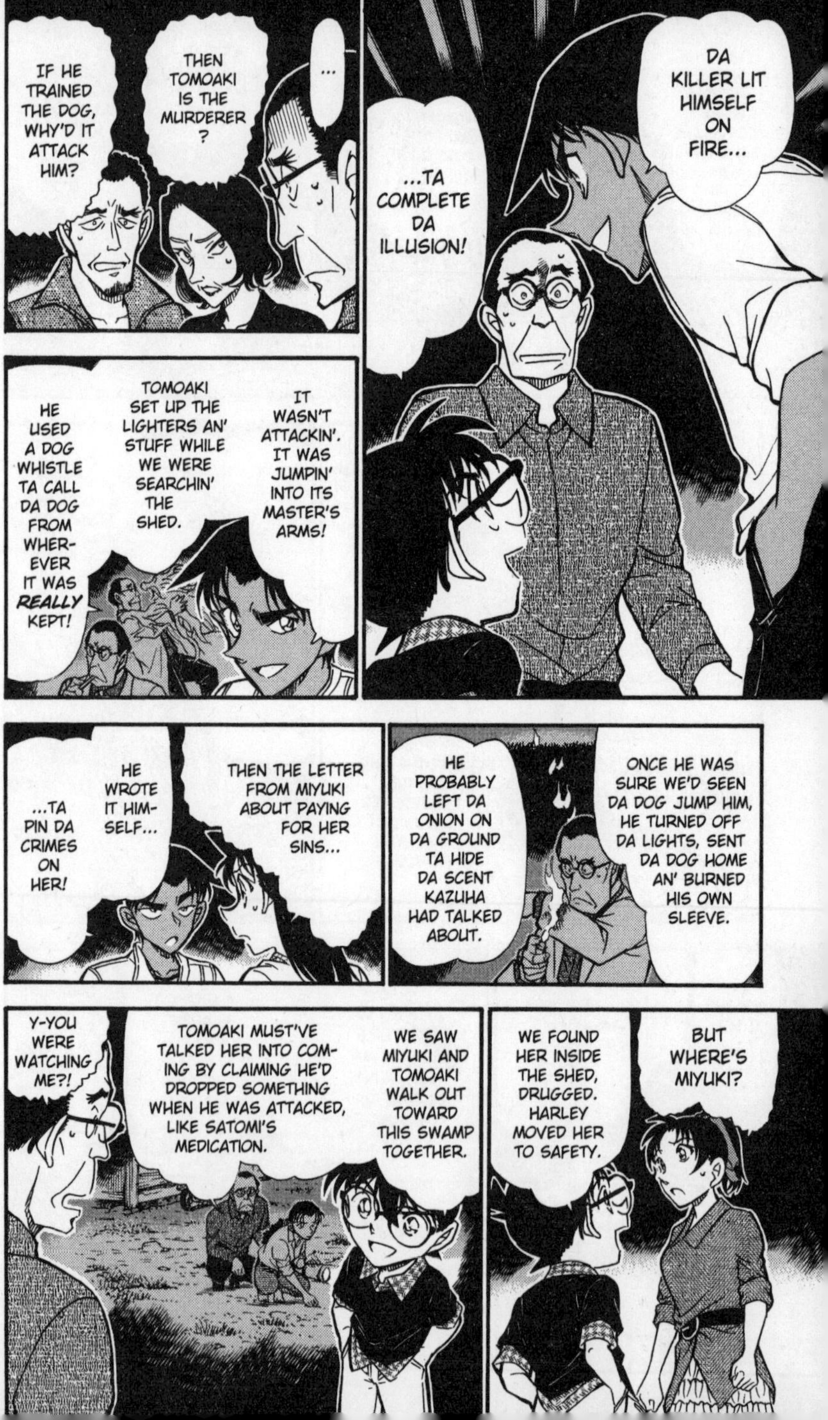
DA KILLER LIT HIMSELF ON FIRE...
...TA COMPLETE DA ILLUSION!
...
THEN TOMOAKI IS THE MURDERER?
IF HE TRAINED THE DOG, WHY'D IT ATTACK HIM?
IT WASN'T ATTACKIN'. IT WAS JUMPIN' INTO ITS MASTER'S ARMS!
TOMOAKI SET UP THE LIGHTERS AN' STUFF WHILE WE WERE SEARCHIN' THE SHED.
HE USED A DOG WHISTLE TA CALL DA DOG FROM WHER-EVER IT WAS REALLY KEPT!
ONCE HE WAS SURE WE'D SEEN DA DOG JUMP HIM, HE TURNED OFF DA LIGHTS, SENT DA DOG HOME AN' BURNED HIS OWN SLEEVE.
HE PROBABLY LEFT DA ONION ON DA GROUND TA HIDE DA SCENT KAZUHA HAD TALKED ABOUT.
THEN THE LETTER FROM MIYUKI ABOUT PAYING FOR HER SINS...
HE WROTE IT HIM-SELF...
...TA PIN DA CRIMES ON HER!
BUT WHERE'S MIYUKI?
WE FOUND HER INSIDE THE SHED, DRUGGED. HARLEY MOVED HER TO SAFETY.
WE SAW MIYUKI AND TOMOAKI WALK OUT TOWARD THIS SWAMP TOGETHER.
TOMOAKI MUST'VE TALKED HER INTO COM-ING BY CLAIMING HE'D DROPPED SOMETHING WHEN HE WAS ATTACKED, LIKE SATOMI'S MEDICATION.
Y-YOU WERE WATCHING ME?!

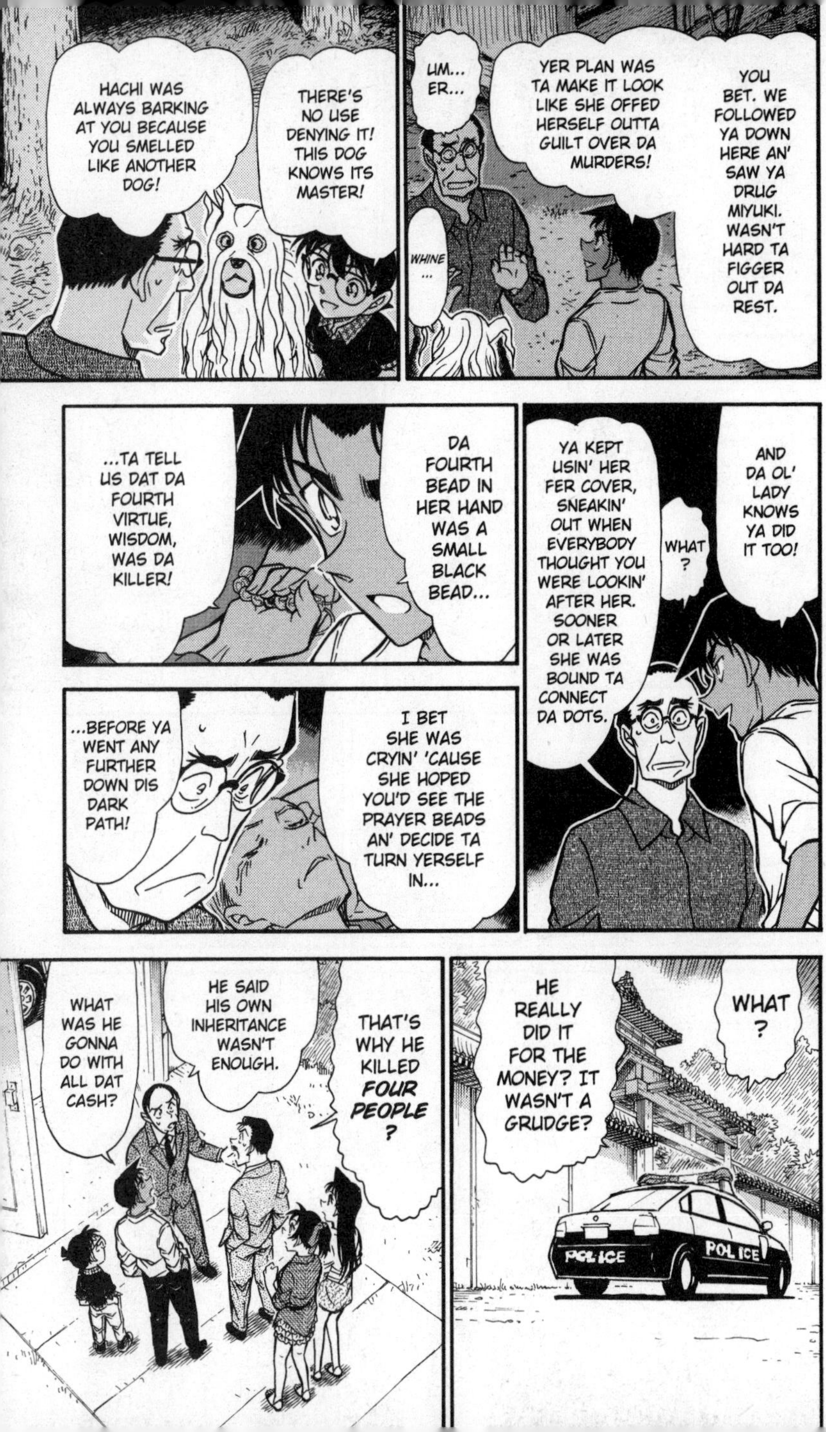
YOU BET. WE FOLLOWED YA DOWN HERE AN' SAW YA DRUG MIYUKI. WASN'T HARD TA FIGGER OUT DA REST.
YER PLAN WAS TA MAKE IT LOOK LIKE SHE OFFED HERSELF OUTTA GUILT OVER DA MURDERS!
UM... ER...
WHINE...
THERE'S NO USE DENYING IT! THIS DOG KNOWS ITS MASTER!
HACHI WAS ALWAYS BARKING AT YOU BECAUSE YOU SMELLED LIKE ANOTHER DOG!
AND DA OL' LADY KNOWS YA DID IT TOO!
WHAT?
YA KEPT USIN' HER FER COVER, SNEAKIN' OUT WHEN EVERYBODY THOUGHT YOU WERE LOOKIN' AFTER HER. SOONER OR LATER SHE WAS BOUND TA CONNECT DA DOTS.
DA FOURTH BEAD IN HER HAND WAS A SMALL BLACK BEAD...
...TA TELL US DAT DA FOURTH VIRTUE, WISDOM, WAS DA KILLER!
I BET SHE WAS CRYIN' 'CAUSE SHE HOPED YOU'D SEE THE PRAYER BEADS AN' DECIDE TA TURN YERSELF IN...
...BEFORE YA WENT ANY FURTHER DOWN DIS DARK PATH!
WHAT?
HE REALLY DID IT FOR THE MONEY? IT WASN'T A GRUDGE?
POLICE
POLICE
THAT'S WHY HE KILLED FOUR PEOPLE?
HE SAID HIS OWN INHERITANCE WASN'T ENOUGH.
WHAT WAS HE GONNA DO WITH ALL DAT CASH?

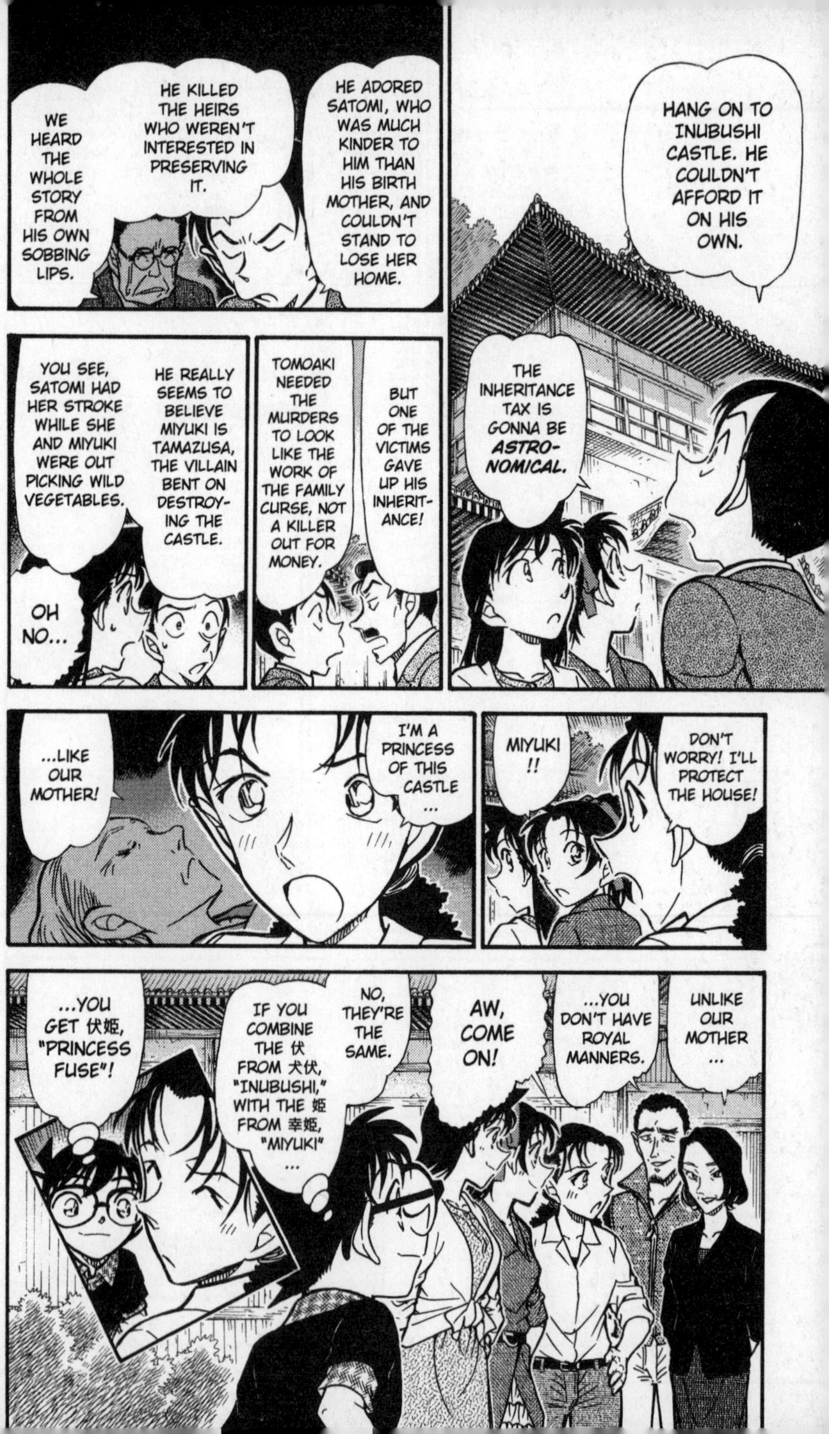
HANG ON TO INUBUSHI CASTLE. HE COULDN'T AFFORD IT ON HIS OWN.
THE INHERITANCE TAX IS GONNA BE *ASTRONOMICAL.*
HE ADORED SATOMI, WHO WAS MUCH KINDER TO HIM THAN HIS BIRTH MOTHER, AND COULDN'T STAND TO LOSE HER HOME.
HE KILLED THE HEIRS WHO WEREN'T INTERESTED IN PRESERVING IT.
WE HEARD THE WHOLE STORY FROM HIS OWN SOBBING LIPS.
BUT ONE OF THE VICTIMS GAVE UP HIS INHERITANCE!
TOMOAKI NEEDED THE MURDERS TO LOOK LIKE THE WORK OF THE FAMILY CURSE, NOT A KILLER OUT FOR MONEY.
HE REALLY SEEMS TO BELIEVE MIYUKI IS TAMAZUSA, THE VILLAIN BENT ON DESTROYING THE CASTLE.
YOU SEE, SATOMI HAD HER STROKE WHILE SHE AND MIYUKI WERE OUT PICKING WILD VEGETABLES.
OH NO...
DON'T WORRY! I'LL PROTECT THE HOUSE!
MIYUKI !!
I'M A PRINCESS OF THIS CASTLE ...
...LIKE OUR MOTHER!
UNLIKE OUR MOTHER ...
...YOU DON'T HAVE ROYAL MANNERS.
AW, COME ON!
NO, THEY'RE THE SAME.
IF YOU COMBINE THE 伏 FROM 犬伏, "INUBUSHI," WITH THE 姫 FROM 幸姫, "MIYUKI" ...
...YOU GET 伏姫, "PRINCESS FUSE"!

Hello, Aoyama here!

I've tried all sorts of popular fortune-telling systems, but I get bad readings on every single one! I'm a Fawn in Zoomancy and my Chinese Zodiac sign is the Rabbit. Why do I keep getting cute animals? But a few years ago I found a "Bakumatsu Era Zodiac" in some magazine and I got Ryoma Sakamoto!! (So cool! ♪)

No big deal or anything, but if anyone wants to create a *Case Closed* Character Zodiac, please tweak it so I get Jimmy or Booker, even if it's just as a joke! (I'm serious....)

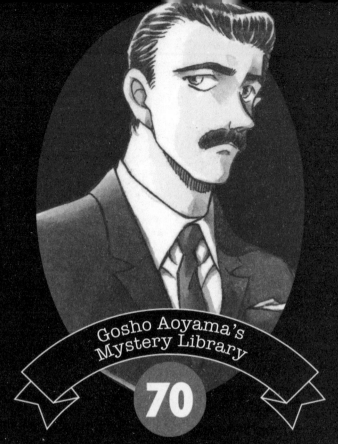

Gosho Aoyama's Mystery Library

70

PHILIP TRENT

A detective should never fall for a suspect...but Philip Trent broke that rule 100 years ago! Trent is 32, tall, single and basically a nice guy. He's an artist by trade but finds himself becoming more famous for his detective work. After he makes a name for himself by solving cases just by reading the newspaper, he picks up work as a freelance journalist covering criminal cases. Trent has a gift for immediately grasping all the details of a case, using his nimble mind and artistically trained eyes to fit the pieces of the puzzle together. But he loses his cool after meeting a beautiful widow who's the prime suspect in a murder!

The author, E.C. Bentley, objected to the tasteless detective novels of his time, which was why he added a light romantic touch to his own story. As the creator of a romantic comedy mystery manga, I'd like to praise him from the bottom of my heart. Hooray!

I recommend *Trent's Last Case.*

Kidnapped by the Demon King and imprisoned in his castle, Princess Syalis is...bored.

SLEEPY PRINCESS IN THE DEMON CASTLE

Story & Art by
KAGIJI KUMANOMATA

Captured princess Syalis decides to while away her hours in the Demon Castle by sleeping, but getting a good night's rest turns out to be a lot of work! She begins by fashioning a DIY pillow out of the fur of her Teddy Demon guards and an "air mattress" from the magical Shield of the Wind. Things go from bad to worse—for her captors—when some of Princess Syalis's schemes end in her untimely—if temporary—demise and she chooses the Forbidden Grimoire for her bedtime reading...

Hey! You're Reading in the Wrong Direction!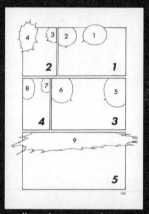

This is the **end** of this graphic novel!

To properly enjoy this VIZ graphic novel, please turn it around and begin reading from **right to left.** Unlike English, Japanese is read right to left, so Japanese comics are read in reverse order from the way English comics are typically read.

Follow the action this way

This book has been printed in the original Japanese format in order to preserve the orientation of the original artwork. Have fun with it!